MW00718156

Authentic Happiness

DEVOTIONS FOR
THE SLUMBERING
BELIEVER

SARAH ROWAN

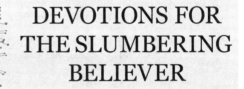

Carpenter's Son Publishing

Authentic Happiness: Devotions for the Slumbering Believer

©2016 by Sarah Rowan

Published by Clovercroft Publishing, Franklin, Tennessee

Published in association with Larry Carpenter of
Christian Book Services, LLC of Franklin, Tennessee

ISBN: 978-1-942587-40-8

Library of Congress Control Number: 2014915531

Printed in the United States of America

I dedicate **Authentic Happiness** *to my two sons,*
Jonah and Andrew,
who are my loving gifts from the Lord.

Boys, I want to take a moment to write just to you. I wrote this book for many reasons. Two of the primary ones that I never lost sight of was you two. I wanted you to always have some of the truth I have learned, while I was with the Lord.

I have been far from perfect in my life. I have made poor choices that I have had to carry along life's path. I had no idea the pull of this world on a Christian. I was naïve, on many accounts, with how easy it was to take my eyes off of the one I called Lord to meet my heart and soul's needs for happiness that was not within His will for my life. I have complete assurance of my salvation despite making those poor choices and being out of the Lord's will at the time. Grace, mercy, and forgiveness are some of the most wonderful things about our Lord. Remember, God promises to be faithful when we are not. Always remember no matter what you do in your life, God will be faithful to forgive and love you.

You have both confessed with your mouth that Jesus is Lord and believed in your heart that God raised Him from the dead. You are eternally saved according to God's Word and promises. Do not let the world take this truth away from you. I promise you, it will try. You are in your adolescent years now, but you have already begun to feel the pull of the world on you away from the Lord. In your own interests, you see that it is hard to stop what you want to do and spend quality time with the Lord in prayer and in His Word even now. This is the beginning of slumbering as a Christian. Even as youths in Christ, you can slumber so easily. It only gets harder to stay spiritually awake as you get older.

You never mean to put Christ second in your life. You think He will wait until you can "fit" Him in your lives as you have learned that He is patient and loving. You think He is okay with letting you have your way, when and how you want it to be. Boys, be very careful, as God commands us not to have idols before Him. If you do not guard your time with the Lord closely, the idol may become you.

You will soon be men and go out into this world. You have to be spiritually awake and strong in the Lord, not just for yourself, but for your future wives and children. Make a difference in this world. Be the men of God that He created you to be, so your lives will always bring glory and honor to Him. Love the Lord with all of your heart and with all of your soul and with all of your mind and with all of your strength.

Love,
Mama

Acknowledgments

The greatest pleasure in writing *Authentic Happiness* was sharing my journals day after day with friends and family. Malachi 3:16 says, "Then those who feared the Lord talked with each other, and the Lord listened and heard. In His presence, a book of remembrance was written of those who feared the Lord and always thought about His name" (NIV). I wonder how many conversations have been heard and recorded by the Lord over the year of writing this book. While there are so many people to thank, I am deeply indebted to the following family and friends:

Kevin, Jonah, and Andrew Rowan. My three gentlemen have sacrificed a lot of Mama and wife time over the last year while I concentrated all of my time and energy on the book. They have been supportive, patient, and loving the whole way through.

Daddy and Mama; Stacey and Dennis Dyson. My sweet parents, sister, and brother-in-law have supported me from day one of writing my journals. They always had an encouraging and loving word for me.

Shannon and Dena Anderson. I couldn't ask for more loving in-laws than these two Godly people. They are a testimony of authenticity.

Natasha Grimes. Without a God-ordained meeting between her and me, this book may have never come to be. It was her passion for growing in the Lord that prompted me to share my personal journals in the first place. She is a Godly young woman with a heart for the Lord.

Robin Hester. My best friend for over thirty years! She has been with me through thick and thin. Now we can add writing a book to the list!

Receiving list. These special people have supported me each morning, as I have shared my journals of what the Lord has taught me:

Laura Hayman. My "Friday" counselor, friend, encourager, and massage therapist. She helped me when my back ached and hands hurt from typing so much. She kept me going mentally and physically!

Steve Preston. My editor who kept me laughing through the most tedious process of the book. Thanks for the "swords' discount!"

Mark Grimes. He is a wise and dear friend that I can trust and share anything with. I have been blessed by his friendship that always includes support and encouragement.

Varne Cummings, Elaine Rowan, Laura Hayman, Mark and Pam Grimes, and Tom and Donna Manry. Thank you for your love offerings toward the publishing cost of Authentic Happiness. It was an unexpected blessing from the Lord.

Contents

Introduction

I remember sleepwalking when I was younger. Whatever I was dreaming of, I acted out as if it were real. One time in high school, my mom heard me in the middle of the night making noises. She checked on me. The next morning, she told me that I was standing in the middle of my room playing what appeared to be softball! I had recently joined my school's softball team. I guess I was playing a game in my dreams? I had no awareness that I was asleep. Everything seemed so real. Just a few years ago, I remember dreaming that I had to get up to do something. I sailed off the end of the bed only to hit my forehead on one of the tall wooden posts! That woke me up in a hurry—as I rubbed my head, disoriented. You can actually get hurt sleepwalking, because you are unaware of your surroundings. What seems to be real is not.

I guess this is the best way I can understand how I have walked in my sleep for the majority of my time as a child of God. I have not walked in complete reality of exactly how serious my personal relationship should be. I have not walked in the reality of how consistent and holy my thoughts and behaviors should be, especially if I call the Most High God my Father and Jesus Christ my Lord. I have justified the minimal relationship with Him as being enough. I have justified my minimal or nonexistent prayer life and Bible study as acceptable. Everything else would get done, but if quiet time was left off, there were no immediate consequences. I justified that God would understand I was busy and I had "things" to get done. He knew I loved Him, but I had a life to live. I would fit Him in when I had the time. He would have to be patient until I did. God was okay that I was in complete control. He would be on the sidelines of my life if I needed Him to help me out. He would accept the fact that I had other gods before Him, mainly myself. All was well.

Who did I think I was really compromising with? I was living in a dream world, and I was sleepwalking. I was in a deep slumber, as if I had taken a sedative. I convinced myself that I was living the victorious and blessed life that God had for me. The only problem was, I was controlling my life and thinking God was going right along with me. I learned that God doesn't "go along" with you. He doesn't follow you. You go along and follow Him. Those directions can look very different. God only goes in one direction and that is His. Oftentimes, I would be walking around and asking "Where is God in this situation?" I found Him standing way back as He said, "I am over here, Child! I don't follow people, especially those walking in their sleep. The Creator never serves or follows the created, but you do."

The Bible tells us many times to, "Wake up," "Be Alert," and "Be watchful!" Who is it talking to? The nonbeliever? No! God is telling that to Christians. Why would the Word of God have to tell Christians to wake up, unless they have not first fallen asleep? Just like dreams seem so real when you are in them that you do not realize you are asleep, you can be slumbering in your Christian walk and not even realize it. Something has to wake you up, just like the wooden poster of my bed woke me up.

Waking up out of a spiritual slumber can be painful, too! It may take a jarring of your system to get your attention, especially if you are sleeping deeply. Waking up to the realities that wickedness dwelled in my heart and that I desired my will more than God's (despite my belief that I was a good person and committed Christian) shook me awake. I woke up and took a long look at my thoughts and consistent actions with the Lord. I found that I was not as committed as I thought I was. Honestly, that was a revelation to me. I had been sleepwalking so long that the mundane and stagnated Christian life seemed alive and fulfilling enough for me. I had measured just enough God out in my life that I was satisfied. It didn't really occur to me that God was far from satisfied.

When I woke up from my spiritual slumber, yawned, stretched, and wiped the temporal blinding matter of this world and myself from my eyes, I started seeing my life the way a Holy God saw it. I was in His reality at that point and no longer my own. He showed me that the happiness that I had sought out while I was slumbering was from temporal and meaningless things. That explained why the happiness was not lasting and fulfilling. My busy life with work, family, church, and hobbies had become a god before Him. I did not consider myself doing horrible things, but anything that comes before God is an idol; however, I wanted to justify it. That idol could be you or me.

Once I was awake, the Lord spoke, "I am your only source of authentic happiness. I desire to be first in your life. I will not accept your justification of Me being in any other place. Every breath you take should be for Me. Every beat of your heart should be for Me. Every desire you have should be for holiness in My will and not meaningless in your own. Wake up! You have slept long enough!" Since I have awakened, the Lord has taken me into the deeper parts of His Word. He has spoken to me firmly at times, leaving me in heaps of tears and conviction at the reflection of my own foolishness as I continue to see His truth and glory. He has brought me so close to Himself, even to His very throne room.

Through my own journey of spiritual awakening, the Lord has given me the strong conviction to write His lessons or dialogues in personal journals. I had no idea when I started my journals that one day the Lord would allow them to be sent out to friends and family and then to be placed in a book that He personally named Authentic Happiness. He told me once that He could move at lightning speed, and He certainly has demonstrated that in the book that you are now holding. I have literally held on to the hem of His robe for the last year as I have tried to capture all that He has shown me. Even this book could not hold it all. I already have enough journals to write a second book. I stand amazed at Jesus, the Nazarene! Like never before in my Christian walk, He has revealed Himself in a real and tangible way to me and others through the writing of this book. I could probably write a book just on that testimony alone.

God wants His children to wake up from their slumber. He wants us to know that He is very real. He wants us to know that He doesn't accept our pitiful excuses and justifications of why He is not at the top priority in our lives as demonstrated by our thoughts and behaviors, not just our words. We should have holy and godly thoughts and behaviors without compromise. That includes not missing time with the Most High God, because we have other "things" that need to get done. There should be nothing, including yourself, that should be more important than your consistent, committed, and growing personal relationship with the one you call Lord and Savior. If you are not doing this, then you are slumbering and sleep-walking in your own dream world. You do not get to create your own alternate reality of how your Christian life should be when there is only one authentic reality in the Lord.

It is my sincere prayer that as you read through the journals that follow, that God will speak as clearly to you as He has to me as He gently wakes you from any slumber in which you might find yourself right now, and that the life you find in Him will be full and rewarding as you serve the living God. If you begin to realize, through reading this, that you are not "slumbering" because you never have been awake before in a genuine relationship with the God of creation, it is my prayer that you seek God at this very moment. He promises that "If you seek Me, you will find Me, if you seek with all your heart" (Jeremiah 29:13 NIV).

Sarah Rowan

Slumbering Believers

Therefore, stay awake, for you do not know on what day your Lord is coming. (Matthew 24:42 ESV)

And do this, understanding the present time: The hour has already come for you to wake up from your slumber, because our salvation is nearer now than when we first believed. (Romans 13:11 NIV)

The New Testament speaks several times about the need for Christians to wake up. It is logical to conclude if the Lord has to tell Christians to wake up, then they have fallen asleep in the first place. They have fallen asleep spiritually while they walk around physically. They assume since they are awake physically that this means that they are also awake spiritually. Nothing could be farther from the truth as the flesh is temporal and the spirit is eternal. These are two totally different realms. It seems much harder to wake up spiritually than it does physically. The fact has been established that a Christian can slumber spiritually.

I wonder how a Christian can tell if he or she is in a deep slumber, and what wakes a Christian up. Have you ever thought about that? To be perfectly transparent, I have never given a second thought about whether I was spiritually asleep or awake. This would have contributed to most of my problems in the first place! I knew I was a Christian. All was well in my little life. I went to church as I knew to do. I was the "good" Christian. I didn't do bad things. I loved on others and tried to act like a Christian was supposed to act. Looking back, I think I started falling asleep years and years ago. I was so busy trying to be the Christian for me and for others that I forgot about being a Christian for God. I neglected having a consistent, intimate, and personal relationship and conversation with Him through the power of the Holy Spirit. I ignored the importance of Him interpreting my words to Jesus and Jesus' words back to me.

Honestly, I don't know how long I have been asleep. How would I know, when I thought I was awake the whole time in the first place? The only thing I can compare it to would be falling asleep unexpectedly in the chair or on the couch. It's not like you intended to fall asleep. It happens before you know it. When you wake up, your spouse or your child tells you that you have been sleeping for an hour. You can't believe it. I think that is how Christians originally slumber. They never intend to; it just happens. You don't know how long you have slumbered as time stands still when you are asleep, or at least it feels like it.

So how can you tell if you are a slumbering Christian? Let me ask you a few simple questions. If you answer yes to any of these or all of them … well … you are slumbering. Is it possible that the only time you open the Word of God is when the preacher tells you to on Sunday morning? Is it possible that you leave your Bible in the car, the counter, or the table only to pick it up the next week for church? Is it possible that you wake up and start your day, work hard, and take care of your family only to fall in the bed like a cut-down tree at the end of the day never once missing Jesus? Do you find it hard to reprioritize your life to give Jesus an hour a day, or even forty-five minutes, or how about thirty consistent minutes a day? Do you feel the amount of God in your life is balanced perfectly with the amount of time you desire to hear and learn about Him at church? Not a lot more God is needed outside of that.

Do you find it hard to check in daily with God, because you are just too busy, but always seem to find the time somehow to check in with people via emails, texts, phone, and Facebook? Do you check in with people more than you check in with God? There is always the time to watch a movie or your favorite series on TV but never a time for a deep personalized Bible study. Does it ever come to mind that He is waiting for you to come, yet you never do, and it doesn't bother you a bit that you missed quiet time? Is it possible that you mumble a prayer to Him either when you wake up, in the shower, or before you drift to sleep? You never wait to hear back from Him. Are you doing all the mumbling and waiting for no reply? Is it possible that you talk at Jesus and not with Jesus? Is there active listening on your side? Is it possible the only time you study the Bible is when you are in a group-led study at church instead of a Spirit-led personal Bible study at home? Did you answer yes to any of these questions? These were pretty simple to put together. I just took all of them from examples of my own life with the God I called Lord but treated Him far less than that.

We can beat ourselves up as long as we want to over that fact that we may have slumbered, but that is not going to get us anywhere now! We need to figure out what wakes us up! If you are reading this journal and you answered yes to any of those questions, then the realization of your slumber should wake you up. It can be that simple. The other option is to say, "What a nice journal. She made a lot of good points there. Then ZZZZZzzzzzzzzzzzzzzzzz …" That is what many people will do. It is just the human way. You recognize truth but you just don't care to have more than you have right now in your life. You are satisfied with the amount of God you have in your life. I can't make you wake up. I can just sound an alarm that you may be slumbering. You have to want more of God to wake up.

The other thing that will wake you up, which is way more painful than just reading my journal, is the sin that you will find yourself engaging in while you are slumbering. Sin is an unfortunate and very costly alarm to the realization that you are slumbering deeply. Some of us are more stubborn than others, and it will take an unexpected sin to shake us awake. So be it. God doesn't cause you to sin, but He can use it to teach you a lot of lessons if you are willing to stay awake and learn them.

Waking up from a spiritual slumber is all up to you. You have to desire it more than the life you have now. You have to reprioritize your life and put your quiet time and personalized Bible study at the center. You may have to sacrifice something in your life that takes up time, so you can use that time for the Lord. You may have to get up an hour early and sacrifice some of your precious sleep. You have to make an appointment with God and not compromise it for any reason. You have to be committed. If you are not committed to a deeper and consistent relationship with the one you claim is Lord of your life, then go get your blanket, pillow, and go back to sleep. The Lord will wake you with His return. If that is what it takes to wake you up, I really wouldn't want to be you.

Starting Point

I really did not have a goal for writing my journals. This was something private that was between the Lord and me. In the whole world, it was something that we did together. The Lord had other plans for the journals, and now they are shared with many people. That is still amazing to me. May the Lord be honored and glorified by anything that has been written.

Since the journals have been sent out, more and more people have come to me and told me that I am a testimony to them. My consistency and passion for the Lord has caught their attention. What amazes me is that they do not know each other, but they are saying some of the same things. They want to hear the Lord in their own lives. They want the deeper truths of God for themselves. They know there has to be more to this Christian walk than they have experienced thus far. They are struggling to figure out how to prioritize God in their busy lives. They love the Lord with all their hearts but don't know how to start to get to where they want and need to be. I can relate to all of these things so well because I was exactly where they are just a couple of years ago.

I have been a Christian for over thirty years, but I was right where the majority of Christians are. I was confessing the name of Jesus Christ but denying His power in my life. I was handling things in my own strength and was in a deep slumber. I was missing out on God, but I didn't act like I missed Him. I was missing His deeper communion with me. I was missing His power. I was missing His blessings. I was missing His voice. After receiving another phone call from a friend about wondering where and how to start a deeper relationship with the Lord, I thought I would write a journal discussing my own starting point.

Recognition is the starting point. Recognition of what I was missing in my life that I just described weighed heavier and heavier on me. The hardest part for me was admitting that whatever I was missing in my life from the Lord was all my own doing. It was by my own choice. No one can make me miss the goodness of Lord in my life—not my children, my spouse, or my busy schedule. Only me. I had to recognize that I had many priorities in my life, but God was not one of them. I loved God, but He wasn't a priority in my life past going to church. I do not feel that I was a horrible person. I just didn't have time for Him. I had to take responsibility for my own growth in the Lord. I had to recognize that I had become very inactive and negligent with the Lord, despite being in church every Sunday.

When I left my Bible in the car after church every Sunday so that I wouldn't have to look for it the next Sunday, I was basically leaving His ability to speak to me sitting in a hot car week after week. I couldn't figure out why I wasn't growing or why I didn't see the Lord's blessings that preacher kept telling me about. Why wasn't the Lord talking to me too?

Well, He was in the car. The only time I had time to pray was when I was in the shower, before "my life" started for the day. That is all He got. The prayer may have lasted as long as it took to wash my hair. If these things do not epitomize where my relationship with the Lord was, nothing can.

I had to recognize my state of being and how serious I was taking the Lord. I had to recognize how much trouble I could get myself in when I was not abiding closely with the Lord. That honestly scared me. It was a hard realization. Many tears of repentance were shed, forgiveness was given, and love flooded my soul. I was awake! Praise God! I was finally awake. As God is my witness, this was the conversation that followed. I distinctly remember telling the Lord, "Show me You." He said, "Are you serious this time?" I said, "Yes, Lord. I am serious." He said, "Hold on. I move like lightning." That last phrase was written just like that in one of my older hand-written journals from 2012.

Structure is the next step. If you are anything like me, you have the best intention to do good for the Lord. You just don't know how to go about it. The Lord was faithful to give me a resource to provide structure for my prayer life. He knew that it needed overhauling, and He also knew that I didn't know how to do it. I purchased the book The Hour that Changes the World by Dick Eastman. This book was written in 1978, and I doubt any of you have ever heard of this book or this author. I had not, either. The Lord put this book in my hand. I devoured it and knew the Lord wanted me to take what I had learned from Mr. Eastman and apply it in my life. The author took different parts of how Jesus prayed with scriptural references and structured it into a prayer wheel. There are twelve parts of the prayer. Each part is prayed for five minutes, and then an hour is done. I kept up with how many hours of prayer I did, but when I passed 250, I just stopped keeping tally. I wasn't trying to meet some goal or something. I have no idea of how many hours of prayer I have completed now. Who cares! I just know I am praying now.

As I was learning to have structure in my prayer life, I was very serious of following the prayer wheel. I think that was good for me in the beginning. After about a year, I started modifying it to meet my own growing needs with praying longer or shorter in some of the portion of the prayer. In the end, God had taught me to pray, based on the scriptures. It changed my life. I can't wait to give Dick Eastman the biggest hug when I get to Heaven. He was truly used by God to change many Christians' prayer lives. His book is written specifically for prayer; it doesn't touch on deep personalized Bible studying.

After I prayed for an hour, I would read one chapter of a book in the Bible per day until I finished the book. Then I would choose another one. I would have a handwritten journal out with pen ready. I feel that is a must. I started having dialogues with the Lord as He showed me His deeper truths. I wrote down what I was learning as I knew I couldn't remember it all. The book that you are holding is the result of those journals.

Consistency is the fourth step. When you make an appointment with the Most High God, He expects you to keep it. If you can figure out a good enough excuse for not keeping it, let me know. I could never come up with one, so I didn't miss my appointment. God expects consistency in our lives if we are awake and He is at the top of our priority list. If we are not consistent, then we are slumbering. The only reason you are not consistent is because you have somehow justified your excuse. I don't care what you have told yourself for not being consistent with meeting God daily, it is an excuse. Your excuse. I have learned that the Lord doesn't take your excuses, however good you think they are and however you have chosen to justify them. It will never be good enough.

Knowing this truth, stop giving excuses to the Lord; He is not accepting them. You have believed the lie that He is. Wake up and understand who you are really talking to! He is the One that existed before time began. He is the One that exists outside of time. Look up at the sun today. He hung it and sustains it. The earth that you are standing on right now is suspended in space on nothing. You can't imagine His power and He wants to share with you. What excuse could you possibly have to deny this kind of power in your life? Please tell me. When you put all this together, you will see that there are no excuses or justifications for your lack of consistency with spending daily quality time in prayer and Bible study. There are no excuses for our own slumber.

An abundant blessing is the last step. God was true to His Word of moving quickly, and He hasn't stopped. Most of the time, I cannot keep up. He wants to show me so much more Truth than I possibly can write down. He has introduced me to new people, and we have had wonderful conversations of the truth that He has revealed. He has given me opportunities to read some of my journals in churches and opened up opportunities to share my testimony. The Lord has used some of my journals to wake some Christians up. The best blessing is that God seems more real to me than He has ever seemed in the past. I understand there is a spiritual revival in each of us, but we have to wake up to experience it.

Beagles

When I was letting my two beagles out the other morning, I noticed long lines that were worn down in the grass. It had taken a long time to wear those paths down. One line went to the right and one line went to the left. Each dog chose its own way, and they followed down their lines exactly. They never deviated from them. They were following the familiar. They were following the ways that they had followed the day before, the month before, and the year before. They absolutely have no intention of ever creating a new line in the grass, a new direction. They will follow the paths that they created until they die.

They are not interested in forming a new path because the ones they have thus far have worked so well for them. I observed as they had their heads down and noses to the ground. They never looked up. They never looked side to side. Not once. Anything or anybody around them would have been missed because their whole world was on that nondeviated path. They only saw what was right in front of them. They seemed satisfied.

I stood against the fence and watched them for a while. I asked myself, "Am I following the same line in the grass as a Christian that I have always been on? Am I looking up or side to side from my path to see whose lives I can touch with mine or new truths I can learn from the Lord? Is it all about my own line in the grass? Would I ever share someone else's line in the grass, or would I share mine with them? Am I doing anything different and more for the Lord today, this month, or this year by taking a different path? Am I staying with the familiar one? Am I like my beagles?" Are you? I have learned that growth only occurs when you go outside your comfort zone or, in this case, your familiar path. That is the only time you create new paths. I am challenging myself to find a new line in the grass this year.

Contentment

Godliness with contentment is a great gain. (1 Timothy 6:6 HCSB)

I think we all search for many things in life. There is one thing, though, that everyone searches for that is the same—contentment. It's the one feeling people would be satisfied with above all others to have. It seems like it's the one that eludes them the most.

People search and search and search for what makes them content in life. It may be a relationship. It may be for others to be pleased with you. It may be that perfect job. It may be a child. It may be something that you feel like you deserve to have and don't. It may be a change in the people in our lives to act like we want them to act and on and on. Paul teaches us that we can never find contentment in any of the things that we acquire on earth. We brought nothing with us, and we will take nothing out. The only thing we have was our spirit, which was God-given.

Paul said, "Godliness with contentment is a great gain." Our gladness, fulfillment, peace, pleasure, satisfaction, and serenity can never be found in the external but only in the internal workings of what God can satisfy within our spirits. Godliness within our spirit and lives is where contentment lies. You can search your whole life, and if you miss this truth, then you will miss contentment. Things and people will always disappoint and take away your contentment if that is where you keep it. That doesn't seem to be a very safe place to keep something so valuable. God never disappoints or takes away your contentment when it resides in Him and in your spirit. This truth has changed my life.

Profound

I was in amazement and in awe of how it was possible that God continues to fill me with immense joy, total contentment, love, and sustaining peace. I asked Him in my hour of prayer to explain how this was possible. This is what I understood Him to impress upon my spirit:

I am the Father, I am the Son, and I am the Holy Spirit. We are made up of joy, peace, love, and contentment. This is our very essence of who We are. There is nothing different We can be as this is Our nature. You have the Holy Spirit in you because you have put your trust in the Son. The Father gave you to the Son. The Son gave you the Holy Spirit that eternally and completely fills you. The Holy Spirit is part of the Father and the Son. He resides in you and acts as a magnet that pulls from the Trinity joy, love, peace, and contentment into you to where He dwells. When you allow the Holy Spirit to reign in your life and do not grieve Him, then you allow Our nature to be felt in you. When you stay close to Me, the Holy Spirit fills you completely with what We are made up of. In turn, Child, this is how you are continually filled.

Profound. Absolutely profound. Thank you, Lord, for explaining this and filling me with the Holy Spirit!

I've Heard about You

Paul oftentimes started his letters with, "I have heard about you." In Colossians, he says he had heard about the Christians' faith in Jesus Christ and the love they had for other people. He had heard about the depth of their hope that is reserved in Heaven to cause them to act the way they did. Paul had heard about their expediential growth by the power of the Holy Spirit and how they were bearing fruit for the Kingdom. What a compliment by Paul! In Romans, Paul tells the Christians that the "News of their faith is being reported" to everyone. In Ephesians, Paul gave thanks constantly because he had heard of the deep faith these Christians had in the Lord Jesus and the love they had for those around them. Because of this faith, he prayed that a spirit of wisdom would come upon them so they would have new knowledge of God.

In Philippians, Paul praises the Christians because of their consistency and faithfulness in the gospel of truth. In 1 Thessalonians, he and the other disciples remembered and spoke about the Christians' strong Godly conduct. In 2 Timothy, Paul points out Timothy's Christian characteristics of sincere faith and heartfelt commitment to the cause of Christ. In Philemon, he says he had, "heard of Philemon's love and faith toward the Lord Jesus and other Christians." He complemented Philemon on his active participation in the faith. Paul said because of Philemon's love that he and others who knew Philemon gained great joy, encouragement, and a refreshed heart. Could Paul have given a higher compliment to a fellow believer?

Paul has been known not to always compliment what he heard about Christians. To the Galatians he said he was, "amazed," but not in a good way. He said he was amazed how quickly Christians turned away from Jesus Christ to different or compromised truth. They were not living out the truth they had already been taught. They were Christians but far from committed ones. He was basically saying that their faith was so weak that they could be easily led astray to listen to different messages of self and the world. They were weak followers of Christ but strong ones for the world. Paul said he was "amazed" at the weakness, despite these Christians knowing Jesus. Their heads should have never turned to the right or the left, yet they were. They found themselves in all sorts of sin and sorrows by not heeding the warnings the Lord had given.

Paul heard different things about Christians. They were either sold out for Jesus—effective, uncompromising, consistent, and had a great impact on others around them—or they were weak, lukewarm, and noncommittal. Paul recognized both groups as called by God but very different. If Paul was around today and wrote a letter to me, what would he say he heard? I'm sure the Lord talks about us in Heaven. What has Paul heard from the Lord about me? When I get there, Paul is high on my list to have many long conversations with. I hope I can hear Paul's first conversation with me go something like this: "I heard you were faithful to Jesus Christ and loved other people. I heard that you were committed and always growing in wisdom and knowledge of our King. I heard that you brought great joy, encouragement, and refreshment to the heart of others as often as it was within your ability to do so. I heard that everyone who knew you, knew that you were sold out for Jesus Christ. Is what the Lord told me about you true?" I pray that I can say with a grateful heart, "Yes, Paul! The Lord told you right!"

Covered

Kevin and I went to Colorado for our twenty-year anniversary trip. During our ski lessons, our instructor asked us where we were staying.

We said, "Mt. Princeton Resort." He said, "Did you hear what happened up there last fall?" We said, "No." He started telling us a heartbreaking story of a family of six going hiking one October afternoon. There had been heavy, freezing rain that loosened the rocks. As they were walking along, a massive rock slide occurred, burying all of them. Five of the six people were killed except one little thirteen-year-old girl. Her mom, dad, older sister, and two cousins were killed. How did she survive? Her dad covered her with himself and shielded the rocks from killing her. Her dad laid down his life to cover his daughter so that she could have a chance to live.

I heard this story, and it impacted me immediately. The daddy exchanged his life for her life. He wanted her to live and was willing to pay the ultimate sacrifice. Can there be any clearer testimony of love than this? On the day they went hiking, the daddy did not know that he would die or have to lay down his life for his beloved child. If he had known, he would not have gone up on that mountain. He would have made a different choice with different outcomes. He and his family would have lived.

As Christians, our Heavenly Daddy knowingly allowed His beloved Child to climb a different hill called Mt. Calvary. It wasn't for an afternoon hike but for a sacrifice. The difference between these stories is our Heavenly Daddy knew what would happen to His child that day at the top of the mountain. He knew the deadly crushing rocks of judgment and wrath would fall on His Child from the very day He was born into this world. He allowed His Child to climb the mountain knowing that there would be no covering or protection for Him. There would be no rescue from death for His Child.

Would any one of us reading this journal make the same choice as this Heavenly Daddy? It is one thing to lay your life down for your child in an emergency situation, but it's quite another when you allow your child's life to be laid down for others. Not one of us would have allowed this to happen to one of our children, especially our only child. This earthly daddy who covered his child had the power to save his little's one life, and so he did. This Heavenly Daddy also had the power to cover His Child so that He could also be saved but chose not to.

What a contrast. Why? Why didn't this Heavenly Daddy cover His Child to save Him from certain death if He had the power to do so? If He had, then He would only have had one Child for eternity. He would have only had Jesus. Our Heavenly Daddy wanted us as much as His firstborn Child! That should stagger your mind. When He allowed that one special Child to die, He in return gained all of us as His children.

We are called "brothers and sisters of Jesus." Our Heavenly Daddy felt that you and I were more valuable than His own Child to have allowed His suffering and death. Our Heavenly Daddy put our needs of salvation higher than His only Child's wellbeing. When Jesus asked to have the cup pass from Him, our Heavenly Daddy said, "No, My Child, I have to have my other children, too. You are the only One to cover them from the crushing rocks of judgment and wrath."

I thought the earthly daddy in Colorado had demonstrated the ultimate testimony of love. No, I was wrong. Our Heavenly Daddy did when He sacrificed His child for you and for me when we were still His enemies. That is called *grace*—receiving something we don't deserve.

Do you know the name of this little girl who was saved by the covering of her earthly father? Gracie. Coincidence? I don't believe in coincidences. Open your minds. What can we learn from Gracie's daddy? Love is so strong that it is worth somebody else's life that you love more than your own. I bet the only other one who can fully understand this type of sacrifice is our Heavenly Daddy. Gracie will live a long, full life because of her daddy's sacrifice. We will live an eternal life because of ours.

I said once before that falling rocks can crush us, but that Jesus Christ told us to enter His strong tower as a shelter. Children of God, listen to me. The rocks never stopped falling. We just never felt them, and we never will because they fell on Jesus instead. No one covered Him because He had to cover us, just like Gracie's Daddy had to cover her so she could live. Somebody has to take the rocks, and somebody gets to be covered. I understand clearer now than ever before this truth. I have been covered; have you? If not, ask Jesus to cover you now. If Jesus has covered you, then get on your knees and thank Him every day.

> Abba Father! My sweet Daddy! Thank you for loving me so much that you would sacrifice Your only Child so that I could be with You. I can't comprehend Your sacrifice or how you restrained Yourself from covering Jesus for my sake, but I accept it. I accept the covering that You provided out of Your love for me. Amen.

Lake Louise

In Canada, there is the most beautiful lake that I have ever seen called Lake Louise. You should look it up so you can have this image in your mind when you read my journal. I have never been there, but I have seen pictures and video of it. It is the bluest water you can imagine. There are tall, majestic mountains climbing thousands of feet above it in all directions. The lake is so smooth that it mirrors the mountains around it. It is the most peaceful place; one day, if the Lord is willing, I want to go there.

My life before an unwise decision or sin is like a still, calm lake. My life is like Lake Louise. It mirrors the majesty of the Most High God. His peace makes my life still. Sin is like a boulder, not a small stone, that I choose to cast into the calm lake of my life. The ripples go on and on through every part of my life. Once the boulder has been removed and forgiven by God, the ripples continue. The ripples are the consequences of my unwise decision to sin. Listen, God only removes the boulder; He never stops the ripples. They are the natural consequence of my sin. The ripples destroy the mirror-like quality of my life so that the majesty of God gets all blurry and is lost. Sometimes it takes a long time before the ripples finally stop, and the peaceful state of my lake is restored. It happens every time I sin.

I have to guard the calm lake of my life from the boulders of this world that I would choose to throw in it. When I sit here writing this, it seems so easy. How could I ever throw something in my life to disrupt the lake? Then one day my human nature steps up and in a time of weakness for my spirit, I pick up a rock and hurl it in the lake. What must God think of me when I know better? It hurts my heart so much that I can look up in the face of the Most High God and throw a rock right in front of Him in my lake that should be full of His stillness. I actually get tears in my eyes just now writing that into words. What am I thinking? How can I be so weak to exchange something so majestic and calm for ripples?

I do understand that we live in a fallen world. While we do need to recognize our own effects of sin, sometimes the ripples that are in our lake are not from our own throwing. I know that others—and they are typically loved ones or those closest to us—can throw a boulder or boulders in our life. While we seek stillness and the mirror-like quality of the

Lord's majesty, they seek disorder, so they throw heavy boulders in our life. Unfortunately, I have learned that the ripples work the same way. It takes a long time for stillness to be restored.

God is not a God of ripples, but of stillness. He seeks to restore the calm again in our life. He promises us a future that is still. Stay in prayer and study of His Word, whether you made the ripples in your lake or someone else did. The path to stillness is the same. Have faith and patience in the Lord. The ripples do eventually stop, and God's majesty will be mirrored once again.

Dandelions

I have this strong image of a big field. There is only one thing as far as you can see: dandelions! I have never seen so many. Then I see Jesus walking along and bending down close to this one or that one. As soon as He stands up, I see the little white parts of the dandelion take off gracefully flying into the wind. They seem to float through the air forever. I see some dandelions that He walks up to, bends over, and then walks on by them. No little flyaways happen. He bends down close to this one or that one and then moves along. What is He doing? It's almost as if He is having a conversation with each one that He bends down to. I get close, almost like I should not be watching this. I get close enough to see and hear what is going on.

On the next dandelion, Jesus bends down so gently. He gets really close. He speaks to it. I can't hear what He says. I can only hear what the dandelion says back. The dandelion says, "Yes, Lord. Blow on me." All of the sudden the soft, light feathers fly off all around me. It is beautiful. I turn around and see Jesus already bending down to another dandelion. He bends down the same as all the others. I hear the dandelion respond, "No, Lord, do not blow on me." Nothing happens. I am standing there trying to put all this together. Some dandelions wanted the Lord to blow on them, and some didn't. While I am lost in my thoughts of what I am watching, I look up and see Jesus walking straight toward me. Oh my gracious! There's nowhere for me to hide! He knows I have been watching Him! He comes up to me and bends down. Wait a minute. He is bending down to me as if—as if—I were one of those dandelions! What? I look down at myself and see that I am a dandelion, too! I am standing there in disbelief. How can I be a dandelion like all these other ones?

Jesus catches my attention immediately as He bends down close to my softness. He starts talking to just me. I can hear Him clearly this time! I look around at the other dandelions, thinking this is so cool! He says:

> "You are my delight. I have made you for My purpose. I know you have been watching Me blow all those soft, white feathers in the wind. You are a curious little one! You should understand that they are really seeds! My seeds. If I blow on you, it will change the appearance of your dandelion, but it will spread My seeds with the wind so that there can be more dandelions in My garden. If you don't allow Me to blow on you, then you will never be used to make more dandelions. Will you allow Me to blow My breath on you?

I start thinking back to the other dandelions' responses. One said, "Yes, Lord. Blow on me," and one said, "No, Lord. Do not blow on me." I look back at Jesus and say, "I have a choice?" He smiles and says, "You are in My garden, and whatever your answer is will never change that. Nothing can take you out of My hand. There are some here who desire to share what I have given them, and there are some that do not. If you allow me to blow on you, I can use you to plant new dandelions in My garden. Yes, it's your choice. I have given you the seeds, but you have to be willing to be blown. Do you understand?"

I look around and see the other dandelions that didn't want to be blown on. They turn away from me almost in embarrassment of making their choice. I do not judge them. I do wonder why they didn't want to be blown on, though. I know they have their own reasons that they have justified as making sense to them. Maybe they are too busy. Maybe they like their dandelion just like it is. They don't want to change.

It's comfortable, and as long as they have their spot in this garden, they are satisfied. Maybe they are scared to ask the Lord to blow on them because they would no longer be in control of what He may do in their life. They do not know where the Lord will land their seeds, so they would rather not trust that He knows best. They rest in their own understanding. They are safe where they are and that is good enough for them.

The Lord looks at me and says gently, "Dandelion? I will ask you once more, for your lack of response to My question is also your answer. I know that so well. Do you trust Me enough to blow into your life?" I look into His eyes for a second, start smiling, and close my eyes really tight as if trying to prepare myself for flight and say, *"Yes Lord! Blow on Me!"* Immediately I am airborne! Oh my gracious! It feels like I am weightless. Incredible! This is way more exciting than just sitting in the garden. I look down to see Jesus looking up at me smiling, then proceeding to bend down to the next dandelion. One by one.

He talks to each one individually, giving them each a chance to choose to be used by Him. I fly over endless fields of dandelions. There are so many! I keep floating until I see ahead where the field starts thinning out. My seeds start landing everywhere. I fall into the soft, prepared soil and wait on the Lord's next move!

What will you say when He walks up to your dandelion? You know He's coming. Be prepared with your answer. Be mindful that your lack of response will also serve as your answer. He will walk on by you and will not be able to use you. There are plenty of dandelions who will choose to be blown on. The question is whether you will be one of them or whether you will be satisfied to sit in the garden. The Lord has been gracious to give such a choice. He can only use those that are willing. He has learned that by now.

Emotional Truth

Trust in the Lord with all your heart, and do not lean on your own understanding. In all of your ways acknowledge Him, and he will make straight your paths. (Proverbs 3:5–6 ESV)

God made us in His image. When I was little, that always confused me. It was a shock to me to learn later that I did not physically look like God! I guess we need to do a better job explaining God to our little ones! We do not physically look like Him. We look like Him spiritually and emotionally. That is a more abstract concept to grasp. My characteristics should look like His characteristics. Who I am should look like who He is. My spectrum of emotions should line up with His truth of how I should feel about myself.

I should not interpret my emotions based on how I feel, but they should always be based on God's truth and His characteristics. People get themselves on a slippery slope when they start making decisions on how they feel instead of on Godly emotions or thoughts. As soon as they listen to their own emotions for long periods of time, then they can expect hurt. This self-inflicted hurt may be to themselves or to others.

Think of God like an emotional measuring stick. When you start measuring your personal emotions, do they line up with the Lord's? Are your emotions spiraling and tossing you to and fro on the waves of life? We have to have a constant with which to compare our emotions, or the enemy will eat us for lunch. He will keep you spiraling so much that you will not know which way is up. It's a tactic, and if you do not understand this, you are emotionally dead in the water.

The world will tell you that you will never amount to anything. God says, "You are a child of a King." The world will tell you that you feel depressed, and things will not get much better. God says, "You have the emotion of hope." The world tells you that you will physically never measure up. God says, "You are beautiful." The world tells the older generation that they are not valuable. God says, "They are the wisest among you." The world tells you that you are not lovable. God says, "I loved you so much that I sent My son who for you."

The world tells you that you can't keep it together. If you were just a little more like that other Christian then you would not be in the shape you are in. God says, "I personally chose you before the foundation of the world to be Mine. I knit you in your mother's womb. You are exactly how I intended you to be. You are perfect in Christ Jesus just as you are. I hold all things together including you."

The world will tell you that you have so many problems. Bad things happen because of what you have done. It's your own fault. While some problems may be the result of your sin, there are many others that are the result of others' poor choices as a result of exercising their free will. Your feelings and life were unfortunately affected by others. The greatest way the enemy can steal your daily victory is not by tempting you in your weakness but to make you believe you have no ability to control how you feel at any given time.

God has a wide range of emotions that are more intense and far ranging than we can ever imagine for ourselves. They are very strong. Since we are in His emotional image, our emotions are very strong as well. They are so strong and can actually create a prison in your head if you allow them to. They can tear you down and leave you bleeding. You feel like you are dying inside. Emotions seem to feed on each other. They can suck you in, leaving you to drown. The more you dwell on one, the deeper it goes and the more far-reaching an effect it has on your thoughts and behavior.

The effects are not only in your head, but they are manifested to others. Emotions can wreak havoc on your thought processes as you continue to make stuff up in your head that is not based on truth. Your whole perception of yourself or a situation is spinning on *your* truth, which is based on your emotions that you created. There may be little reality in your emotions, but you live in what you have created. Are you beginning to see the problems that emotions can create and how the enemy can paralyze you and spin you like a top?

Proverbs 3:5–6 says, "Trust in the Lord with all your heart, and do not lean on your own understanding. In all of your ways acknowledge Him, and He will make straight your paths" (ESV). I can paraphrase this as heart and mind are very closely associated. "Trust in the Lord with all of your mind which is the source of your emotions, and do not depend or rely on your own understanding. In all your ways acknowledge Truth, and He will make straight your paths." Why would the Lord tell us not to depend or rely on our understanding? Simple. He knows the self-talk we tell ourselves. He knows how we make stuff up in our head. He knows how we feed our unhealthy emotions then react off of them.

How you are understanding things to be may not in fact be reality. The minute you lean on that which is not true in your head, then how can your paths be made straight? He wants your truth to line up with His truth. He wants you to only lean on His understanding. He knows the power of emotions. He created them. They can be used by us for our own good or our own self-destruction.

Sisters and brothers in Christ, you are not okay or okay in life, based on how you feel at any certain time. This is the lie you have bought from this world. You are okay because God is real. He has made promises to you that He has the inability to ever break. He is holding your today and all of your tomorrows. His ways are not your ways, and His thoughts certainly are not your thoughts. Trust Him with what He says before you trust yourself with what you are thinking. This is the emotional truth.

Spiritual Truth

I have spoken about being made in God's image. We understand that we are like Him emotionally. We love because He loves. We hurt because He can hurt. We have righteous anger when things are not the way they should be in this world because He has righteous anger for the same reasons. We seek justice and fairness for everyone because He is just and no respecter of people. Everyone is equal and should be treated as such in His eyes. We care for others because He cares for us. We are emotional beings because we were made by an emotional Being. We do not just share God's emotional image; we share His spiritual image as well.

The atheist and agnostic don't have to believe we are spiritual beings to make it real. God putting spirit within us does not rely on their faith or affirmation of this truth. Did you know that if no one believed in God, that would not negate His existence? God is not dependent on our belief in Him to make Him who He is. That is very comforting to know. If you looked at people groups and cultures across millennia and locations, there is one thing they always share. They all worshipped something.

By this time in our history, there is probably not one thing that exists or doesn't exist that people haven't worshipped. People have worshipped demons, angels, suns, trees, water, sky, wooden idols, gold idols, stone idols, money, material goods, deeper knowledge, stars, universe, flesh, animals, false gods, or themselves. Through time, people have worshipped anything but the one true God. Romans 1:25 says, "They exchanged the truth about God for a lie, and worshipped and served created things rather than the Creator Himself, who is worthy for eternal praise." It is not that people lack something to worship, it's what they choose to worship that is the problem as Paul so eloquently said.

The point I am trying to make is all people worship something in the first place. Have you ever stopped for a moment and thought about the why of this truth? On the sixth day, God scooped up clay from the freshly made earth. He formed it into the shape of the first man. He bent down and breathed into the lifeless soil. Instantly, the soil wrapped itself in flesh and started inhaling and exhaling. That man stood up and looked at His Creator. Because Adam was made in the spiritual image of God, there was immediate worship and fellowship that first day of Adam's life. As created beings, angels also instantly worshipped God. The only reason we yearn to worship is because we have been given a spirit by the Most High God.

We have each been given free will. With that comes freedom. Even though we have been given a spirit, that doesn't mean we will worship with it appropriately. God never demands we use our spirits to worship Him. He doesn't need our worship. It is for our spirits' sake, not His, that we worship Him. He only desires deep and unforced worship from us. I think so many people miss this truth. If you can truly wrap your mind and heart around this, it will completely change your worship of the Most High God. The spiritual truth is that you will worship something in your life, no matter if you are a believer or nonbeliever. The most important question in your life is, "What is your spirit worshipping?" If you are worshipping anything in your life but your Creator, then you are worshipping a lie. So what are you worshipping in your life? God or a lie? Make no mistake: you are worshipping something as this is spiritual truth.

Disgusting!

I woke up this morning, and as is often the case, the Lord brings to mind a verse out of the blue. Some of the verses catch my attention like, "Where in the world did that come from?" I know by now when the Lord gives me a specific verse that He wants me to write a journal about it. I wasn't awake for thirty minutes this morning before He gave me today's verse clearly. I said, "Yuck, Lord!" He said, "Exactly!"

Proverbs 26:11 says, "As a dog returns to its vomit, so a fool repeats his foolishness" (NIV). Now you know why I said, "Yuck, Lord!" I have to write a journal about vomit? Ugh! How do I even start a journal on this? The Lord doesn't much care how I do it just so I do. So here it goes. To understand this verse, I need to answer the question of why dogs vomit in the first place. A dog will vomit when there is some sort of irritation occurring—something doesn't settle well with its system. Vomiting may be a sign of serious trouble as well.

Why do they return to their vomit? No matter how well a dog is fed, it will still rummage around for food from trash cans or anything else they can get a hold of every chance they get. Whether that is food or vomit, dogs do not distinguish between what is good and what is bad. As disgusting as it is, the dog's vomit smells good to them, so they eat again that which they had expelled due to the irritation it originally caused in the first place. Makes sense? They eat something that they should not have. It caused irritation so they expelled it. They got rid of things that should not be there, but since they cannot distinguish between good and bad, they return to it over and over. This verse is starting to make a lot of sense.

How often in my own life have I not distinguished between good and bad? I partook in sin that was an irritation to the Spirit of God within me. He said, "Get rid of that! We cannot have that as a part of you!" I repented of that which I took into my life. Within a very short time, I start smelling that which I got rid of. That trash that I expelled has an aroma that seems to be calling me back.

I return to the same sin that originally irritated the Holy Spirit. I sin again in like manner. It would not be so bad if I returned to that which I repented of and expelled once or twice. No, I return to it many more times than that. In fact, if it were not for the heavier and heavier convicting power of the Holy Spirit, I would re-eat my sin which I had previously repented continuously. Sin–repent–re-sin; again, repent–re-sin. Again, eat something that is irritating–vomit–return to the vomit; eat something that is irritating–vomit–return to the vomit. Sin–repent–re-sin again; repent … Are you starting to see the correlation that God wants you to understand? I am.

This is an indication of some serious problems in our lives. We love our sin too much to stop eating it. A dog eating its own vomit is one of the most disgusting visual images that I know mainly because when they are eating it they make it look like they are enjoying it. Why would we sin–repent–re-sin again usually on the same sin? Because we enjoy it just as much as a dog enjoys his vomit. *Disgusting, right?* All of us fools need to wake up out of slumber to start seeing sin as God sees it!

God is telling us that we disgust Him with our own return to our sin. He says that we are fools that return to our own foolishness. We are disgusting fools because we are in la-la land, justifying the secret sins in our lives. Sin that has been expelled from our lives that is taken back in over and over taste so good to us; otherwise we wouldn't take them back. I don't care how much you minimize sin your life; I speak the truth.

Returning to sin that should not be there is like a dog returning to its vomit. We are doing no differently than what a dog does. You can paint your sin all pretty and justify it all you want as not being that bad. It looks like vomit to God. It smells like vomit to God. He watches as you re-ingest that which should be disgusting to you, yet you act like you enjoy it. Oh how far have we fallen from the goodness that the Lord has for us.

We need to wake up from our foolishness and understand that we are children of the Most High God. We have tasted Divinity. We are dressed in white robes. We have been cleansed whiter than snow. The Lord has blessings that we can't imagine when we live within His will for our lives. Let's not be like dogs when we are children of God. Let's not return to that which is disgusting to us and the Lord when He has invited us to eat at His table where there is only sweetness and holiness.

Hiding and Grieving

Lord, how long will You continually forget me? How long will You hide Your face from me? (Psalm 13:1 HCSB)

Do you ever feel like God hides from you? What a strange question to ponder. Sometimes I lie down in prayer time, with eyes closed and still. I pray, but I feel like there is no dialog. At times in the past, I felt like I was talking to air. Has God heard me? Is God there? I don't see the circumstances that I have prayed about changing around me. Sometimes I have prayed for certain things for years, yet nothing happens. When I am in the middle of my trial and things do not improve, is it wrong to think that God is not listening or hiding from me?

There are references in the Bible such as Deuteronomy 32:20–21 that say God hid His face from the children of Israel. The verses say "I will hide My face from them; I will see what will become of them, for they are a perverse generation—unfaithful children" (HCSB). Several verses following reveal God's righteous anger at the children for choosing idols over Him. He calls them worthless idols. Do we have any of those in our life today? Have we been unfaithful to God by putting Him anywhere but first on our priority list? Have we then justified His placement? I have.

God is the same God of the Old Testament that He is today. Malachi 3:6 says God does not change (NIV). If He became angry with His ancient children, could we also make Him angry? I would have to ask myself, "Am I doing the same behavior of the children of Israel?" While we do not share the same sort of idols of the past, we certainly have our modern idols. We may justify them, but they are still idols. Anything that takes God out of our center focus is an idol. I wonder how many times I have made God hide His face from me because I have made Him angry due to the idols I have in my own life.

While God has not changed and still has righteous anger for what He observes in this world and things in our lives, we are now under the New Covenant. The Holy Spirit does not descend, stay a little while, and then ascend. Because of Christ, the Holy Spirit is clearly put within us. The Holy Spirit does not leave us. While I do not believe that God hides His face (by that I mean hides His plan from us), I believe we have moved now to grieving the indwelt Holy Spirit (1 Thessalonians 5:19; Ephesians 4:30–31 HCSB) with our thoughts and actions. Grieving the Holy Spirit may feel the same to us today as God hiding His face from the children of Israel in the past. I cannot say for sure.

Grieving the Spirit can be simplified to choosing your way over God's way. You can look at the scriptural references for the specifics, but it says in order to avoid grieving the Holy Spirit, put aside all wickedness. A synonym for wickedness is iniquity. A synonym for iniquity is sin. Every time you choose your way over the Most High God, you are sinning; you are in disobedience to His perfect will for your life. For a Christian to grieve the Holy Spirit is a very serious matter, one that today's Christians don't think twice about. We justify our idols. We justify our way. We justify our sin. God justifies none of this. He will be talking to us personally at the Judgment Seat of Christ about what we have justified so easily while we were on earth.

According to the Word, we make God angry, and we grieve the Holy Spirit when we sin. Stop justifying truth. Wake up. He is Holy and expects holiness from His children. It would be best to stand in front of the Most High God's throne as transparently as possible at all times. It makes discerning God's will much easier with a clear conscience. Confess your sins immediately, and pray for strength to stay away from temptation. You place yourself in temptation most of the time, not the other way around.

You choose your own way. You are in control of your sin as each one is a choice. If you are not careful, soon your sin will be in control you.

You will find that when you want to stop, sin grips you with the pleasure it provides. When I lie down or kneel in prayer, it is my responsibility to ensure there is no sin between me and God. We will not have a productive conversation until that happens.

I would like to add one last thing about feeling like we don't hear God. We have to remember that God's thoughts are not our thoughts and His ways are not our ways. When we pray with a clear conscience for something and we haven't received our answer, then we have to trust that His way is higher and better than ours. Be mindful not to ask for something that you already know would be out of His will in the first place. He will never answer you in the affirmative. You may see it one way and He sees it another. He will only answer in the way He sees that is best for you according to His will. You don't have to like it; you just have to trust Him. So while you think He is not listening and answering your prayer, He is behind the scenes working out all things according to His will. He will reveal it to you when it is time. Your job is to be faithful in prayer, in petition, and to maintain a clear conscience. God hears you.

Choices

We have two choices. We can wait for the Lord, or we can wait on ourselves. The two choices contradict each other, yet we try so hard to fit them together, tied up with a nice little ribbon. That is delusional. The Lord says:

> Wait on Me. My timing is perfect in all areas of your life. If you move ahead or behind My timing, then you are waiting on yourself. I am the Most High God, yet you actually think with your finite mind you know the best timing for things in your life? Child, I invented time. You can have faith in My perfection of it.

How can we justify, as children of God, that we trust Him if we say back to Him, "You invented time, but I live within it, and You move too slowly!" We have numerous stories from the Bible of consequences for people who were too impatient to wait for the Lord. Ironically, I am named after one of them! You would think we would be wise enough to learn from others' mistakes. But no. We are just as impatient as everyone before us.

I am beginning to understand that waiting on the Lord comes with a deep trust and spiritual maturity. Waiting on the Lord and not yourself requires discipline. The question I have to ask myself is, "How disciplined and spiritually mature am I to wait on the One who created perfect timing? How badly do I want my own way to go it alone without the Lord?" Waiting on the Lord is one of the hardest things you will ever do, but the heavenly blessings will be heaped upon you if you do. Have a nice day waiting on the Lord. It is truly an honor. It shows our trust and respect of His will. It should never be a burden.

"Where are you?"

I had never contemplated the first question of the Bible before. Do you remember when the Lord asked Adam and Eve, "Where are you?" I know He was calling out to His child, and I understand why. The child had previously shown affection toward God. The child previously had time to tell Him the things on his heart and mind. He previously had joy in the communion. The child had previously heard God's voice, sought His truth, guidance, and wisdom along with feeling His affection. All of these things happened daily in the fellowship between the child and God.

Then one day, God shows up to continue to give and receive affection. He shows up to hear what is in your heart and on your mind. He shows up to share truth and wisdom. God in His consistency and devotion to you as His child simply shows up. Then He looks around and asks the same question of His first child millennia ago, "Where are you?" I have never contemplated that three words could possibly hold that much convicting power. What am I to a say back to the Most High God when He calls?

I fervently pray that I can be like the boy Samuel when God called him. Samuel answered boldly, "You called me? Speak, Lord. I am here. I am your child, and I am listening." How can we justify saying anything else to God? The fact of the matter is we do. I challenge you that God never shows up in your life and has to ask, "Where are you?" It is a fair question. What will you say to Him?

Feeling Saved?

I am sure there are very few of us that have never doubted our salvation. Have you ever thought of one of the following statements before? "I don't feel as close to God as I used to. Am I really saved?" "I don't have a deep desire to tell other's about Christ. Am I really saved?" "I'm hit-and-miss going to church. Am I really saved?" "I am not hearing the Holy Spirit talking to me like that other Christian. Am I really saved?" "I really don't love people as much as I should because I like my comfort zone. Am really saved?" "I just don't feel saved. Am I really saved?"

"How could salvation have been that easy in the first place? Surely I missed something. Am I really saved if I didn't do everything that I thought I should?" "If I am not all of these things then I must not be saved." The possibilities are eternal of why we don't "feel saved." I say they are eternal, because the enemy that you are listening to speak doubt to you is eternal.

Do you remember the story of Adam and Eve? When Satan came to Eve to tempt her, Eve spoke truth. Satan cast doubt on the truth that Eve had in her mind and heart by saying, "Did God really say?" Before Satan said this statement, there had been no doubt in God's truth in the human heart. Think of the power of doubt cast into Eve's thought processes. Think of the power of doubt that we have in our thought processes. Truth was exchanged for a lie that very second, because the doubt was believed. This was Satan's first tactic on humans; it worked so well that he still uses it to this very day.

"Do you think someone would want to love you?" "Do you really think this marriage is going to get any better?" "You have to know that this whole situation is really your fault, and no one has the guts to tell you." "As long as you have been divorced, do you really think anyone is really out there for you?" "Do you really think you will ever amount to anything?" "Do you think God would forgive you for that?" "Do you think you are worthy to even call yourself a Christian?" "You know what kind of person you are. Do you really think Jesus loves people like you?" "You know you are not the Christian you need to be; is it possible that you were never saved in the first place?"

"Did God really say all you have to do is believe that He rose Jesus from the grave, and Jesus was the Messiah to be saved? Don't you think that is a little too simple? Don't you think you have some work you need to do for that salvation to be complete?" "You know you don't feel saved sometimes. You need to realize the only reason you feel that way is because it is true." On and on, the enemy of your soul goes as he tries lie after lie on you to see which one will finally work. He never rests.

God would never call you to Himself and then cast doubts in your mind of His love and acceptance of you. The truth of the matter is that you are sealed by the Holy Spirit on the day you confess Christ. Ephesians 1:13–14 says:

> You also were included in Christ when you heard the message of truth, the gospel of your salvation. When you believed, you were marked in Him with a seal, the promised Holy Spirit who is a deposit guaranteeing our inheritance until the redemption of those who are God's possession to the praise of His glory. (NIV)

The very instant that you realized you were a sinner in need of a Savior, the Holy Spirit was put within you by God. Any person with the indwelling of the Holy Spirit is God's child. Nothing can take you out of His hand, certainly not your negative human self-talk and the Enemy's lies.

God never said that you would "feel saved." Feelings are based on human emotions. God's plan for salvation had nothing to do with emotions but everything to do with reality. God's plan for salvation had everything to do with what He did, not how you feel about what He did or any doubts you may have about what He did. He didn't seek counsel with humans to see how they felt about His plan before going through with it. What humans thought and felt about it was irrelevant, just like human's thought and feelings are today when it comes to God's plan for this world.

Satan has infused emotions into it because he knows human emotions fluctuate. He knows he can keep them riding the waves. If everything is going well, then the human will feel saved. If the human hits some trials, backslides a bit, or doesn't meet the standard, then he or she won't feel saved. It is an ingenious tactic by the enemy. Remember you are not saved by what you feel inside; you are saved by what God did. Salvation is based on what God did. You have to accept that as truth or deny it. There's no emotion that salvation is based on—it is based on truth. As soon as you base your salvation on emotion, then you are setting yourself up for doubt and enemy attack. You are building your life on shifting sand. You set your salvation on what God did for you, and then you are building your life on solid ground.

When the attacks come—and they will—they do not negate your original assurance of salvation. God doesn't snatch away the salvation promise or Holy Spirit that He gave you if you doubt your salvation. He gave you His Word. He gave you Christian fellowship. He gave you the avenue of prayer to come to Him when you are struggling with emotions and feelings. He hasn't left you alone in your doubts. The Enemy will tell you that you are though.

Be very careful which voices you listen to in your mind. The Voice of Truth? The voice of lies? God knows the enemy's tactics better than we do, which is why He went to great lengths to give you the resources you would need to travel the Christian road, including how to deal with doubts. You have the strength inside of you, by the power of the Holy Spirit, to listen to the Voice of Truth. Romans 8:16 is one of my favorite verses of the entire Bible. It says, "The Spirit, Himself, bears witness with our spirit, that we are the children of God" (ESV). Hebrews 6:18 says, "It is impossible for God to lie" (ESV). If God says you are His child, then it doesn't matter how you feel at any given time, you are His child. Nothing can change this. That is the Voice of Truth.

All Lies

I have a deeper understanding of how crafty our enemy can be with just one lie. I am learning that he goes around and keeps selling lies until we buy one. The following are some examples of such lies that some of us may have bought. "There is no God." "You are unworthy." "You will never be good enough." "You will never have what you have prayed for." "You will always be alone." "No one wants you." "God has forgotten you." "You will always have these same problems." "You will never be more than you are now." "God is not listening to you." "You deserve to follow your own will and there will be no consequences." "It is okay to skip your quiet time today. God will understand how busy you are." On and on the lies can go.

You may say, "Oh, I would never buy one of those lies!" My question would be, "Are you lying when you say that?" The enemy never stops trying out different lies on you until you finally buy one from him. When you do, you will immediately see it only makes you empty, sad, lonely, and defeated. In the end, that is the enemy's only objective. Friend, listen! Wake up, and do not buy a lie from the Enemy. Stand firm, and buy the truth from the Most High God. It has already been purchased at an extremely high price.

Aerial View

I had a dream last night. I know it had multiple meanings for me. This morning at 2:30, the Lord woke me up to tell me this one particular meaning. I had been lost in a woody, swampy area for what seemed like a long time. I remember being very frightened and weary. I found a platform in a tree that I climbed on to. Once I did, I could see the path clearly out of the woods. I was saved.

The Lord showed me that while I was walking on the ground trying to find my way out, I only had a limited linear perspective. I had no idea if I was going in circles, deeper into the woods, or in the right direction. I was in complete uncertainty. Once I climbed up on the tree's platform and looked out, it gave me an aerial perspective. I could see the right path clearly and, more importantly, immediately. The Lord has shown me that when I am walking in life, walking through a difficult situation, walking through hard decisions, and even walking through sin, I will either go in circles or get myself deeper in trouble with my limited perspective. The Lord says:

> My Child, look up! Heaven is My throne, and the earth is My footstool. I have the ultimate aerial view! I know the right way you should travel in any area of your life, because I can see if clearly from My view. Walk closely with Me, and I will always guide you.

So we are faced with our limited linear view or God's unlimited aerial view. Which one will I choose? Should it even be a difficult choice for me to make? Our flesh screams, "Linear! Go with what you can see." God whispers to our heart, "Aerial. Go with what I can see."

Trusting

We form a trust bond for many reasons. I believe one of the biggest contributors for trust is consistency. The more consistent someone is in your life, the more trust deepens. The less consistent someone is, the less you naturally trust them that they are truly who they say they are. This is fair.

God says, "I am the same yesterday, today, and tomorrow. You can trust that I am who I say that I am. I will do what I say I will. I consistently show up in our relationship. I act the same." When we self-reflect on who we are, our thoughts and our actions as Christians, can we be trusted? Trust in a relationship depends on consistency. Are we being consistent in our relationship with a Holy God? Can God trust us in this same relationship like we trust Him?

I believe we have it all wrong. We always tell others to trust God. Preachers tell us to trust God. He has met the conditions perfectly for that trust. We never turn that question around in our head. It is fair for God to ask, "Can I trust you in a personal relationship with Me? Can you be consistent?" How much do you think God can trust that you are who you claim to be in Him based on your current consistency?

Do you meet the conditions for the Lord to trust you? Again, don't worry about the ability to trust God. Be very concerned what you would say to the Lord if He asked you the trust questions. He has every right to ask because He is holding up His side of the relationship consistently. Are you? By the way, I've learned that God doesn't much care about what you say with your mouth. It's your thoughts and actions that He is concerned about the consistency of. Be very mindful of that. That took me a while to get!

Wickedness

I know when the Word of God repeats a truth that I should always stop and think, "Why is this so important?" Paul tells us to have a pure heart, good conscience, and a sincere faith: a pure heart so that no wicked way can be found in me and a good conscience, not just in front of friends and family, but at all times. I think we are so glad they really can't see in our hearts and minds. God says, "You better be more concerned with having a good conscience in front of me. I can see your heart and mind. Nothing is hidden from Me."

We are to have sincere faith. By faith, Paul says, we can engage in battle. Who or what is this battle against? If wickedness can be within you as the Bible teaches, then we are to be strong against our own flesh. Jesus says that since He sees that you are faithful to Him, He will strengthen you in this battle. You may say, "Wickedness in me? No! The devil comes and brings his wickedness to me." This may be true in some accounts, but all sin is chosen. You can blame the Devil all you want. All he does is gives suggestions for sin. You are the one that says, "Yes" and "More." Wake up! Wickedness can be in you. Get a hold of that truth, Friend!

Torn Paper

No one cannot serve two masters. (Matthew 6:24 NIV)

Choose you this day whom you will serve. (Joshua 24:15 AKJV)

I was in quiet time just now. I had cleared my mind and was focused on bowing before the throne of God. I praised Him for His existence. I praised Him for loving me so completely. I was being still in front of Him. I prayed that I would remain humble. I prayed that I would hear His voice when He chose to talk to me.

Suddenly, in my mind's eye, I saw a piece of paper floating down from Heaven. I saw it floating down slowly as if carried by a gentle wind. I could not take my eyes off of it. It hung in the air in front of me. I looked at it and inwardly knew that was my life. There were no words on it, but that paper was my life. Slowly, a small corner of the paper started tearing by itself. I watched as nothing was touching the small piece of paper as it was being torn from the whole sheet. The small piece of paper floated to land at the throne of God. The rest of the sheet landed firmly in my hand, and I gripped my life. Jesus looked at me and said, "I don't want a torn little piece of your life. I died for all of your life. I want all of you. Why do you give Me just a piece?"

How have I justified to myself that I have given the Lover of my soul only part of my life—not even half, but just a corner? How do I reason with my human logic that I can take care of the rest and not only can I take care of the rest, but I can do a way better job than the Almighty God? The depth of pride of my lifestyle starting with the smallest thought processes! I can't live three quarters of my life under my own control and give Him a quarter of it and expect that I will be who He created me to be in Him. Yet, that has been my thinking. God is a God of miracles right? He should be able to take one quarter of my life and make things how they should be for the rest. That makes logical sense.

I can't live with one foot in this world and one foot in His. A house divided against itself will fall. Because of pride, I think I am different than this divided house. I think I am above doing things exactly as God has laid out in His Word. I reason that I don't have to do everything He says. I act like I can pick and choose what part of this Christian life that I like and don't like. I live the parts that I like, and ignore the others.

The other would be the part that God really needs me in. I don't have the power to divvy up my life between God and myself, yet I act like I do. I don't have to be totally committed. I don't have to relinquish all control. I don't have to give God the whole paper of my life to be okay. Justification. Reason. Logic. Lies.

I have been living a lie with all of my justification and human logic of how a Christian life should be. God never compromises with one of His children; I am no different. Knowing this, I have unilaterally compromised with God. I actually think I get somewhere in the relationship with Him by doing this? I think He's okay with me taking the lead reins most of the time and consulting Him when I get in trouble, at the end of myself, or in need of an answered prayer? I actually think I can use God when it is convenient for me.

You may have never shared this same compromised life with God, the same torn disproportional Christian life. If you have, I am beginning to understand what we have done. We haven't robbed God; we have robbed ourselves. God is perfect and complete. It is we who are not. We need to give all of ourselves to be perfect and complete in Him. We tell ourselves we are okay with a little God in our lives, but look at our lives. Look what we are capable of doing in our minds and actions when we hold the majority of the torn paper. Where's the goodness in that? Where is the glory in that? Where do we get ahead in that?

I have heard once, "If you tell a lie long enough, it becomes your truth." I think we have good hearts and mean well, but I think mentally we lie to ourselves of how much of God we need in our lives. I never contemplated that the two masters that could be served were me and God. That is where my pride showed itself. I was blinded to the truth. I have one life to commit to one master. I choose to completely serve God, not myself. I have controlled the majority of the paper long enough. God says, "I want every piece of your life." Let's stop justifying giving Him the top corner.

Get Your House in Order!

Do you not know that your bodies are temples of the Holy Spirit, who is in you, whom you have received from God? You are not your own. You were bought at a price. Therefore honor God with you bodies. (1 Corinthians 6:19–20 NIV)

Raise your hand if you like to clean! Those who raised your hands are weird. Put your hands back down! My closest girlfriends can testify that I do not like to clean. I remember when I was a little girl, my best friend would help me do my house chores before my mom came home. My friend didn't want to see me get in trouble. That is true! I have never liked to clean. The stack of towels that are on my couch for a week are clean. That is close enough to being put up. The only time my whole house is in order is when company comes.

The only logical reason to clean is to invite company over at Christmas. Think of the time and energy I saved cleaning! When we start cleaning, the children ask, "Who's coming?" That is the honest truth. I have actually had nightmares that people have come over and peeked in each room in my house to see how untidy it is. I wish I was kidding. Now that my boys are old enough, they have a lot more responsibility in the house. They can push a vacuum cleaner and clean tubs!

Every time I see them cleaning a part of the house that I don't have to clean, I have an inner joy that comes out of me. There's a permanent smile on my face—as though I have hit the lottery! Why didn't I have more than two children? Think of the work the other children could have done in the house! It's really bad when you tell your child, "Go clean your room," only for them to look at you and say, "Why? Yours isn't clean?" Then I say, "I'm the mother! Go clean your room!" That's the best comeback I have.

Why don't we keep our houses in order sometimes? I can think of many reasons. There are other things to do that seem more pressing for your attention. There are other people that need to be attended to. There are other places that are more fun to be. There are other activities that are more stimulating or relaxing to be involved in. There never seems to be enough time. There doesn't seem to be a point as it only gets back to the way it was before.

There is no direct impact in our life if it is not kept. There is no excitement in it. I have rationalized all these reasons in my head at different times. When I have, every one of them makes sense to me, depending on which reason I chose. Knowing that my body is the house of the Lord and knowing that I have had it unkept, I can look back at these same reasons to understand how I rationalized it. I do not think when my house of the Lord was unkept that I was doing horrible things against the Lord. I just wasn't using my house in the best way for Him. I wasn't being very hospitable to the Holy Spirit to let Him have free reign in all the rooms.

The clutter in my house of the Lord was strewn about. I couldn't see everything clearly because there was that clutter, which needed to be thrown away. There were things that needed to be washed. There was some updating that needed to be done. There was some rearrangement of some items that would make the floor plan easier for the Holy Spirit and me to maneuver in. It's hard to honor the Lord when my house is not in order.

The first thing you have to do to get your house in order is to recognize that it is in disorder right now. That sounds easy enough, but it is not really. If we have lived in a disordered house for long periods of time, then the phenomenon of desensitization may occur. To desensitize means to make indifferent, unaware, make inactive, make less sensitive, deaden, anesthetize, and numb. Even though your house of the Lord is indwelt with the Holy Spirit doesn't not necessary mean that you are not desensitized to Him. You may be numb to Him.

You may behave indifferently to Him. You may not be sensitive enough to Him. You may have grieved Him so much that He isn't active in your life. You are so desensitized to this truth that you are totally unaware of the presentation of your house. When I say you have to recognize that your house is in disorder in the first place, this means you will have to wake up a bit and do some soul searching. You need to ask the Lord what kind of shape your house is in.

What is the second thing you have to do to get your house in order? When the Lord starts cleaning house, let Him. You can't give Him two of the five rooms of your house. That is not how it works. God says that He bought your house at a price, and it is no longer your own. That would be like selling my home but telling the new owners they are not allowed in the master bedroom and bath. We would never do that in real life, but that is exactly what we do with the Lord. We justify it so well that is makes sense. God knows better than we ever could how to put our house in order. He built it in the first place. He knows every square inch of His own house.

He knows what needs to be swept and put in the trash can. He knows what old clothes you don't need to wear anymore. He knows what literature needs to be burned. He knows what thoughts need to be renewed and filtered. He knows what Internet sites need to be blocked. He knows which emails need to be erased. He knows what pantry and refrigerator items need to trashed. He knows what debt needs to be paid before anything else is brought in the house. He knows what people need to be coming or going in the house. He knows what programs need to be playing in front of us. He knows what grudges need to be forgiven. He knows how to clean your house better than you ever could.

Have you ever had a salesman come to the door and you go hide? You hear him knocking, but you pretend like you are not home. You are hoping he will go away quickly. I can't be the only one who does this! Sometimes that is the way we treat the Lord. He is the salesman that I am pretending like I don't hear. The Lord doesn't have to knock on His own house!

He is already in it, and you can't hide from Him behind the couch. He sees everything that takes place in your house. You have never swept a thing under the carpet. I don't care how well you think you have covered it up. Don't buy your own lie that He has. Your house is His house. You willingly sold it to Him. He signed the papers in blood. Recognize who the rightful owner of your house is. Recognize if it is in disarray. Allow Him to do some deep cleaning to put it in the order that is best for Him and you. Make sure that once He gets your house in order, you maintain it. I have learned that houses can get messy really quickly.

Now! Not Later

I truly believe that Christians have good intentions in their hearts to prepare and nurture close personal relationships with the Lord. Since we assume that we have a tomorrow, we put ourselves first today: our needs. Our plans. Our schedules. Our errands. Our business. Our work. Our school. Our family. Our everything. We put ourselves first today with anticipation of putting God first tomorrow. If He can only be patient enough until after you get everything done, then you will put Him first. How is that going for you?

The thing is—we are not guaranteed a tomorrow. Just because you "feel" that you will have a tomorrow, doesn't make that a reality. It doesn't matter anyway because God doesn't dwell where we can meet Him in our tomorrow. He can only dwell with us in today because of our own temporal restraints of our humanity. You are telling God that you will dwell with Him in a time that you physically cannot live in and you have no guarantee of? Think about it. If the whole truth be told, you only have now. You also can't tell Him that you will meet Him tonight. You can say it, but that doesn't mean your soul will not be required of you before that time. Who really knows? Since we don't know, then it would be wise not to assume.

We really need to stop taking time for granted and meet God in the now. Don't buy a lie that God won't miss you today. He has already showed up and is waiting for you. Would you ever keep an important person waiting? If the Apostle Paul came over for a visit, would you say that you would meet up with him tomorrow? How about Abraham or Moses? Are you insane? How in the world do you justify keeping the Most High God waiting? I'm sure when we get to Heaven God will not ask, "Where are you?" but "What took you so long?" How will you answer? I can promise you that you don't have a good enough excuse. So just save it, because you are the only one buying it anyway.

"Yes, Lord"

There are many reasons God gave us children. One reason is becoming clearer as Jonah and Andrew get older. They seem to be requiring more repetition to obey requests. They are slower at following through on requests. They question our requests. Yes, they at times disobey and ignore our requests. As a parent, I stand in disbelief of my children's thinking and actions. It's like sometimes they act as if I'm not even there speaking to them.

It was on such an occasion this week that God stopped me cold in my tracks as I was saying to Jonah, "Why aren't you listening to me?" The Holy Spirit got a hold of me with such power that I felt He had me by my shirt collar and said clearly, "How are you any different than him in your behavior toward Me? I am your Father, and you are My child!" It just took my breath away. I had to go sit in my room and ponder His words.

How many times has God repeated, "No, don't do that anymore," and I still continue. God says, "I want you to spend more time with Me in prayer and in My Word," and I say, "I'll do that later. I'm busy." God says, "Do this" and I say, "Why and what for?" God says, "I'm here and trying to talk to you, Child" and I say, "Huh? I can't hear you. I don't have time for You." How many times have I acted toward God exactly as my children act toward me? Yet my Father happens to be the Most High God!

The Holy Spirit has an amazing way of putting things in perspective for me, leaving me no room for argument. The Lord has made it abundantly clear to me that He is only interested in two words out of my mouth when He speaks to me and that is, "Yes, Lord." Anything besides that and I am choosing disobedience of my Holy Father. I act just like my own children. You can accept this truth or choose to believe that saying something different like, "Wait, Lord" or "No, Lord" to the Most High God is acceptable. If you actually sell yourself that lie, then that makes you disobedient. God gives you free will. Choose wisely what you will say to Him and how quickly you respond.

Let's Go for a Walk

I love a good contrast. It really helped to solidify what I am learning about. I like to see why I should do one thing over another, why I should make one choice over another. If you are successful in convincing me which side of an issue that I should be on or which decision I should make, it will be very difficult to convince me to change direction in the future. I take my time in making choices as I want to do what is best for my life and those people my life affects. I believe the majority of you share my thinking.

Let's go for a walk. We have two choices on which walk we take. One I will call the "Death Walk" and the other I will call the "Life walk." Now, I know what you are thinking! "Death Walk? I would never choose to take that." Sure you would. Don't overestimate yourself. If the truth be known, you have already taken this walk. If you are not a Christian, you are still walking it. Some have walked this way for longer periods than others. Let's start out with the "Death Walk" as it sounds so inviting. Ephesians 2:1–3 says:

> You were *dead* in your trespasses and sins in which you previously *walked* according to this worldly age, according to the ruler of the atmospheric domain, the spirit disobedient. We too all previously lived among them in our fleshly desires, carrying out the inclinations of our flesh and thoughts, and by nature we were children under wrath, as the others were also. (HCSB)

Before accepting Christ, think of yourself as a walking dead man or a walking dead woman. You were so dead that you didn't even know that you were dead. You took this Death Walk for three reasons. Paul said, "You walked according to the worldly age." The world says, "Do whatever feels good! Promiscuity, fornication, alcoholism, adultery in your heart or action, pornography, lying, cheating, and hiding things from others are all okay. There is no real accountability anyway. There will be no consequences for your choices later in life. You are just fine."

What this world lies that is okay to think and feel, you believed it hook, line, and sinker. You were a dead man walking and loved every minute of it. Paul says we walk this way according to the ruler of the atmospheric domain. A ruler is usually a real being. The very real being that controls the atmospheric domain is Satan. Ephesians 6:12 says, "For we do not wrestle against flesh and blood, but against the rulers, against the authorities, against cosmic powers over this present darkness, against the spiritual forces of evil in the heavenly places" (HCSB). Satan and his demons are very real. Do not underestimate their tactics and intelligence when it comes to you taking the death walk. They would like nothing more to suck you back in and see you lose your daily victory in Christ.

Finally, Paul added that you take the Death Walk due to your own fleshly choices and thoughts. You can't blame everything on this world and Satan. You are ultimately responsible as no one or nothing can force you to sin. Every one of us has taken this walk, "But God, who is abundant in mercy, because of His great love that He had for us, made us alive with the Messiah even though we were dead in trespasses. By grace you are saved" (Ephesians 2:4–5 HCSB). By the grace of God in the sacrifice of Christ Jesus, He has changed our walk from death to life.

This new "Life Walk" is a stark contrast to the previous walk. Once you start walking in life, you should not want to walk in death. You have victory over death by Jesus. I will have to add though, due to our own weakness of the flesh and the strength of the world around us, we compromise far too often by walking the line between life and death. We can never lose our salvation, but we can still be in our trespasses and sin if we spend time there. Nothing good comes from it. No matter what comes your way, walk in life.

Paul describes in Ephesians 4:1–3 the Life Walk that we should take since accepting the grace of God. He says, "Walk worthy of the calling you have received, with all humility and gentleness, with patience, accepting one another in love, diligently keeping the unity of the Spirit with the peace that binds us" (HCSB). As you are on the Life Walk, the very characteristics of the Spirit will be evident in you. "Keeping the unity of the Spirit" is a very interesting phrase. If you want to be unified in the Spirit, then you should avoid creating disunity in your life and in the life of others. Disunity takes the peace away from our lives. We are one in the Body of Christ. We all drink of one Spirit.

Ephesians talks about the "Spirit of disobedience." Once you allow a spirit of disobedience to enter into your life, your thinking is affected first. Once you justify the disobedience of God's way for your life, your actions are affected. I have learned a hard life lesson. Once you entertain the spirit of disobedience, you have lost the unity of the Spirit and the peace that binds you unravels quickly. It has amazed me in the past how easily I could move from walking in life to walking back in death. The pull that you feel from the Death Walk can be very strong. Diligently stay unified in the Spirit where there will be only peace for you no matter your situation.

Remember Paul says, "Walk worthy of the calling you have received." This Life Walk that has been received by us is the better way. It is God's way. We once were dead, and we walked in it. Now we are alive. The Life Walk we have received by our own choice is honorable, admirable, and useful. God, in His grace, has told us how to walk in life. May you and I be strong enough, by the indwelling of the Holy Spirit, to do it.

Thought Life

I think about my Christian walk when I have allowed sin to come into my life by either thoughts or actions. I used to distinguish between thoughts and actions as thoughts being the lesser of the two sins, but the Lord has shown me differently. They are the same. The Lord really wants us to know this truth. In Psalms 139:23, David tells the Lord, "Search me, O God, and know my heart! Try me and know my thoughts" (ESV)! King David understood that holiness and godliness start with the thoughts. It was his thoughts that followed with action that lost for him the honor of building God's temple. He lost his holiness and godliness so quickly by not controlling what was in his mind, and there were huge consequences.

I am convinced we think that there are no consequences for our thoughts, only our actions. How wrong we are. You fool yourself, because you have already fallen from holiness and godliness way before the action occurs. When that happens, you are out of communion with the Most High God. You have opened yourself up to full enemy attack. You think there are no consequences for your thoughts? Think again. God knew every single thing David was thinking. Nothing was hidden, nor are our thoughts hidden. Why do we act like they are? The Lord keeps bringing me back again and again to this truth. It's like He is saying, "We are staying here at this one truth until you understand how important your thoughts are."

I'm learning what you think really is where your heart is. You can put on a good front to others every day and even to your family, but what you think is who you are, way more than what you do. It's the person that God sees and knows. You lie to yourself and say, "Nobody really knows, not even God." There is power in the four letter word, "M-I-N-E." Once our thoughts say, "Mine," we lose accountability, we justify, and we hold on to those thoughts with a vice grip. We exchange godliness and holiness for what we think is ours. Good trade, Right?

The Lord is not going to play tug a war with your will. He doesn't play games; we do. He will let you have your own way by His gift of free will, but if you think you got the better end of the stick, then you are a fool. You know what the Lord asked me? "Why don't you hold on to Me as tight as you do your thoughts and things you think are yours?" If we did, I can promise you our word should change from M-I-N-E to Y-O-U-R-S. Holiness and godliness would be on the road to being restored. So what word are you saying today? Mine or Yours? My thoughts or His holiness?

Sitting in the Lord's Presence

Then King David went in, sat in the Lord's presence, and said, "Who am I, Lord God, and what is my house that You have brought me this far? What you have done so far was a little thing to you, Lord God." (2 Samuel 7:18–19 HCSB)

Do you know what fascinates me about God's written Word? It is how another person can read the same verse as I read, but we come away with two totally different messages. The messages are not contradictory to each other at all. The Lord just shows us different things according to what He wants them to focus on. I think it is depends on where we are in their lives, as well. The Spirit guides each one of us as the Word of God is alive and active (Hebrews 4:12 HCSB). It is an experience each time you open the Word of God. The problem with Christians is that they don't open it enough. They don't spend enough time waiting on the Spirit to speak before they close it and move on with temporal and meaningless stuff. That is for another journal!

My friend and I were emailing about this verse. He was contemplating different things about this verse. He was pondering why God allows bad things to happen to good people as David had some bad things happen to him through the years. The trials of Saul with David's life being in danger, losing his best friend Jonathon, as well as his first-born son were all very bad things. My friend also was asking why God allows good things to happen to any of us as the world we live in is dying, and we are certainly not deserving or worthy of anything good from the Lord. These are all very deep things to ponder.

When I read this same verse, the Spirit guided me to ponder something totally different than my friend. The question of good or bad things happening to good people did not come to my mind when reading these verses. The part that stopped me completely was five words of the verse. David "sat in the Lord's presence." David was so humbled that he started out as a poor shepherd boy but was now sitting in a palace as the King of Israel (2 Samuel 7:8 HCSB). God reminds him of this fact so David speaks back, "Who am I, Lord God, that you have brought me this far?" David recognized God's power as he tells the Lord, "What you have done so far was a little thing to You." He knows God can do much mightier things than this and will. David goes on in the next few verses to tell the Lord, "Not only have you made me what you have made me, but you speak about future events as well." David was in awe of how insignificant he was and how significant the Lord God was. He goes on to tell God, "You are great. There is no one like You, and there is no God besides You."

David's prayer of thanksgiving wasn't spoken under a tree or in his palace. Verse 18 said, "King David went in and sat in the Lord's presence." Where on earth would that have been? David went into the Tabernacle. This was the holiest place in Israel. That is where the Lord's presence was. David was serious about his relationship with God. He got as close as He could get to God on Earth and "sat down in His presence." What boldness. David even talks about his own courage on doing this later.

The only reason David would have been able to do this is because he had a close relationship with God. There was no fear. There was only communion. You stand up in the presence of important people. You don't sit. I doubt people would even sit in King David's presence, but yet David sits in the presence of the Most High God. This says that he had spent so much time in God's presence that he felt comfortable. David says later in chapter 7, "Your servant has found the courage to pray this prayer to You. Lord, God, You are God; Your words are true. Please bless your Servant's house." Not only does David sit in God's presence, he speaks courageously and boldly to ask God to bless him and his family. He expects something from the Lord.

There is so much packed, not only in these couple of verses that I talked about, but all of 2 Samuel chapter 7. I highly encourage you to take time to study it. This chapter is very important as God lays out a Messianic prophecy of Jesus coming from the House of David. I think that so often Christians stand stiffly in the presence of God, maybe even feeling awkward of what to say or do. They say what they need, spend little time waiting for a reply, and get back to their lives—mostly due to the fact that they don't know what God's voice sounds like in their lives. For Christians to "Sit in the Lord's presence" would indicate that they may stay a while. They are very busy, so sitting never comes into their thinking.

The other reason Christians don't "sit in the Lord's presence" is they have not formed that close relationship with Him. They may not feel that sitting is an acceptable position to be in when they talk to Him. Let me tell you something. The longer you spend in God's presence, the more relaxed you become. He wants us to be so close and comfortable with Him that we sit in His presence. David "sat in the Lord's presence." The Lord accepted this posture, because David sat with a humble, respectful, and courageous heart. He was human and a forgiven sinner just like us. We have every right to sit in the Lord's presence as well. Ephesians 2:6 says, "He also raised us up with Him and seated us with Him in the heavens, in Christ Jesus" (HCSB). David sat in the Lord's presence, and by His grace we also sit with Him.

The Five Senses

As I sit here in quiet time, the more I contemplate God, the less I can understand Him. *God*: who and what is He? Who can know Him? No one has ever seen Him. What is He made up of? The Bible says He is invisible. God is Spirit. God is eternal. I certainly can't wrap my head around an eternal, invisible Spirit. The cool thing is God knew that He would be hard to understand. In fact, He knew that it would be hard for us to fully connect to Him because of His own characteristics.

God made humans to experience everything they know through their five senses, even their God. He knew becoming man was not at all for His benefit but only for ours. It was the only way humans could really know Him on a deeper and personal level. We were able to hear His first cry in the manger and His last cry on the cross. Many touched Him for their healing. We touched His nail-scarred hands and the wound in His side. We got to see that Love would die for humans undeserving of that Love. We tasted the wine He handmade. Jesus poured His sweetness out for us to drink. We smelled the fish He cooked on the Sea of Galilee.

Through these examples and many others events that satisfied our five senses, we experienced God. Understanding what great extremes He took to allow us to know Him, reminds me of one my favorite verses. Psalm 8:4 says, "What is man that you are mindful of him?" Why did He go to all this trouble for me? No one can tell you and me that we don't have intrinsic worth. The Most High God allowed us to experience Him in such an unimaginable way. We must be more special than we could ever imagine. God chose us over Himself. Why can't we choose Him over ourselves? We should choose Him out of gratitude alone. He had so much more to sacrifice than we ever will.

Run!

God must be a runner, or at least He likes the sport of running. There are so many references in the Bible about running. The most familiar example is Galatians 5:7, "You were running a good race" (NIV). Have you ever wondered that if there is a good race then there must be a bad race? He is saying there are two races, and He wants us to choose to run the good one. Interesting.

What does the bad race look like, and what do you win? Paul tells us when you run the bad race, there is a possibility that you will fall into temptation, shipwreck your faith, lose your logic and become foolish, have harmful desires, become trapped, have ruin, destruction, disputes, understand nothing, slander, be in constant disagreement with men, depraved from the truth, wander away from the faith, and—the best prize yet—pierce yourself with many pains. Wow! What a race! The prizes are so exciting and irresistible! We get all that and more for running the bad race? That's tempting.

Are we insane? Are humans so willful that God actually has to tell us, "Now, children! Listen. There are two races on earth. Make sure you run the good one!" Why in the world does He have to tell us to run the good one? Think about it! Which one do we normally run if we were honest? Our own. This most likely is the bad one if we are following the way that satisfies us the most. That's a problem.

What does the good race promise us? Righteousness, godliness, faith, love, endurance, gentleness, glory to the Father, thankfulness as demonstrated by our actions for what Christ did for us, peace, contentment, and a beautiful, flowing, white linen robe as you cross the finish line in Heaven. Why does God have to tell you to, "Run the good race?" Shouldn't that be the only one we ever desire to run?

Fire Memories

One thing that people seem to like about my journals more than anything is the analogies that I come up with. The Lord has His hand on these as I could not put all them together. I understand more and more that Christians are seeking how to make the Word of God fresh, relevant, and functional in their lives. That is what I seek. That is why I write. When I am able to put an analogy together to help me understand life better and how it works, then I can go back to it time and time again. It is sort of like a mental anchor to hold me to reality when thoughts and situations come up.

With that being said, I want to talk about fire ants! If you are not from the south, you may have never heard of them. We are blessed with them in the southern states! Now, these horrible creatures are in the same insect order as bees and wasps. Fire ant stings and bites are different than bee and wasp stings; a single worker ant can bite and sting numerous times. Once attached, it stings over and over. Because fire ants attack in a group, there will be many ants doing this at the same time. The fire ant's venom contains potent poisons. The only result is intense pain and burning. They are not normal ants! I am pretty sure they are of the Devil.

What in the world could I compare fire ants to that would be relevant our daily lives? What is one thing that all humans share? Memories. To put things in perspective of how many memories our brain can hold, let's compare it to hours. I read once that our minds can hold three million hours of TV shows. We could leave the TV running continuously for more than 300 years to use up all of our memory storage. That is a lot of memories.

Of all those stored memories, which ones seem to bother us more than any others? The ones where we received a new bike on Christmas morning when we were ten? The ones where we received our high school high school or college diploma? The ones where you were saved and baptized? No. All those memories are there, but they don't come up to the front of mind to relive and dissect to pieces. The memories that come up are the ones where you did wrong or the ones that wrong was done to you in the past.

You know these particular memories that I am referring to. I have mine. You have yours. The amazing part of the human mind is that it can pair emotions to any memory that you go mess with. The memory is lying dormant in your mind. It is not bothering you. Then you disturb it or something triggers it. Instead of taking your thoughts captive immediately as the Lord instructs, you stay with the memory longer and allow it to reform in your mind. The longer you dwell on it, the stronger the pain gets from it. It may be a past hurt from someone, a grudge that you have tucked away, a sin that you committed, or a disappointment of a past choice you made. The memory can be anything that had intense emotions from the day it was made. With time, you would think those emotions would dissipate, but they seem as strong as ever when you start thinking about them again.

Do you know the best way to avoid getting stung over and over by a fire ant? Do you know the best way to avoid the pain and suffering? Recognize what fire ant beds look like and avoid them. It is the same way with our hurtful memories. What do we do? Do we recognize and avoid them? Oh goodness no. Sometimes, we go looking for them. Sometimes, if they pop up we do not take them captive. If bad memories were like a fire ant bed with all its poisons, instead of avoiding them, we say, "Oh look! Fire Memories! Oh, goody!" We take a stick and start poking to see if the bed is still active.

We think of one memory then that memory hooks to this emotion, and then that emotion grows more intense until the whole memory is actively crawling everywhere. It's like that one memory multiplied hundreds of time. It fills our minds. Once those fire memories are disturbed, they start injecting their painful poison in our hearts. The pain and suffering is intense. Slowly, they subside, and the bite heals. Weeks, months, or years later, we are walking along in life; we stop and say, "Oh look! A Fire memory bed! Oh goody!" The process starts over again even though we knew what the fire memory bed looked like just liked we knew what a fire ant bed looked like. We have a mental stick in our hand, stirring them right back up for them to bite us again.

Who are we hurting when we disturb these old memories? The person that wronged you? The situation that you wished didn't happen? God? No. You are the only one hurting yourself. You are the only one stinging yourself. It's like you have a fire ant bed right between your ears. Whenever you stir it, you get stung over and over.

It is one thing to address old memories, especially if there was abuse involved, to bring them to resolution, but it is quite another to live in the past and frequently dwell in the middle of it. There are so many of us who are dwellers by nature. We can't let things go. We hold on to everything. The best way to avoid all of this pain and suffering of a fire memory is avoid getting stung in the first place. Recognize what fire memory mounds look like and where they are. Stay as far away from them as possible. If you get stung again, it will likely be your own fault.

Spiritual Gifts

I ponder all of the spiritual gifts. They absolutely fascinate me with the mere concept of them. At the point of our salvation, God put a gift in our spirit, no matter what our age was at our time of salvation. The gift or gifts have been "deposited." I think of my boys. They accepted Christ at an early age. Right now in their spirit, a gift given by the Most High God just waits for discovery. I can't imagine many more exciting things to discover than a gift left by God to be used by Him and for Him!

I see Andrew (13). He has an unashamed boldness for sharing the gospel with anyone that will listen. He witnessed at a local college during his own summer camp that he was attending there. When Andrew was nine or ten, he witnessed at a play park in our town. He came back crying to me that no one would listen to the gospel that he was trying to share. He wanted people to know the Truth in their heart. He watches videos on how to defend his worldview. We continually have deep discussions, that I would think are atypical for a thirteen-year-old, on how to state the cause of Christ to the unbelieving world. As a mother, I ponder if he has the gift of evangelism taking shape. It's still very rough, trust me, but something is there. Is he testing his gift out and getting his feet wet on how he will be used for God and not even knowing it?

I see Jonah (16), my introverted thinker. He sees others that no one else sees. He talks about what they must be feeling and how they got to the place they are in. He tries to relate and understand their hardships. Is the gift of mercy slowly manifesting itself? I believe that I have two spiritual gifts. I have been given the gift of teaching and the gift of discernment. I have so many people tell me how much they enjoy reading my journals. I am using my gift of teaching when I write. I pray that God uses my gift to strengthen you in Him. That is their only purpose.

Our gift or gifts will lie dormant until we are spiritually mature and spiritually-minded enough to discover what they are. If you are a Christian, you don't have to wonder if you have one. You just need to figure out what it is. Once discovered, we are expected to strengthen the gift by the utilization of it. The more you use a spiritual gift, the more effective it becomes. Spiritual gifts, while given by God, are not actually a true gift in the way we understand gifts. Why do I say that? The gift wasn't given to you to be used for your gain at all. In fact, it is impossible to use your gift on yourself. I can't use my gift of teaching on myself, but I can use my gift for you and others.

The purpose of gifts is to bring others to Christ and strengthen them once they have come to know Him. Please do not belittle your knowledge and usage of your gift. It is possible that when you stand before Christ on your one-on-one with Him, He will ask, "I gave you the spiritual gift of _____. How did you use it for My kingdom?" Your ignorance will not be an excuse. Do not fool yourself. Please don't think you are going to get off the hook regarding answering His question.

If you are a Christian, you are not here for own your good. You are here for God's will. Jesus did not come for His own good but for the Father's will. I believe Christians sweep the amount of accountability they will have for the utilization of their gift(s) under the rug. We would never treat a gift that a loved one gave us by ignoring it, sweeping it under the rug, or never using it. Why do we treat the Spirit's gifts like that? It is just not right. I believe one reason that we do not explore, use, and develop our spiritual gift is that it may move us out of our comfort zone. We may be asked to step up and do something that may make us uncomfortable or take time away from our busy lives. Our Christian life is supposed to be *none of us and all of Him.* A lot of us live our Christian lives as if it is all of us and a little of Him. Wake up! Stop the excuses! Use your gifts!

Stop Talking

I love words. Anyone that knows me knows that I love to speak words. I love to string them together in really long sentences for long periods of time. Breathing is overrated. I love writing words in long journals. I don't know if anyone has noticed that yet. I love hearing other people speak words to me.

The Lord has noticed all these things as well. He made me like this, and He loves me! Sometimes when I am praying in quiet time, I'm sure He is shaking His head and smiling at all of my words. He impresses upon my spirit, "Ssshhh, My Child. Listen." Immediately I'm quiet and peaceful and nothing is on my mind. All words are gone. I just dwell with my hands holding one hand of Jesus. He has His other hand on my head as I bow before him with chin down in reference. Again, "Ssshh. Rest. I know every word you have ever spoken and ever will speak. Just be still with Me now."

It's in these times that I feel the closest to the Lord. He doesn't need one of my words. He wants my quiet so that in these times I can hear Him whispering. He wants my stillness so that He can be the center of every thought. After an intense year of lots of words with the Lord, I love it when He gently tells me to hush. I know He is getting ready to fill me and teach me in the moments that follow. The anticipation is almost too much, yet I am quiet.

Be still and know that He is God. How mighty He is in our lives if we would only talk less and listen more. He is mighty to love us enough to tell us, "Ssshhh, My Child. Listen." If you do this, I promise it will take your personal relationship with Jesus to a whole new level. How ironic that I, among all others, am going to advise you to, "Stop talking so much."

Two Natures 1

When I think of things that are strong, I can think of a big African elephant that I have seen flipping over Safari jeeps on YouTube. I think of the space shuttle as the power it takes something that heavy to break through gravity of the earth is mind boggling and on and on. Even if I think of the strongest things on earth, one of the top ones that I never gave credit to is the flesh. When I say flesh, I do not mean necessary sensual, but I mean the human will.

We are made up of two natures. The spirit nature and the human nature (flesh). When the Bible says we were created in God's image, it is referring to the spirit nature as God is Spirit. The Bible says there is always a battle against the two. That is why Paul says he did things that he knew he should not do, but the things he knew to do he didn't do. He described the battle perfectly. People battled 2,000 years ago with the same things we battle with today because we are still made up of the same two natures in the 21st century. Just because time has passed does not mean that the make-up of humans has changed one bit. It hasn't, and it never will.

The flesh only understands the temporal and can only be tempted and fed by the five senses (touch, sight, smell, taste, and hearing). If you fall into temptation, the flesh has become weak in one of these areas. It could be the taste of alcohol, the sight of a good looking person of the opposite sex, the delightful smell of food that you really don't need any more of, or a hundred other things. It could be self-defeating thoughts or ungodly thoughts that you can't stop and on and on. Once the flesh is weak in an area that you may not have known it was weak in, then your thoughts start spinning. The flesh starts making plans of how to fulfill that which it is weak in. It only desires self-satisfaction. Can you start understanding the strength of the flesh? The kicker is the flesh will not stop until it is satisfied. The flesh only understands the temporal. How can I be satisfied right now?

The spirit side is totally different. It can only understand the eternal as it was created in the image of God. Here's the bottom line. If your human nature is stronger than your spirit nature because you have not prepared yourself as God has instructed, then your flesh will win the battle. You are foolish to think otherwise. If you have strengthened your spirit nature, then when the temporal temptations come to tempt your flesh, you will remain strong. This is truth.

Two Natures 2

I started praying this morning, and I felt that I should write a follow-up to yesterday's journal. That has really never happened before so this is interesting to me that the Lord wants this known. Remember in yesterday's journal, I spoke of two natures: human nature and spirit nature. One can only understand temporal, and one can only understand eternal. They are typically at odds with each other. I talked about the strength of each one and spoke of things that could happen if one was stronger than the other.

When I sat down in preparation for quiet time this morning, the Holy Spirit immediately impressed upon my spirit:

> Sarah, do you see what you just did? You literally laid down your human nature in front of Me. You were physically and mentally preparing your temporal body to be sustained for a while to allow your spirit nature to communewith Me. Your human nature is still there, but you willingly placed it in a position of submission. Your spirit nature is dominant at this moment in time. By doing this you have set aside time so that your spirit nature will be stronger than your human nature.

Wow. I'm pretty taken aback that this truth, while so simple, was explained to me in this way. I can wrap my mind around this. I can willfully choose whatever nature I want. Whichever the stronger one is will be most be the "go to" nature—the one that feels most comfortable. The more I spend time in placing my human nature in submission to my dominant spirit nature, the more that they will not be at odds any longer. If your human nature is always stronger, then the two will always be at odds and you will struggle in your life. The Lord wants us to know this truth.

The last thing that I know for sure is that you have to want to place your spirit nature in a dominant position—not just talking about it and saying you are going to do it but actually disciplining yourself to reprioritize your life to put the spirit nature first. The problem for Christians is that it takes too much time, effort, and commitment to strengthen the spirit nature, so they continue with their dominant human nature. Until you are serious about which nature you want stronger in your life, God is not going to be serious with you. You have to show Him that you are serious before He will move. You do that by your actions in front of Him including prioritizing Him in your everyday life. He doesn't care so much about what you say you are going to do or how good of person you think you are. That is irrelevant.

Two Natures 3

The Lord is just not letting go of further teaching me about the two natures. I certainly do not mind not moving on to a new lesson until this one is done. I understand the two natures and understand that whichever one is dominant will be the one that rules my life. What would my life look like if I let my human nature be dominant? There would be poor choices, hurt, and stagnation. That is very easy to picture as my human nature has been dominant for pretty much my entire Christian walk if I were to be transparent. Knowing where I am now, I can say that I have been a true Christian all this time, but my priorities may not have always been in order mentally—at least consistently.

There are so many "gauges" of which nature is dominant. If I took two simple gauges to read to see which nature has been dominant in my life, I would take prayer time and reading/studying the Bible. Prior to September 2012, I prayed either in the shower in the mornings, or I prayed right before I went to sleep. Forget deep reflective consistent daily Bible reading and study, because that didn't happen. So I prayed in the shower for one reason only. It was the only time I had in my day to fit God in my schedule. I'm just being honest. I would pray right before I went to sleep, because I had a few minutes. Typically, I would fall asleep about mid-way through my second sentence. Oh, but look at me praying twice a day! My spirit nature was just soaring over my human nature! The sad part is I did this forever and thought all was well. This was my time with the Lord? He sacrificed Himself and this is the best I gave to a King? *What?* What must He be thinking of me and how willing should He be when I ask Him to answer my prayers and protect me from enemy attack?

The audacity I had to actually think that I was doing what I needed to do as His child that I could even go before His throne and ask for a thing takes me aback. Anyone who knows me knows that I give 110 percent to everything and everybody. Yet what percent was I giving to the Most High God whom I call my Lord? The scarier part is that I thought I was doing fine with my pattern. It was good enough because the Lord knows how busy my life is. He is appreciative that I gave Him fifteen minutes while I was taking a shower and five whole minutes prior to going to sleep. I'm good! What planet am I living on? I can change the Lord's standards just that easily, and everything is fine? I'm okay with the ways things are so that means He has to be okay with how it is, as well?

The Lord is not okay even though I think I am okay! When I woke up from my slumber, I know that the Lord has not been okay with what I have given Him thus far. He expects and demands that I have my natures in order. I do not get to choose the order. No! He expects that if I am serious about what I say with my words, then my actions have to follow. Until they do, my natures are not in God's order. It is as simple as that.

When we get to Heaven, one of His questions could be, "If you knew which nature to make dominant, why didn't you do it?" We can hum and dance around nervously all we want to avoid His direct question, but there is only one answer that is the same for all of us. "We wanted our way, and we didn't have time to fit You in our daily life. Something always more important came along to prevent me from spending quality quiet time in prayer and study daily. Something or someone always prevented me from putting my spirit nature first."

The only "thing" preventing you from putting your spirit nature first in your daily life is *you*. Go look in the mirror if you need a visual. It's you. Stop justifying it any other way. It's you. When the Lord asks, be honest and just say, "I was more important than You." You can tell me a thousand excuses. I have young children. I have a busy job. I have school. I have all my running around. Again, when the Lord asks, be honest and just say, "I justified in my head that what I had to do in my life or care for in my life was more important than You."

As for me, my appointment with God is coming. I want to ready myself now with the prioritization of my two natures that among all the questions He will ask of me, He won't ask why I didn't put Him first. Frankly, I do not want to tell the Most High God that I was more important than Him. Not sure how I can sell that lie convincingly. If you are thinking, "I would never say that now or then that I am more important than the Lord. " Remember He doesn't care about your words, only your actions. You show Him daily what nature is dominant without ever opening your mouth. Think about it.

First Day

I picture my first day in Heaven. I am standing on the outer gates with my hands placed on them, ready to slowly open them and peek inside. Before I open them and enter, I turn back to look at my life one last time. To ponder all of my most memorable moments that will pale in comparison to the moment I am presently in. I see myself walking down the aisle to reach out and get my Master's diploma. I look down at it, knowing that I have achieved something great. I have something that no one can ever take from me—knowledge.

I see my Daddy opening two great, white, wooden doors to a magnificent church. I hold on to his strong arm so tightly as he walks me down the aisle to give me away to my sweet husband. I see the nurse wrapping my baby boys in soft blue blankets and laying them in my arms for me to look into their eyes, to know them and for them to know me. I see young children sitting around my feet, listening to me explain to them how much Jesus desires them. These memories and so many more fill me to overflowing. Each memory is precious to me and will always be a part of me no matter where I am.

Today, though, is different. Today is the day that I enter Heaven. I push the gate open, and the purity that surrounds me is almost tangible. I can breathe it in. I reach my hand out to touch it but find that I am a part of it. I look down, and the street on which I walk is almost transparent. I look from side to side and see others also walking in their own experience as I am in mine. I slowly walk into a field. There are tall, swaying, purple flowers signifying the majesty of my surroundings. I turn around and they are as far as I can see in any direction I look. It's beautiful.

I see a figure slowly walking toward me. He looks strong. He is wearing a long, flowing, white linen robe. I know it is the King coming to greet me. The anticipation that is building in me as I walk toward Him is indescribable. I reach Him and He looks at me. I look up at Him. A big smile fills His face as He says, "Finally! My Child, you are home. Oh I have been waiting for you from before creation. Welcome, My faithful one." I bow to my knees and put my head down slowly until it touches my chest in the deepest respect that I have the ability to show to a King. I reach up to grab one of His hands. He reaches and has all of me in just a touch. He puts His other hand on my head. There we stay for what seems like eternity. I have no desire to move from His presence.

This is my first day with my Lord. I start singing quietly, "Oh Lord, My God. When I am in awesome wonder consider all the worlds thy hands have made. I see the stars. I hear the rolling thunder. Thy power throughout the universe displayed. Then sings my soul, My savior God to Thee. How great thou art. Amen." I can only imagine what it will be like on my first day of Heaven. Whatever we can imagine will pale in comparison to what the Lord has in store for me and you.

Holy Ground

When Moses fell on his face in front of the burning bush, what did God say? "Do not come near; take your sandals off of your feet, for the place on which you are standing is holy ground" (Exodus 3:5 ESV). "And the commander of the Lord's army said to Joshua, 'Take off your sandals from your feet, for the place where you are standing is holy.' And Joshua did so" (Joshua 5:15 ESV). What made the ground on which Moses and Joshua stood holy? Was it the location? Was it the person? No. God made it holy by His presence. Wherever the Lord is, there is holy ground. We would all agree with that.

Did you know these passages are the only times "holy ground" is used in the Bible. Stephen used the term in the New Testament but only to reference back to Moses' experience. It is interesting that there are not more mentions of holy ground when Jesus came. Why? Wherever Jesus went was holy ground. If He was standing on the ground, it was holy. If people were standing near Him on the same patch of land, they were standing on holy ground. Just like Moses and Joshua, the land was holy because the Lord was present.

Do you think we have holy ground today? People would say, "Yes. Churches, synagogues, and any place of worship would be holy." Possibly. It isn't the building that makes it holy though. No building in the world is holy on its own. I don't care what the religion claims. It is impossible. If one authentic Christian enters the building, then the building becomes holy. If people who say they are Christians but are not authentic enter the building, it is not holy.

Wherever the presence of the Lord is there is holy ground. The question is, "Where is the Lord today?" When Jesus left the earth and before the Holy Spirit was sent on the day of Pentecost, I personally believe there was no holy ground earth. Why? The Lord was not dwelling in any form on earth. The very day that the Holy Spirit was sent to dwell within us, everything was changed. When that happened, it literally changed our bodies to a sanctuary of the Holy Spirit which was given to us by God (1 Corinthians 3:16; 6:19 NIV). Once this bodily change took place, we had the ability to be holy, because God is holy (1 Peter 1:16 NIV). Never before did a human have the ability to be holy in the sense of having holiness live within them. It would have been impossible. We need to understand by accepting the Holy Spirit, we became holy.

We have scripturally established that where the Lord dwells is holy ground, because His presence is there (Exodus 3:5 NIV). We have scripturally established that according to Luke 11:13 and many more references, such as "The Heavenly Father gives the Holy Spirit to those who ask Him" (ESV). We have scripturally established that we become a temple or sanctuary to physically house the Holy Spirit within our bodies, once we receive Him (1 Corinthians 3:16; 6:19 NIV). We have scripturally established we have the ability to be holy like God because of this truth (1 Peter 1:16 NIV).

My question to you is: if you are an authentic Christian based on the above scriptural truth that is the Word of God, are you not standing on holy ground right now? Have you once ever stopped to think about this? People say, "This is holy ground or that is holy ground." My question would be, "Was there an authentic Christian standing with the indwelt Holy Spirit of the Most High God?" If yes, then it was holy as the presence of the Lord was there. If no, then the ground was just plain ground. A mere man, just saying ground is holy, does nothing to change that ground. A Christian, being present, changes the ground completely. When a Christian walks across the ground, carrying the presence of the Lord in them, every step they take makes the ground holy.

Theologically, you may disagree with me. That is fine. Scripturally, the Lord is clear that where His presence is there is holy ground. I have the Holy Spirit's presence in me, and so do you if you are authentic. According to what I understand, the ground where I am standing is holy. Not at all because of who I am or who you are, but because we have the presence of the Lord dwelling in us. We are holy like He is holy.

I have been thinking about this for a long time, and when I put this together in my own mind with the supporting scriptural understanding, it makes me speechless. The deeper I dwell on this truth, the heavier accountability I have for where I put my foot and my presence as a Christian. Where I go, I take the presence of the Lord with me. I am to be holy as He is holy. The ground on which I walk as a Christian is not normal ground but holy ground. Praise God.

Smoke and Mirrors

One time one of my friends used the term, "smoke and mirrors" to describe a situation that appeared one way but really wasn't the way it was in reality. It was made to appear better than it truly was. In my quiet time, this term came to my mind. I had another friend say to me recently that you can talk the "Christian talk" all you want, but if you don't walk the "Christian walk" then you have no witness of the Lord being who you say He is in your life. I am pondering these two comments. They are saying the same things, but in different ways. I do think that there are some people who call themselves Christian who talk but don't walk the Christian life. They could be blowing some reflective smoke around. Some people reflect the things of God, but they truly do not have His image in their heart's mirror of being anything like Him. Interesting.

I would have to contemplate who some of these people who call themselves Christians are trying to impress. God said, "You can't please both man and Me." The Pharisees and Sadducees, the godliest people of Jesus' time, were all about man. They were so sure of their safety in the Kingdom of Heaven, according to their standards. I know that today some people who call themselves Christians are as sure of their safety in the Kingdom of Heaven for the same reasons. That is the most dangerous thing for a soul. Deafening alarm bells go off in my head. No alarms bells go of in theirs, though.

Jesus is clear. He knows His sheep and He knows goats. They will be separated, even though today they are all together. He states clearly that there will many people who think they have safety in His kingdom because they have "talked" and "blown smoke" so well for so long that they even fooled themselves! When they arrive in front of God's throne, the discussion per the Gospels will go something like this. "Lord! Finally! Glad to get here. Where's my mansion?" The Lord will look at them and say, "I'm sorry I don't know your name. I don't know where you come from. You certainly haven't come from a deep personal relationship with my Son." Then they say, "Whoa, Lord! Wait just a minute! You didn't see all that talking I have been doing? You haven't seen all that smoke? You must be blind! Now where are my rewards?" The Lord will look at them while shaking His head and say, "Depart from me! I do not know you and from where you come from! Leave My presence at once!"

Some people who thought they were Christians will find out that they truly never were. They were truly never lovers of God but only of themselves. All they did was talk a lot and blow smoke. If they ever stopped long enough from doing these two activities to be seen by man, then they would have figured out that they were not authentic! They pleased themselves. They had time for their highest priorities, none of which was truly the Lord. They fooled themselves and man, but their eternal mistake will be that the Most High God is no fool.

The Christian walk is not a game that you can play seriously when it is convenient and for show. Do not think you will get a second chance at authenticity when you get to Heaven? No. That is not how it works. Either you are authentic when you arrive there, or you will be turned away. For any person reading this, I urge you to reflect on which category you are in. Are you an authentic Christian that has a deep personal relationship with the Most High God so He knows your name and where you come from? Are you someone who just "talks" a lot about having that and feels you are a really good person that God would never turn away?

If you are producing no fruit in your life for Him, then are you truly connected to His vine or your own? The conversation that the Bible describes occurring is probably one of the most sobering passages in the entire Bible to me. You can "play" Christian all you want but know that God is no fool. He knows His sheep. If you have breath in you, then I suggest you use the next few to talk to the Lord to make sure He knows your name and that you come from a committed personal relationship with His Son. It seems crystal clear that He better know your name and where you came from by the time you arrive or you will not make it past His throne. You can fool yourself and others all day; you will never fool God.

Priestly Shepherds

I love studying Biblical history! Did you know that there were priestly shepherds who tended large herds of sheep? The place where this occurred was only located in Bethlehem. It was called Migdal Eder. It consisted of a two-story tower that stood in a pasture. The remains of this place have been discovered. These sheep were looked after by rotating priests because the lambs were to be examined at each birth to see if they were without spot or blemish. When a lamb was approved for a later sacrifice at the Temple, the lamb would be wrapped with strips of cloths made from old priestly undergarments. This was done to keep the lamb from getting blemished. They would place the lamb in a manger to make sure it was not injured in any way.

Jesus' birth in Bethlehem was prophesied in the familiar verse of Micah 5:2. People gloss over the prophecy of Micah 4:8 because they do not think it is relevant. The verse reads, "And you, watch tower of the flock, fortified hill of Daughter Zion, the former rule will come to you, sovereignty will come to Daughter Jerusalem" (HCSB). Other translations say, "Unto thee shall it come, even the first dominion. The kingdom shall come …" (KJV). This verse prophesied that the Messiah would be announced at the "Watch tower or tower of the flock." In those days, this tower was called Migdal Eder.

Did you ever wonder why the angel announced to these particular shepherds in Luke 2 that Jesus being wrapped in swaddling clothes laying in a manger would be a sign to them? I always did! These shepherds were not ordinary shepherds. They were priests! When the shepherd priests were greeted by the angels and told to go see this special baby, they would know they had the right one because of the sign given. They knew that this baby would be like no other. When they saw the baby Jesus wrapped in priestly cloths, lying in a manger, the image and significance would have been stronger to them as compared to a typical poor shepherd.

The significance of seeing a baby wrapped in swaddling clothes lying in a manger just like a sacrificial lamb would not escape them. The Messiah that had been prophesied had finally been born. The cloth that He was wrapped in was most likely made of the same priestly undergarments that the sacrificial lambs were wrapped in. How could this be? Mary's cousin Elizabeth was married to Zacharias who was a priest in the Temple. Mary was with Elizabeth earlier in her pregnancy. Elizabeth could have given Mary some of Zacharias' priestly undergarments to wrap Jesus in, because Elizabeth already knew who Jesus was. This is all very interesting.

Jesus had to be born in Bethlehem. This was not only the city of David, but it was the only place on earth that sacrificial lambs were born that one day would be sacrificed for the sins of the people. Jesus had to be wrapped in torn pieces of priestly robes and placed in a manger, just like all the other little lambs in that very special field watched over by Temple priests. One last parallel: Jesus died on the cross at the same hour that the lambs were to be sacrificed at the Temple. Jesus was treated like a sacrificial lamb from His birth to His death. All of this leaves me speechless and in awe of the Most High God. Our Lamb lives!

Adapted from Norten, Michael. (2012). *Unlocking the Secrets of the Feasts: The Prophecies in Feasts of Leviticus.* West Bow Press.

Freedom from Sin

Now the Lord is the Spirit, and wherever the Spirit of the Lord is, there is freedom. (2 Corinthians 3:17 ESV)

Have you ever watched a dog on a long leash anchored to a tree or the ground? He thinks he is pretty free, but in reality he has a finite circumference in which to walk around. His whole world is inside that circle. He can see outside the circle, but he is anchored within it. Sometimes the dog may forget that he is tied down. He makes a mad dash toward freedom, only to be snapped back to reality. We have all seen dogs that have been pulled back hard by their own chain. It's easy to forget he is tied down, until he tries to leave.

The other truth of the situation is that even though the dog can always see what is anchoring him, there's little he can do about it in his own strength to free himself. He can try to break that chain all day long, and he will be defeated. If his master comes out, the dog gets so excited. Why? The dog has learned that his master is the only one who can break the chain and allow him to run around in freedom.

Sin works just like this. We are the dog. The chain and the anchor is the sin. Whereas the master puts the dog on the chain to create a finite circumference in its life, we put ourselves on the chain of sin. We limit the circumference in our own life by anchoring ourselves to sin. It takes us a while to figure out that the circumference around us is finite, as we have loads of fun exploring. It takes us a long while before we figure out that we are walking around in a circle. At some point, we get bored with what is in the circle. We make a mad dash for freedom, but within a short time our necks are snapped back just like the dogs. We are not blind to what has pulled us back. David said in Psalms 51:3 "For I acknowledge my transgressions and my sin is ever before me" (KJV). David was clear that he knew what was chaining him down. He says his sin is always before him, just like the anchor is always before the dog. Our sin is always before us as well.

We know sin is holding us in the finite circle. We think we can just walk away. We find out quickly that it has a hold of us and not us of it. Does the dog hold the chain or does the chain hold the dog? We are the dog, remember. We are not going anywhere! I'm not sure how deep into sin you have to go before the control switches, but in my experience it is not too deep. I have not only tied the chains of sin around my neck, I have hammered the anchor down, creating my own circle. I have volitionally limited my perspective. I have stayed in sin for long enough until the chain is holding me. I have taken my own freedom of having a clear conscience away. I did that. No one did that to me.

What must the Lord be thinking when He watches me chain myself down to a sin? I am always in the presence of the Most High God, and so are you. How weak and pathetic we are to fall for the meaningless chains of sin. Sin is limiting every time. I haven't chained myself down just once but many times. You would think I would learn. My mother always told me I was a strong-willed child. That is the nice way of saying I was stubborn. It's true. People who know me are shaking their head in agreement right now.

I have been in sin that I no longer wanted to be involved in, but I couldn't figure out how to get myself out of. Has that ever happened to you? I kept committing sin that I knew that I shouldn't, but I couldn't do what I knew was right. It is easy to get into sin but hard to get out of it. The best way I can describe is it is like quicksand. Before you know it, you are shoulder deep, and you need help to get out. For those sinless souls out there, you may be thinking, "Just walk away from the sin. It's easy!" For those sinful souls out there, you are shaking your head.

If no one in the world can understand what I am saying, at least Paul does. He had obviously chained himself down a few times and tried to dash for freedom as well. Romans 7:15–21 (NIV) says:

> I do not understand what I do. For what I want to do I do not do, but what I hate I do. If I do what I do not want to do, I agree that the law is good. As it is, it is no longer I myself who do it, but it is sin living in me. For I know that good itself does not dwell in me, that is, in my sinful nature. I have the desire to do what is good, but I cannot carry it out. For I do not do the good I want to do, but the evil I do not want to do this I keep on doing. Now if I do what I do not want to do, it is no longer I who do it, but it's sin living in me that does it. I have discovered this law at work, although I want to do good, evil is right there with me. This law is waging a war against the law of my mind and making me prisoner of the law of sin at work within me.

Paul said all of this to say that he was a prisoner by the sin in his life. Prisoners always have chains. Chains are always anchored somehow, so the prisoner can't escape. Do you think Paul would understand the dog and chain scenario? It sounds like to me that Paul made several mad dashes to freedom, too. He had to figure this out somehow. I bet he figured it out just like I did—by experience. He clearly saw the right he should be doing in life, but his neck was snapped back to what was right in front him the whole time, his own sin.

Paul made another realization that I talked about earlier. He was anchored by his own sin. He needed rescuing. He needed to be released from the chain just like the master of the dog released it. Paul says in verse 24, "What a wretched man I am! Who will rescue me from this body that is subject to death?" He gives us the answer in verse 25, "Thanks be to God, who delivers me through Jesus Christ our Lord! So then, I myself in my mind am a slave to God's law, but in my sinful nature a slave to the law of sin." Romans 8:2 continues to say, "Because through Christ Jesus the law of the Spirit who gives life has set you free from the law of sin and death" (NIV).

We are the dog. Sin is the chain and anchor that is always before us. We are weak in the flesh and cannot free ourselves. We are prisoners of our own making. Christ Jesus is our Master who comes to the yard while we walk around in our finite circle of sin. He releases the chain so we can run in the freedom of His mercy and grace. John 8:32 says, "Then you should know the truth, and the truth will make you free" (NIV). I have told you the truth that offers you freedom.

I have been a chained yard dog one too many times. I bet you have, too. If you have sin right now that has you chained down, ask the Master to come release you. You may be in sin so deep that you have become imprisoned. It can happen so easily and quickly. Remember, it is like quicksand. You have to repent, and He will release you from the prison you created for yourself.

You have to turn from re-chaining yourself down to the same sin again. That is very easy to do. I know. As soon as the Lord releases you, it seems that you run around the yard once and go back and hook yourself back to the same chain. There is strength and power in the Lord. When He releases you, stay as close to Him as possible. The strength of that sin you were just released from will dissipate with time if you stay close to the Lord. If you don't, you will re-chain yourself. You know from experience that I speak the truth.

Catching God's Attention

Is it possible to catch the attention of a Holy God? Actually, many men have caught God's attention through time, such as Job, Abraham, Moses, Samuel, David, and many more through the New Testament. We could dissect how each one of these men caught God's attention, but let's talk about Job. He is one of the most loved men of the Bible. He is certainly one of my favorite people to study.

Picture two scenes from the Book of Job. The first scene opens up on Earth. Job was going about his life. He was making a living, raising a family, being a good husband, and fearing his God. He desired nothing more than these things. Everyone around him knew what kind of man he was, but how was he any different than his neighbors? The Bible says he had "perfect integrity, feared God, and turned away from evil" (Job 1:1 HCSB). Obviously, these three "God catching" characteristics of Job happened in combination with each other not in isolation.

His neighbors certainly could have exhibited one or two of these characteristics, but Job had all three. This set him apart from those around him. We may think, "It only takes these three things to get the attention of a Holy God?" It almost seems too easy on the surface doesn't it? But if it were easy, why didn't the neighbors catch God's attention? Why didn't other members of Job's family catch God's attention? We know it is not easy. We struggle with maintaining integrity, fearing God, and turning away from evil, just like everyone did then and everybody does now. No one caught God's attention at the time but Job.

The second scene is in Heaven. Satan enters the Almighty's high court and approaches the throne of God. As he walks, he looks side-to-side at the Holy ones and sneers. God knew that Satan had just returned from roaming the earth. Satan was walking around like a hungry animal looking for someone to devour. Job 1:8 says, "Then the Lord said to Satan, 'Have you considered My servant Job? No one else on earth is like him, a man of perfect integrity, who fears God and turns away from evil'" (HCSB). Satan insinuated that God had a hand of protection on Job, and that is why he had never tempted him previously. So not only did God bring Satan's attention to think about Job, Satan already knew about what kind of man Job was. If you think about that for a minute, that is amazing. Job caught God's attention and Satan's, too.

So many things fascinate me about God saying, "Have you considered My servant Job?" First and most importantly to me, Job caught the attention of a Holy God. Who does that? When I really wrap my mind around that truth, it is very difficult to comprehend. A human can catch God's attention by his or her heart and behavior? I believe that Job did not recently catch God's attention. He had sustained it for a good long while, waiting for Satan to return from roaming. What also interested God about this particular human is God said, "There was none like him on earth!" At least there was none like Job at the time he was alive on earth. That's quite a compliment as God knew every person's thoughts, motives, and actions.

Secondly, what made Job different? I talked about it earlier. He had what God considered perfect integrity, the ability to recognize sin, volitionally turn away from it every time, and intimately knew and respected God for who He was.

Finally, remember Job was a human, like you and me. That is abundantly clear as we know what happens to Job's physical body later in the book. But, think about this: God didn't supernaturally make Job have perfect integrity, recognize sin and turn from it, and fear the Lord. Job chose to do it. He had to make a conscious choice every day to maintain these characteristics. The point I am trying to make is that if Job was a mere human and by choosing perfect integrity, fearing the Lord, and turning away from evil caught the attention of a Holy God, why can't we? I don't know about you, but I want to catch God's attention!

Oneness of Christ

There is one body and one Spirit just as you were called to one hope when you were called. One Lord, one faith, one baptism, one God and Father of all, who is over all and through all and in all. (Ephesians 4:4–6 NIV)

On March 7, 1990, Abigail Loraine and Brittany Lee Hensel were born in Minnesota. They are dicephalic parapagus twins. This means that they are a very special and rare type of twin. They have two heads but one conjoined body. One of them completely controls one side of the body and the other controls the other side of the body. They can independently control isolated movement on the side of the body that belongs to them such as eating, brushing teeth, hair, and putting on makeup. They can independently write their thoughts out with the hand that they control.

Movements such as walking and driving a car have to be done as a coordinated effort. I have read about these young ladies before. Their success in life is a testimony of what two people can achieve together. They know how to have a like mind to work together for the body's good. If they don't, they would never make it. They share life in one body. They have to be unified on the important things to take the body where it should go.

I was praying this morning. As always, I ask the Lord if there is anything that He would like me to write about. He is always faithful. This morning, He brought Abby and Brittany to my mind very strongly. I opened my eyes and couldn't believe that of all things to write about I would be writing about conjoined twins. There was no mistaking what I heard though. He quickly showed me the why of it all. He wanted me to understand how the oneness of Christ should work. He knew I would understand if He explained it this way. Abby and Brittany have figured out "oneness" beautifully. They are our examples to follow. With all respect to these ladies, God knew they could teach us so much! He never makes a mistake.

Every Christian has two heads in one body, just like Abby and Brittany. While it is literal for them, it is metaphorical for us. When we were nonbelievers, we only had one head with one body. Before accepting Christ, we did what we wanted, thought what we wanted, and went places that we wanted. There was one selfish mind that controlled one body. There were no problems of having a divided mind. Our mind was worldly. One Mind. One body. No struggles. When we became Christians, a transition took place. A Christian took one mind of the self and joined it with the mind of Christ. Now we have two heads with one body. These two heads had their own thinking and way of doing things. They were independent of each other but shared one body, just like Abby and Brittany.

The Lord knows that there will be a transitional period back to one mind with one body after leaving the world. That is to be expected when anyone makes such a radical turn in a new direction that directly affects lifestyles and thinking. There are many reasons that God gives us grace, but Christians certainly need a ton of it during the time they are trying to sort everything out in their mind of the new life they will lead in Christ.

I have been a Christian for over thirty years; up to this point, I have had two heads and one body. I have only now recognized it by the revealing of the Holy Spirit. I have one head that I keep for myself and one head I keep for Christ. I walk around in one body, thinking all is well because

I use the head that works best for me at the time that I need it. The problem is that the Lord does not want that transitional period of having two heads to last very long. Thirty years is a little excessive to figure this all out, but I may be the norm and not the exception. Christians think the Lord is okay with sharing the mind or head with us. He is not!

We justify two heads, because it works for us. It doesn't work so well for the Lord. In fact, it doesn't work at all. We buy the lie that it does. While He is trying to use His head to guide the body in one direction, we are using our head to pull it in another direction. Mark 3:25 says, "If a house is divided against itself that house cannot stand" (NIV). Can I paraphrase this verse to say, "If a person's mind is divided against itself, the body can't move?"

Abby and Brittany have to move together if they are going to move at all. They do not have divided thinking on moving the body, despite their condition. We do though! That is exactly what causes our poor conditions and stagnation in the body. We never move due to our divided mind. Think about it like the game of Tug of War. The Lord has one end of the rope and self has the other. There is a pull on the rope just like there is a pull on the body, because self-will is so strong against the will of God. Think about it like a car. The car is the body and can only go where the person that is steering leads. Abby and Brittany drive with a like mind. We try to share the wheel with Jesus and steer the car in all different directions. It just doesn't work.

The Lord is mighty and perfect. He wants you to only have the mind of Christ because that is what is best for you, not Him. He doesn't have two heads. You do. He will not enter a power struggle with you over which head is in control of the body. You have to choose. You can't keep both heads when you enter the body of Christ and think you will be blessed and grow. It doesn't work that way. That is why Christians struggle. God will allow you to have a divided mind until the point at which you wake up and see that your body isn't moving and growing. God doesn't have a divided mind; you do. God doesn't play games; you do. God doesn't justify thinking outside of His will; you do. God's desire and will for you is to have His mind:

> Make my joy complete by being likeminded, having the same love, being one in spirit, and of one mind. (Philippians 2:2 NIV).

Who has known the mind of the Lord so as to instruct Him?' But we have the mind of Christ. (1 Corinthians 2:16 NIV).

And be not conformed to this world; but be transformed by the renewing of your mind, that you may prove what is good, and acceptable, and perfect will of God. (Romans 12:2 AKJV).

Let this mind be in you, which was also in Christ Jesus. (Philippians 2:5 KJV).

"Love the Lord your God, with all of your heart and all of your soul and all of your mind" (Matthew 22:37 NIV). Why would it say, "all of your mind?" God knew that you may still be holding back on Him. Again, He doesn't want to share your mind. He wants all of it.

Once we have the mind of Christ, not only will our body be led by the Lord, we will also fall into the larger body of Christ. He tells us that we are of one body. Romans 12:4–5 says, "Just as each of us has one body with many members, and these members do not all have the same function, so in Christ we who are many form one body, and each member belongs to all the others" (NIV). First Corinthians 12:12 says, "The body is a unit, though it is made up of many parts; and though all its parts are many, they form one body. So it is with Christ" (NIV). He makes it very clear that He is the head of the body (Colossians 1:18 NIV). First Corinthians 12:18 says, "God in fact has arranged the parts in the body, every one of them, just as He wanted them to be" (NIV). Verse 25 says, "There shall be no division in the body, but that its parts should have equal concern for each other" (NIV). Christ adds in Colossians 3:15 that the body has been called to peace. He dislikes division. Whether that division is in you or in the larger body of Christ, take great measures that you remain in peace.

Not only do we have one mind and one body, but we have one Spirit. First Corinthians 12:13 says, "For we were all baptized by one Spirit in the one body. We were all given the one Spirit to drink" (NIV). Romans 5:5 says, "God's love has been poured into our hearts through the Holy Spirit who has been given to us" (NIV). Ezekiel 36:26–27 says, "And I will give you a new heart, and a new spirit I will put within you. I will cause you to walk in My statutes and be careful to obey My rules" (NIV). The oneness of my spirit and His Spirit is mostly affected by my own spirit of fear, self-reliance, self-doubt, and disobedience. The enemy uses these emotions more than any other to affect the unity of the Spirit. I always need to be on guard and protect the oneness of the Spirit given to me. I suggest you do the same.

Just as there is one mind, one body, and one Spirit, there is one hope (Ephesians 4:4 NIV). Romans 15:13 tells us, "May the God of hope fill you with all joy and peace in believing, so that by the power of the Holy Spirit you may abound in hope" (NIV). First Corinthians 15:19–20 says that we have eternal hope because of Christ resurrection (NIV). Paul tells Timothy that the Lord Jesus Christ is our hope (First Timothy 1:1 NIV). Acts 4:12 says, "Salvation is found in no one else, for there is no other name under heaven given to mankind by which we must be saved" (NIV). There is only one hope for the world, and His name is Jesus.

When you become a Christian, you "lose your mind" in a sense. Typically, that would require a short stay at a psychiatric hospital and heavy medications, but not in this case. Losing your mind means you exchange yours for Christ's. You will be physically, mentally, emotionally, and spiritually better for it. Those around you will also benefit from you having the mind of Christ as well. When you have the mind of Christ, you are given one Spirit. By having Him, you are one in the Body of Christ. You are used as a vital member of the body according to His will. You may have an "out-of-body experience" and be "out of your mind," but He is never out of His! When you have oneness with Christ in mind, body, and spirit, you have hope for eternal things. You are in the center of His holiness. We have two choices of how to live our lives. We can live in self-inflicted division or in the oneness of Christ. Seems like a simple choice, doesn't it?

Thank you Lord for Abby and Brittany and the testimony they are to the world. They have blessed people more than they could ever imagine. They are Your miracles. I will never meet them this side of Heaven, but they have taught me so much about You. Amen.

No One Is Good

No one is good except God alone. (Mark 10:18 NIV)

I volunteer with a ministry called Walk to Emmaus. It is a three-day Christian retreat. I was a pilgrim on this walk in October 2012. It was an amazing time with the Lord and my sisters in Christ. When you are the one walking, you have no idea how many people are behind the scenes making your walk special just for you. After you walk, the Emmaus community encourages you to become involved as a worker for others. Everyone who works at Emmaus is a volunteer. I have worked four walks so far, and I absolutely love serving the Lord in this ministry. I feel blessed each time I give back to what was originally given to me.

It was on my third time working a weekend retreat that a friend of mine back home texted me, "You are awesome! I wish I was just half as good as you." I texted back, "There is no one good but the Lord! I am not being good. I am just serving Him!" As I continued working, the Spirit wouldn't let go of the fact that since my friend saw me working for the Lord that I was somehow being "good." I started thinking how some people that are Christians and nonbelievers see those highly energized and on-fire Christians as being somehow "good." Somehow they are elevated like they have more Jesus in them or something. There is nothing good about doing what the Lord has asked you to do. Being good indicates a self-righteousness.

Paul says in Ephesians 2:10, "For we are His creation—created in Christ Jesus for good works" (HCSB). James says because of our faith, we should show good works for Christ. Good works can manifest themselves in countless ways. The Lord gives many ministries in which Christians can work. It is up to us to find a ministry of some sort to be involved in. If no good works comes out of your life, then how is your faith? There is a direct correlation. If you are one of those Christians who sit in church and watch other people do good works for the Lord, then your faith is dead. That should be very concerning to you. Of course, dead people have no concerns.

If you ever look at other people and think, "If I could just be a little like them, or if the Lord had given me something to do like them, then I could do it!" This is said the whole time you are warming their bottoms on the church pew. It is easy to sit there and have all the wishful thinking that you want to do good works for the Lord, but it is because of your dead faith that you are ignorant to that holds you back. Stop talking and wishing. That gets you nowhere fast. The Lord wants us to demonstrate our living faith for Him to this world by doing good works for Him. Hebrews 6:10 says, "God will not forget your work and the love you showed for His name when you served the saints—and you continued to serve them" (HCSB). He goes on to say that as hard as you serve the Lord by working that you should demonstrate that same diligence for the hope in you so that you won't become lazy but imitators of those who inherit the promises through faith and perseverance.

There is a line between being good and doing good works. They have never been nor ever will be equal in the Lord's eyes. Jesus says in Mark 10:18, "There is no one good but One—God" (HCSB). Jesus took the simple word *good* very seriously. If He did, then we should, too. He tells us to do good works, but we are not made good for doing them. The people who are sometimes doing the good works may think they are good. They may do more and more good works because of the way it makes them personally feel and not for the sole purpose of serving the Lord. No one is good in and of themselves as we have the sin nature in us. Until we are given our resurrected bodies, we never will be "good."

Integrity

The Lord is near to all who call out to Him, all who call out to Him with integrity. (Psalm 145:18 HCSB)

In September of 2012, my husband and I went to an amazing cabin in the Blue Ridge Mountains in North Georgia for a long weekend getaway. It was a time of relaxation for us and a time for me to reflect on where my Christian walk was with the Lord. The road was very long and winding up the side of a mountain. When we arrived, there was only peace and quiet waiting for us at the top. I hoped some of that peace and quiet would fill my soul. The cabin was located on a high ridge; in the morning time, the clouds would cover the valley. You could look across and see the other ridge line above the clouds. It was serene. The scene was very majestic as well.

The wooden cabin had a long porch all the way across the back. It was there that I sat for long periods of time and looked over the ridge. I shut the whole world out, and I wanted to hear from the Lord. I am learning that is what we should all do sometimes. Get away from the world and go to a quiet and peaceful place just to listen to Him. Sometimes our lives are so busy that we don't have time to listen to God's still, small voice of direction or correction.

At that time, the Lord looked in the mirror of my life; it was not Him that He saw looking back, but me. I love that analogy of the mirror. It's so simple, but powerful. He should have seen His own reflection if indeed I am to mirror Him in all of my thoughts and actions, right? There was no reason to try to hide from a Holy God who knows me intimately and knew that it was my image that stared back at Him. I did not have the integrity it took for God to see Himself. I was embarrassed when I finally stopped my life long enough for Him to examine me. I was ashamed that I had not given Him better thus far in my Christian walk.

I think sometimes Christians would just like to work hard at home, work, and church because as long as we think the Lord sees us working that we are okay. We are being good little Christians. But are we really? Do we keep busy as not to let Him catch up to us long enough to examine us in the first place, knowing that He would not see Himself in the mirror of lives if we did? Do we not think Jesus died for more than that? Honestly, I really did not want Him to look at me, but He reminded me that He was big enough to handle anything in my life. He paid a precious price for that privilege to make all things new again in me, regardless of my own doings. All I had to do on my side was let Him.

Why was that so hard? Besides, I was mentally, spiritually, and physically tired of doing it my way and being the Christian I thought I should be. I had just enough Christianity that I thought I could handle most anything that came along. How foolish and naïve. How very dangerous as well when the enemy is prowling around looking for Christians to devour. If you haven't been attacked by the enemy for a while, you get a little too confident with a false sense of security that you have things under control until it's almost too late. Some Christians have already fallen before they knew what hit them. Again, that is an extremely dangerous place for a Christian to be. Beware.

I asked Him to reveal why I made poor judgments and sinful choices when I was a daughter of a Holy King since childhood. I thought that if I had been a Christian since childhood, I should be at some level or point on a graph far past where I was currently. What that place was in my head I had no idea. I didn't know who I was measuring myself against, either. It was just my truth. I was hard on myself and placed pressure where pressure should not be. Or should it? If I didn't pressure myself to meet some arbitrary level of Christianity, who would?

I didn't need to worry about other things that more baby Christians would have to deal with, right? After all, I was a Sunday school teacher and lifelong Christian since the age of nine. My life was far past the chance to be caught by a surprise enemy attack, or so I thought. I learned that the enemy cannot read your mind but can and does watch your behavior. He will watch for however long it takes to finally put just enough temptation out there until you take it. He doesn't care how far you fall, what you lose when you fall, and how hard you hit after the fall, just that you have fallen. We all need to wake up.

It makes no difference how long we have been Christians. When there is a lack of integrity at any point, there is automatically a lack of wisdom. When there is a lack of wisdom, there are always poor choices made that could lead to sin. Who knew these things went together? I surely didn't. Maybe I did, but was my life way too busy to care? I'm not sure. In my head, I felt that I was stronger in the Lord. I would do things in His strength, not mine. It shocked me that I wasn't. Is this another way Christians fall, too? Just based on the belief that, "I got this, Lord. I say it with my lips that You are my strength, but I got this on my own. I'm good!"

I can see how these two misconceptions could be disastrous. On one hand I have been a Christian a long time so I would never make "that bad choice," whatever it may be. That would happen to somebody else, but that would never happen to me. On the other hand, I say with my lips that I trust in the Lord's strength, but I really know that I trust in myself to be strong in even the most dangerous of circumstances that could lead to sin. We all know Christians who make sinful choices that you would never think they would ever make nor did they. Well, they made the bad choices somehow, didn't they? Nobody made the poor choices for them. They did it. The Lord was starting to show me some possible ways of how they got there and in turn was protecting me from arriving at the same place one day.

The Lord was gentle and started the process of teaching me some very valuable lessons. It was truly my responsibility to reflect Him in my life's mirror, but my heart and mind was not going about it in the right way. I had the drive, but it was Him who drives out the best of me. Not me. I tried to do it in my own strength so it didn't seem like I was growing in the Spirit. This also gave me a false sense of security from the evil one's attacks. Again, this is a very dangerous place to be. I started understanding that the Lord does expect things out of our lives. It is only when He draws out that desire in us to become more like Him that we start growing deeper. The most amazing thing is that not only do we grow, but others around us grow as well. When we do it in our strength nobody grows. That's not hard to understand. God is not a God of confusion. We are the ones who confuse things. He calls us to a life of integrity. That is a pivotal foundation in every growing Christian's life.

My Offering

Lord God, Maker of the heavens and the earth. You are holy. All Your ways are delightful to me. When I taste the blessings that You have laid before me, they are sweeter than honey to my mouth. You have ordained every step I have taken and have pulled me back from the boundary of sin so many times. You always pull me back. You have mended my broken heart and redressed me in white linen. You have never left me as I have the inability to ever leave your presence. I am secured and anchored in You when storms toss me to and fro. You are there. You hold me steady when I am in unsure situations. You give me peace to walk on, despite my lack of understanding. I can't see over the next hill, yet You are calling me to cross over. There are no hesitations in You, Lord.

You saw me when I was in my mama's womb. You touched my heart and made it beat for the first time. You knew every one of my heartbeats would beat for you until the last one. You saw me take my first breath of life, and you will see me take my last. Every breath in between that time will be counted by You. Nothing in my life escapes You. You see every thought, you know every dream, you watch every action, and you hear every prayer. You have sanctified me as your vessel that I am to give you my reasonable service all the days of my life. You have bought me with Your love. Set my paths straight before me. Protect me from my accuser. Let me live my life in such a way that he will have nothing to accuse me of before the brethren.

Do not allow me to give him something to embarrass me with in front of the brethren as he longs for me to fall. Keep me from temptation, Lord. Stir up the Holy Spirit that you put within my soul to protect me for choosing my own way in this world. Make me miserable until such time that I am doing things Your way. Give me the strength to be obedient to the knowledge that you have given me. Make me wise in all of Your ways, Holy One. The rewards that wait for me that I have stored up in heaven are all Yours. There is nothing I want now or for eternity future but You. This world that I dwell in offers me nothing, wrapped up like it is something. Help me to recognize authenticity.

Guide me to know Your movements. Speak to my spirit about the deeper things of You, God Almighty. Forgive my iniquities and the hurt I have caused you. I want to be holy as You are holy. Help me not to grieve the Holy Spirit within me. I know the only way I can hear you is through Him. I want my body to be the living tabernacle of the Lord. I want to be hospitable to the Holy Spirit as He is my link to God the Father and God the Son. I know when you called Him to Heaven that He will bring me to You. There is no greater hope under Heaven than that. I praise You, my Redeemer. I praise You, my Beloved. My soul rejoices over You in my life. There is no one like You. No one has ever loved me as completely as You, Lord. Please accept this prayer as my offering to You today. The only desire I have in my life is to serve and dwell in the House of the Lord forever. Amen and Amen.

The Field

As when one plows and breaks up the soil, turning up rocks ..." (Psalm 141:7 HCSB)

The Farmer rises early again. There is much work to be done in the fields. He owns many fields, but some are far away. As He walks down the road He comes to the first field. He sees a fence around the whole field. He investigates the fence and sees that it has been well built. He has never been in the fence-building business. He knows that fences keep Him out of the field and hinder His work. He's never cared much for them. There has been much time invested in the construction of this particular fence. If the owner took more time in other areas of the field besides trying to build fences to solely keep the Farmer out, what a field it could be! As He examines the fence, He also sees that there is no gate for Him to enter if He desired.

The Farmer notices an old sign tacked up on one of the fence posts that reads, "Private Property. No farming allowed." He has tried many times to purchase this field, but it seems that the landowner is not willing to sell no matter the price the Farmer is willing to pay. He checks on it every day, hoping to see a "For Sale" sign each time. The Farmer would never climb over the fence as He respects the free will of the owner to choose how he cares for the field. As the Farmer leans on the fence, looking across the field, the odd appearance is interesting to Him. The owner takes such care to construct such a sturdy fence to keep Him out, but all He sees is barren land inside the fence. Why would the owner want to keep a perfectly experienced Farmer out of such a field when the Farmer could have an abundant harvest out of it? It's a mystery.

He turns back toward the road to only walk a little way before He comes across another field that is very closely located to the previous one. He would prefer that there be more space between this field and the last one because He recently purchased this newer one some time back. He is greatly concerned that the weeds may cross over to His new field and make the sowing more difficult. The pesticides the other owner uses may contaminate His field's future harvest. Unfortunately, the Farmer has seen it happen so many times in the past. When His fields are too closely located to other fields that He does not own, the results can be disastrous. He walks upon the field and starts to inspect it. He is disheartened to see that even though He owns this field, there has been another fence put up around most of the perimeter. There is only a small amount of land that He is allowed to till. He does what He can with the amount allowed to Him but shakes His head. He knows this field has greatly limited its own harvest to come. He has worked hard in this field for many seasons, but the part of the area that He is not allowed has a sign posted that says,

"Limited Farming." The Farmer never puts up or takes down fences; the owner does. He does what He can. He continues to walk quite a ways down the road. There are many more fields that He passes, but most of them are similar to the first two.

The Farmer never has favorite fields that He owns. He understands that the size of the field, the type of soil, and whether it is fertile in the right season will be different. Some of His fields lay dormant for many seasons as He waits for the soil to prepare itself for planting. There are many of His fields that have larger pieces of land they allow to be planted, but never all of it. Fences are put up then taken down whenever the original owner thinks he or she can plant and harvest themselves. The Farmer laughs at the foolish thoughts of the owner. It's never a very good harvest. If it does yield something, it will only be used for itself. The Farmer is patient though and never forgets one of His fields.

In the far distance, He sees a field that He has been waiting to till more of. The first thing that excites Him is the location! It has removed itself far from the other fields that the Farmer has passed by so far. This field is different. The last time He checked the original owner had a fence around some of the area, but it has recently been totally removed. He smiled as He puts His first footprints in the soil and proceeded to walk across it, unobstructed by barriers. The Farmer knows that He has other fields much greater than this particular field. Ones that produce bountiful harvest season after season with little preparation. These other fields that He is thinking of are used to His ways, and they always seem to produce strong fruit. They may have been in His possession for a short while or many years but seem to really understand the sowing and reaping process. This field has caught His attention today.

The field senses the Farmer's footsteps and is in great anticipation of being planted. It can hardly wait to see what the Farmer decides to do with it. The Farmer bends down and grabs a hand full of soil to examine it. He looks at it for what seems to be a long time. The farmer stands up and with a big smile says to the field, "Yes! Your soil is ready. It is rich, moist, full of life, and willing for sowing. I have been waiting so long, and this field is finally ready."

The Farmer pulls His plow onto the field. As He is walking behind the plow, He hits a rock. The field felt that, and it didn't know that particular rock was there. The field knows that it has scattered rocks here and there and mostly knows where they are. It didn't have an idea that the Farmer was going to remove them before the planting or even that it was needed. It certainly didn't have an idea that He would find this particular one. The field thought that the Farmer could do His work and then move on to the harvest, especially since the owner took down the fence. As the Farmer continues plowing and the soil is being turned up, another rock is hit, then another, and yet another. The field wants the Farmer to move along and ignore the rocks because it seems like the process will take forever to clear the field for planting at this rate. The field thinks to itself, "What are a few rocks here and there?" It really doesn't have an idea of how the rocks got there in the first place. Some have been there so long, and others just appear. The field seems to have grown accustomed to the rocks, and some don't even bother it much anymore.

The Farmer comes across yet another one and stops. He knows the field is growing impatient with His preparation of the soil. This time, He bends down and picks up the rock and holds it over His head. He is silent as He looks slowly over the field from corner to corner. He speaks very loudly across the field so every inch of it hears Him clearly, "This is My field! I have paid for it in full. This rock and all the other ones should not be here. I will turn them up and remove them for proper preparation for if you could remove them then you would have already done so. Without the removal of all these obstructive rocks, you will be unable to produce to your fullest potential according to My work. You can only see the planting, but I see the harvest. I know every rock in you before I hit it. I know how long it has been there and how hard it will be to remove. No planting shall occur until the field is prepared. The time in between the preparation and the final harvest will be the most important for you."

The field was stunned and thought about what the Farmer has said. It slowly started to understand that before the harvest and even the planting, it had to figure out why all the rocks were there and how could it avoid more as to not prevent a bountiful return for the Farmer. The field now welcomed the preparation. It may be timely and painful at times, but it is a process that it has to go through. It knows the Farmer sows in love and reaps by the Spirit. The Farmer is willing, but the field has to yield. It's not what the field thinks is best for itself, but what the Farmer knows is best.

I think a lot of our Christians' lives are like this third field, only after we moved through the second one. They are wide open, far stretching, and capable of growing amazing fruit so that others will be fed. They also have the ability to grow the most fragrant flowers to be used as incense to honor the Lord. The Christian life has to be prepared before any good harvest comes from it. I mistakenly thought my field was ready for planting because it had belonged to the Farmer for so many years. How can it not be ready? I know that I have choices to make in this life before the final harvest and those choices will determine the extent of what is produced.

I used to be the field that only gave the Farmer part and fenced in the majority for my personal property. The sad part is that I thought the small harvest that the Farmer produced from the space I provided Him in the past was something to be proud of. That was enough and if the truth be known that I could extend my fence even a little more. I felt my life needed more space and was confident that the Farmer would always understand and still bless me with a bountiful harvest. Where did I get the audacity to erect fences in parts of my field in the first place? Assuming that I could till those parts myself? How selfish and naïve.

Then one day the Farmer hit my last rock. I looked around the field of my life and realized that not only did I not mind the rocks, I had justified them as not all that bad. After all they are my rocks in my field. In my opinion, they are not hurting the overall field or other fields around it. I believed that the rocks would not hurt the harvest. While the Farmer was turning up the rocks, the soil in my life was covering them up just as fast. I sat back, shocked at my actions. If I sold my field to the Farmer, how could I not also let go of every corner of it and everything in it? Why was it important to hold on to certain pieces? Knowing and accepting these truths as it relates to my thinking and behavior, I was very far from catching the attention of a Holy God.

The more I pondered these questions, the more driven I became to walk up to the Farmer and ask Him to show me the why of it all. If rocks equaled preventing Him from properly preparing the field the way He saw fit, then before they could all be removed, I had to understand how they got there and stayed in the first place. I do not want my life to have off-limit areas or stumbling rocks to the Lord. I do not want to give Him what I think He should have, but I want Him to give me what He thinks I should have. I understand that the Farmer wants to give me, not just a life but an abundant life. Again, there is an incomprehensible gap between these two things. I understand the rocks better now. I understand how they look to Him and why He is so happy when I allow Him to remove them. When I finally gave all the rocks to Him then the planting and growing began.

The Lord has shown me that before I can have perfect integrity, fear Him, and turn away from evil, I must have a solid foundation on which to build my own understanding of how to even achieve these goals. The farming analogy has resounded in my mind as the simplest and clearest way to understand how a field of life yields itself, is sown by God, and is reaped by the Spirit. If parts of my life are blocked off by fences that I erected, then how can I have His total harvest? The soil has to be broken up to turn up the deep rocks hidden underneath. It is through my own doing if I don't allow this preparation to occur, thereby again limiting God's work in my life.

We have to build our field of life on rock-free soil with no fences. Friends, as much as I can gather from what I have been shown by the Spirit, it seems like this is one of the keys to the beginning of understanding. You can't go much further in a deeper committed life with Christ if you have fences and areas that are not opened to God. You have to pray and ask the Lord to reveal where fences and the rocks are. Ask Him to help you remove them. Figure out what parts of your life that you are holding back from God while thinking you can handle it. Fences limit God. Technically, you own no part of the field that you call yours. You sold it to the Farmer which He paid dearly for. Trust me when I say it's not easy, but the tradeoff is more space in your life for the Farmer to do His work. This leads to an abundant life. More space equals a bigger harvest. The field always yields a bountiful harvest if you allow the Farmer to do His will.

Hard Coverings

I bought a new laptop just before Thanksgiving. Kevin gave me a really nice laptop carrying case for Christmas. I have never seen one quite like it. It has a really nice argyle design. It looks so nice on the outside. The thing that caught my attention was that it had a hard case. I have never seen a hard carrying case for a laptop before. This hard case will do well to protect my very valuable laptop with all of my writings. It was a nice-looking hard case on the outside to protect something very valuable inside—interesting and very functional. In reality, it really is the best protection from any damage.

I started thinking about my own life. I listened to people talk about their life experiences of hurt, disappointments, and disillusionment with how they thought it would be for them now. Because of these things and many more that I may not be able to give examples of, I think sometimes we put our very valuable hearts and emotions inside a hard case—a mental one, which may be stronger than anything else in reality. It is not because we may really want to but for the protection of our mental and emotional well-being.

Sometimes it seems that it's better to be protected in a hard case than a soft one where you put your heart out there one more time, only for no one to protect it, appreciate it, accept it, cherish, and love it the way you know it needs to be treated. You may have learned from repeatable incidences that having a hard case is your best bet in staying okay and functional. This is a learned behavior, again based on your life experiences. Not only is the case we place our valuables in a hard case, it still looks nice on the outside. That is important because we all know those closest to us can hurt us the worst. You want them to see the niceness of your presentation but never let them know that you have a hard case to protect you from their possible hurts, rejection of you, and what you have to offer of who you truly are. These people may be the ones directly responsible for requiring that we have a hard case protecting our immensely valuable hearts, minds, and feelings in the first place.

I am not wise enough to give advice on how to lay down that hard case and let your valuables come out once again, unprotected. It probably took years to make it just right so you could walk the tight walk of the line of emotions. It is a deep desire on your part to present as okay as possible but still remain in protection mode of who you are way down deep. I had a very hard case once from past hurts. I carried that hard case around for a very long time. I did so well protecting my valuables that I almost exchanged it for the life that God had planned for me. My best advice is to evaluate if you are protecting yourself in a hard case and some of the reasons why. Find a trustworthy friend, a confidant, or maybe even a professional to talk with in order for you to successfully share who you really are with the ones closest to you. Maybe you could have a heart-to-heart with your loved one and express that you may be carrying a hard case but you desire to lay it down in order to share your valuables inside with them. I know my own hard case made me miss out on a lot of good years. I can honestly say my life is so much better now that I do not carry it anymore.

Beautiful One

Before time began, God created the angels. Just as God created all the animals at one time on earth, God also created all the angels at one time in Heaven. The angels were created prior to the creation of the earth as Job 38:4–7 tells us they rejoiced and sang when the foundation of the earth was laid. They could have been created within the creation week but just before the earth's foundations were laid. It is believed that the angels had not been created long before the earth. As a child, I thought angels always existed with God. John says there are legions upon legions, ten thousand times ten thousand angels. John used the highest number he knew at the time to describe what he saw. The number would be most likely larger than we could count, as well. I want you to get the concept of the number of angels that God created.

God made different positions of angels. Some were messengers, some were leaders of legions, some were guardians, and some were worshiping angels. There are likely more positions than these. Whatever position the angels were made in, that is the position they would be in until God changed it. According to the last encounters in the scriptures, the angels had not changed in position. The reality is they may never change positions. For example, from the first time Gabriel was mentioned to the last time in the New Testament, He was a messenger angel. He never changed position. If you study Michael, the archangel, he is a leader of angels. He also is a warrior angel. At the time Michael was created, there was no reason for Him to be a warrior; however He was still a leader. God didn't change His position. He just used Michael fully in it.

God made all of the angels individualized and purposeful, just like us. One particular position of angels is called the cherubim. They were very powerful. The purpose of the cherubim was to be guardians of light and of stars. Another primary purpose is one of protection. We all remember that God put cherubim to swing flaming swords to protect the Garden of Eden.

God made one of the cherubim unique among the other cherubim and the other angels. God named this particular cherub Lucifer, which means "Bright Morning Star." He was called the Beautiful One. He was God's greatest creation. It is believed that Lucifer was more powerful than Michael, the archangel. As a cherub, Lucifer stands very tall. I have read some articles that He could be as tall as eighteen feet. He has four wings and under each wing are like hands of a man (Ezekiel 10:8 NIV). He has four faces including a face of a cherub, a man, an eagle, and a lion (Ezekiel 10:14 NIV).

God made him perfect in beauty. Lucifer is described as very colorful and almost prism-like in appearance. Lucifer was unique in the fact he had the ability to create music out of his body (Isaiah 14:11 NIV). The verse speaks about Lucifer creating the sounds of harps or some kind of string instrument. Ezekiel 28:13 describes, "The workmanship of thy tambourine and of thy pipe was prepared in the day that thou was created" (KJV). We know that Lucifer could create at least three different types of sounds from his body. According to the Bible, the sounds included stringed instruments, tambourines, and pipes. There could be many more sounds that were not recorded in scriptures.

God placed this ability in Lucifer to bring honor and glory to Himself. He loved to sing and shout for joy about the glory of the Lord (Job 38:7 NIV). God said Lucifer was, "anointed." This set Lucifer apart as he was dedicated to the service of God and was sacred. Lucifer was closest to God's throne. God made him perfect in wisdom. God allowed Lucifer to come and go in between Heaven and the Garden of Eden even before the first man was created. God allowed Lucifer to walk on the holy mountain and in the midst of the stones of fire (Ezekiel 28:12–18 NIV). It seems God wanted Lucifer to enjoy all of what belonged to Him both in heaven and earth.

Lucifer had everything any creature could ever want, but he wanted one more thing. He wanted his own way. He wanted to be in control. He wanted to make the decisions. The only problem with this was that it deflected attention off of God and His will for Lucifer's created purpose.

Nothing would do for Lucifer until he made everything about self. Once he used his gift of free will, he did just that. His name is now called Satan, the accuser of the brethren. The pride of the lifestyle changed his name and even the meaning of it. God didn't do this to him. Satan did it to himself.

We would call Satan a fool for exchanging God's way for his own. He was a fool to move one step outside of God's glory. He was a fool to exchange God's divine purpose for his existence over the one he would create for himself. As Christians, we can sit on the outside with a clear perspective and see how Satan was wrong, why Satan was wrong, and what Satan lost for his own poor choices. Of course, it seems we can do this for anyone but ourselves. We can clearly see that Satan exchanged God's truth for his lie. He was such a fool. Don't we do the exact same thing? Aren't we just as foolish?

Romans 1:25 says that we can exchange the truth for a lie just as easily (NIV). People exchange God's truth for what they want to be true in their lives, which is a lie. They justify their own thoughts and behavior at the altar of self. This is just another way to define sin. If you have to justify yourself, for any reason, in front of God then you have sinned. You have exchanged God's truth for your lie. While it seems harsh, which angel are we really more like? We don't want to believe it, but we each carry the same pride of our own desires just like Satan.

We want our way over God's way just like Satan. We exchange the glory of the Lord for the meaningless of our choices just like Satan. We each want one more thing that God hasn't given us. We want our way just as bad as Satan wanted his. We exchange the blessings and honor of the Lord in our lives just like Satan exchanged his name, all for self. Even though Christians shouldn't struggle with self, we know we do. We would be lying if we said we didn't. We have to sacrifice "self" daily on the altar of the Lord.

The Beautiful One or his demons are roaming around in your life looking for ways to devour you. Be alert! He is using the cover of lightness to fool you into helping you exchange the truth for a lie. Sin is never going to appear dark to you when you enter it. It is light and satisfies your wants and needs at the time you are involved in it. Sin will always be satisfying to you.

Satan is conniving and extremely wise. He knows your weakness as he tries to throw things out for you to take the bait. Once you do, he's hooked you. Stop taking the same bait every time! Be strong in the Lord. Stand firm in the Truth. Do not be prideful in your lifestyle. Be on guard at all times as the Beautiful One is alive and well. He is just as beautiful as the day he was created, and he will present sin as such. Don't fall for it.

Lost Blessings

Have you ever wondered if God gives us a certain number of blessings for our lifetime? I wouldn't necessarily think that each person would receive the same blessing of another, but they would be individualized and fair. I would have to believe this to be true as God is fair and just. We do not know how many blessings we will each receive as they may even in the end be innumerable. God does love to bless His children.

The best that I can understand is that blessings are earned, based on behavior. When I say behavior, I mean obedience to what the Lord has commanded for a life as a Christian individual and even a Christian nation. I also know that we can miss out on blessings that God had intended to give us—again, as an individual and as a nation. Our sin, even if repented, can cause us to miss out on some of the biggest blessings of our life. We don't want to think about that. You can choose to ignore this, but it is truth. If David would not have sinned, he would have been able to build God's first temple. That is a huge missed blessing!

If Moses would not have sinned, he would have been able to enter the Promised Land and not just have looked at it. After forty years, I am sure that he was disheartened to say the least that he missed that blessing. If Adam and Eve would not have sinned, they would never have had to leave the blessing of the Garden that was created just for them. If Solomon wouldn't have sinned, then He would not have had turmoil and division in his kingdom. He missed the blessing of having a unified nation.

If I stepped back and looked at how God's blessings work, it doesn't take a lot of intelligence to understand. If I obey His Word, wait for His timing, and follow His plan for my life, there will be blessings of protection and prosperity among countless others. If I choose—and that is the key word: choose—to disobey Him and do it my own way out of impatience, arrogance, self-centeredness, or pride, then He has every right to hold back a blessing from me. It's His blessing to give, and it's His blessing to hold back. We cannot claim that is unfair at all. His blessings. His rules. Fair.

I want to add something else that some may really claim as unfair. This is very important so listen closely. David repented. Moses repented. Solomon repented. Adam and Eve repented. All before the future blessing was withheld. Guess what? Despite their acknowledgement and repentance of their disobedience and sin, God still held back humongous future blessings from them. Think about that for moment.

We may think, "Okay, I was in active sin so I *deserve* to not have my blessings, but *if* I am repentant in my sin then God should fairly have to give me my blessing in the future." Nope. He doesn't have to do anything of the sort, and if His track record holds, He certainly may hold back future blessings for your past sins. He is obligated by His promise and nature to forgive your sin, but He is not obligated to give you a later blessing for a poor choice you made in the past. I am not a preacher or theologian. I am just Sarah. I am just interpreting what I am reading as simply as I can and trying to understand how blessings work. The best way to logically do this would be to look at how others gained and lost theirs in the past. History is man's best teacher.

The reason I feel confident in my understanding is that God doesn't change. If He held future blessings from Moses, David, Solomon, and so on, for their past sins/disobedience, who am I that He would respond any differently on handling my future blessings? I have to sit and seriously ponder today: how many blessings have I missed up to this point in my life due to my past sins of disobedience of God's will? I do believe it's possible that the tears in Heaven that He will wipe away may be because He was showing me some of them. At this point in my life, there is nothing I can do to change God's mind on what blessings He will hold from me due to my sinful choices in the past. God has already decided what He is going to do. If these other people couldn't talk Him into changing His mind, I suggest you save your breath.

I accept this as part of the consequences of going my own way in the past. What I can control is how I conduct myself now and in the future according to God's ways. I am more committed now than ever before to be mindful of temptations that can lead to sin. Besides not wanting to hurt my Father's heart, I want to prevent myself from losing any more blessings that He wants to give me later. I can only do this by disciplining and strengthening my spirit nature to be placed above my human one and heeding the convicting power of the Holy Spirit.

Broken Hearts

The world as we know it today is not the world that the Lord wanted for us in the beginning. We must understand this truth. When you start thinking about the far-stretched arm of sin and the ripple effects that are still happening even in our lives today, it is mind boggling. I can think of each ripple individually. The one ripple effect that is heaviest on my heart for me and others actually deals with broken hearts. Can a heart really be broken? If the Lord addressed the brokenhearted, then yes, our hearts can be broken. Our spirits can be so beaten down by the world that it literally and completely breaks our heart. It feels this world takes from us that which does not belong to it and leaves us with brokenness. That is not a good trade.

The truth is, it is usually people that are closest to us that are the best breakers of our hearts. I have to sit back and wonder if people actually have a clue about the power they possess over others. Some people's lives are totally shifted off course to become completely derailed because of what has been done to their hearts at another's hand. Things they could have never imagined that their hearts would break for broke them. We say, "Oh my heart will never be broken for that or for this." If you live long enough, your heart will be broken by someone's words and behaviors. It is, sadly, the ripple of sin. Again, it is by those that have been close to you in the past or are currently close to you now that will do the breaking.

Do you think for one second the Lord didn't know that our hearts could be broken? He made them. He wanted them to be tender. He knows how delicate and precious they are, especially to Him. He doesn't desire a broken heart for even one of His children, but He knows this world better than anyone. He knows His children's hearts will be broken sooner or later by something or by someone. In those times, it feels that you are more alone than you have ever been. Your emotions tell you over and over that you are alone in this, and you are hopeless. You can listen to emotions and the enemy that lies to you or you can choose to listen to the Voice of Truth.

What does the Truth say? "I am the Lord your God, and I am close to those that are brokenhearted. I will save your spirit because I know it has been crushed" (Psalms 34:18, paraphrased NIV). What else does Truth say? "I am the Lord your God and I will heal your broken heart, and I will personally and tenderly bandage your wounds" (Psalms 147:3, paraphrased NIV). What else does Truth say? "I am the Lord your God, and I will send My appointed people just like I have in the past to bind up and comfort whose hearts are broken so that you may hear My Voice of Truth. I want you to know that I hear you and send my people out to tell you My truth" (Isaiah 61:1, paraphrased NIV).

My sweet brothers and sisters in Christ, you are pretty much guaranteed a broken heart over something or somebody. If you are reading this journal, I can't believe you have even missed one by now. I haven't. Some of my younger readers may not have had one, but unfortunately the world will see to it that they will have one in the future. Are we going to listen to the voice of our emotions that there is no hope for our hearts— or the Enemy's voice? The Lord's truth is the only truth to listen to in these times. It is the only truth that will heal your heart. He is closer to you when you have a broken heart more than any other time in your life.

His heart hurts when your heart hurts, so in His compassion He comes very close to you. Can't you just picture Him taking your tender heart in His big hands and gently turning it over and bandaging it so that it can heal? It heals under His watchful eye. What an image of truth for your mind to dwell on. There's nothing the Lord cares for more than your heart. I can promise you this world doesn't care about it. Listen to the Voice of Truth, and get the healing from the One who is the cardiac specialist!

Your other choice is to continue to carry around a broken heart. The truth is that the Lord will allow you to do this unless you come to Him. Draw very close to Him, and He promises to draw close to you. Do it your own way, and He will let you. Do it His way, and He will heal you. That's just how He works. If you are one that may have some brokenness of heart today, may the Lord be with your spirit as He heals it. I am learning that hearts can be broken more than once, so I know that He is faithful to heal them every time. That is a comfort to know.

Sign-in Sheet

I went to the county law office yesterday to take care of some minor business. They had a sign-in sheet that had name, county, and reason for visit across the top of the paper. I put my name on the last line on the page. I scanned over the column for reasons for others' visits. I was curious about what people would come to a county law office for besides my own reason. There was one word that reappeared over and over: divorce.

Next line, "Divorce." Next line, "Divorce." Next line … I think you get the picture. All these names on the paper represented lives and marriages. Real people. They all were seeking the same thing. Fifty percent of the names on the paper were seeking a divorce. I started thinking isn't that a coincidence. Fifty percent of the marriages end in divorce in America. Coincidence? No. It was confirmation that the national statistics are correct.

I walked out of that law office and thought at one time my name could have been on that paper. Divorce is such an easy word to fly around in a head when things are not right. I had a hard time collecting my thoughts. That simple sign-in paper was all I could think of. I knew the Lord had already started pricking my spirit to write about what I had just seen, and I didn't want to do that. He reminded me that it wasn't about me. It has never been about me and never will be about me.

I'm not going to disclose more of my personal life as I do not feel the Lord would expect that of me. I do think I can share my lessons learned and other lessons that I have learned from friends. I recently celebrated twenty years with Kevin. We are both exceedingly happy to reach such a milestone together! No marriage is ever perfect, and mine certainly has had its issues. I look back on the years and where I am today. We are in a lot better shape this side of twenty than the other side; that is for sure. I don't necessarily believe that marriage gets better with years, but I do believe that in my case, that can certainly be true. What I have learned from other friends who have had struggles that led to separation, then divorce, is there is no place for judgment in that. There is only support as I am not a judge. None of us are.

I have learned that when one spouse breaks the Lord's commandment for godly conduct, there are harsh consequences for the marriage. I have learned that when one spouse has unhealthy thoughts that they have either brought in the marriage or have picked up during the marriage, there are harsh consequences for the marriage. I have learned that spouses have polar opposite personalities. They can't understand their spouse's personality because they can't even understand their own, and that has harsh consequences for the marriage. I have learned that communication and active listening skills are not innate and don't go home with you from the church after the reception. When these skills are lacking, there are harsh consequences for the marriage. I have learned that if spouses do not take care of each other's physical and emotional needs *consistently*, and one is not greater than the other, then there could be harsh consequences for the marriage. I have learned when one spouse cannot control the tongue, there are harsh consequences for the marriage. I have learned when spouses don't spend enough time to deeply understand the other to love them like they need to be understood or loved, there are harsh consequences for the marriage.

If you think your marriage is untouchable by sin of the past and/or the present, then you are a fool, and because of your lack of awareness it will come under surprise attack. You can be attacked. Your spouse can be attacked. Your marriage will be attacked by internal and external forces. Literally attacked. Bombs going off and things flying. Attacked! That is a guarantee. Why? Our enemy is roaring and roaming around constantly looking to take down any Christian he can get his filthy evil claws on. We are in a battle, and it is all spiritual. We are completely clueless.

Spouses are fighting against something so much bigger than each other. They have no clue who and what they are up against for the defense of their marriage. They walk around blind and unprepared. Wake up! Satan doesn't have to attack both spouses. If he can turn one spouse against another, he has taken the marriage. If he can just get the attention of one, then he can write their names on the county law office sign-in sheet.

None of us had any idea how hard marriage could be when we walked out of that church, even the ones who are divorced now. No idea. We had no idea what battles lay ahead. I think we have marched so many times unprepared and have received many war wounds because of that truth. Some have lost the war, not by their choice though. Some marriages have had too many harsh consequences to survive. Some marriages are battle weary and are barely hanging on and will not survive one more wound. I understand. The Lord knows you can't sustain one more wound. Maybe you have hardened your heart so that you wouldn't feel if another wound did come. Knowing the past battles in my own marriage, I know it is sometimes hard to see over that next hill. Really hard. You just close your eyes and hope that you reach it. You are not sure what will happen when you do.

For those marriages that are still marching on but have sustained wounds, I would encourage you to read this journal together. Start some much-needed dialog about those things under the carpet that everyone keeps tripping over, but bombs go off when you talk about them. Sometimes you have to have outside help with that. I am a true believer in seeking help. A lack of honest dialog and understanding is a land mine just waiting to be stepped on. The marriage will sustain injuries when it gets stepped on either now or in the future. Get a battle plan together. Prepare yourself and protect your spouse. Guard your marriage.

I learned that battle wounds are self-inflicted by either one spouse or both. We are our own worst enemy to our marriage when we fail to admit that to ourselves and to our spouse. We need to band together against the enemy. We need to stop being the enemy to our own marriage. We want to be right and have it our way at the cost of everything. Why? Why do we have to come out on top when the mountain peak has enough for two to stand side-by-side on? It took me a long, long time to figure out that the top had enough space for two, and it wasn't all about me. That seems so simple but powerful enough to destroy everything.

I don't want to be on the county law office sign-in sheet with reason for visit "divorce." If you have already, then by the healing power of the Holy Spirit, it doesn't mean that you ever have to be in the future. The past does not need to define your future. I have learned it certainly will if you let it. It's difficult to write a journal that addresses both situations, because of the compassion I have for both. Take what you can from my words as they were difficult to put together. This was by far one of my hardest journals.

Believe me, when I went into the court house, I had no idea I would be writing a journal on divorce later on that day. God did, which was probably why I had to go in the first place. The ironic thing is the clerk said I could have printed off the paperwork from my home computer. I was meant to go in person because I know I was supposed to see that sign-in sheet. The Lord uses many situations to teach me. I try hard to listen and be faithful to what He impresses upon my spirit to write about. Please wake up and guard your precious marriage.

Thinning and Cooling

O taste and see that the Lord is good. Blessed is the man that trusteth in Him. (Psalms 34:8 KJV)

I absolutely love eating peach oatmeal for breakfast. I have a cup almost every day. I add the milk and warm it up in the microwave. I stir in some butter. There is perfection every time. The only thing is, when I take a bite it is too hot! Usually, I just let it sit and cool like normal people do. This morning, I was impatient with my peach oatmeal cooling because I was hungry. I wanted it now! I added several pieces of ice cubes. This cooled it down really fast, but as a result it also watered the oatmeal down. It didn't taste as good watered down. The flavor had been affected.

As I was stirring the ice cubes around the hot cup of oatmeal, the Spirit spoke to me. He said, "You put ice cubes in the cup of your life that belongs to Me. You water down the power I want to give you. I want to give you a thicker and more flavorful life than the one you keep thinning and cooling down by your own choices." Wow. I just looked at my cup of thinning oatmeal and the ice floating in it.

I started thinking about the ice cubes I stir in my own Christian life that cools and thins it out. A flood of thoughts came to my mind. Each thought was like its own individual cube of ice. There was lack of trust in the Lord, impatience when He took too long to answer, complacency, working according to my own strength, lack of consistency of choosing God's way, wanting things in my life that He had not given and justifying why I should have them, compromising, poor prioritization of the things of God, self-defeating thoughts, justifying my own thoughts and behaviors when I know the Lord would not approve because sin is satisfying, not using my talents for the Lord, minimal prayer time, lack of consistency with reading and studying the Word that He wrote to me, becoming inactive with the eternal Lord as I become more active in temporal things, and justifying the lack of fellowship with my Christian brethren.

I have never once thought that these things were like ice cubes thinning and cooling my life. I was stunned of how the Lord taught me this and how clear things seemed now. I knew that I should not have these ice cubes in my life, but I never really saw them harming me in the long run. Honestly, I was only thinking and living in the now. Each ice cube were good for how I needed them to work for me right now.

The Lord has tested the temperature of my life and watched it drop from hot to lukewarm. He watched while I thinned down my Christian walk. I have walked on dangerously thin ice. Underneath it was cold water that would cause my life's temperature to drop even further. He watched how I changed the sweetness of my walk with Him to a bland flavor. This happened all because I was dropping ice cube after ice cube after ice cube into my life. I was to the point in my life that I was making the Lord physically sick. Jesus said in Revelation 3:15–16, "I know your works: you are neither cold nor hot. Would that you were either cold or hot! So, because you are lukewarm, and neither hot nor cold, I will spit you out of my mouth" (ESV). Matthew 5:13 says, "You are the salt of the earth, but if salt loses its taste, how can it be made salty again? It is no longer good for anything, except to be thrown out and trampled by men" (NIV). I never intended my life to lose its heat and flavor.

I understand my life to the Lord is like my peach oatmeal to me each morning. The Lord desires my life to be hot, thick, and flavorful. When He stirs my life and tastes it, it should be to His liking, not mine. It should be good to Him. I am learning that He doesn't want me to drop ice cubes in my cup of life. As long as He is holding my cup, I am perfect in Him.

God's Faithfulness

If we are faithless, He remains faithful. (2 Timothy 2:13 NIV)

When we are not faithful, God remains faithful. God is bound by His nature to behave this way. If I am His true child, then He has the inability to be unfaithful to me. I have the ability to be unfaithful to Him through His own gift to me of free will. This is such a big and important truth. Some would read right over this and miss the importance. Christians should fall on their knees, thanking God that He cannot act any other way than the way He does. I'm thankful that He is true to His nature.

If you were honest, how long would you hang on to a relationship with someone who went against you and hurt your heart by following their own desires? They follow their own way, requiring you to constantly bring them back, and at times they don't believe what you say. Sometimes, they will not talk to you. They never have time to spend with you except maybe once a week if that, and there would usually be other people around. They rarely listen, even though you gave sound advice every time. They always place other things or people before you. They disregard the notes that you have spent time writing for them to read and respond to. How would you respond to that kind of person? What would your nature tell you to do? Continue to be faithful? No. We would be done with a person like that.

When we lose our faithfulness in how we should behave in a relationship with the Most High God, He remains faithful. Stop. Think about that. Now think about it some more. He remains faithful to us, anyway! Not one of us would remain faithful in a relationship like I described. How often in my own Christian life have I treated the Lord just like this? I pray, "Thank you, Lord, that regardless of the lack of my faithfulness in maintaining my relationship with You, You remain faithful in your relationship with me. Praise God that when I do not have my will and Your will in the right priority, You remain patient and faithful until which time I do."

Surrounded

Elisha was one of the most powerful prophets that has ever lived. He was Elijah's protégé. Before Elijah was taken up to Heaven, Elisha asked for a double portion of his spirit. Some say He was even more powerful than Elijah due to the granting of this double portion. Every heartbeat that Elisha had beat for the Most High God. He totally rested in the power and protection of God. He not only believed it, he saw it displayed around him. By the power of God, Elisha multiplied food, healed sickness and diseases, raised the dead, multiplied the widow's oil, purified water, and changed inedible food to edible food.

What was interesting about Elisha is that he always saw the invisible hand of God's power. It was almost like he was used to it. When other people did not see God's power and lost faith that God would take care of them, Elisha would almost be in disbelief of their little faith. The people had seen God's power demonstrated in the lives around them, but they so easily forgot as new problems or trials came. How we are like them. We will be on a mountain and have so much faith in God's power, but when we hit that valley, our faith dries up as we cry out for the Lord to move and show His power. The same power that was present on the mountain is the same power in the valley.

Second Kings 6:15–18 tells of such an incident. There was an evil king of Aram that rose up against Israel. Every time the Arameans made plans to attack Israel in several different ways, Elisha would already know it because the Lord notified him. He would go tell Israel's army so that they would be protected. The king of Aram found out about Elisha's gift of prophecy and went to kill him so that they could then attack Israel without their knowing it. They went to shut up the man of God. The Lord has stated in 1 Chronicles 16:22, "Do not touch my anointed ones! Do my prophets no harm" (NIV).

There is one thing you do not want to mess with and that is an anointed prophet of God. Bad things can happen! Elisha was not worried one bit that he would be harmed. He saw the power of the Lord and trusted in it. When the king of Aram heard that Elisha was in Dothan, they went by night and surrounded the whole city. They had horses and chariots and a massive army. The king was going to get his man, or so he thought.

The next morning when the sun came up the army became visible to the inhabitants of the city. Elisha's servant looked out and saw the great army and knew they were coming for Elisha. I can just see him wringing his hands in hysterics saying, "What are we going to do?" Elisha in verse 16 calmed the scared servant and said, "Don't be afraid, for those who are with us outnumber those who are with them." Can't you see the servant's face as he looked around an empty house at only him and Elisha? That servant probably thought Elisha had lost his mind.

Remember, this servant most likely had been with Elisha with all the miracles and power that had been displayed through him. All that was in the past for the servant, he was only living in the now. He only saw his trial. He saw no power of God even though it was surrounding him. Again, we are just like this servant. That trial comes in our lives, and we forget all power of God. We shake in our boots, "What are we going to do?!"

Elisha prayed, "Lord, please open his eyes and let him see." Instantly the servant's eyes were open to behold the power of the Most High God. He saw the entire mountains covered with heavenly horses and chariots of fire. The power and protection of God were all around Elisha. The servant finally saw what Elisha already saw and had confidence in. Elisha knew that the power of God would never leave a child of God. The servant had to be visually reminded of that same truth. The servant only saw the circumstances in front of him and not the power around him.

This story was written approximately 2,500 years ago; we have not changed much, have we? Many of these ancient people are just like us in almost every way. You would think we would have more faith in the power of God as time has passed, but we really don't. We sometimes have no more faith in the power of God than this servant did. We see our circumstances instead of God's possibilities in our lives. We are just as blind as this servant was to the power of God all around us.

I am so guilty of this as well. I wish I could say that I had the eyes of Elisha to see the power of God all the time so my worries and fears would be calmed, but I am so much like this servant. My prayer for us as Christians is when the next trial comes or our enemy attacks, we can lift our eyes to the mountains to see the power of the Most High God surrounding and protecting us. He is there. God never leaves one of His children powerless and unprotected. We just have to have enough faith and trust to see like Elisha.

Crowns of Heaven

As hard as it is to believe, Jesus considers us his brothers and sisters. We are God's children, but Jesus calls us, "brothers and sisters (Hebrews 2:11 NIV). He calls us heirs to the Kingdom of God (Romans 8:17 NIV). Jesus' sacrifice enabled us to become brothers, sisters, and heirs. I wanted to explain that because Jesus is a king. Kings wear crowns. We are heirs to a kingdom, and we are brothers and sisters to a king. If we are related to a king, then we will wear crowns, too.

There are five crowns that we may wear. We earn them now, but the

King will crown us when we get to Heaven at the Judgment seat of Christ. At that judgment, you will have a one-on-one with the King. No one will be with you. It will be just you and Jesus—nothing to dread at all, but I do feel that it will be intense. He will want to talk with you and maybe ask you some questions. He will reward you with one or more crowns according to your lifeworks on earth. Once you get to Heaven, you cannot earn these particular crowns. They are only administered there and only earned on earth. That's important to understand. I will go through each crown and explain it to the best of my knowledge. Some crowns will be more difficult to earn and even one you may not want. I will point that one out to you!

If you have a deep longing with all your heart for the glorious appearing of Jesus and you are actively looking for it to occur, then you will be given the *Crown of Righteousness* (2 Timothy 4:8 NIV). Again, you would rather Him return this second, rather than to take another breath on this earth, not that it would just be a nice thing that could happen! Nothing is more important: not that loved one, not that child, not that animal, and not that spouse—nothing. Jesus is above all others and everything in your life. You are actively engaged in eagerly waiting to see His face.

If you are disciplined with strict self-control of placing your spirit nature as the dominant nature in your life as your norm, then you will be given the *Incorruptible Crown* (First Corinthians 9:25–27 NIV). You are running the good race with great purpose. You run with a centered life, firmly focused on Jesus Christ. You are absolutely confident and unwavering in Him. Jesus Christ is in complete control of you so that there is actually none of you and all of Him.

When you have intense testing, temptation, or suffering for the cause of Christ and still continue to be strong, you should be very happy. In doing this you have proved your faith. You will receive the *Crown of Life* as you have endured patiently through trials. Again, these are more than hard times in your life that you trusted Christ. You had to suffer for Christ. The key to this crown in my mind is your faithfulness to the end that He will be faithful to what He says, and you believe Him even when faced with the toughest situation (James 1:12; Revelation 2:10 NIV).

I think of the American Pastor Sayeed who has suffered imprisonment and abuse in Iran for his Christian faith. He doesn't know if he will live or die, but he has not renounced his faith in our Savior. He will receive this crown. This crown also has been termed the martyr's crown. Those persecuted unto death will receive this for sure. I do not believe you have to die to receive it, but I imagine you would have had to endure some intense testing, temptation, and suffering. This is the crown that I was talking about that you may not want to earn or at least it would not be pleasurable to qualify for it! None of us want to suffer or possibly die for our faith, but we have to pray that the Lord will strengthen us to endure if we are called upon to do so. His grace will be sufficient for us if we do.

The *Crown of Glory* will be given to those godly leaders who were examples to the flock (1 Peter 5:2–4 NIV). They could be pastors, elders, missionaries, or teachers of the Word. They have a deep willingness of the Spirit to instruct others in the Word because they are very eager to serve God. They lead by good examples of their own lives. I think of them like earthly shepherds tending the Chief Shepard's flock until He returns. They help others grow and understand the things of Christ in a very loving and encouraging way. Not everyone is called in the body of Christ to do this, so not everyone will earn the Crown of Glory.

First Thessalonians 2:19 talks about a crown that everyone is eligible for, but sadly so many Christians will not earn (NIV). It's the *Crown of Rejoicing*. This is the soul-winner's crown. Jesus says, "Go and make disciples of all nations" (Matthew 28:19 NIV). Daniel 12:3 says that those who lead many to righteousness will shine like stars forever (NIV). This is the scenario I think of about telling others about Christ. Let's say there is a fire in a building.

One hundred people are in the building. You know that there are others, and you are the only one who knows the one door out of there. Instead of telling others, you quietly slip out the door. The saddest part is when you get to safety, you never worry about those 100 people. All that really matters is that you are personally safe and sound. Why? Because you justified in your head that someone else would tell them how to find the door out of there. It's not your job or really your problem. It is definitely not your priority. It never has been and you do not see that you even want it to be.

Wake up, Christian, from your very deep slumber! If you know the door to safety from an eternal fire for others, open your mouth, and tell a hundred people so they can go through the door with you! The door should not be a secret! Christ is not your little secret! "I found Jesus, so you can find Him for yourself." What is wrong with us? What are we thinking? Are we truly that weak and timid in our faith? Are we truly that selfish to keep Christ to ourselves?

We have justified this so long that we are quiet while others perish. Again, as long as we don't personally perish and our life is comfy, all is well. Christian, if I'm describing you, all is *not* well. You have bought your own lie that it is. If you tell a lie long enough that it becomes truth for you, then you create your own reality around that. The truth may be that you are very much asleep. Sleeping Christians who are only interested in the safety of their own salvation and spiritual maturity are not in the running for the Crown of Rejoicing.

The Church in America is dying. Slowly, attendance numbers are dwindling. Where are all the people going? Who cares! That is none of our concern. Even if 3,500 to 4,500 churches permanently close their doors every year, as long as ours is still open, all is well, right? Do you know that you could be a member of a dying church right now and not even know it? I've heard it said that if a church is not growing, then it is dying. There is no in-between. How can this be if we are even contemplating getting the Crown of Rejoicing?

The truth is that few Christians are contemplating getting this crown. Honesty, they don't care if they get this one or not. They think, "I'm okay with not getting this crown as long as I get to Heaven." That may be their attitude for all these crowns. The mentality of most Christian and maybe even yours says, "Just let me get to Heaven. I don't need anything more" or "Let me just get there, and I will be okay watching other people get their crowns. It's not a big deal to me." We wonder why the Church is dying in America. I know why it is dying. I can assure you it's not the world killing it. It's the Christians. How you ask? By doing absolutely nothing.

Things die pretty easily when you do nothing to them. Marriages. Friendships. Relationships. Life. Churches. If I had a plant and did nothing to it, it would die. That's how it works. I could be the best gardener in the world. I could have all the knowledge in the world of gardening, but if I never watered or fertilized the plants, they would die. That's how I look at Christians in the church. They are the gardeners. They make sure they are very well taken care of, but they don't care for or forget about the plants.

We step back and see the plants become weak and die and say, "I don't understand; I am such a good gardener!" We have so many Christians who care about nothing more than making sure their personal day-to-day lives and Christian walks are okay. They have all the knowledge but never tell a soul about the saving grace of Jesus Christ. As Christians, we may help other Christians grow, and that is all well and good, but when you cocoon yourself in Christian circles, how does that reach the outside? The nonbelievers live on the outside of the church walls and functions. We have to move from the inside to the outside. I am guilty of doing this in my own life.

When will we want to stop being fed and deeply desire to feed others? We say we are alive and living for the Lord. Are we alive and well by God's standards or our own? Have we, in reality, been useless in furthering the Kingdom of God? In the last year, have you told one nonbeliever about Jesus Christ? What is more, has it even crossed your mind once to do it? I'm not trying to give anyone a guilt trip. I am right there with you.

I have been convicted of this myself this year, and I have tried to do better with my verbal witness. I am finding it is not as hard as I thought. My priority in the past has been to personally grow and teach my Sunday school class. Again those things are not bad, but it is not sharing the Lord with the one that needs to hear it the most—the lost person. I have read my Bible, and this is what God says is one of His primary reason for saving you. He wants you to tell others about Him. When we stand in front of Him and He asks you, "Do you love Me?" you say, "Oh, yes, Lord."

The next question may be, "How many people did you tell of my Love that you profess with your lips so that they may love Me, too?" Christian, you have been bought at a very high price. You have a purpose, and that is more than your own spiritual growth. As I said before, the Crown of Rejoicing is available for everyone to earn. I do not believe the majority of Christians will get one. Only 20 percent of the church are faithful tithers; there are probably less than that of consistent verbal witnesses.

Do you know what people do with these crowns they earn? Wear them and parade around in Heaven and say, "Look at us?" No. As soon as they get them, they worship the Lord by casting them down at His feet in Heaven (Revelation 4:10 NIV). It was never about these particular people on earth, and it will not be about them in Heaven. If we can worship the Lord by casting our crowns, ask yourself how much more can you worship the Lord right now by earning them? Think about it! How can it not still be worship on this side of Heaven? It is!

Do you really want to be standing on the sidelines of your Christian life thinking you don't need to worship the Lord in a way that He says later He will give you crowns for? Obviously, this is all pretty important to Him! What is important to Him should be your highest priority, but the reality is it's not. How much clearer can He be in what He desires of us? Which nature is dominant again—the spirit or the human one? How you look at your desire to earn these crowns is a good way to gage that answer. Please understand that these crowns do not signify your salvation. You can be saved and not earn one crown. Why wouldn't you want to? The crowns signify lifeworks after your salvation for the Most High God.

Being a Christian is not a game that you can pick and choose what parts you want to follow. There is a responsibility when you carry the name of Christ. Few Christians deeply understand that. They quickly accept Christ's name but not the responsibility that comes along with it. They change the rules and standards all the time to fit Christ into their life. You are the one who is supposed to change your life to fit into Christ's. If you call Christ Lord, then you are bought at a high price. You are no longer your own. Why do we still think and act like we are? When will we start caring about what the Lord cares about and not what we care about? When will the Christian wake up from his or her slumber?

Some have been sleeping for a very long time. This was me. I am no different than you. The Lord woke me up, and I haven't dozed since that day. I pray my journals are like alarm bells going off in your head that are deafening to wake you up if you have been sleeping, too. The Lord is coming soon, Christian. Will He find you all nestled down in your slumber or worshiping Him now in such a way so that you can cast crowns at His feet in Heaven later? I would take some time to answer that question.

Remember Me

Look! I stand at the door and knock. If you hear my voice and open the door, I will come in, and we will share a meal together as friends. (Revelation 3:20 NLT)

The Spirit has impressed upon my spirit to start having a personal communion with the Lord during my quiet time. At first, I did not believe the impression that I was receiving could be accurate. I felt that I was supposed to be given communion in a church by an ordained minister. Jesus reminded me that He was the High Priest, and He would serve me communion. For about two weeks, I kept hearing, "Have communion with Me. Come. Have communion with Me." I felt unworthy to partake in communion with just me. The Spirit kept saying, "Have communion with Me."

After this two-week period of having this strong impression, I talked to one of my close friends about my concerns. I told her what I thought the Lord was telling me to do and how I thought I must be hearing wrong. She became really teary and went over to a special place in her desk. She took this leather container out. She brought it over to me and handed it me and said, "The Lord has told me to hold this for you but not to offer it until you told me that you were supposed to have communion with Him. I have had it for a long while. I never knew when you would tell me that the Lord had asked you to do communion with Him. This is yours."

I opened it up and it was an individual silver-plated communion set. It had beautiful etching on the silver containers with a bread holder and two small silver cups. When I comprehended all that was going on, I became in awe of the Lord once again as He continued to validate what He wanted me to do. This communion set confirmed that I was hearing Him correctly. I couldn't believe it.

After a couple of days, I went to the Christian book store. I walked back to the back of the store to look at the communion bread. I still felt like I should not be in that section of the store. I felt very uneasy. I just stood there looking at the different boxes of the little crackers. A man came up to my right and stood very close to me. I could feel someone to my right, and I thought it was my son so I turned to say something then realized it was a man. He was short, balding, and wore glasses. He wore this very large wooden cross on a leather string around his neck. I had never seen one just like it, mostly due to the size. It was very eye catching, and I looked at it.

I said, "I'm sorry. I was going to say something. I thought you were my son. I'm trying to figure out what kind of crackers to buy. I have never bought them before. I really don't know which ones to get." He smiled and pointed to one box and said, "These round ones do not taste good.

They taste like paper. I wouldn't buy them. They do come in wheat, but you can't buy them here." The strange thing is that before he said that, I was going to buy the round ones! He then pointed the second box that said "soft" on the front. He said, "These advertise as soft, but they truly are as hard as the normal ones in these boxes over here. So they are the same." I told him, "Thank you that helped a lot."

I looked back at the shelf of the communion crackers then back to my right, and he was gone. It was like he came out of nowhere, and then he was gone. When I went to the front of the store, I didn't see him again. Did the Lord send someone to help me pick out communion crackers? What are the odds that a man wearing a very large wooden cross was in the same store looking at the same shelf of crackers as me at 5:00 on a Monday? The strange thing is he knew a lot about communion crackers, yet he didn't buy a box. He was there telling me about the different types of crackers and then he was gone. Take this story however you want. I am still in awe.

This morning I took my little silver cup out of my communion set and poured the grape juice in it and set it aside. I took my little piece of bread and held it in my fingers. I started my quiet time listening to the song, "Spirit of the Living God, Fall fresh on me." Then I listened to "Spring up O well, I have a River of life flowing out of me." I read 1 Corinthians 11:23–26 and meditated on the words of my Lord. I asked for forgiveness for all iniquity so that I could stand in His presence with a clear conscience. I told Him that I felt uneasy and unworthy to partake of communion this way.

I closed my eyes. I clearly pictured Jesus in front of me with a round piece of unbroken bread in His hand saying, "This is my body broken for you. Take. Eat." I saw Him tear the bread and stretch His hand out for me to take a piece. He held it there, and I finally took it out of His hand and held it to my lips. He said, "You live because I live. Eat." I put the bread in my mouth, and it was so soft. It melted in my mouth like no communion cracker has ever melted.

I then picked up the little silver cup. I pictured Him holding a large silver goblet. He said, "This is my blood shed for you. This is My new covenant. As often as you drink of this cup, you remember My cleansing blood that I poured over you. You live because I live. Drink." I drank the one swallow of juice, and it was so sweet to taste. I had my hands put together as in prayer. He come up and closed His hands over mine. We just stood there together in the sweetest communion.

God is alive. I was the one who was dead. I was like a dead man walking before the day I accepted His broken body and shed blood. I was without hope. I was walking in darkness, and the enemy laughed as I stumbled in my own weakness, reasoning, justification, and sin. I was destitute and didn't have a realization of my condition. No power in this world could release my captive heart and heal me from my condition.

The Lord wants me to commune with Him and take His broken body and shed blood. He never wants me to forget the magnitude of His sacrifice for my heart and soul. He never wants me to forget who I was without Him and who I am now in Him. He never wants me to forget how significant and valuable I am in His eyes. He never wants me to forget His power. So I will accept my Lord's invitation to sup with Him. I will always approach communion humbly with a clear conscience and with a great fear of the Lord as I consume His broken body and shed blood.

Time Management

Lost time is never found again. (Benjamin Franklin)

None of us like to waste time and certainly do not want others to waste our time. When we sin, we are not only wasting our time but God's time. We are using precious time that we could be maturing in the Lord or helping others mature, yet we are expending it on sin or ourselves. We do not have the right perspective on the time God has given us. We will be held accountable for how we use our time. God says we have wasted too much time doing what nonbelievers enjoy (1 Peter 4:3 NIV).

If you do not think He notices when His time or a Christian's time is wasted, think again. When we became Christians, we punched God's time clock. This is a very special time clock in that there is only one clocking and that is in! You never clock out of God's time. It's 24-7. You do nothing on God's time unless it is part of His will for you. He has already paid for all of your wages in advance, so He fully expects your time. When you are out of His will, you are cheating Him out of time that He paid for.

You wouldn't cheat your employer out of paid time, would you? Would you cheat a Holy God out of His time? What kind of logic is that? Where are your ethics? Just because you can't see God, and your wages will not be garnished, you think you can cheat Him? You rob God out of time that He paid for when you are in your will. It is not right to give time to God only if you have some left over. The truth is that is how most Christians manage their relationship with God. Your time already belongs to Him. He says, "Tonight your soul may be required of you." He knows how much time you have, not you. You act like you do when you plan and think you will prioritize God sometime in your future when your life slows down. How very foolish. We have a very distorted perspective of time according to our own reality. That doesn't mean it is truth. The only reality we had better live in is the Lord's. He says your time belongs to Him.

How do we display poor time management with the Lord? I have already mentioned that being out of the will of God is poor use of His time and yours. This simply means sin. Sin is one of the biggest contributors to nonproductive time. Sin is a time eater. You know it, and God knows it. Think back when the last time you sinned or think about the sin you are in now. How has that sin robbed your productive time for the Lord?

I know when I have been in sin, it is like a time warp. You are having so much fun with the flesh being satisfied that you lose all track of time. I know the Lord wants us to mature, not at snail pace but at a steady pace. When we do not spend the time being disciplined enough to stay in His word, our ability to spiritually mature is significantly affected. Why should we desire a holy life? First Peter 2:2 says it is so that we may grow and become fully mature in Christ along with being like Him in our hearts, behavior, and actions (NIV). Finally, understanding deeply by hearing His voice come out of the Word of why it is so important to rid ourselves of all wickedness of heart assists in our spiritual maturity as well.

Worry is also an example of poor time management. The Lord tells you not to worry about one thing. He has everything under control. He takes care of the birds and the flowers, and you are much more import-ant. How do we use our time and His time? We analyze every little thing. We pick it apart 100 times, then put it back together. We play possible scenarios out in vivid detail in our head of how things may go or how they should go. Most likely, not one of the scenarios will be that way in the end.

Even if they are, what did it benefit you to worry about it prior to them happening anyway? It didn't. The amount of time I have wasted pouring time and energy into worry makes me feel sick to my stomach. The time I have spent dwelling over things I have done in the past or worry about things that may happen in the future is time I will never recover. Since I have decided to use my time for the Lord today, I have been at complete mental peace. I now fully understand why He tells us not to worry.

Last, I think another example of poor time management is delayed disobedience. Technically, delayed disobedience is sin. Besides that, delayed disobedience to a Holy God will rob you of timely blessings. It may even rob you of missed blessings that you will never know of. We never consider these consequences when the Lord tells us to do something. We tarry because we are not quite sure where He is on the timeline of getting things done. There are reasons that God tells us to do things at certain times. He sees the big picture and knows what has to fall in place where and when to achieve His goals.

If you delay in your obedience to him, He may choose another Christian to accomplish the task. Make no mistake; God will have His way. You just may not get to be part of the grander design as you are still trying to figure out if you are going to obey yet. Delayed disobedience is very poor use of your and God's time. I can't tell you how many people have told me that they have delayed obeying God. I am just as guilty, too. You do not want to move until you are comfortable. I would have to ask you, "Why have faith in God, if you only move when you are comfortable?" You are only demonstrating faith in yourself at those times. Who needs an all-knowing God? Therein lies the fundamental problem with the Christian thinking, doesn't it? We still cling to our control, and all along we are wasting valuable time.

Benjamin Franklin said in his wisdom, "Lost time is never found again." So true. We should try really hard starting today not to lose any more time. Time is one thing you can't make more of. You can always make more money, but you may not have the time to spend it. Time is the most precious resource that God has given us. Time makes all the difference in how we use our lives and how productive we are for the Lord. We can live for ourselves and be totally unproductive, or we can live for the Lord and be 100% productive.

Where's the dilemma? If there is a dilemma over how to use time, God didn't create it. You did. On the day you were born, the Lord turned over an hourglass. The sand is pouring from one side to the other even as you read this journal. You could have ten grains of sand left or half the hourglass left. You don't know. Why do you want to chance one precious grain and live outside the will of God? Don't waste the time you have left on this earth living for yourself and your priorities. Use good time management and spend the rest of your time living for the Lord and with the Lord.

Who Is in Control?

The clock went off at 5:00 this morning like it does every day. I got up and turned the alarm off. I got back in bed and momentarily contemplated sleeping in. Quiet time always starts promptly at 6:00. Sometimes I can even get in the sunroom earlier, which is all the better. This morning though I lay back down. Instead of being able to drift off to sleep, the Lord impressed upon me, "Slumber? Slumber is all it takes to keep you from being with Me?" I still lay there. The Lord basically told to me to get up and write a journal on what pulls people away from time with Him. After that I was awake. I got up and started my morning routine and was in the sun room by 5:40. I immediately started writing this journal.

The simple question is this: what pulls us away from personal quiet time with the Lord? Every one of us should be honest and answer that. The Lord certainly already knows, so it's not like He's in the dark about the reasons. The disciples gave us one reason. What pulled them away from their quiet time with the Lord? Fatigue. Just being plain tired. As humans we get tired. If I should stay up, let's say, to 11:00 at night and I know my quiet time is at 6:00 in the morning, what frame of mind will I be in when the clock goes off at 5:00? Tired. Too tired to stay awake and focused on the Lord. Now, whose fault is that? Should the Lord get shifted, because I couldn't manage my bedtime better? Who is going to get their way—me or the Lord?

We justify to ourselves and the Lord, "Oh, Lord. You know how tired I am. I promise to go to bed earlier so that I can spend quiet time with you tomorrow." The Lord waits. The Lord is faithful when we are not in our relationship to Him. The Lord says, "I had something to tell you very special that was just meant for today. You missed it, because you chose sleep over Me."

Sleep certainly is only one thing that pulls us away from our quiet time. Busyness. In whatever way you are busy, it makes no difference to the Lord, whether it is due to school, children, work, friends, or family. You could be busy doing good things, and most of us are. You could even be busy for Christ and still miss your quiet time. The Lord says that working hard is part of the Christian conduct. He also said "being still and knowing Him" was part of the Christian conduct. He fully expects you to balance your busyness with being still and knowing Him. Stop justifying it in your head that when things slow down or the kids get a bit bigger that you won't be so busy.

Satan will ensure if this is the one thing that keeps you from spending time with the Most High God that you will always be too busy. I guarantee it. It's a trap set by the enemy, and the majority of Christians have been ensnared quite tightly. We say, "Oh, Lord. You know how busy I am. I promise to rearrange my schedule so that I can spend quiet time with you tomorrow." The Lord waits. The Lord is faithful when we are not in our relationship to Him. The Lord says, "I had something to tell you very special that was just meant for today. You missed it, because you chose busyness over Me."

Sleep and busyness are not the only things that pull us away from our quiet time. Self. That dirty four-letter word. S-E-L-F. How in the world can it be so strong? Our will. Our wants. Our way. Our timing. Our control. Our priorities. We choose the way that seems right for ourselves but in the end leads to our ruin. We are clueless. We think we know better. We don't need a daily quiet time, because an hour of church is good enough. We justify and justify only to end up in the deepest stagnation of our Christian life. We are in danger of turning into lukewarm Christians, which absolutely sickens the Lord to the point of nausea.

We play the Christian game. I call it a game because many Christians have changed the rules to play it the way they think it should be. The Lord says, "Witness about me to nonbelievers." We change the rules and can't remember the last time we talked to someone who didn't know the Lord. The Lord says, "Be holy and as I am holy." We change the rules and have secret sins including maybe the sin of complacency of our Christian walk. We can't remember the last time we had a revival in our lives where we felt on fire for God.

The Lord says, "Be still and know Me." We change the rules thinking we are too tired, too busy, and too into self to have quiet time. And on and on it goes. Whatever game you want to play with the Lord, I can promise you will be playing by yourself, and it will lead to your stagnation. The thing about quiet time is it is not for the Lord, but for you. You miss out. The Lord doesn't miss out because He's complete. We are not. We need to spend that important time with Him each day, preparing our hearts with a Christ-like mind and ensuring our vessels are ready for service.

When we miss quiet time, we miss the Lord. How often though does that not seem to affect our lives so much? If it did, we wouldn't miss it again. A lot of Christians have some serious heart conditions when they justify that they don't really need quiet time. When they do have one, it is not consistent. I would hazard to guess that many Christians never even contemplate setting serious focused time out of their lives for the Lord. I mean more than just a quick prayer if you have time. I mean serious, shut the world out, focused attention, hearts bowed, and Bibles opened quiet time. The Lord says, "If you want an experience with Me, then come near to Me." If you don't want to experience the Lord, then go back to your fatigue, busyness, and self. It's comfortable there, primarily because you are in control.

The Way

There is a way that appears right, but in the end it leads to death. (Proverbs 14:12 NIV)

Sin is the ultimate deceiver. It has a slow way to make wrong things look and feel right. It never does this suddenly as you would never fall for it. It is slow and subtle, often as a slight compromise. Sin never shows you or allows you to even imagine what happens in the end. When a Christian, who may not be abiding close to the Lord, turns his or her head to the left or right, they notice an alternate "way." That "way" would satisfy the temporal flesh. Again, when I talk about "flesh," while it could be sensual, I am using it in the broader term of self.

Even though they may think it is not the best way, the longer they look and think about whatever it is that the flesh wants, the "way" starts appearing not so bad. It is even fun. It even starts appearing right to his or her own justification. They step a few more steps away from the Lord, and He immediately says, "Child! That is not My Way. Come back now!" We have convinced ourselves that the way that seemed right is right. At least it feels right at the time.

Why would we want to travel a way to which the Lord says, "No"? Primarily because we want our way more than the Lord's way. Our way leads to destruction in our lives: destruction to our witness, destruction to our families, destruction to our mental and sometimes physical health, and destruction from being used by God until repentance comes. There is only one way that is right for man, and in the end it leads to the Most High God with abundant life. Don't be fooled by any other way.

Paul warns us that foolish and harmful desires plunge people into ruin and destruction. He says when we choose our way we are throwing ourselves with full force into our own peril. Who is doing this to us? Others? God? No. We are. We are all intelligent and logical people. Yet when we choose our own way that appears right to us, it leads to our own ruin. Where's the logic in that? Even more, we choose our way over and over again. I do this. You do this. All of it pretty much blows my mind when the Lord states so clearly what is going to happen every time I choose my own way. There are so many places in the Old and New Testament that state why we do this. The Lord says, "They will not listen …" (Jeremiah 7:27 NIV). "They have ears, but cannot hear" (Psalm 135:17 NIV).

I know what I do and why I do it when I choose my way. I am without excuse. So are you. What are we going to say when the Lord asks us, "Why did you choose your way when My way led to life? Why would you choose your own ruin?" I think of all the heartaches I could have saved myself if I would have just listened to the Lord's way. I am very regretful and repentant to my own pride and stubbornness against the Holy Spirit. I pray I have learned to listen. Only time will tell.

What Is Truth?

What is truth?' Pilate asked. (John 18:38, NLT)

After Jesus' arrest and illegal Jewish trial, He was taken from the High Priest Caiaphas's house to the Roman governor's palace. The innocent Lamb of God would have walked bound with guards surrounding him, as though He was a flight risk and danger to society.

When Jesus arrived in front of Pilate, He was some sort of an anomaly to him. He was perplexed as to why the people wanted this seemingly innocent man to die. Pilate said on three occasions, "I find no grounds to charge him," yet without Pilate's approval, Jesus couldn't be put to death. Pilate had never met a man like Jesus. Jesus stood in front of Pilate completely calm and in full control of Himself and the situation. Jesus did not tremble or fret without wringing of His hands or worrying. Jesus spoke with authority.

Pilate thought he was directing this situation but quickly found out after meeting the crowds and Jewish authorities that he wasn't. He knew somehow that Jesus was different and not worthy of death, which is why he ceremonially washed his hands of Him. Oh, if it were that easy to wash away sending the Lamb of God to the slaughter. Pilate has paid for the mishandling of Truth with his eternal soul for about 2,000 years now. He only has eternity to go.

At one point, Pilate did try to understand a little deeper as he and Jesus had a conversation. In John 18: 37, Jesus explained that the reason He had come into the world was to tell people the truth. Jesus said, "Everyone who belongs to truth listens to My Voice" (NET). After hearing this, I can just see Pilate disregarding Jesus' words as meaningless as he sneered and asked, "What is truth?" Pilate liked to hear himself talk and had little to no active listening skills. After he asked Jesus one of the most profound questions of all time, "What is Truth?," Pilate didn't give Jesus a chance to answer him. Jesus just said "Listen to Me for the truth."

If someone knew what truth was, then it would give that person freedom and power to live it all the days of their life. It would change all of their perspectives so that they could be guided by complete wisdom. I think that Pilate did not give Jesus a chance to answer because Pilate didn't think a peasant from Galilee would have that kind of wisdom to answer his question sufficiently. How very blind and foolish of Pilate to not take the time to listen for Jesus to answer the question "What is truth?" John 18:38 goes on to say as soon as Pilate asked this question, he went out (NLV).

I have to think how much I have been like Pilate at times of my life. I ask good questions, but I don't stick around long enough in the presence of God to get the answers. "Jesus, what do you want me do to in this situation or in my life? Never mind. Don't bother answering; I have to go now. I'll do what feels right." Pilate paid dearly for not taking the time to hear Jesus; I think I have, too. I have been as arrogant as Pilate for not having the time to hear Jesus speak truth to me. I don't want to think that I could have one characteristic of Pilate, but I do. To deny that would be denying truth.

While Jesus was not given a chance to answer Pilate's question of truth, Jesus did answer it earlier in His ministry. Thomas asked Jesus, "Lord, we don't know where you are going, so how can we know the way?" Jesus said, "I am the way, the truth, and the life" (John 14:5–6 ESV). The magnitude of this one statement has changed the entire world. Jesus packed so much truth in this brief statement that you could study it for years and still be in awe of all that it implies.

Jesus says, "I am the way." It's interesting that He uses this term, *"the way."* Did you know that the early Christians used this terminology to distinguish their beliefs from the world? They adopted that terminology from Jesus' own description of Himself. Jesus would only differentiate that He was *"the way"* if there were choices of different ways in the world. There are ways in the world that lead to different paths, but Jesus said, "I am *the* way, not *a* way." There is clarity with just one simple word *the.*

He was letting us know which way to choose. His way led to life. Proverbs 14:12 says, "There is a way that seems right to man, but in the end it leads to death" (NIV). This verse is interesting. It says a way that "seems right." Have you ever sinned? Why did you do that? It seemed right to you.

Your own way felt good to you as you sought after self-gratification, self-logic, and self-will. You were going down the path of least resistance for your life. It was as if you were going down a slippery slide and having fun all the way down. That slide ended, didn't it? While at the beginning, it "seemed right," at the end it led to death. That may have been a death to blessings for your life, happiness and joy, a friendship, marriage, or closeness to God.

Listen to me. The way that seems right to man will always end eventually. It will always end badly. That may be when you close your eyes for the last time. When you stand in front of the Father's throne, life will not be waiting for you. You lived in death while on earth with the way you chose, so you will continue to live in death for eternity. This is for the nonbeliever. People always say, "How can God be loving if He sends people to Hell?" God doesn't send people to Hell. They send themselves there.

Remember the verse, "There is a way that seems *right* to man, but in the end it leads to death." They chose their *way*. It was their perception that their way was right. That was their truth. Unfortunately, that wasn't reality. It's not God's fault, yet He gets blamed for their poor choices? That is interesting.

For the believer, sin will always hurt you personally and those people around you. That is what sin does. It only hurts people. While you are sliding down your way, you justify and lie to yourself that it won't hurt. The Word of God says it will. Who are you going to listen to? Your fallible, self-seeking flesh or an infallible, eternal God who knows all and sees all? How arrogant we are in our thinking. We deserve anything that happens to us when we choose our own way. Thank God there is mercy and forgiveness for the believer when we do.

Jesus says, "I am the Truth." If there is one thing I want from my children, my husband, my employees, my manager, my friends, and anyone that I come in contact with, it is truth. Every one of you wants the same thing as me. It seems so simple. Where truth gets really complicated is when it is based on people's beliefs and perceptions. I have a friend who is an atheist. He is a good guy and very kind. He works hard to have a productive life. His perception is there is no God, that there is no evidence of God, and I am worshiping some sort of ancient man-made mythology. This is his truth. His focus is on his job, being a good citizen, a good husband, a good friend, and an overall good person. There is nothing wrong with that, and I am glad he wants to be good.

What is the point of being good in all these areas if the truth of the matter is that everything is meaningless in the end anyway? Why is there meaning at all in his job, marriage, friendship, and overall presentation? What drives him to be good when there is no absolute truth of good in the first place? How does he measure the truth of good? If we had to prove the truth of God, how would we do that? We would have to recognize and prove that there are absolute objective moral values and truth. This type of truth would not be based on a person's perception. In this, I mean we would have to agree that something that is wrong in our culture is also wrong in every other culture that is in isolation of any other and also wrong through all time.

Can we agree that absolute truth exists? Well, let's take a very harsh example of a rape of a two-year-old child. Would that be wrong in every culture of our world? Yes. Would the world cultures have to come together to discuss and decide the absolutely morality of the event? No. Would this event be wrong no matter when it happened through all time? Yes. This is an example of an objective moral value or truth. Rape is wrong to anyone, at any age, across cultures, and across all time. Believers and non-believers can all agree on that. If you don't agree, then you are saying you don't mind your two-year-old or any other two-year-old around the world being raped. I can't imagine anyone reading this would agree with that. We have established objective absolute truth.

The next thing to ask ourselves is, "How did this absolute truth become known to us in the first place?" If objective absolute truth exists, how does man know it? I can assure you it is not by a slow, gradual process of evolution. Evolution is a mindless, nonemotional process. It can't even begin to explain emotions and feelings or even absolute truth for that matter. Evolution can't explain truth because it was created by man to live in a universe void of God. Jesus said, "I am truth."

We are created in the image of truth of the Lord our God. He has given us basic knowledge of truth in each one of us. You wouldn't have to tell my adolescent children rape was wrong and explain it. They know in their minds and hearts that it is wrong as does every one of us. Absolute truth is in us. If there is absolute objective moral truth, then we have established there has to be an absolute, objective, moral truth Giver. Again, the truth has to come from somewhere.

The Word says we are inherently wicked, yet the only way we would know our own wickedness is to know truth in the first place. My atheist friend has made some choices in the past that revealed some wickedness within him, like every one of us have. How did he know his actions were wicked in the first place? How did he move from that point and turn toward the truth of having a "good" life? There has to be some absolute objective standard of truth to understand how far we strayed from it in the first place to seek better. Jesus says, "I am truth." To paraphrase, He is saying, "I am the truth Giver. Because I exist, you have the knowledge of absolute truth in you. If I did not exist, there would be no truth, yet there is. So therefore I exist." When Jesus said, "I am truth" what He was saying is, "I transcend all time and every culture. I am absolute truth." Who else can do that? Jesus says, "I am the life."

I always remember the saying, "There are two things you can be sure of—death and taxes." Not necessarily. The secular world, with its belief that "time plus chance" gave us everything we see around us, would have us to believe that when we close our eyes for the last time, all life ceases to exist. Naturalists love to use science to prove their theories, but how can they prove that life doesn't exist after death? They can't, but they have immense faith that what they preach is truth. They have nothing to base their truth on, but it is truth to them nonetheless. This goes back to people's perception and what is true to them is true for everyone. Not so.

Jesus says not only am I the way, not only am I absolute truth, I am life." He is saying He is like walking and talking "Life." Those who abide in His life live because He lives. Those that do not abide in His life will have an eternal consciousness after they close their eyes for the last time, realizing their mistake just like the rich man did who saw Lazarus in the bosom of Abraham. It will be too late when the prison doors of Hell close for the last time. These people, who have chosen their own way because it seemed right to them, will receive death instead of an abundant life with eternal God. Again, this is by their own free will.

My atheist friend said one of the hardest things mentally to let go of was the threat of Hell one day. He said it took him a long time to accept this new truth but had immense mental freedom once he believed Hell didn't really exist. I wonder if he knows that Jesus spoke on Hell more than on Heaven. I wonder if he knows that Jesus Christ died because Hell was such a real and tangible place that He did not desire one person to go there. My very kind friend has bought the biggest lie told by Satan hook, line, and sinker, and that is: "God doesn't exist, and I don't exist, either. All is well. While you think you are enlightened, you are walking in complete and utter darkness. I have an eternal cell with your name on it." Jesus wanted us to know He is life, because He knew the reality of death and Hell.

I talk so much about the simplicity of Christ in my journals. The way, the truth, and the life in Jesus Christ are simple truths. We try to go our own way, we try to twist the truth, and we try to justify that nothing bad will happen in our life if it is not lived in Jesus. Neither the world nor the believer is without excuse. Jesus has made everything about Him very simple to understand and accept. If we choose to complicate simple truth, that is our own fault.

Strongholds

The Lord is the stronghold of my life. (Psalm 27:1 HCSB)

God tells me over and over in Psalms that "He is my stronghold." If I think how strong some sin is that takes so much of my time and energy, it really shocks me. When sin is active in your life, it will become your stronghold. You are fooling yourself if you think it won't. Sin is way stronger than you. If God is the stronghold and nothing else in my life is in competition of Him, the changes He can make in me would be inspiring to say the least. It's not about the external investment, it is about the spiritual investment on whom or what will be the stronghold in my life.

How much time and energy am I willing to invest in my spiritual growth if God is truly my stronghold? I have learned clearly that we can say that we want God to be our stronghold in our life, but if we are honest, our actions say something totally different. I think it is important to take a stronghold inventory. What do we have in our life that has a stronghold over us? Could it be something like a situation, work, our past, our thoughts, our desires, life circumstances that you wish were different, dwelling on things that we can't move on from, enjoyable sin, our hurts, our negative self-talk, somebody or a group of people, and so forth. What stronghold do we spend more time and energy thinking about or dealing with than Jesus? We all have strongholds in our lives. God only wants us to have one—Him! I suggest you get rid of anything else you can deem as a stronghold other than Him, as fast as possible. Your actions need to line up with your words.

The Good Samaritan

Please read Luke 10: 25–37.

This morning I woke up with the story of the Good Samaritan on my mind. I never anticipated that I would write on this story, but I should have learned by now that any topic is possible with the Lord. His desire is to pour deeper truth after deeper truth in our hearts to see Him clearer. I was wondering what I could learn new from this well-known story. When I reread it, one thing that Jesus asked leaped off the page. It was when the expert of the Law or what we would call a lawyer stood up to test Jesus. Jesus answered by asking a question back. He asked, "What is written in the Law? How do you read it?" This can be interpreted as, "How do you understand it or how do you interpret it?"

The lawyer was one of those ambulance-chasing lawyers who was looking for a quick open-and-shut case. He was sadly mistaken on this attempted entrapment of Jesus. I love how Jesus could spin things on a dime! Not only did Jesus give a functional and meaningful story of who a true neighbor was, He made it personal to everyone that heard it. Jesus immediately changed their thinking by giving them a fresh perspective. He often did this when He taught, which is what made people amazed by His teachings.

I think we can learn so much by Jesus question's back to the lawyer. We all understand the Lord's ways. At least we should. Where we get into trouble in our lives is when we do not interpret situations or our ways in the same way Jesus would have interpreted it. See, your behavior and thinking is all based on how you interpret something. How radically would it change our lives if *before* we enter into a temptation, sin, or an uncertain direction that we turn to Jesus and ask a few questions?

If we as Christians can slow down, be disciplined enough, and be truth seekers, we could go to the throne of God and ask Him, "Lord, this situation has come into my life; how do You interpret it?" "Lord, this emotion is so strong in me that it is tearing me apart; how do You understand it?"

"Lord, this person is affecting me in ways that I may not understand the magnitude of; how do You read them?" I never contemplated this until today. We need to C-A-R-E about how the Lord sees everything and every person in our lives. The lawyer asked the Lord a question. Jesus told him exactly how He understood and interpreted things to be. Complete clarity followed. If the lawyer would have never asked, he would have missed this truth and new thinking that Jesus so easily revealed. I'm afraid if we don't ask, we will miss the truth, too.

I go on to think of the poor man that was beat up and left for dead on the side of the road in the story of the Good Samaritan. While I do see Jesus' moral of the story of teaching about which neighbor we should be like, I see so much more. This man was beaten up by robbers who stole personal possessions from him, hit him repeatedly, and then kicked him to the curb. They didn't care if the man lived or died because the man had no value in their eyes. If I could relate the robbers and the passersby being the world, we being the man and Jesus being the Samaritan, this story just became three dimensional. Matthew 6:19 tells us, "Do not store up for yourselves treasures on earth, where moths and vermin destroy, and where thieves break in and steal." If I could paraphrase this, I would say, "Do not store up things in your life that are meaningless and only valued by the world. You have been blinded to believe what is valued by the world also holds value for your life as well. When you set yourself up with this thinking, your life becomes vulnerable as you leave a door or window open for robbers. They will creep in and steal parts of your heart and soul."

In my paraphrasing, do you think that the world lifts you up when your life has been robbed of the sacred place of your heart? How about when it is torn apart by something or somebody? What does the world do when your life is in shambles, when you are lost in unrepentant sin, and when you can't see the light of day? It kicks you and keeps you down. After that, it passes you by. It doesn't care if you live or die, because you are insignificant in its eyes. There are seven billion more just like you. One more man down will not be missed. The world will leave you in the ditch of life to be forgotten because everybody has their own problems to deal with. If you look for the world to help you, you will be without hope.

While you are lying in the ditch and looking around at your life, you cry out for one thing, "*Mercy! I need you!*" You know that you do not deserve better because you have found yourself in this current situation, poor emotions, and sin by some of your own actions. You know the world passes you by just like you have passed others by in their own distress. Maybe you were truly innocent in your current situation, and life attacked you anyway, with the world writing you off. You still cry out while you are on the side of the road beaten and bruised, "Grace! I need you!"

We have all been beaten up in life either by our own doing or someone else's. We have all been passed by. We have all been left in the ditch. We have all cried out in need of the Lord's grace and mercy. Jesus asked the lawyer, "Which person do you think was a neighbor to the man who was attacked?" The lawyer said, "The one who showed mercy." I ask you now, "Who in your life has shown you mercy? Who in your life has never passed you by? Who in your life picks you up out of the ditch that sometimes you put yourself in and brings you back home to bind your broken heart?" I believe that Jesus Christ was painting a picture of Himself. He is the only one with enough mercy and grace to be the Good Samaritan to us when we are left for dead by the world.

Citizenship

This has got to be one of the coolest new understandings that the Lord has shown me! Very exciting! Psalm 87 teaches that those who have acknowledged the Lord have a literal spiritual birthplace in Zion, the City of God. God himself registers the people. The Lord will record and say, "This one was born there.... He will mention those who know Me" with saying "each was born there" (NIV). Zion is a Christian's spiritual birthplace. It is where we dwell spiritually from our birth into the family of God. Albany is my physical birthplace, and Zion is my spiritual birthplace. It's where we come from the Lord. He says we were born in the City of God, the "Holy Mountains." The Lord states that His city is "glorious."

Our name is recorded in the Lamb's Book of Life, and we are numbered as citizens of the City of God called Zion. Understanding this makes Luke 13:25–27 a little easier now to make sense of. It has confused me in the past. God will say to some people on the Day of Judgment, "I don't know you or your name or where you are from" (NIV). Since all Christians' names are registered, it will be easy for God to check this once people of all nations get in front of His throne. I am pretty sure He has it all in His head. He's a pretty smart guy. Still, He tells us that those names that have acknowledged Him have been recorded.

If a certain person comes in front of Him and tries to pass as a citizen, He will call them on it pretty quickly, declaring that He doesn't know their name. Then He tells them that He doesn't know where they come from. That is interesting. He seems to be only taking registered citizens born in only one place. Where is the one place that all Christians call their spiritual birthplace? The City of God. Zion. The Holy Mountains. If you are not from this one place, He will say, "I don't know where you are from."

If you do not have a deep, personal, authentic relationship with Jesus Christ, but you just act like you do, and you hang around church occasionally or maybe a lot, your name has not been registered as a citizen of the City of God. You either have a registered birth certificate stamped with your hometown of Zion when you arrive in front of His throne or you will be turned away. I hate to say it, but it is that simple. There are no second chances on securing birth records for citizenship once you get to Heaven. Some people actually believe there are because God is so loving. Don't forget He is just. People so want to ignore that part of God's character. He has told you what to do. Do not be naïve to think He will change the rules for how to secure citizenship for me and you. I can promise you He won't.

Authentic Happiness

I understand the older I get, the more I see people seeking happiness in many ways. That includes me as well. If we find our happiness in ways that are a part God's appointed will for our lives, then the accompanying emotions, self-fulfillment, and excitement is acceptable to the Lord. The Lord desires for His children to be happy because He is happy. First Timothy 1:11 says, "That conforms to the gospel concerning the glory of the *blessed* God, which He entrusted to me" (NIV). Blessed means blissfully happy! Our God is blissfully happy! What a thought. You can think of all the beatitudes when they say, "Blissfully happy is the man" that does this or that. God tells you all the ways to be blissfully happy in Him if you want to know how. Psalm 144:15 says, "Blissfully happy are the people of whom this is true; blissfully happy are the people whose God is the Lord" (NIV). Matthew 5:3 says, "They are blissfully happy are poor in spirit, for theirs is the kingdom of heaven" (NIV).

In October of 2012, my gracious Lord allowed me to hear two words that changed my perspective: "authentic happiness." Who could have thought one little phrase could have that much power? When the Most High God speaks to the innermost part of your heart, it is always powerful. I heard the words while being led on a three-day Christian weekend retreat called, "Walk to Emmaus." I have had people try to sponsor me for the walk for seven years, and I said, "No, I'm good." Year after year after year, one faithful friend never stopped asking me to go to the Walk to Emmaus. Every time, I said, "I'm good. Thanks." I thought arrogantly that others needed it more than me. I was doing okay in my little Christian walk. How the enemy can sell that lie so convincingly to our hearts, and our minds believe it.

The truth of the matter is I wasn't doing okay in my Christian walk. I was so stagnant in the Word and neglectful of the presence of God in my life that I saw how easy it was to seek happiness outside of the will of the Lord. I do not think that one Christian intentionally seeks happiness outside the will of God. I think that they have fallen into the deepest slumber, and that is how they make choices that they would have never made if they were awake. The poorest choices we have made in our lives are when we seek happiness from the world or other people. The happiness looks authentic. It feels authentic. It smells authentic. It looks authentic. The emotions are authentic. But they are all lies.

The Spirit told me that I was to go the Walk to Emmaus as clearly as I just typed that. He was getting ready to do some house cleaning and soul searching. He said, "I have something to tell you. I will meet you at Emmaus." I went through the whole weekend, straining to hear what the Lord wanted to tell me. I listened intently to every word that was said, never knowing which words were just for me. On Saturday night, I was sitting in a candlelit, old, wooden church. I had not heard *the* word from the Lord yet.

I started thinking I had misheard the Lord, but I knew He spoke so clearly to my heart to come to Emmaus. The women were singing soft acapella worship music which, if I close my eyes now and concentrate, I can still hear being sung. What sweet worship. The director was talking to us. I was sitting there with a quiet spirit with a clear conscience, waiting on the Lord to speak to me. The director started another sentence. Honestly, I had heard so many words up that point. I wasn't hearing everything she was saying until she said, "*authentic happiness!*"

The Spirit just about flipped me off the pew bench! I opened my eyes and it was like I was the only person in that little church. The Spirit spoke with authority, "Listen to Me! I am the only One in your life who can give you authentic happiness. You can seek it in people and things outside My will for your life and you will never find it. I am the only person you should ever desire to fill you with authentic happiness." I just sat there and kept repeating, "Authentic happiness—Jesus is my only source of authentic happiness. Authentic happiness—if He is the only true source, then any happiness I find in people or things that He has not ordained to be part of my life is all a façade and imitation." I was awake! My deep slumber was over!

Finding authentic happiness radically shifted what my senses sought after. The flesh is weak and will lead you astray every time because it seeks the tangible things of the world instead of the invisible things of a Holy God. By flesh, do not limit your thinking to just the sensual. There are so many more ways the flesh can become weak than that. I am referring to flesh broadly as self-will—going your way and not thinking God notices or not caring. The flesh seeks what it can only see, touch, hear, smell, and taste. The flesh goes after perceived happiness in different areas, while hearing the Spirit says, "Come back!" Your response is, "When I am done with what pleases me first!" It is like the flesh takes sleeping medicine and goes into a deep slumber. The mind becomes numb and the heart no longer cares as deeply as it once did about grieving the Holy Spirit. We fool ourselves that the imitation happiness that we are now experiencing is lasting. Sometimes, the Spirit has to get in our faces and shake us out of our deep slumber. He has to speak to our soul to start waking up the whole body as it has traveled far from authenticity.

A disciplined, spirit-soaked mind and life is the only thing that can keep the flesh on the narrow path. The minute you lose focus on the Lord and lack spiritual discipline is when the enemy sprinkles sleeping dust over you once more. He is waiting close by to pounce on your vulnerable and slumbering flesh. The cycle starts again as you fool yourself into exchanging imitation happiness for authentic happiness. It may include moving from an active to inactive state in the Lord. As soon as this happens, authentic happiness is affected. It can happen before you know it.

The consequences of this exchange will rob you of more blessings in your life than you could ever imagine. In the end, you are just fooling yourself. When you are living in the happiness of the flesh and going your own way, you are living in an alternate reality. It is very hard when you return to truth. Take my word for it; you will return either now or in front of a Holy God. You gain nothing from imitation happiness except heartache. Stay awake and seek authentic happiness from the Most High God. The happiness He has ordained according to His will is always blissful and best of all authentic. It will fill you to overflowing so you will be drinking from your saucer. Would we want anything less for our lives?

Secret Sins

You have set our iniquities before You, our secret sins in the light of Your presence. (Psalm 90:8 NIV)

Have you ever had a secret sin, a sin that no one else knows about? If it's in your control, no one ever will. You would fight to the death before anyone ever found out. You would do anything to protect your secret of what you have done. It may have destructive power for your life if it ever came to light. Could it be:

A sin of the flesh?
A sin against a loved one?
A sin that fed the flesh and starved the spirit?
A sin that you never thought you were capable of committing?
A sin that you never intentionally planned but just couldn't stop?
A sin that you knew full well was wrong, but you did it anyway?
A sin that you covered so well that no one would ever find out?
A sin that the years have dampened the effects of?

Have you ever had a secret sin in the past, or is it possible that you have one now? Everyone's heart rate probably just went up after reading this! If we were honest, we have all had secret sins that we would never want anyone to know about us as they would bring deep embarrassment and shame upon us. Shouldn't all sin hold that kind of weight? I just think it is fascinating that a verse in the Bible written approximately 3,500 years ago could make everyone's respiratory rate get a little faster just thinking about their "secret sin." Humans have not changed a bit! I didn't make up the phrase, "secret sin." Moses did, at least according to what I understand. He certainly knew about secret sins! He clearly reminded us in Psalms 90:8 that God has set our unjust ways before Him. Our "secret Sin" has been put in the light of His Holy presence.

Wrap your mind around this; the whole time we are sinning in secret, we are doing it in the full light of God's Holy presence. Oh my gracious! I am worried about other people finding out what I did and keeping it under wraps?? The Most High God sees every single second of it from start to end. Talk about embarrassing and shameful. It's unimaginable. This is truth, though. We each know it in our hearts. Nothing is hidden from the Lord, yet as long as we think we have hidden it from others, we are okay. How messed up are we in our heads?

If you have not already repented of your secret sin, do it right now! Whatever it is and however big the sin is, ask the Lord to forgive you and He will. Make every effort to put as much distance between you and committing that sin again. Ask the Lord for strength and healing. He is faithful. I am no different than anyone reading this journal. How could I have written this if I too didn't know about secret sins? I know about them, but even greater is my knowledge of the healing power of the Lord over any sin that I have held secret in my heart.

The Lord does not want our sin to become millstones around our necks. That is not His plan and purpose for us. Just like you sinned in His Holy presence, you go ask for forgiveness in the same place. There is hope to set a new path and reconciliation with our standing with the Lord. I promise. He is such a good God. He seeks to forgive and, most importantly, heal His children's hearts.

Brevity of Life

Someone asked Billy Graham what was the biggest surprise in life? He responded, "The brevity of life." There are a few equalizers among all of us. We are all humans, and we all live inside the restraints of time. I don't have more time in a day than you do, and you don't have more time in week than I do. We each have 24 hours or 1440 minutes or 86,400 seconds in a day. It doesn't mean I will use all those minutes and make it to the end of the day. We have no guarantee of one of those thousands of seconds. We treat life and God as we have all the time in the world. We act like we have plenty of time to reprioritize. James 4:13–14 says:

Some of you say, "Today or tomorrow we will go to this or that city, spend a year there, carry on business and make money. We will stay there a year, do business and make money." Why, you do not even know what will happen tomorrow. What is your life? You are a mist that appears for a little while and then vanishes. (NIV)

Isaiah 40:6–8 agrees with James and says

All humanity is like grass, and all of the goodness is like the flower of the field. The grass withers, the flower fade when the breath of the Lord blows on them; indeed, the people are grass. The grass withers, the flowers fade, but the word of our God lives forever. (HCSB)

Paul understood time. I think that he knew his time was always limited and that is why he worked tirelessly for the Lord. He made sure he wrote as much as he could, he preached as much as he could, and met as many people as he could to tell them about the saving grace of Jesus Christ. He devoted every second of every day until he died for the Lord. His time was committed. In Ephesians 5:15–17, he said, "Be very careful how you live. Do not live like those who are not wise, but live wisely. Use every chance you have for doing good. Do not be foolish, but learn what the Lord wants you do to" (NCV).

The faster you learn what the Lord wants you to do, the better use of time you will have and the wiser you will become. If it takes half your Christian life to get serious for the Lord, think of how foolishly you have used your time. Think of all the good things that you have lost the chance to do. This is not a truth that I wish to dwell on very long. We have to go forward with where are today in our new knowledge. Psalm 90:12 says, "Teach us to realize the brevity of life, so that we may grow wise" (NLT). We come into our Christian walk really not understanding the brevity of life. The Word says we have to be taught. That doesn't mean it should take long to learn the lesson, but it seems like it does. I think the only way we know we have learned the lesson of the brevity of life is if our actions change on how we use our time for the Lord. Makes sense to me.

Isn't it interesting that the Bible seems to have a theme of understanding time in relation to you either being wise or foolish? I have never put that truth together before this journal. I love it when I learn something new. The scriptures spend a good amount of time explaining the brevity of life. I never knew why. The longer you take to figure out what to do with this precious resource, the more foolish you are. If you think you have all the time in the world, God says in Luke 12:20, "You Fool! This very night your life will be demanded of you" (NIV). The Lord doesn't desire for us to remain in foolishness but to move toward wisdom.

We need to seek truth on how to become wise. Proverbs 9:10 teaches, "The fear of the Lord is where wisdom begins and knowing holiness demonstrates understanding" (ISV). Understanding time, how to use it, and the brevity of life makes wisdom continue to develop in us. Understanding that the time we have in life is given by the Spirit deepens our wisdom more (John 6:63 says, "It is the Spirit that gives life. The flesh doesn't give life. The words I told you are Spirit, and they give life" NCV). When we do not understand time, according to the Lord, we live in the flesh which leads to foolishness and death. Ecclesiastes 8:1 says, "No one is like the wise person who can understand what things means. Wisdom brings happiness" (NCV). As we continue to wake up from our slumber, I think we are beginning to understand what things mean. The Word says we are becoming wise and happy! It is interesting that Billy Graham references hisis understanding of time and happens to be considered one of the wisest among men. Coincidence? I don't think so.

Tangible Consequences

I dropped my oldest child off at school this morning. I was driving back home and passed a speed limit sign that said 45. There's no reason to disclose how fast I was going, but let's just say it was higher than the recommended speed limit. I tapped the brakes and slowed down. I came up to a traffic light that was yellow. I knew what color would come next, so I slowed down. I saw the red flash of color so I stopped. I entered the expressway and saw that I was to yield to oncoming traffic. I slowed down. I entered a work zone with a change in speed limit. I slowed down. It seemed like every sign that I passed instructed me to slow down or stop.

What if I didn't want to follow the signs? When I turned on the last road to my house, I was reminded of the tangible consequences that it would cost me if I didn't. Let me give you a hint. He was sitting very still in the median in a dark car with the new low-mounted lights that you can't see the outline of at a distance! If I had not chosen to obey the posted sign, I would have had an unavoidable conversation with that nice man sitting in the car. It would have gone something like this: "Good morning Ma'am, license and registration please." Ka-ching $$! My husband will be pleased to know that I was following the posted sign, at least this time! Nobody is perfect all the time!

For the rest of the way home, the Spirit spoke to my heart about all those signs that told me to slow down and even the ones that told me to stop. I only obeyed them because I knew there would be tangible consequences if I didn't. Disobedience to the signs posted would cost me more than I would be willing to pay, but I would have had to pay in the end. The consequences of my actions would have been real rather than imaginary. They would have been tangible.

The Spirit reminded me that I speed through God-posted signs all the time. If He says, "You need to yield to Me. I am coming into the lane of your busy life," then I need to slow my life down to let Him in, but I don't yield. If He says, "You do not have a green light on this but a bright flashing red one. Stop going your way!" I keep on going and run the red light. I rarely look back. If He posts a speed limit sign in my life, for my own good, to slow down my emotions and or actions in a situation, I become like a super speeder. I hit the gas and pay little attention to any of

God's road signs in my life. Why? I like my own speed, and I like going my own way.

The Bible talks about being a fool so many times, which is why I use the word in my journals. I have never liked the word fool. It is so degrading to be called that. A fool is defined as someone who lacks judgment. The old saying of, "If the shoe fits …" would be appropriate in the times when I have lacked godly judgment and not obeyed clearly posted signs by the Lord. He didn't just post one sign, but many. I have ignored even the U-turn signs. I have sped and run red lights that were there for my own good.

I was a fool to think that there would be no tangible consequences. I have paid out more than I was willing to pay for my sin and my way. The Lord forgives my sin, but oh, don't think for a minute there are no tangible consequences that are real, rather than imaginary. If you believe there are not, that would make you the fool. I have learned after all these years of ignoring God's signs that sin requires emotional payback as its tangible consequence more than any other kind. Occasionally there are physical consequences, but I have found with my sin, it is mostly emotional. That may be the most costly to pay. It certainly hurts, I can tell you that!

If I had to ask myself why I have ignored God's road signs placed in my life, I would have to be honest and say it was for two reasons. One, I didn't think there was going to be consequences. Two, if there were, they would not be that bad. F-O-O-L! Another definition of fool is to be tricked or deceived. So not only have I lacked poor judgment to slow down, stop, or do a "U-e," I have deceived myself that there would be no consequences. I tricked myself into believing that if there were, they would be minimal at best. No one tricked or deceived me into believing this. I tricked myself.

Talk about a revelation in my mental processing. It seems so easy to go your own way when God is way up in Heaven tending to the entire world's business. Surely there will be no tangible consequences for my little ole sins. I deceived myself by slumbering, not knowing and accepting truth. That would make me a fool by definition. I have learned that you do foolish things when you are not fully awake in the Lord. These are hard lessons learned.

I am reminded of Psalm 147:3 when God says, "I heal up the brokenhearted and bind their wounds" (NIV). How do you think we get brokenhearted and wounded in the first place? Sometimes, it is due to other people breaking God's posted signs, but sometimes it is our negligence of the signs and the fact that sin has tangible consequences. Our spirit and emotions are affected by every sin that we commit against a holy God. God says in Psalm 147:5 that His understanding is infinite. He is not being harsh when He posts certain signs in situations that we find ourselves in. He is not being uncaring when He posts U-turn signs on some people that we meet who are not in our best interest.

Even though we can't see it in the moment, if we do not obey His posted signs there will be tangible consequences of broken hearts and wounds. He knows best and that is why He posted the road signs in the first place. When we disobey and become foolish, our wounds and hearts will need to be bound up again, forgiven, loved on, and taught about obeying the posted signs. When we start back down on the road of our Christian walk, we should travel a little slower and pay closer attention to God's signs. Slow down when He says yield or flashes a yellow light. Slow down when there is work ahead for you to do. Stop when you see the Spirit walk in front of you with a crossing guard stop sign. Stop when God flashes a red light. Turn around immediately when He posts a U-turn sign. Do not be foolish, Christian. Just obey the road signs.

Waiting on the Lord

Wait for the Lord; Be strong, and let your heart take courage; Yes, wait for the Lord. (Psalm 27:14 NASB)

I like choices. I always tell my children that they have choices. The Lord gives His own children two choices when it comes to waiting; however, only one is right. We can wait for Him, or we can wait on ourselves. The two are contradictory of each other, yet we try so hard for them to fit together. We package it so nicely in our mind with a little ribbon and shiny paper. I think we are trying to convince God to compromise somehow. We are trying to convince Him that our timing is right at least sometimes. We think if we pitch it to Him just the right way that He will see it our way.

That is delusional thinking. Being deluded is misleading or deceiving the mind. Do we delude ourselves when we fail to wait on the Lord and make things happen in our timing? Sure we do. The Lord says:

> Wait on Me. My timing is perfect in all areas of your life. If you move ahead or behind of My timing, then you are waiting on yourself. I am the Most High God. I am omni-temporal. I see past, present, and future at one time. You actually think your finite mind knows the best timing for things in your life? Is it possible that you have deceived yourself? Child, I invented time. You can have faith in my perfect timing.

While some words can have many different meanings, one Hebrew word for "wait" is *yachal*. The King James Version sometimes translates *yachal* as "trust." Isaiah 51:5 says, "All the faraway places are waiting for Me; they wait for My power to help them" (NCV). If I changed the wording and added the word trust, it would read, "All the faraway places are trusting in Me; they trust in My power to help them." That is a fresh reading of the Word of God when it comes to the word *wait*. When you wait for the Lord's timing in your life, you are literally demonstrating trust in Him. When you are impatient and make things happen according to your will, you are looking right in the face of your Lord and saying, "I don't trust You." That should take you aback for all the times you have been impatient with the Lord's timing. It does me. Knowing that waiting can mean trusting really gives you a different perspective.

We can all think of people from the Bible who did not wait on the Lord: King Saul, David, and Solomon to name a few. I have seen people not wait on the Lord. I have seen them move before they should have on a situation or maybe with a person in their life. I have not waited on the Lord many times in my own life. I can tell you there have always been very costly emotional consequences to my impatience. I regret those times to this day. I pray that as I learn more about waiting on the Lord that I will recognize when I am getting even a step ahead or behind Him. I think the only way that we can be disciplined and patient to wait on the Lord is if we are spending the quality time to trust Him enough for His timing, however slow.

The phrase "Wait on the Lord" is used sixteen times in the scriptures. He wants us to hear His instruction clearly for our life. He doesn't want us to miss His blessings. What does the Lord promise us if we wait on Him? Lamentations 3:25 says we get the Lord's goodness if we wait for Him. Isaiah 25:9 says that salvation comes to those who wait for the Lord.

Psalm 27:14 says waiting will strengthen our hearts. Psalm 37:7 says waiting makes us mentally restful in the Lord by not fretting ourselves.

Psalm 37:9 says waiting will ensure an inheritance. There is a hope of something coming that the Lord will give. Anything the Lord is willing to give is worth waiting for. We can trust that anything the Lord gives will be good. Psalm 130:7 assures us, "For with the Lord there is loving kindness and abundant redemption." People who rush through life at their own speed will miss this loving kindness that the Lord has for you in any given situation or when meeting a sweet new friend that He has ordained for you to have. You will miss all of this if you wait on yourself.

Psalm 62:1–2 says that our souls (should) wait in silence for God only. I love this verse. There never seems to be silence in the noisy life that we live. If I wait for the Lord, my soul is silent, and that immediately fills me with peace. I can take a big exhalation and just be quiet. Isaiah 30:18 says, "Happy are those who wait on the Lord. Mercy and grace are bestowed by the Lord for those that wait on Him." Isaiah 40:31 says they shall not grow weary (all verses are NIV).

I think about Jesus going to Lazarus' tomb. Remember when Mary and Martha waited on the Lord? When they waited on the Lord with their own physical eyes and mental processes, they thought He was late. Did they really wait on the Lord because they trusted Him to do His will, or did they wait on the Lord so He could do their will? I think the answer is clear in their chastisement of the Lord when He arrived. He doesn't want us to wait on Him with Mary and Martha's attitude. They give us a clear picture of us, though; don't they? I think we should wait on the Lord like Job. When we do not understand God's delay, we trust His heart with all of ours. No matter if bad or good comes into our life while we wait, we strongly trust that we are being strengthened, quietened, loved, mentally rested, and hopeful—and we have His mercy and grace.

I have learned that waiting on the Lord comes with a deep trust and spiritual maturity. Waiting on the Lord and not yourself requires discipline. I have to ask myself, "How badly do I want the blessings of the Lord in my life? Can I wait long enough for His will to be done?" I have also learned that you can't wait on the Lord when you are slumbering. You have to be fully awake to wait on the Lord. If you are not, He will come and go. You would have missed His blessings. If you are a little sleepy-eyed for the Lord, wake up and wait on Him with great expectations!

Field of Vision

Sin is like looking through a paper towel roll. The next time you get an empty paper towel roll, put it up to one of your eyes and close the other one. What do you think you would notice? Your peripheral vision is non-existent; the whole picture is lost. Your focus is narrowed down, which then distorts your reality. When your perspective is limited, you make choices on the information you have. Typically, these will be poor and affect the bigger picture of what life will look like once you stop looking through the paper towel roll.

Let's take King David. He had great perspective when he initially took the throne. He saw the big picture and made good decisions, understanding all that he saw. Then one day he picked up a paper towel roll that was lying on the balcony. He used that to look down at a sin. He immediately lost sight of the big picture. He only saw what was at the end of that roll. He did everything he could to make what he saw in that limited focus his everything. He forgot all the things that still existed outside that narrow field of vision, mainly God. His new focus created a new vision and direction for him regardless of everything else to the contrary. That is what sin does.

Once you limit your own vision with sin, you will make what you see at the end of the paper towel roll your greatest desire. Nothing else will matter to you until you have what you see. Poor decisions will be made. Hurt feelings and pain to you, others, and God will be the result when you limit your view. That is how sin works.

There are countless examples of great people in the Bible picking up a paper towel roll. If you think it works any differently for you, then you are fooling yourself. My best advice is to stay away from paper towel rolls! Don't even pick one up. They are very dangerous. If you have to pick up anything to look through, then pick up a kaleidoscope. Where sin is like a paper towel roll, God is like a kaleidoscope. God never narrows your view; you do that all by yourself. He provides continual beautiful, vivid, and breathtaking possibilities for your life. That seems like a no-brainer. We can expect the world to pick up paper towel rolls; however, as Christians, what is our excuse for picking one up when God is handing us a kaleidoscope?

Crossbeam

Have you ever thought about Christ's literal wooden cross? Not the symbol of it. The literal cross. You know some images have depicted that He carried the whole cross. It would be more accurate that He only carried the crossbeam. There would have been no way for Him to carry the whole cross after what He had been through. I wonder how much His crossbeam weighed. From what I could find, it would be around forty pounds. That's heavy. I also found out that wood was sparse in that region, and they reused crossbeams over and over. Jesus wasn't the first one to be crucified on that piece of wood and wouldn't be the last. I've never thought about that before. To the Romans and the world, Jesus was just another man to be put to death on forty pounds of wood. Jesus was just a man to them but God to us.

After thinking of the literal cross, my thoughts turned to the symbolism of the weight of that crossbeam. Jesus' crossbeam was different than other typically used pieces of wood. It was so much heavier than forty pounds. It was actually 6 sextillion metric tons. *What?* That is the estimated mass of the Earth. Isn't it true that we said the weight of the world's sins from past, present, and future was upon His shoulder? I think we all agree with that. We just never put a number to it. It gives a new perspective, doesn't it?

If Jesus Christ carried 6 sextillion metric tons on His shoulders, where in your thinking can He not carry what you have in your life? *Hello?* Any sin you have committed. Any poor choice you have made. Any broken heart and spirit you have. Any problem that you have in your life. Any marital problems. Any prodigal child. Any difficult person in your life. Any divorce. Any addiction problems. Any hurt or disappointment. Any financial problem. Any decision about your future. I think 6 sextillion tons covers pretty much any weight you have in your life from your past, present, and future.

If Jesus carried this very heavy crossbeam, I promise you He can carry you. He's the only one strong enough, you know. Your friends and family are not strong enough. It's obvious that you are not strong enough. *He* is the only one with the strength to do it. Why should you carry yourself and all your problems, when He died just so that He could? Why do you try to carry a crossbeam with the weight this world tries to place on you or you place on yourself? Think about it.

Praise God that it belongs only to Him. Christian, stop trying to take it from Him! "You who are heavy laden, come to Me and I will give you rest." What are you heavy laden with? It is the crossbeam that you are carrying that only He is strong enough to carry, and you wonder why you are so tired and weary.

Human Frailty

For He knows how weak we are; He remembers we are only dust. (Psalm 103:14 NIV)

God made humans in His image. He put a spirit in us then wrapped it in dust. He used the material of the earth to make you and me. Earth is as a synonym of dust. This dust elevated itself quickly by having a prideful heart. The dust knew better than its Creator. Sin entered the world through the dust of the earth. Death entered through the sin of the dust. Death comes to all because all dust came from the original dust (Romans 5:12). Every little granule of dust is now contaminated with death and sin. It is impure or unsuitable to come in contact with a Holy God. The dust has now become weak.

Remember hearing about the Chernobyl nuclear accident in Russia? Every single speck of dust in the whole area is unusable by man. Every speck of our dust is contaminated in the same way. The ground in Chernobyl didn't ask to be contaminated, but by one event it joined all the other specks of contaminated dirt. That is how the first sin contaminated us. We didn't ask for it, but we are made up of the same dust. We are unusable. We are no good to God in our contaminated condition.

If men could think of some way to clean the dirt in order to make the Russian land usable and viable again, it would. It cannot. The land has been abandoned. When Satan tempted Eve and she sinned along with Adam, he knew that God would not be able to use us in a contaminated or impure condition. I truly think Satan thought God would have to abandon us, just like the Russian people had to abandon Chernobyl. This is pure evidence that Satan does not know the future. He is like us in that sense. We firmly understand that contamination came through the original dust of Adam.

To decontaminate a substance, it has to be sterilized. The original contaminate of sin in the dust had to be neutralized. The dust had to be purified. All harmful substance had to be destroyed. Some synonyms of decontaminate are "cleanse" and "wash." How interesting. The Scriptures talk so much of being cleansed or decontaminated from our sins. First John1:9 speaks about being decontaminated from all unrighteousness.

Isaiah 1:18 says that our sins were washed away. They were scarlet, but now they are white as snow. First John 1:7 speaks about being cleansed from all sin. Revelation 1:5 says Jesus Christ Himself washed us from our sins with His own blood. God says in Acts 11:9, "Do not call anything impure that I have made clean." What was originally seen as impure has now been decontaminated. Satan has made us believe that we are still impure and not worthy enough to be used by a Holy God. Jesus has said numerous times in the scriptures that He has decontaminated us by the power of His life, death, and resurrection. We are clean because He is clean. Decontamination for every granule of dust comes from the gift of God, which is Jesus Christ (Romans 5:15–17).

Knowing we are clean, I still look at the frailty of humans living in a fallen world. I know that I have believed the enemy's lie in the past, "How could God use dust to do anything great for His Kingdom?" God has His reasons. First Corinthians 1:27 says, "But God chose the foolish things of the world to confound the wise; God chose the weak things of the world to confound the strong." This is really an ironic verse. The foolish and the wise are both dust. There are some contaminated people who consider themselves wise as they look down at the foolish. By what standard do they consider themselves wise, I wonder.

God chooses us to confuse, amaze, or surprise the world by using the simple dust of the earth. The disciples completely amazed the preachers and the teachers of their day. Why? They were supposed to be the most foolish among men, yet they spoke with authority and displayed the power of God. The Lord received all the glory. The world counts us as nothing, but God calls us His children (1 Corinthians 1:28; 1 John 3:1). What a contrast of opinions.

God uses the foolish because He knows that the pride of life and the world is what contaminated the dust in the first place. God chooses to use us because we know where we came from. We will never boast about our accomplishments in the presence of God (1 Corinthians 1:29). There is no pride in our hearts because we give all the credit to the Lord. He uses us in our weakness so that He will be glorified. The world can see Jesus Christ in us despite our dusty, contaminated origins.

When we do Kingdom work, we do this in His strength (Psalm 18:32–34; Philippians 4:13). Our dusty souls get weary so we have to rely on His Word (Psalm 119:28). We recognize our own weakness. He wants us to be available and follow the work that He has laid out for us. If we can do it in our strength, then we are not doing Kingdom work. It's when you know the task it is too big and you are too weak that God says, "It is okay Child, I remember that you are only dust. Let My strength work through your weakness." I don't know about you, but Psalm 103:14 takes a load off my mind, especially in those times that I try to do the best job I possibly can do only to find several mistakes later. We do not glorify the Father in any greater condition than when we are weak and He is strong. This is the only condition that we are useable in. It is with this knowledge that we have a fresh understanding of the dust of the earth.

Baggage Claim

It never ceases to amaze me how much I can learn when I look at ordinary things with spiritual eyes. When I traveled through the airport recently, I couldn't help noticing that everyone had at least one or more things that they were carrying. That's lots of baggage! Even the little kids had cute little bags that they were pulling behind them just like their parents. There were some people who had disproportionately sized bags. They were way bigger than the person carrying them, or so it seemed. The person appeared strained to even carry such a load. There were others that had too much baggage for one person to carry. I thought, "Those poor people. They are going to be exhausted under that load."

Kevin and I packed one carry-on bag between us as we checked in all the other baggage. We put a lot of stuff in it. Pretty quickly, the bag became heavy to carry very far. Kevin would carry the bag for a while, and then I would offer to carry it for a while so that he could rest. We took turns sharing that one piece of baggage in order to help the other along the way. We wanted to help lighten the load for the other.

I couldn't help to compare what I saw in the airport to what we do as Christians. All Christians carry baggage that they have picked up along life's travels. Some baggage they didn't want, but it was dumped on them by others. Some baggage they have created on their own by traveling down paths that they should not have been on. Some baggage happened by life circumstances. In any case, the baggage is there and adds weight to their lives. Baggage creates drag, and it affects their mobility in the Body of Christ and in their own personal lives. Some people carry disproportionate baggage, and some carry just too many bags.

I am paraphrasing Jesus as He reminds us in Matthew 11:28:

> Come to Me and hand Me your baggage. Every one of you are weary because the burdens you carry are very heavy. Please come to me Child. I will take your baggage and in exchange give you rest. I am the only One that can do this. You can try all you want; however, you are just fatiguing yourself more. Bring me the baggage of your marriage. Bring me the baggage of your divorce. Bring Me the baggage of your regrets. Bring Me the baggage of your lost dreams. Bring Me the baggage of your helplessness in your current situation. Bring Me the baggage of your loneliness. Bring Me the baggage of unreconciled relationships. Bring Me the baggage of not having the life you thought you would. Bring Me the baggage of all of your longings. Bring it all to Me. This baggage makes you so tired and weary, but I died so that I could carry it.

God is so good in His provision for us. I think of God like a big baggage rack. We can pile all of our baggage on Him. He just smiles and then rolls them away. You don't even have to tip Him! You have to put the baggage of your life on His rack in the first place.

Oh, there's one last thing. When Kevin and I had that one heavy bag between us, what did we naturally do? We shared the burden of the weight. As Christians, we are to share others' burdens that life sends them. It could be a financial burden, burden of a prolonged illness, burden of a widow, burden of a friend with a prodigal child, burden of a recent loss, or burden of a recent divorce. There are countless burdens that we can come along our Christian brothers and sisters to help carry. Pray for them; then actively help carry their burdens. As the Lord gives you rest from your own baggage, be there for others to give them rest by just sharing their burdens until they pass. One day they will, in turn, help carry your burden.

Jesus Christ loves us so much that He takes our baggage. It is for your good and for the good of others around you that you release the heaviness you are holding on to. He can carry it from now on while you rest. You will be all the lighter for doing so.

Falling Rocks

When Kevin and I were in Colorado, we had to travel an hour into the mountains to reach our destination. The elevation climbed quickly as evidenced by my ears popping. The snow increased greatly the higher we went. I have never seen so much snow! It covered the rooftops and all the trees. It was the purest white. Everywhere I looked was the softest snow. As we traveled up the mountain, the most breathtaking scenery started to unfold around every bend. The only words that came to my mind were, "Perfect, beautiful, and majestic." My eyes could not turn away as I wanted to see more and more of this beauty. It was serene, like I was looking at a postcard.

While I was caught up in all of this, I looked to see a sign posted to my right. It was half buried in snow. The road sign read, "Watch for Falling Rocks." Immediately, my attention was pulled from my original experience to the high cliffs above us. I looked with fresh eyes to see rocks just clinging to the side of the mountains. There were some large rocks and some small. I had not noticed them before. I imagined what would happen if one of those rocks fell down on us. How would that change my experience?

The Lord allowed an immediate analogy to form in my mind of how life works. Because we live in a sinful and dying world, there will always be falling rocks in our lives. I know so many friends who were living a serene life, one they would call near perfect, when the falling rock of an affair fell into their lives. After one rock fell, then the landslide of divorce occurred. I know of friends who had beautiful lives full of health and happiness until a falling rock of a debilitating disease or illness fell into their lives. I know of friends who only wanted a peaceful life, but the falling rocks of addiction prevented it.

There are countless falling rocks all around us. We each could name our own. Even as I was traveling through those beautiful mountains, an unexpected falling rock could have changed everything, even permanently. Falling rocks seem to happen quickly; that is why the sign said to watch for them. The sign was trying to put you on the alert that they could occur so be prepared. The sign was put there so that you would not be caught off guard. It was for your own protection. I can promise you, no matter how beautiful and peaceful your life is, rocks will eventually fall. You will never know when they are coming. It could be one rock or a landslide. Until they fall, you will never know how it will affect your life.

Do I think you can prevent at least some falling rocks? Yes. I believe we assist some rocks falling into our lives by our own poor choices and sinful actions. If I should have an affair, and the falling rock of divorce falls into my life, whose fault is that? If I should have an addiction, cheat, lie, or steal, and the landslide of rocks fall into my life, whose fault is that? If I should step outside of God's way to go my own and rocks fall, whose fault is that? If I push the rock off the mountain, why should I be surprised when it falls into my life? My own personal choices could bring falling rocks into my life. Other people's poor choices could also bring falling rocks into my life, as well. We all know that this happens all too frequently. Our lives are so connected that if a rock falls in someone else' life who is close to us, it might as well have fallen in our own life. We all have examples of this occurring.

When falling rocks happen we need a strong shelter. God promises us in Psalm 61:3 that He Himself is our shelter from the falling rocks of life. He is not only a refuge but a strong tower in which we can enter while the rocks are falling. He is our protection when we see a sign that says, "Watch for falling rocks." All too often we seek the wrong shelter when the rocks fall. That one mistake may lead to other rocks falling. Be mindful that He is the only One that can give you full protection until the rocks stop falling.

Hidden Majesty

During the week Kevin and I were in Colorado, I had so many things that inspired me to write a journal. There was one thing that kept coming back to my mind as a new way to look at, not only a nonbeliever, but more specifically someone with a naturalistic or evolutionary worldview. People say that God doesn't exist for many reasons. They say that Theists can't prove God because no one can see God. I may have never seen God, but I have read about people who had no reason to lie that they have. The disciples saw God in the flesh. His name was Jesus. They died for what they proclaimed to be the truth.

I may have never seen God, but He says we are without excuse to know about His existence by just the nature and the order of the universe around us. I may have never seen God, but I know He exists based on the evidence of the power of the Holy Spirit in my life. I may have never seen God, but I know that Israel exists. Israel exists by fulfilled promises of the Most High God to the Jewish people. In my mind, if Israel exists then God exists. What more do you need? All of these reasons are too simplistic to an Atheist. Do they want God to tap them on the shoulder and say, "Boo?"

Who knows what will make them believe. In the end, whether they like it or not, they will bend their knee and confess His Lordship. Besides all of that, I am always trying to understand atheism. I try to make sense of it in my head, and I just can't. I mean as big as God is, how can anyone miss Him? The Lord answered this question for me.

After arriving late in Denver, we met our friends to take us back to their house. It was dark, so I rode with them as I had no idea where to go. As we were chatting, my friend said, "Over to your right is Pikes Peak! It's really big, but you can't see it in the dark. Tomorrow when it is light, you will be able to see it clearly." I looked over to my right and sure enough just blackness. I tried with all my might to see this massive mountain that climbs 14,115 feet in the air. I could imagine all I wanted that the mountain was there, but I couldn't see it through the darkness. I had to trust my friend that it was there because she had seen it in the light. I had to trust my friend that it was there because she had touched it by hiking it last summer. I had to trust my friend that it was there because she had experienced the mountain.

Just like the disciples saw, touched, and experienced Jesus. I have to trust them like I trust my friend. What I couldn't see because of the darkness, she had complete faith in the mountain's existence. Why? She had seen it in the light; therefore, she could never deny its existence. All the passages in the Bible about being in the darkness versus being in the light hit me like rock. She had been in the light and could see clearly what had always been there: the mountain. Even though it was now dark, and she could no longer see it, she still knew it was standing over to our right. I was in the dark and had never seen it in the light; therefore, technically, it did not exist to me.

The next morning when I woke up, I looked out her back porch, and there was Pike's Peak in all of its beauty, all 14,000 feet of it. Only one variable changed my experience. The light is what exposed the existence of the mountain.

The Bible tells us in John 12:46 that those that do not believe in God are in darkness (NIV). God is there in all of His majesty the whole time, just like Pike's Peak. The person can't see Him because they can't see through darkness. They can't see God; therefore, they conclude He doesn't exist. This is a very dangerous deduction with eternal consequences. Just because I couldn't see or touch Pike's Peak physically did not negate its existence. Just because people can't see or touch God does not negate His existence, either. God is way bigger than 14,000 feet, yet people can't see Him because they are looking through darkness. I couldn't see Pike's Peak due to physical darkness, and they can't see God due to spiritual darkness.

In John 8:12 and 9:5, Jesus declares that He is "The light of the world" (NIV). Jesus is the *Son* who reveals God's majesty to the world, just like the sun revealed Pike's Peak to me. Both are light that reveals something you could not previously see. *Son. Sun.* Coincidence? They both reveal majesty through the darkness. One is spiritual and one is physical. Jesus says once you believe in Him, you will no longer be in darkness (Ephesians 5:8–9 NIV). Once we see God's Majesty that was hidden because of our spiritual darkness, we are then to share the Light that has been revealed to us in Christ Jesus by the power of the Holy Spirit (Philippians 2:15 NIV). No one should miss the majesty of the Most High God because of darkness, especially when you can share the Light source. I was right that God was too big to miss. What I didn't understand until now was that when you are in the dark, you can miss just about anything no matter the size.

Disciple

When I study the lives of the disciples, they can be summarized by one statement: "They never stopped." Words or phrases such as inconsistent, conflicting, uncertain, if they felt like it, or if they had the time or energy never entered into their mental processing. Do you know that witnessing and living for the Lord in their world was never convenient, comfortable, or in their best personal interest? While they were assured a mansion in Heaven, their life on earth was never a bed of roses. Every one of them risked his life living for Christ. Every one of them, except John, lost his earthly life for the personal cause of Christ.

Once the 1st-century Christians gave their lives to Christ, it was never about them personally again. Their time, money, worship, thoughts, and energy were focused on Christ. Their personal well-being never crossed their mind, despite their continued maltreatment. They never compromised for Christ in their thoughts and behaviors. They never justified their own will to the Lord. There was no consideration of their wills existing after Christ. Not one of them went their own way again after having an encounter with Christ. There was only one will that was to be followed, and that was Christ's. They thought and behaved with a Christ-like mind for the rest of their lives. Do I think and behave that way? They gave Christ every piece of themselves and never looked back at the old creatures they left behind.

What pieces of the disciples' lives did they commit to Christ without compromise? If we knew the pieces, would it help us to live more victorious in Christ? Would it help us to wake from our slumber and stay awake? Luke 10:27 helps define the pieces a little clearer. He says, "Love the Lord with all of your heart, soul, strength, and mind" (NIV). The first thing that I see in this verse that corroborates the life the disciples lived in Christ is the word "all." Psalm 119:2 says, "Seek Him with your *whole* heart" (NIV). Jeremiah 29:13, "Search with *all* of your heart" (NIV). Psalms 138:1 says, "I will praise you, Lord, with *all* my heart" (NIV, emphasis added to all of these). The disciples gave *all* of their heart, soul, strength, and mind to Christ. Do I?

What did the disciples' hearts look like? Heart means our will and our desires. What do we really want in the deepest part of our hearts? We say, "*Christ!* His will!" I have learned that our heart's desires will reveal itself in actions, not words. Slumbering Christians say their desires for the Lord are demonstrated by just words. They can act anyway they want. They say, "I love the Lord. I don't have to pray and read His word to show Him that! He knows it because I tell Him."

I wonder how long a marriage would last if one spouse only told the other spouse how much they loved them but never demonstrated it. There may be a marriage, but it would be stagnant. We justify this exact thinking when it comes to a relationship with our Savior. How? You have been sleeping for a long time if you tell yourself that your heart's desire for the Lord can be in words only. That is exactly how I stayed asleep.

Do you compromise your relationship with the Lord by going your own way? Are you inconsistent with your time with the Lord by not having a strong enough desire to seek deeper wisdom for yourself? Do you enjoy being spoon-fed by other Christians whom you perceive as stronger? Do you seek their input more than personally spending time with the Lord to get His? Second Chronicles 16:9 says, "The Lord searches all the earth for people who have given themselves completely to Him. He wants to make them strong" (NCV). Proverbs 4:23 says, "Keep thy heart with all diligence, for out it are the issues of life" (KJV). We are always so concerned with what others think or desire of us.

Do you know that the Lord doesn't care what one person says about you? Why do we? Oh, there is such freedom to live in that truth. Do you know that God looks straight at your heart above anything else? (1 Samuel 16:7 NIV). There is such freedom to live in Christ's perception of ourselves rather than others'. You can exchange your desires for His. You can rest in His will as there is none in your own. You don't have to keep everything going like you are spinning plates on every part of your body. You stay paralyzed in fear of the consequences of one falling. When you are focused on all of these external things, you can't be focused on the Lord.

The Lord does not desire this for our hearts. The disciples did not know what would happen to them from one day to the next. Their desire of the heart was to listen to the will of God to direct them day by day.

Their desire was to see themselves as God saw them. Their desires were perfect and diligent toward God's heart all the time. Everything else became less important and prioritized appropriately.

What did the disciples' minds look like? I have learned in my own experience that no action can occur without a mental thought first. If you stop and think about that, it is life changing. Control your mind, and you can control your life. No one can tell you that they did something without thinking. That is impossible. They may not have thought very long about an action, but they still thought! Your body can do nothing on its own. It can only move, do things, and go places by the thought and direction of the mind. If your mind is not focused on the Lord, then your body will not volitionally crack a Bible, fold its hands in prayer, or bow a knee. It is impossible.

We look at our lives and wonder why we do not do those actions. We are perplexed why we get ourselves into the situations that we do. We are confused as to why we emotionally feel the way we do. Why? It shows a complete ignorance of the power of the mind. We deceive ourselves and fail to understand that the mind totally directs how we feel and behave. The Bible says, "Guard your thoughts!" Why? Sin starts there. All self-destruction of who you as a person starts there. All perceptions that are not necessarily reality start there.

How you will interact with your husband, your friends, your coworkers, your children, and your family start with what you are saying in your mind. Your behavior is 100 percent based on how you sort out your mental thoughts in a situation or a relationship. Your justification of those mental thoughts may be contradictory to the will of God, but since you are in control, nothing that He wants matters much. Christ did not come to tell you how to think and what to think but to renew your entire mind so that it would be Christ-like. Everything of the old should be gone, and that includes self-will of your thoughts. I assure you this is for your mental well-being. The disciples had exchanged their minds for Christ's. Their godly thoughts directed their behavior. In turn, they changed the world with their actions.

What did the disciples' strength look like? When they saw Christ conquer the grave, they had assured victory. Even if their bodies were killed, they would still win in the end. When you go into any situation with the strength of victory, how can you have defeat? Sometimes, I think as Christians, we do not believe the strength of victory in our lives. We walk around saying, "Woe is me." We don't act like emotional or physical victors all the time. The disciples operated in the strength of victory (Deuteronomy 20:4 NIV). There was rest after they used their strength for the Lord. When they labored and carried heavy burdens, just like us, they had assured rest (Matthew 11:28 NIV). They understood working in their weakness only made the power of Christ rest on them. They understood and were even contented when they were weak because Christ made them strong (2 Corinthians 12:9–10 NIV).

The disciples had to wait on the Lord exactly how we have to wait on Him. They believed the Lord would renew their strength if they waited on Him (Isaiah 40:31 NIV). The disciples had assurance of their strength based on many truths, but I love the one in given Joshua. Joshua 1:9 says, "Be strong … the Lord your God is with you wherever you go" (ISV). The disciple could say anything, do anything, and go anywhere with confidence that the Lord their God was with them. Christian, we serve the same God who gave the disciples their strength. How can we see ourselves as weak if God is also with us? The disciples never lived in their strength but in God's. Whose strength do we consistently live in?

What did the disciples' souls look like? I read many commentaries, looking at Hebrew and Greek translations to understand the biblical definition of soul. Many of our English translations unintentionally mistranslated what God was really referring to. I know with certainty that the soul and the spirit are not the same as God speaks in Hebrews 4:12 about dividing them. I am a simple person trying to learn more about the Lord, but it seems to me that the soul refers to our lives, including how we feel or interpret things with our sensations. I'm not referring to our five senses but the deeper part of what you feel. You have heard people say, "I feel that down deep in my soul." This is the only way they can describe how they feel because they know that it is more than surface-level emotions of happiness or sadness. It's a deeper sensation. I never understood why they used it in that context.

My review of information seems to point to the soul as being a source for life and sensing things of God. When we became a soul, we became a sensual living being. The disciples lived with purified souls. They achieved this by obeying the truth through the Spirit unto everyone they came in contact with (1 Peter 1:22 NIV). They understood that people could exchange their souls for the world (Mark 8:36 NIV). If I paraphrased this, I would say, "They can exchange their life for the life of the world." In this, the person would lose everything and gain no profit. The world takes everything, even your very life, and hands you back emptiness 100 percent of the time.

We can certainly think of people who have done this. My mind automatically goes to things I have heard and seen out of Hollywood. We know personal examples of people who have done this as well. I think of people who have addictions. They have exchanged their souls for the world. They get back nothing, and they never see what is happening to their lives. I think part of the consequences for exchanging your soul for this world is blindness to truth and reason. It's the only thing that makes sense of how people stay in addiction and other chains of this world. The disciples never compromised their souls for the things of their day. The temptation of the world was all around them, and we know that it is all around us. We should always be protective of our souls and never exchange them for what this temporal world can offer us, which is absolutely nothing!

The model that the disciples set for us should make us take a collective gasp. When we look at their minds, souls, strengths, and hearts, they give us hope that we can truly live victoriously this side of Heaven. Each disciple had his own mission that the Lord gave him to do. This is still true of us today. There was nothing that came into their lives to stop them from living consistently, diligently, and wholeheartedly for Christ. We should live our lives in like manner and never sell our Christian walk short. The disciples demonstrated that we can be more than conquerors while we live on this earth, through the power of the Holy Spirit. Praise God!

Confirmation and Comparison

Some personalities are so strong that they never have a need to be confirmed by others. They do not feel a need to be accepted on the basis of who they are or how they look to the outside world. They approve of themselves even if no one else agrees with them. Some might say they have strong self-esteem. They have a favorable impression of themselves. This doesn't mean they are necessary conceited, but if not monitored, they could appear that way to others. There are some who do not look for affirmation from others at some detectable level. Then—there are the rest of us.

There are people who are free spirits who never compare themselves to others. They could care less what other people are doing or about striving to be more or less like them. They don't care what happens to other people. I don't mean this to sound ugly, but they live their life and they let others live theirs with little care. Some people never look at others and think, "If I could just be a little more like them in this way or that way, then I would be doing so much better." Then—there are the rest of us.

I'm not judging you on what side you are on. Only you know that. Most people try to hide this part of their personalities as they may see it as a weakness of some sort. If you are a confirming and/or comparing person, I think it has a lot of emotional needs hooked to it. I'm not a psychologist, but it seems plausible. I will be honest and say I am on the "rest of us" side. It comes as second nature to me. I am more of the confirmation-seeking person than the comparison person, but I have done both. I have been and still do have to fight against those strong emotional needs.

I have wanted to write this journal for a while now but have been putting it off. That's mostly because I did not know how to lay it out and what I wanted to say. I will let the Spirit lead it and just write honestly and freely. This journal may be more for me just to discuss some of my real struggles as I continue to learn to seek my confirmation from Christ instead of from people. You would think that would be so easy. "Oh, Sarah, you are a strong Christian; how would you struggle with seeking confirmation from others?" People sometimes think they know me so well yet they do not know what I struggle with. They see only what I want them to see and know only what I allow to be known about myself just like you. In reality, they only know as much as we allow them to know, no more and no less.

I may present a strong front, but the Lord knows what I struggle with. He is working with me on many things, so I can look more like Him in the end. I have found lately if I am waiting on confirmation from people on something I said, wrote, or did, the Lord will whisper, "I approve of you. I love you." Every time He says this I say, "I was seeking confirmation from men again, Lord. Please help me to only desire to please You! Please help me not to *need* others' approval on what I say, what I write, and what I do. If I do it with a pure heart for You, then it has already been approved." I think I have improved, but changing my thinking has not come easy. Where I picked up needing confirmation or approval is unknown. Where do any of us pick it up? It just seems a part of us, doesn't it?

I have always been a people pleaser even as a very young child. I felt if people approved of me, confirming that in their words or actions, that I was liked or even loved. When I break that down, I have based being liked and loved on other's confirmation of how I appear to them, how I make them feel, or what I can do for them. It doesn't matter if that is not other's perception, it is mine. That has always been my truth. I have learned that your perception is not always reality and truth, no matter how long you have been telling yourself the lie. When we have a hard time distinguishing between our reality and true reality, we are somewhat in bondage to seeking others' approval of us instead of Christ's.

God says plain and simple that He looks at our hearts. That shatters a false reality for a person like me. God doesn't care about what people look at, whether I am that person, or it is referring to others. His reality is that He looks at our heart. When I engage people with a pure heart for the Lord, and I am in His will while doing it, then there is no confirmation that I should seek when I already have the Lord's. What freedom is in that truth! I think it is a process to move from needing strong confirmation from people to needing less.

In the end, we should only need the Lord's approval. Only recognition of our alternate reality, spiritual maturity, and discipline by the Holy Spirit can get us to a healthier and freer mindset. I understand that now. I am on a healing journey of looking who I seek my confirmation from. Men or God? I'm not where I need to be, but I am diligently working with the Lord in that area. He reminds me all the time, "I approve of you. I love you."

There was a verse in the book of John that always confused me. When I planned to write on confirmation and comparison, the Spirit made it all make sense. We are not the only ones that compare ourselves to others. We are not the only ones that think we may have got the shift of the upper hand and left with just the crumbs. Peter, the Rock, the one that the Church was to be built upon, had problems with comparing himself to others. Not only did Peter compare himself to others, but all the disciples had the same problem. This should make every one of us feel better about ourselves immediately! It does me.

There were two occasions that I recall that comparison was an issue. The first comparison is found in Luke 9:46 says, "An argument started among the disciples as to which of them would be the greatest" (NIV). After all the humility that Christ had shown them, they actually were comparing themselves on who would be greater in Heaven. It would seem unbelievable if it wasn't a testimony to the disciples' own humanity and flawed thinking. I am so glad this was added to the Bible. I think it is so important that we see the great men who spread the Gospel of Christ around the world as just normal people with thinking just like ours.

The second account of comparison is found in John 21:18–23. It tells of an account of Peter being told by Christ of the manner of Peter's future death. Peter would not die a natural death; he would be bound and killed by men. Peter would die to give glory to God. Can you imagine being told that? What would your first thoughts be after being told this? Numb? Blank? Not Peter. The very first thing he did was look behind himself and Jesus to see John the Beloved, walking. He compared himself to John's fate and said to Jesus, "What about him?" I can see Peter pointing at young John. Peter wanted to see if John would also die, maybe because he now knew he would. What did it matter to him what happened to John? Peter had a problem with comparison just like a lot of us.

Jesus understood what Peter was doing and made a severe remark, "If I want him to live until I come back, that is not your business. You follow me!" *Ouch!* If you look at the narrative, Peter did not say one word back to the Lord. What could he say? To my knowledge, that is the last time he compared himself to another. He focused fully on the Lord and not on other's lives from that day forward.

What lessons can we learn from people comparing themselves to others? Let me repeat the words of Jesus to you, "It is not your business. You follow me!" So you are divorced, and you compare yourself to all the other married people, wanting to be like them. *Follow Jesus!* So you don't have children and you compare yourself to people who do. Follow Jesus! So you are single, and you compare yourself to others that have happy progressing relationships. *Follow Jesus!* So you have to struggle more financially as you compare yourself to your friends that don't. *Follow Jesus!* So your job is not the greatest, and you compare to others that have better. *Follow Jesus!* Jesus made it plain and simple that it is none of your business what He does in others' lives. He has a plan just for you whether you understand and like it or not.

Do you think Peter liked being told he was going to be killed? Good grief, no! He was going to bring glory to God through his trial and suffering, though. If you are one of those people comparing yourself to others because of your own trials or perceived shortcomings, you can bring glory to God, too, in what He does in your life! Do you like it? No more than Peter, I can assure you. Jesus never said Peter was going to like it. He said, "Stop comparing you to others. You are not them. Glorify Me in the life I have ordained you to live. Mind your own business. Follow Me!"

Those of us who can move past seeking confirmation from people and comparing ourselves to others find freedom and give glory to the Lord. Matthew 6:33 came to my mind so clearly just now. It says, "Seek first His kingdom and His righteousness, and all these things will be given to you as well" (NIV). When we are seeking confirmation and making comparison, we are not seeking His kingdom first. We are seeking ourselves first. This is hard truth, but it is Godly reality. He says if you seek Him first that you will receive a kingdom and righteousness.

This seems so much better than trying to make ourselves feel better by meeting some emotional need by looking at mere men. We have got to be mindful where our focus is! Is it on Jesus or our flesh? Is it on the temporal or the eternal? Is it on His kingdom or on a shack? If you have problems with either seeking confirmation from men or comparison to others, please take your burden to the Lord. You guys need to have a heart-to-heart talk. He will help you see His perspective if you are willing to give up your own.

Puzzle Pieces

Have you ever thought about how complex a 1000-piece puzzle is? There are so many little pieces that have to fit together perfectly in order for the picture to unfold as intended. You cannot force one piece into another, but you have to wait patiently for the right pieces to fit. Timing is certainly involved. You can't fit some pieces together before others are fit together first. What if I took away the picture on the box to make it even more complex? So all you know is that you have a 1000-piece puzzle but not what it should look like in the end. Where would you start?

Not only that, what if I dumped another 1000-piece puzzle where you were sitting over to your right then another one over to your left. I dumped another one behind you and in front of you. You didn't have pictures for those different puzzles, either. What would you do? The complexity of the situation just keeps increasing. What if I told you that your puzzle and some of those other ones around you all fit together to make even a larger picture? What if I told you that every individual life on this earth is like a 1000-piece puzzle? Already very complex in itself, but some of those lives around you fit together perfectly with yours, while others don't. It is absolutely mind-blowing when you contemplate the magnitude of it all.

Isn't this similar to what is happening in our real lives? Each of our lives is so complex on their own even before they fit together with other people's lives, which makes them even more complex. None of us have the final picture of what our life will look like. We don't understand why some pieces, whether people or situations, come into or are taken out of our lives when we were just thinking that we had our picture just about figured out. It has the potential to suddenly and dramatically change the whole picture that was in our head, leaving us at times confused.

Sometimes we try so hard to fit pieces together ourselves so that we get the picture that we think we want or should have. When we force those pieces, it only ends in disaster. You can never force two pieces of puzzle together that were not originally made to go together and expect a smooth fit and good picture. It just doesn't work that way.

God is the only one with the puzzle box that has the picture on the front. He has the picture of what my puzzle will look like and yours, too. He has the picture of how my pieces at some point have hooked up to yours. I have friends tell me that they pass my journals on to their spouses or onto their friends. That is absolutely fantastic as the Lord gets the honor. I will never meet some of these people on this side of Heaven, but one day God will show those of us that have never met how our puzzle pieces have fit together, even through these journals. Think about that. The best part is they fit together for His glory. Who in the world do you think can control something that complex? You and me? Never.

God tells us , "Hey, Children! I have the plans for this big massive puzzle, not only for this generation but all of the puzzles that have been linked to other generations through time. How do you think your puzzle has been linked to all generations? You are a Christian, are you not? I have been linking puzzle pieces through time since I created Adam's puzzle. Any one linked to Me has their puzzles linked to everyone else that believes in Me. I can do this because I have the master plan and have fit all the pictures together into one perfect one."

There is no way your finite mind can begin to understand the complexity of My puzzle. All you have to do is trust that I have the plans for the puzzle box for your life and every life around you. I will show you how they all fit together for good when I come for you! As hard as it is, it is not meant for you to understand every piece of your puzzle. It is for you to trust that I will follow My plans for your life. If you abide in Me, then the puzzle of your life will look like the picture on My box when I am done."

Awake in the Lord's Presence

I woke up this morning, and one word came to my mind as I made myself get moving: slumber. I was slumbering, and I liked it. As I started waking up more, my mind went to the Garden of Gethsemane. I pictured the Lord speaking with his closest disciples: Peter, James, and John. When the Lord was close to them and they were in His presence, they were alert and awake. As soon as they were removed from His presence, they physically slumbered. Everything of Christ went away. When the Lord returned to them, it was His presence that awakened them from their slumber. When the disciples were removed from His presence, they physically slumbered again. When the Lord returned to them, they awoke. They only awoke from their physical slumber to enter a spiritual slumber. They were far from being awake.

When the Lord was forcibly removed from their presence, their spiritual slumber manifested itself clearly. With Peter in denial and the others going into a tailspin, they all entered the deepest slumber imaginable with eyes wide open. There was only one that did not go into a spiritual slumber: John the Beloved.

As I kept thinking about the correlation of when the disciples slumbered, it became evident that it happened every time they were not in the presence of the Lord. What is interesting is that John was the only one that figured out the correlation. He slumbered in the garden when he was out of the Lord's presence. He wasn't going to leave the Lord's presence again. John was the only one at the cross. He was spiritually awake while all the other disciples were in spiritual slumber. John stayed in the Lord's presence no matter what. John never slumbered once more until the day he died. Why? He never left the Lord's presence.

The only time the other disciples awoke from their spiritual slumber is when they entered the Lord's presence again after the resurrection. Once they woke up, they too never went back to sleep. They understood the correlation as John had.

You have to stay in the presence of the Lord in your life at all times to prevent spiritual slumber. The minute you leave it, you might as well have taken a sedative because you will go sound to sleep. Things don't happen in your life when you slumber; don't expect it. *Wake up! Rise up! Get in the Lord's presence.*

Sin Unveiled

Sin is so powerful. Those three simple letters S-I-N, put together, make up such a deep and complicated word. We never fully understand the truth of sin until we are already deep into it or coming out of it in self-reflection. Sin lies to you at a foundation level. It promises you something, and you get nothing. You think you will get fulfillment for your flesh because your will is being immediately gratified. At the same time it robs your spirit.

Sin is like a thief. It steals your opportunities for abundant blessings. Sin narrows your field of view. Instead of recognizing the thievery of sin, we get tunnel vision. We totally miss its effects in our lives. We are willing to adjust to our new visual deficits because we want our way so badly. Not only does sin lie and steal; it also blinds you. I can testify that sin certainly blinds you. Sin immediately takes the light away and leaves you stumbling around in darkness. You are guaranteed to get hurt. Sin lies to you, robs you, and blinds you. There is hard truth in the unveiling of sin.

Sin is unquenchable. It demands more and more of your time and energy until it feels all-consuming. You have to have what you want when you want it with little regard for much else, especially God, at times. It feels that even if you wanted to stop the sin, it has control of you now and not the other way around. So we can also determine that sin is selfish.

Sin is isolating. When you are in sin, you usually go it alone. If other people are involved, then they are just as alone in their sin as you are. You don't go around telling everyone you are sinning. Sin is an individual thing between your body, mind, heart, and spirit. You heart has to have the desire. Your mind has to be willing for your body to follow. The poor spirit has to witness it. Sin is an individual thing, but it completely affects every part of you. It's just you and the sin. It isolates you from the throne of God.

Let me see if I have this right. Sin is a liar, thief, blinding, selfish, isolating, and hurts our relationship with our Lord, but we say two simple words to it, "Yes" and "More." Can anyone explain how logical and intelligent that is? It is a clear reminder of how strong self is. You have to be less like self and more like God in order to keep this human flesh in check. Don't give yourself a free pass and say, "I have to sin because I'm human." You know what sin is, and you choose it. You can say, "No," but you don't. Don't act like sin is forced upon you like you can't help yourself because you are just a little, weak human.

Wake up and remember who your Father is. Jesus says, "Go. Sin no more." How else would you interpret this verse? You sin because you want it more than holiness. That is truth. God knows it, and so do you. Stop with the excuses. God is sick of them, and you should be, too. He says, "Be holy as I am holy." That is His expectation for His children. He will never lower that for you. God has made Himself abundantly clear.

Learning to Be Quiet

There are people who are naturally quiet. Then there is me! Those who know me personally can testify that I never stop talking. Honestly, I sometimes want to stop talking so much, but it's like my vocal track is somehow separated from my body. It has the inability to stop talking. I skyped my friend recently. We talked for about an hour and half. I was told that I talked all but fifteen minutes of the entire time! I told my friend that was progress because that was five more minutes that he got to talk compared to the last time we skyped! Where's the problem?

When I am in a conversation, I am one of those people who don't like to be quiet for more than a few seconds. If they are not talking, I will be more than glad to fill in all the gaps! I am learning to have a true conversation that I need to have better active listening skills and just be quiet. I need to talk less and listen more, but it goes against every grain in my nature. It is just so hard for me.

I think about my "talking behavior" with my friends and family. I have been convinced that I do the exact same thing to God. I am coming to understand that I do more blabbing than praying sometimes. He doesn't care about my babble! When I do this, I am basically having a one-sided conversation with God. In essence, I am talking to myself. That is going to get me nowhere fast. I picture God on His throne thinking, "Whenever she hushes with all this meaningless talk, maybe she will give Me a chance to say something."

I have learned He is so patient with me. I sometimes come away from prayer time and think, "God hasn't said anything in a while. Wonder what is up with that? Do I have some unconfessed sin that I need to address? Why isn't He talking?" I can just see God rolling His bright, fiery eyes saying, "Heeeelllllloooo! You never gave me a chance! I actually did have something to say."

I understand now that sometimes I, not the Holy Spirit, am running my prayer time. I have prayed both ways. I can promise you there is a difference. Recently, I have seen my desire to "control" quiet time a step further by not listening. I wrote the last journal called "Balanced Desires" at a time that I was in control of prayer time. It was written one morning when I was blabbing to the Lord and not listening to the Lord. It was written one morning when I was *not* quiet during quiet time. I didn't hear or feel that the Lord gave me anything to write about that morning, so since I was in control, I wrote something anyway. I wanted to write, so I wrote. I wanted Sarah's way, so Sarah got her way. I totally disregarded the Spirit, which I am sure then grieved Him, with writing without Him.

How very self-sufficient, rebellious, and arrogant I am. I was exercising my human nature in every sense of the phrase. The Spirit saw me writing. I knew when I was writing it that it was all of me and none of Him. He let me do it though. He let me have my way. When I was done, I felt Him say, "That wasn't from me and you know that. Don't send it." I looked over it and said, "But Lord, it's not that bad. I mean it has some basic truth in there. It is just one journal that I didn't feel led to write, and it will be okay."

From the very day I wrote "Balanced Desires" to the day that I sent it out, the Holy Spirit kept bringing that journal back to my mind and saying, "Don't send it." I would pull it back up and tweak it here or there and still justified that it was adequate to send. When the morning came to send it, the Spirit said again, "It is not from Me; don't send it." I read back over it again and again justified that it was adequate. I knew that it was ordinary. I knew that it was flat. I knew that it lacked the Holy Spirit's touch, yet I sent it anyway. After all these things that I have said about sin in my past journals, in the end I have sinned with my disobedience with sending a journal that He didn't approve of. Consider the irony in that!

I am telling you all this because I want you to see how sin works first hand. Using me as an example, I want you to see sin right in front of your eyes. Sin equals self. Sin equals what you think is best. Sin equals justification. Sin equals "my way." Sin equals willfulness against a Holy God. As much as I have learned about sin on my journey, I fall right back into it like a perfectly fit glove to my hand, like a soft, cozy, comfortable blanket. The very moment in your life, in any situation no matter how minor you think it is, when you start justifying your thoughts or an action to God is the moment you are already head deep in sin. Forget ankle deep. Forget knee deep. No. Head deep and quickly rising. If God says, "Do this" or "Don't do that" and you say, "But, Lord," you just sinned. You just took one big step out of His will. It's as easy as that.

When the Holy Spirit said, "Don't send that journal," the first thing I said back was, "But Lord." I was convicted all day long on the day the journal was sent. The Holy Spirit was extremely displeased with me. I could feel it. I was embarrassed that I had not obeyed.

Last night as I was continually thinking of what I had done and asked for forgiveness, I asked the Lord, "What can I do? I can't take the journal back." Then as sure as I am sitting here, the Lord whispered so gently to my heart, which lifted it immediately and said, "Tell them." He said, "Tell them what you did. They already know that wasn't from Me anyway. Tell them so that they may take away in their own life the lessons you are learning in yours. Tell them." This time I didn't say, "But Lord." I said, "Yes Lord." I am learning to be quiet.

For now on, when the Lord is quiet, I will not write. If that is a week or a month, so be it. If I am going to be His sanctified vessel, I can't be my own, too. Why do I have to keep learning this lesson over and over? I have no ownership of these journals; they are His. They are my worship and communion that comes out of a conversation with God while I am practicing my active listening skills. I think of the image of the Potter and the clay. Sometimes, when God is molding me, big chunks are removed at one time; that is quite painful. I know that the finished vessel will be exactly how He wants it. It's His vessel; He gets to fill it with what He wants to, not me.

Please pray for me as I continue to write that I will be strong enough to die to self and say what He guides me to say. You don't want to read empty, flat, ordinary words from me. They are meaningless. I pray that I will stay focused on what the Holy Spirit is saying from now on. I pray I do not turn my head to the right or to the left. Our God is good. He disciplines His children, that He calls His own because He loves us.

If you have not been disciplined by the Lord, when you have sinned, that is a very serious matter that you need to address. If you have never been disciplined by the Lord by coming under conviction of your sin, you are not His child. It is never easy to be disciplined by the Lord, but by this process, I am once again confirming that I am a child of the Most High God. I am slowly and painfully conforming to a Christ-like mind. For this truth that comes out of His discipline of me, I praise Him and thank Him! It is not easy to be transparent to others; however, if anything I said can increase your understanding of what the Lord expects out of your own life, then may He be honored and glorified. My embarrassment of the admission of my own lack of obedience to the Lord is minor in comparison to His honor and glory.

Time Period

One of the best things that has come out of sending my journals to people is when something they read speaks to them, they respond with heartfelt thoughts either with a call, text, or email. I had all three yesterday! The journals never cease to open up wonderful dialog with someone. The Lord receives the glory. It is rare that I write a follow-up journal based on a previous journal, but the verse, "All things work together for good for those that love Him" certainly was true yesterday (Romans 8:28 NIV). Several people who didn't know each other had similar struggles that came out after reading my journal about my own transparency of disobedience and struggles to move past some things. After the 4th conversation with a person, I felt led to share some further thoughts of how I have dealt with these things.

I have come to believe one of the strongest vise-grips that the enemy has on a Christian is the regrets of poor choices in their past. They also struggle with past sins. They accept the Lord's forgiveness but not their own forgiveness in order to move on. They are guilt-ridden over the things they never thought they would do or the choices they never thought they would make, but they did. Another grip the enemy has, which many Christians struggle with, is their uncertainty and worry about the future, not just thinking about it occasionally but constantly. If the Enemy doesn't do it to us, then we do a pretty good job of keeping our own selves beaten down for all of these same reasons. This took me forever to figure out so stay with me as you are entering "Sarah logic."

It seems people can *choose* to live in one of three time periods. You have no idea how strong your mind is; it will go to the time period that you choose to take it to. Notice I italicized the word choose. The first time period you can choose to live in is the past. There all you can do is remember all of your mistakes, regret them again and again, relive them, pump emotions back into memories, and revive them. You start your sentences as your mind goes back to the event, "If only I had done that or this," "If I only I had made a different decision," "If only I would have been wiser," or "If only I would have been stronger." If only … If only … If only.

This is my analogy. The past is like a fire that once was strong and hot because of your own poor choices or those poor choices of others that affected your life. As with any fire, it burns down as time goes by. When you go back to the past and rehash all of the regrets and sin, it is like you found one little ember left burning and started fanning it. The longer you spend in the past, the more you are fanning the flame until—poof! You have a little fire going again. It is a fire that you have created, a fire that you injected emotions back into that are as real to your mind as if it had just happened.

Who is *choosing* to fan the flame? I know a lot of people who can throw your past back in your face, but if we were all honest, it is you who throws it back at yourself more than anyone else. What do we hope to accomplish with our behavior? We relive regret and remorse and sadness all over again. What do you hope to accomplish? And we *choose* to do this? Yep. Where is the logic in that? Oh yeah, there isn't any.

Do you know all that waits for you in the past? *Nothing.* There is no hope there. There is no healing there. There are no changes you can make there. All you can do is roll it over in your mind a thousand more times. There is just nothing there. Yet we go back to nothingness quite a lot and dwell there, don't we?

When we dwell in the past too much, it affects our today and our tomorrows. Because nothingness is all you can change in the past, it kind of leaves you feeling empty today after you relive, revive, and rekindle. It can even leave you depressed. Nothingness can be depressing. You can't live in the past even for one day. God is the only One who can live in the past as He is outside time. You technically don't even have a past to live in as you are a temporal being and can only live in today. You just lie to yourself or fool yourself that you can.

You actually buy that lie from the enemy. He would love nothing more than for you to get mentally stuck in the past. If you did, you would be useless for Christ today. You think if you spend enough time and energy wishing things were different in the past, maybe they will magically be different. The truth is, and you know it, you can only live in this very minute. Now is all you have.

The next time period is the future. I think there are some Christians who are more captive to the past than to the future. I am really not sure what keeps them in bondage to either time period. It just is. You have those in between that like to dwell in a little of each. As long as it is not today, all is well.

The Lord tells you over and over not to worry about the future. He knows that only anxiety waits for you there. He wants you to be anxious for nothing. He tells us not to go into the future, but as fast as our little minds can carry us, we are there. What does the Lord know? You are planning and creating a thousand scenarios in your mind, all of which will most likely never happen. Smoke is coming out of your ears as the all the wheels are spinning and planning. See, that is all you have when you mentally live in the future. It is okay to lay out some life plans; however, when it starts consuming you and causing anxiety, that is not normal planning any longer. We take it too far. We are so proficient at it. We are almost like professional worriers. Show me a worrier and I know exactly what time period they are stuck in.

God says He knows the plans He has for you—plans to profit you and never harm you. What else do you need to know about your tomorrow when God lives there already and says that He has it planned for you? His plans must surely be better than anything that we can imagine. When you try to live where only God can dwell, then there are some serious trust issues you guys need to work on. When you are so concerned and anxious about your future that you don't trust what God has already promised and has yet to reveal, then you are basically telling God He is a liar. You can justify that any way you want, but it makes no difference. God says He has your future, so you don't have to worry. You either trust Him with it while living peacefully in today, or you don't—thereby calling Him a liar.

The last time period is the present. It is the moment that you are reading this journal. You have this breath. You have this heartbeat. You have this moment. We want so much control of our lives. The reason living in the past and the future is so frustrating and anxiety provoking is that you can't control one single thing. If you live in the present, then you have complete control. I have learned that living in today is way more peaceful and easier than living in the past or future.

I was the type of Christian that did both. Once I figured the truth that I have shared with you today, I experienced total freedom. I can't change my past, and I trust the Lord with my future. I am to live for Christ today. There is so much peace and freedom in that truth; you cannot begin to imagine. The enemy will not like that you know this truth as he loses his stronghold on you. He will have great cause for alarm. When you live for Christ in today, you will continually grow deeper. More than likely, you will also be spiritually attacked. If you are, then just smile, knowing that you are on the right track. He only bothers with Christians who threaten him by living in truth and growing in the Lord.

One last thing: so many Christians want to meet up with the Lord. Listen up! He will only meet you today. You will miss Him if you are living in a dead past and a made-up future. If you are wondering why you are stagnant, can't move on, anxious, in a place that you replay things over and over in your head, or even depressed, check what time period you are living in. There is complete freedom in living in today. God bless and may the Lord meet you there.

Expiration of Happiness

I was talking to a close friend recently who is going through the toughest time in her life. She is carrying burdens that no one should ever have to carry. You may relate as you have your own heavy burdens. It seems like there are enough burdens for everyone to have one. She used the phrase, "expiration of happiness" in one of our conversations. I asked her if I could borrow this phrase to put my thoughts together in a journal. She was agreeable. I told her that I had never put this concept together before, and it highly intrigued me.

I had to ask myself a question, "Do I believe that happiness can expire?" I wanted to go into the Word and see if the Lord gave any examples of when happiness expired. I really needed to see how the Lord defined happiness first. In Psalm 1:1–3, He wrote

> Happy are those who do not listen to wicked or who do not walk in the counsel of the ungodly, who don't do what evil people do, who love the Lord's teachings and they think about those teachings day and night. They are strong, like a tree planted by a river. The tree produces fruit in season and its leaves don't die. The Lord takes care of His people. (NCV)

Happiness would come pretty easily if we always loved the Lord's teaching and thought about them day and night. What if your happiness was connected to someone else who did listen to the wicked, who did walk in the counsel of the ungodly, and who did do what evil people did? Are we not all connected to others in our lives that can affect our happiness? Surely, this is truth. What would happen to our happiness? It would end; in other words, it would expire.

If a drunk driver hit my family, and they died, my happiness would expire. If my husband came home and said that he had found another woman? My happiness would expire. If one of my boys came home and told us he had chosen an alternate lifestyle, my happiness would expire.

My happiness would come to an end as I understood happiness to mean to me. Someone who could affect my life did not live Psalms 1:1–3. I can cause the expiration of my own happiness or the happiness of those close to me by my own lack of living out these verses. So it goes both ways.

There are numerous examples in the Bible of people's happiness expiring by their own failure to live out these verses: Adam and Eve, Moses, Lot, King Saul, King David, Solomon, Peter, Judas, Noah, Cain, Mary Magdalene, and on and on. At some point these people's happiness expired by their own choices. The happiness of others connected to these people certainly expired as well. Do you think Bathsheba's happiness expired when she lost her firstborn son? Do you think the disciples' happiness expired when Peter, the Rock of Christ's church, denied ever knowing Jesus? Do you think the happiness of Lot's two girls expired when they were brought into Sodom and only later barely escape with their lives? You can cause your own happiness to expire, someone else's happiness to expire, or they can cause yours to expire. All based on choices. It is as simple as that.

We have confirmed that happiness can indeed expire. We have determined pretty much the avenues in which it is possible to expire. There are certainly more. The one thing I am seeing, though, is that whatever the cause of the expiration of happiness, it seems to be temporally bound. If it is indeed temporally bound, then all happiness will expire at some point in time. It has to due to its very relation to the element of time. That is not a pleasant statement, but I think a true one. Now it may expire in ninety years, but someone's death will eventually contribute to another's expiration of happiness.

One of my closest friends and I talked about this whole concept. His insight was enlightening. He said, "Happiness is our emotional response to the events of our lives." Any event that we can define is temporal, so happiness is temporal. He added a new word in the conversation: *joy*. He stated that joy is different than happiness. Where happiness is from temporal things, joy is from the eternal realm. The Bible is clear that joy comes from the Lord (Romans 15:13 NIV) and from the Holy Spirit (1 Thessalonians 1:6 NIV). The Lord and the Holy Spirit are both eternal, thus making joy eternal, as well. Joy, *not* happiness, is a fruit of the spirit (Galatians 5:22–23 NIV). All this is very interesting.

Happiness is temporal, and joy is eternal. Happiness can expire due to its source, but joy is infinite. Your happiness can expire in a situation, but it is possible that you can still have joy to carry you through because they are not from the same source. Think of the power in that truth. You need to remember this the next time you have a trial. Don't be surprised when your happiness expires, but you hold on to your joy. How comforting to know that it will never run out.

"Can You Hear Me Now?"

Recently, my cell phone wasn't working properly. The hearing piece was not allowing me to hear people talking, but they could hear me speaking perfectly. Have you ever tried to have a conversation like that? It was frustrating to say the least. I had to continue to say, "Please speak up. I can't hear you!" No matter how loudly they spoke on their side, I couldn't hear them on mine. Their phone was working fine. It was all on my side. Their phone was perfect while my phone was impaired. The hearing piece used to work. In the past, I could hear perfectly, but then one day it just stopped. Did I drop it? Did I get it wet? I was trying to think of what I had done to cause the problem.

After I recognized the problem, I took it to the store. The professional that knew everything about the phone turned it over in his hands, evaluating this or that. He found that the primary problem was an internal malfunction of the hearing mechanism. I had to get a new phone so that I could hear people's voices loud and clear again. I needed one that I could communicate on; otherwise, it was useless.

When I received my new phone, I told my friends with great excitement, "I can hear you now! You are loud and clear. We can have a conversation now!" They were all tired of yelling, so everyone was happy. Why did I have this particular phone problem of all people? I asked around, and no one had ever had this phone problem with their phones. Only me. Why?

It took me a while to make the correlation, but when I did, it was like a lightbulb went off in my head. I told the Lord, "That was brilliant! You probably did that on purpose, so I could write this journal!" After thinking about my phone trouble, a clear analogy started forming in my mind. I have heard this from so many Christians, "I used to be so close to the Lord. I used to hear Him speaking, but I haven't heard Him in a long time." I have to wonder if they think the Lord has stopped talking. Is it possible that they have a hearing malfunction, and they just can't hear Him talking? He could be talking away in His Word and all around us, but we can't hear Him. Is the problem on God's side or, in the case of my phone, is it on our side?

When God tries to talk to you, and you can't hear what He is saying, how can you respond back to have a productive conversation? You can't. That's not how conversation works. If God had a cell phone and you had a cell phone, and His worked and yours didn't, then that's a big problem. The problem with your connection to the Lord is an internal malfunction. It needs to be evaluated and assessed. How is it that you used to have a good connection with the Lord and could hear Him, but now you don't? What changed internally? If you ever hope to have another conversation so you hear Him, you have to dig deep and be transparent to fix the internal malfunction.

I couldn't just hope that my old cell phone would just start working again. I had to actively do something about it. I had to go to the store, send my old one back, and reprogram my new one. You can't just hope that you will hear the Lord again with your unfixed internal issues. You too have to do something actively about it. You have to do this because the problem is on your side, not the Lord's. Hope is not a strategy! Action is.

The sad thing with so many Christians is that they haven't heard from the Lord in so long that they doubt that He will ever really talk to them again. They wrongly believe that He talks to others but not them. They want to hear His voice, but they are not willing to fix their own internal malfunctions. That would take too much time and work. In the end, they reason that they have been getting by all right this long anyway. They start accepting their connection problem with the Lord and that becomes their new norm. Life goes on.

The whole time the Lord is saying, "Hello … Hello? Can you hear Me now? Do you even want to hear Me? I'm right here, still talking. Please fix this connection. You have to fix it on your side; then we can have a conversation. I have so many things to tell you, but you can't hear Me."

What are some possible internal malfunctions on our side? If you haven't heard the Lord in a while, have you stopped to evaluate this problem or have you just accepted it and moved on as everything is okay? There are different reasons that you may not be hearing the Lord. The biggest and most obvious one is sin. Sin will immediately interfere with a connection with the Lord. You need to confess and ask for forgiveness now. Do not fool yourself by thinking you can have ongoing sin in your life and hear the Lord at the same time. Don't be foolish. It doesn't work that way.

Busyness is another internal malfunction on your side that affects you hearing the Lord. You just don't have time. The Lord is talking, but you are too busy to hear Him. It is amazing that something as trivial as our daily schedules and temporal priorities override hearing from the Most High God. Some priority He is in our life, but we call Him Lord. Sure. We have justified this as well.

The last thing I can think of that interferes with hearing from God is that we just don't have the desire to hear. We think we have all the basic information about the Lord, and we are satisfied with what we have heard so far. We reason we have already accepted Him as Savior so what more does He have to tell us? Wow. We wonder why we are so stagnant.

At some point in my Christian walk, I have experienced all of the above internal malfunctions that have affected my connection to the Lord. I can write this because I have lived it. I know how it works, and I understand now what has affected hearing Him on my side. I have fixed the connection, and so can you. The sad thing that I had to realize was, just like with my cell phone, the problem with not hearing from the Lord was totally on my side. It is my responsibility to fix it, as it is yours.

Selfless for Christ

There are no selfish people in Heaven. There will be no one there concerned only for themselves with regard to their interests, benefit, or welfare. I have never thought about selfishness when it comes to Heaven. They are truly incompatible. God reminded me that Heaven is all about Him. From the day we accept Christ until eternity future, it will never be about me, and it will never be about you. It is not about what we think or what we want; it is only about what God thinks and what He wants.

I look at my own Christian walk and have to confess that I have been selfish and concerned with my own interest, benefit, and welfare. I have held on to the old sinful creature with regard to wanting things my way. I have never looked at myself as being selfish, though. I looked at myself as a generally nice person. However, if I look at the definition of selfishness, I would have to confess that is exactly what I have been.

I have to ask myself, "If there are no selfish people in Heaven, at what point in my life will I put off this characteristic in order to prepare for my entrance? At one point in my life will I be selfless for Christ?" I believe I was supposed to make that mental switch at the time of my acceptance of His salvation. I have been a Christian for thirty-three years. I think I should have made the switch! Heaven is closer to me now than it was at that time of my salvation, and yet I'm not sure how much closer I am at becoming selfless for Christ. That contemplation somewhat concerns me.

I can see in the last couple of years as I have awakened from my slumber that I have improved on my thinking with choosing God's will over mine. There are still times when I want to dig my heels into the dirt and stand my ground. This is an example of selfishness. There are still times that my flesh wants to justify missing quiet time for something that I would rather do or just the busyness of the day. This is an example of selfishness. There are still times the Holy Spirit pricks my hearts to call this person or send a note to that person, but I put it off or disregard it. This is an example of selfishness. Am I truly selfless for Christ even today? I really don't think I am. I think I have a lot more waking up and spiritual maturing to do before I can say that I am totally selfless for Christ. I still want it to be about me sometimes, maybe in small ways. I can't justify that thinking because then I am justifying selfishness.

Luke 6:35 says, Do good ... expecting nothing in return" (ESV) Do you expect nothing in return? I do expect things in return, though. I expect words of affirmation by people. I expect people to make time for me. I expect encouragement if I feel I have done well. I expect these things because in some way, I feel like I have earned it. I do mentally and emotionally expect it. The Lord is really putting me on the potter's spinning wheel with this one. He is taking chunks of clay off of me as He molds me in His image. *It hurts!* I don't like it when the Lord touches a sensitive spot. Christ says, "You live for Me in thought and action from now until eternity. Expect nothing in return. There are no selfish people in Heaven. It is all about Me now and it will be all about Me in eternity."

People are selfish because they want to have things how they want them and when they want them. They think their way is best. I am learning, however painfully, that I have to continually move from a selfish mindset to a selfless one. I understand that this can only occur through the power of the Holy Spirit over the flesh. I am learning that I have to tap into that power to live selflessly for Christ. In that, God will receive all the glory. None of me and all of Him.

Little Wooden Crosses

It is strange what catches my attention sometimes. There are some things that don't escape me every time I pass them. They are the little wooden crosses that are put up on the roads, on curves, or at red lights. The little crosses mark where someone lost his or her life. At times, I have seen multiple ones at one location.

I don't want to be morbid, but every time I see one, the same verse comes to my mind. Luke12:20–21 says, "But God said unto him, 'Thou fool, this night thy soul shall be required of thee: then whose shall those things be, which thou has provided?' So is he that layeth up treasure for himself, and is not rich toward God" (KJV). Jesus was telling of a man who was constantly making plans for himself because he thought he had all the time in the world. He was going to and fro. Life, as he knew it, would go on like it always had. No worries. He was putting his own priorities in order, not thinking once about putting God as His top one.

Everything crossed his mind as more important than His relationship with the Most High God. Everything always took precedence. The Lord said that things were being stored up in this man's life but not for the Lord. Nothing ever happened bad in the man's life by not having a priority relationship with the Lord. One year rolled into the next. It got easier and easier not to worry or miss time with God. He lived his own life.

The Lord called the man and people who live like him fools. Why? Their souls would be required of them at an hour that they never expected. They will not have time to prepare their lives with the right priorities later. They would have no time to put God first at the end.

I wonder how many crosses on the side of the road mark people's lives that were just like this man's life that Jesus was talking about. They left their house just to go down the road and never made it home. Never once did this ancient man think his life was going to end, and neither do people today. We make so many plans and store up so many temporal things in our lives. We have so many priorities, but Jesus may not even have been on the list. We are never guaranteed that we will do any of them. We are never guaranteed that we have time to truly get our priorities right. The Lord says the very day we make all of our plans, that very night He may require our soul to stand before Him. If we don't recognize that storing up eternal things in Heaven is more valuable than temporal things on this earth, then we are fools. If we think we have all the time in the world to put God first later while we live for own priorities now, then we are fools. These are not my words, but the Lord's.

I do not know when my soul will be required of me. I want to strive to have my priorities right. This doesn't come easily. It is a daily struggle, as there is so much pull on our lives from the world today. I want to store only eternal things, so I will be prepared to meet the Lord. The only way I see these things as a possibility is to be in a constant state of self-reflection and awareness. I have to rank my priorities correctly and respect the brevity of life. I want to be ready when the Lord requires my soul.

Spirit

"Spirit, I feel you within me, stirring and moving. You are my witness. You are my internal accountability partner. You are my compass that guides me north or south, east or west. Every step I take is ordained by your directions. You settle me when the self-doubts overwhelm me and when I want to stop the work that has been given to me to do for the Kingdom. I never realized that the more I work in your strength, the less confidence I have in myself. I thought it would be the opposite. The less control I have makes me feel like the less I can hang on. I feel like I am hanging on the side of a cliff with only my fingertips. Spirit! I can't hang on much longer."

I hear you whispering, "Let go. Let go, Child. Why are you hanging on to the temporal with all of your strength? Why are you hanging on to the meaningless control that you see as your savior? When you let go, I will take you to the Savior. Nothing is in your control. It never has been. That is all a façade. You have been given a lie that you are in control. God is the only One in ultimate control of everything, including the very breath that you just inhaled.

Why do you feel that you have one bit of control in your life when you agreed to give it away so long ago? I love you. I have dwelt within you since you were a child. I have watched you grow into who you are today. I have never left you for one second. I am in you and around you. I love everything about you as you are made in My image. Rest your mind. Put aside your mental worry of how things will work out or if people will accept your work or not. I accept it and have ordained it.

I am jealous for you. I take you to the Son and the Father. I intervene in dialogue with them from the deepest part of your soul. You do not realize that your soul has a language of its own. It is on a spiritual level that only I can interpret and understand. I hear your soul speaking to Me, Child. I understand your emotions more than you do. I know what you need, before you think it. I know how you feel, before you feel it. I see every part of you and accept you as Mine. I have sealed Myself around you so tightly that you will never fall out of the grasp of the Most High God. You are not secure because of men's approval of you but because of My approval. Your security in every part of your life is found only in Me. You are loved, not in what you can do for Me, but in who you are to Me. I need nothing from you, but you need everything from Me.

I loved you before you even understood who I was. I hovered above the waters in the beginning. I led armies to victory countless times. I am like the fire that penetrated hearts after Christ's ascension. I am the one that moved nations for God. I am more powerful than you can comprehend, and God the Father has put Me in you to dwell for eternity. When your heart needs binding up, I am the one who binds it as I live in it. When God the Son has a message, I am the one that brings it to you.

I never close my eyes in rest. I never take My eyes off of you for one second. I am always active in you and speaking to your spirit. I will take you to meet Jesus in the clouds when the Father calls His children home. Even then, I will not leave you. You are never alone. You are my child who I find pleasure in and protect. I am a part of who you are and who you continue to become in Christ. When your mind becomes overly active living in the past and the future, and when it creates an alternate reality that causes you undue worries, I will be here to pull you back to the present in order to give you the correct perspective. I will never let go of you. I adore you. You are My child in whom I am well pleased."

"Self-Like" Mind

There is deeper truth to learn about our Lord. I know our time is very short on this earth. I have a sense of urgency to stay in prayer and the Word to get as much knowledge and wisdom as I can so that I can share it with others and be adequately prepared to meet the Lord.

When I was in deep slumber, I never contemplated what little quality time in my life I had for the Lord. I thought that when the Lord came back that it would almost be like a vacation. I would have more time to devote to Him in eternity. All would be well then. My busy life could stop, and I could focus on Him and give Him the attention I knew He deserved. If He could just let me get through life first, then I would be all His. I honestly justified this thinking, and it controlled my behavior for most of my Christian life.

If I had more time at some periods in my life, then I would give Him more time, but if not, I wouldn't. Notice the word *if*. That all depended on my thinking of how time and priorities worked in my life at any given time. If the Lord had something to say, or if the Lord wanted my attention, it was never considered. I never contemplated the fact that He was standing there waiting to commune with me day after day. In the end, I didn't miss Him enough from day to day to really care that He was standing there. As I long as I knew He was there, holding the world together, I was fine.

I never held myself accountable to be consistent in the amount of time I gave the Lord or what priority He fell in on the pecking order of my things to do list. Nobody else held me accountable for my spiritual maturity. This was neither their job nor concern. Just as theirs was not my concern. When is the last time you really contemplated and cared for your friend's spiritual growth and maturity? Why? We are all too busy looking at our own needs, spiritual or otherwise. Truth? I think so.

I thought if I had no time for prayer or Bible reading that the Lord would always be patient and understanding. He knew I had a lot going on in life and that I would prioritize Him when I could. Days turned into months, which turned into years, which turned into decades as I conducted my Christian thinking like this. I wrongly thought I was in charge of my Christian walk. My Christian walk belonged to Him the day I accepted His Lordship, right? Therein lies the problem though, doesn't it? I accepted His blood and broken body, but I didn't accept His Lordship with my time, mind, and energy. It is if I said, "You can have my heart, because I certainly want Your blessings. Everything else though is still mine. When I get to Heaven you can have the rest of me." Oh! How privileged the Lord should feel!

Jesus says in Matthew 22:37 to love Him with all of your heart, with all of your soul, and with all of your mind (NIV). If we do not prioritize Him as first in our lives, with none of our justified excuses, do we really love God with all of our minds? This is my opinion, but I really don't think we do. I have read over this famous verse many times as you have. Have you ever considered what loving the Lord with all of your mind would look like? He says to have a "Christ-like" mind. How can we do that when we hold on to our "self-like" mind with a death grip? I think when we do not love the Lord with all our minds, that is when we begin our slumber. As long as we keep our "self-like" mind, we sleep.

My priorities in life were upside down with the thinking that I could later put the Lord first. In later, I meant maybe when the kids moved out of the house and I retired. I'm not kidding. Realistically, that is the only time when I saw my life slowing down enough to devote the appropriate attention to the Lord. The Lord says:

> You put Me first on earth, and you put Me first in eternity. This mental mindset is not conditioned on whether you are on earth or in Heaven. The Creator never waits for the created. You wait for Me. That is how it works. When you don't wait on Me, then you will miss My blessings in your life. You also affect your treasures in Heaven that you can't begin to understand.

I can't imagine how tired the Lord was of my excuses. Honestly, I just stopped offering them. I would give Him my few minutes of prayer time in the shower each morning and would give Him Sunday mornings. Everything on the outside of that was mine. My time. My priorities. "Mine." I am learning more and more as I wake up that there is no "Mine" in this God-child relationship. There is only His time, His priorities, Him. Remember when you can't fit prayer time and studying of His word into your life, then you are slumbering. When you see your time and priorities as more yours than His to manage, then you are slumbering. Truth? I think so.

Jesus Paid It All

Come into prayer time with me. Shut the door and put a "Do Not Disturb" sign out. You may want to lie down comfortably. Get a soft blanket. You may want to sit in your favorite chair. You may want to play some of your favorite praise music softly, or you may prefer it quiet. Close your eyes. Relax. Take a few really deep breaths. Every time you breathe out, exhale the temporal world holding on to you. Inhale the breath of Heaven. Sit quietly as Jesus knows you are coming.

Picture yourself slowly feeling lighter with your mind wandering from where you are. You are traveling to Him. It seems as if it is a great distance, but you look up and He is standing right in front of you smiling. Walk up to Him. Go on. Walk up to Him. Look at Jesus. He's right in front of you. He loves you so much and is honored by your presence. Kneel before Him and bow you head. Fall prostrate if you want. Get as low as you want so He is all you see when you look up. Allow Him to put His hand on your head. Allow Him to bless you. Reach up and grab His robe or His hand. Be still. Worship. You don't have to say anything. Just be still.

Praise Him, the Creator of your soul. Praise the one who paid your debt and raised your life from the dead. Praise Him for who He is and who He has always been. Praise Him for His faithfulness when you are unfaithful. Praise Jesus for paying it all for you. Praise Him that He washed you and has mended your broken heart. Worship the Eternal One. He will never forsake you.

When everyone and everything in your life passes away or falls apart, Jesus will be right in front of you. He never moves an inch from you. He is your faithful witness. You are never alone, friend. He is the lover of your soul. Jesus accepts you exactly as you are right now. You don't have to do anything except recognize who He is and love Him.

You hear the Savior say, "Your strength indeed is small. Child of weakness, watch and pray. Find in Me thine all and all. I paid it all. All to Me you owe. Sin had left a crimson stain. I washed it white as snow." You whisper back, "Now indeed I find my power in you alone can change my spots and melt my heart of stone. Before Your throne, I stand complete. You died, my soul to save. My lips will always repeat." You stand up in front of the Holy One. You put your hands around His face. You look right into His eyes and say, "I praise the One that paid my debt and raised my life from the dead.

Do you hear me, Jesus? Do you want me to shout it so all the angels can know that I am here? Angels, I praise God! Jesus, I praise and worship You in my life! There is none before you, Lord. There is nothing in this temporal world left for me when I compare it to anything that You offer me. You are my heart, Jesus. Praise the One that paid my debt and raised my life from the dead. You are my beloved. You are the lover of my soul. You are my Savior. I love you Lord."

Christian, come pray with me. Come praise Jesus with me. Come and let Him touch you. Come. He's waiting for you. Don't delay. Come.

Twenty Ounces of Peace

Peace is a funny thing. It seems when you get all filled up with it, someone or something is pouring it right back out. It is like they were slowly pouring water from a bottle. You can actually feel the level of your peace slowly going down. Twenty ounces of peace, then fifteen, then nine, then five, then three, and then the last drops spills out. Have you ever felt your peace draining out of you slowly or maybe quickly? You try to hold on to that last drop of peace with all your might, but when it falls out of your bottle, that is it! All peace is gone.

When my last drop of peace falls out of my bottle, I actually feel different. I certainly do not feel like I did when I had twenty ounces of peace or, for that matter, even three ounces. It is something about that last drop that changes everything. You feel like you are somewhat okay as long as you have a drop left. You know when that last drop is gone. First of all, I get irritated when I see peace leaking out of my bottle. When the last drop falls out, I am upset that I allowed my bottle to empty again! How is that possible? Why can't I keep a lid on my peace bottle! Why is it so hard to hang on to? Why is it so easily poured out? Ugh! The other thing that makes me madder is the circumstances that caused my peace to be poured out in the first place. In my mind, it wasn't worthy of an ounce being lost in the first place, yet it emptied half my bottle or more.

I never volitionally pour out my peace. Whether it is true or not, it seems like others are the ones slowly draining my peace. I want to yell, "Get your greedy and uncaring hands off my bottle of peace! Don't you know I only have twenty ounces? Good grief!" I know I cannot be the only one that feels this way. You keep trying desperately to get the lid on your bottle, but you just can't. It's like once there is a slow leak, it gets bigger and bigger. You watch helplessly as it continues to go down. It feels like it is out of our control to stop it. The reality is that it's going to happen. People and circumstances are going to tap into our peace reserve. No matter how hard we try to keep the lid on our bottle, a slow leak will occur. The Lord knows this, which is why He said, "Peace I give you."

In my mind, this is how peace works. When I am drinking a bottle of water and it is empty, I go to the sink, turn on the faucet, and fill my bottle up. Jesus is saying, "I know your peace bottle is empty. Come. Give Me your bottle." He takes it and fills it back up with twenty more ounces of His peace and sends you on your way. He personally refills our bottles with peace. Nothing else can refill us sufficiently and completely. You wouldn't take your water bottle and put it under a table to be refilled would you? How about your stove? A bike? No, you can only refill your water bottle at the sink.

This is just like your peace bottle. You can only refill it by giving your empty bottle to Jesus. Wait for Him to give you more. If you try to fill your peace bottle with any other source, the twenty ounces you do put in will evaporate a lot faster than if God filled it. You will have something in your bottle, but it will be false peace. God will only fill you with twenty ounces of peace at a time. Why? If you had any more, you would rely on yourself longer. God knows this and so do we. We need to remember that Jesus never runs out of peace. He desires for us to be dependent on Him to refill our bottle every time. He is the source when we lose our last drop.

It Is Well with My Soul

If I could have been an observer at the greatest event that changed the world, what would I have heard? After God walked among the garden in the cool of the day and heard the confessions of the first sin, what would have been the follow up conversation in Heaven? Let's listen. I can imagine it going something like this:

God said, "Son, although the sins of mankind are not Yours to carry, I send You to do that which they cannot. I know that You will want this cup to pass from You, but You will carry out My will. Your perfection of obedience and love will bring all nations to My Throne. By Your own sacrifice, everyone will have a choice of where to spend eternity. Without this, they have no hope. I send You, Son."

Jesus, the only Son of the Most High God, said, "It is well with My Soul."

God the Father goes on, "I will pull you down from Your position to make You lower than Our own creation of angels. Your throne will be exchanged for a manger. You will be wrapped in flesh and made a baby in all of its fleshly weaknesses."

Jesus, the Son of the Almighty, responded, "It is well with My Soul."

God continued, "You will live sinlessly. You will have temptations by the very hand of the one that use to worship You, before the foundations of the earth were laid. You know the Bright and Morning Star, Lucifer. He will do everything in his power to make You fall. He will even infiltrate those closest to You. Those that tell You that they love You will deny ever knowing You. Hatred will burn in the hearts of the people and leaders of Israel against You. The enemy will blind them to who You really are. Israel will not believe You are My Son no matter how many ways and times You explain it to them."

Jesus, the Son of the Invisible Holy One, responded, "It is well with My Soul."

God said, "At thirty years of age, you will start ministering about Me. You will teach both day and night from one side of Israel to the other about how people can come to Me by way of You. You are the appointed bridge between them and Me. They will ask You to show Me to them. Tell them clearly and with authority, if they have seen You then they have seen

Me. I will only allow three years for You to testify all the truth that they need to understand to make a decision. No more time will be allowed. If they don't get the truth in that amount of time, they will never get it."

Jesus, the Son of the Great I AM, said, "It is well with My Soul."

God added, "As My appointed days of Your ministry come to an end, You will be taken by the authorities under the cover of darkness to receive an unlawful trial. When they tell You that they will take Your life, make sure You tell them that they do not have that authority. Tell them the only reason Your life is being laid down is that I have authorized it, not them. You will clearly explain that You are the Son of Man. Tell them You sit at My right hand. Tell them You have the power to judge, and You will come back on the clouds of Heaven. When they ask You if You are a King, Tell them You are what they say. Tell them Your Kingdom is not of this world."

Jesus, the Son of the God of Abraham, Isaac, and Jacob, said, "It is well with My Soul."

God sadly said, "Son, they will take You and bind you. They will spit on You, hit You, pull Your beard out, strip You, mock You, scourge You, push thorns in Your head, nail You to a piece of wood, and leave You to die. You will carry the sins of the entire world past, present, and future upon Your shoulders as appointed by My will. At this point, You and I will be separated for the first time in eternity." God paused.

Jesus thought to Himself and said, "Father, I remember when You told Me that I would want this cup to pass from Me. I can take all of what You have said thus far, but to be separated from You is too hard to bear."

God continued, "Son, this cup of My wrath, including separation from Me, is the only way. It cannot pass from You."

Jesus, being of like mind and spirit as the Father, said, "It is well with My Soul."

God added, "On the third day after Your death, I will raise You Myself. After people see all of these things take place, if they confess with their mouths that You are Lord and believe in their hearts that I raised you from the dead, they will be saved."

Jesus looked into the fiery eyes of the Eternal One and said, "It is well with My Soul, Father. I am ready."

After this conversation in Heaven, I heard a baby cry out from the hills of Bethlehem. I turned toward Jerusalem and heard the cries of the Son of God from the hill of Calvary. It has come to pass. I dropped to my knees, looked up into the heavens, and cried out in a loud voice, "It is well with my soul, God the Father. It is well with my soul, God the Son! Let it be as You both willed it to be."

The Blood Covering

In fact, the law requires that nearly everything be cleansed with blood, and without the shedding of blood there is no forgiveness. (Hebrews 9:22 NIV)

When I was praying during quiet time, I submitted a petition to God like I often do. I asked for a deeper understanding of the things of God. Immediately, Jesus gave me a complete picture of Himself walking from the Garden of Gethsemane to the cross.

Jesus said quietly, "What was I doing in the Garden?"

I said, "Praying."

He said, "What else was I doing in the Garden?"

I said, "I'm not sure besides praying."

He said, "I was bleeding."

I thought back and said, "Yes Lord. You were sweating blood while you were praying."

He said, "That was my first drop of blood spilled for you, but all of My blood had to be spilled for you, not just one drop. One drop was not sufficient to cover your sins and the sins of the world. You see, when the priests slaughtered the sacrificial lambs at the Temple, they made a large gash so that as much blood could be drained as possible. They didn't prick the lamb's leg to get one drop. There had to be as much blood as possible drained for the sacrifice."

I said, "Yes, Lord. I hear what You are telling me. Why did all the blood have to be drained? Why couldn't it just be a drop?"

He said, "There had to be enough to cover your sins and one drop wasn't enough. All the blood had to be drained."

The Lord asked, "You understand that life is in the blood, don't you?"

I said, "Yes, Lord."

He continued, "When all of my blood was drained for you, then you had all of My life in you—not just one drop of My blood, but all of My blood, not just one drop of My Life, but all of My Life. That was the only way. Not only did all of My blood have to be drained, it wasn't all drained in one place."

I said, "I don't understand what You are saying that it was not all drained in one place."

"My first drop of blood fell in the Garden of Gethsemane," He added. I was then taken to the High Priest Caiaphas where I was hit blindly from several people. Blood was drained from Me. That blood sprinkled the Jews as I was in their high courts. A sentence was passed that I would die. I was then taken to Pilate. There I had a crown of thorns pushed through my scalp. More blood was drained from Me. That blood sprinkled the Gentiles, as I was in their High courts.

A sentence in that court was passed that I would die. The two people groups that existed both agreed that My blood would be drained. I was tied to the whipping post where as much blood as possible was drained from Me without killing Me. So much blood was drained there that it weakened Me, and I could not walk unassisted to Calvary. I fell several times on the way; each time more blood was drained. As I walked through the streets, people would pull out my beard and mock Me. More blood. I continued to stumble through the streets. I became weaker and weaker as I sprinkled the streets of My beloved Jerusalem with My blood that was slowly draining from Me.

When they nailed My hands and feet to that cross, more blood drained. While I hung on that cross for all those hours, more of My life was drained from Me as blood dripped down the wood and pooled at the base. I thought back and remembered that when My first drop of blood was drained, I was praying to My Father. On the cross, when my last bit of blood was drained, I was praying to Him as well.

Why do you think I am telling you all of this about the sprinkling of My blood and how it was slowly but completely drained throughout My last day?"

I answered humbly with tear-filled eyes and a wet cheek, as my heart was so heavy at this point: "I'm not sure Lord. I don't know what to say."

He said, "I could have had all of my blood drained at one place, but my blood was all over that city by the time it was all over. It was in the garden, the courts, the streets, the people, Calvary, and you. My Child, it was all over you, too. I wanted you to know that My blood covers everything and everywhere. I literally covered every part of the city of Jerusalem with My blood, just as I have spiritually covered every part of your life with the same blood. Do you understand? My blood was slowly drained, as it had to cover every part. I had no blood left when it was all over. I emptied My life's source for you so that you may have My life's source in you.

I have already walked down them sprinkling My blood ahead of you on the many streets that you have traveled in your life that you committed sin on or the streets that you will travel that you will commit sin on, just like I walked down the streets of Jerusalem. There is not one part of your life that My blood hasn't covered. There's not one place that you have gone that My blood hasn't covered. You need to understand that it was a complete covering and a complete emptying. You are My child. You have My life in you because My blood was completely drained for you. I gave every drop. I love you. "

All I could do was cry when He spoke this to me. What in the world can I say back when the Most High God tells me such things? I tried to find the words to speak back to Him, but all I could say was, "Lord! Thank you for Your blood." It seemed so inadequate. Who am I that God is mindful of me? Who am I? Who are we that He would drain His life's blood to completely cover us and give us His life? To know He did this while we were still His enemies is beyond comprehension. What kind of love is this? I cannot answer. There are no words.

Awesome Work

God works so that people will be in awe of Him. (Ecclesiastes 3:14 HCSB)

I was looking through Ecclesiastes last night because there was this one verse that I liked. I wanted to include it in a card that I was writing to a friend. I was scanning the third chapter when I came across verse 14. I read it, and the verse just absolutely flew off the page and screamed, "Look at *Meeeeee*! I bet you didn't know I was hiding out here in this old book! I was just waiting for you to finally discover me!" I started smiling and wrote it down.

I ran to find Kevin and said, "Listen to this awesome verse!" He thought it was just as amazing as I did. He wasn't giddy or anything, but thought it was really cool. I ran to find my two boys who were playing video games. I said, "Look at me as I need to see your eyeballs! I have something to say!" They were so excited! Not really. I said, "Do you have *any* idea why the Lord shows His work to us?!?" They stared blankly at me. One wiped drool off the bottom right corner of his lip. Not really.

I said, "So everyone can be in awe of Him! We can sit back and look at everything He has done and just say, 'You are so awesome, Lord. Look at you go!'" My oldest son looked at me very seriously and said, "Mama. That is good. Do you think you should be a preacher?" I said, "No son. I am just excited over this new simple truth that I found in the Word, but I am going to write a journal about it!"

Sisters and brothers, look at this verse! "God works so that people will be in awe of Him." Get excited! Wow! I can't stop saying that verse over and over. If you looked at some other Bible translations you will see, "God works so that people will be in fear of Him." To understand what fearing the Lord means, we can cross reference Hebrews 12:28–29, "Therefore, since we are receiving a kingdom that cannot be shaken, let us be thankful, and so worship God acceptably with reverence and awe, for our 'God is a consuming fire'" (NIV). To have reverence and awe means to fear the Lord.

What does reverence mean? It is a feeling or attitude of deep respect. What does awe mean? An overwhelming feeling of admiration produced by that which is grand or extremely powerful. Let's paraphrase this amazing verse in Ecclesiastes. "God, the Creator of everything seen and unseen, works by the power of His spoken word to all people for the primary purpose that we can be completely overwhelmed with admiration by His great power, resulting in an attitude of the deepest respect of who He really is!" How's that? I'm sorry, but if this verse doesn't excite you then something is wrong with you! I hate to break that truth to you.

Look at the universe. There are billions of stars, millions of galaxies, our life-giving solar system, and our earth that are held by nothing yet supports you and me, our sun, our moon, our oceans, our animals, and us! Each one of these things in their own right can blow your mind. That is exactly why God did it all. He wanted to blow our minds. He wanted us to stand back at look at Him and say, "Wooooowwww. Just amazing! God, You indeed are worthy of all of our praise and honor and glory! You! You, God, are absolutely awesome in the work that You have done. You have outdone Yourself, Lord!"

Look at the Jewish nation. Millions of people living today are descendants of a promise made 4,000 years ago to a man named Abraham. These chosen people have been persecuted from the very beginning of their existence as Satan has come up against them in order to destroy them from the face of the earth. Even to this day, that threat is ringing out from countries around the world. There is a small piece of land of only 8,000 square miles that holds God's promise to Abraham. God says, "They will be my people, and I will be their God. All of my people will be saved. Israel is the apple of My eye (Jeremiah 32:28; Romans 11:26; Zechariah 2:8 NIV). The Jewish people and nation by all account should not even exist today, but they do. I have been to Israel and have seen the Jewish people. They are alive and well. God says to the world, "I have held my promise to Abraham and My people still live in the Promised Land that I have given them. Look at My work! All people should be in awe of Me."

High Priest

We all know enough from the scriptures to understand that priests came through the tribe of Levi. One of the reasons it is believed that God chose this particular tribe is because they did not bow down and worship the golden calf in the wilderness when Moses had left them to go up to receive the Law (Exodus 32:25–29; all following verses are NIV). Another reason is that Moses was a Levite, and he was the one that originally received The Law from God to give to the people (Hebrews 7:11). It only makes sense that other Levites would pass the Law down as well. A man from any of the other eleven tribes of Israel could never be a priest. Historically, it is believed that the priests of the Old and New Testament came from the firstborn males from the tribe of Levi.

There were different levels of priest. I am most interested in the high priest. Hebrews 5:1 says, "Every high priest is selected from among the people and is appointed to represent the people in matters related to God, to offer gifts and sacrifices of sin." Verse 4 goes on to say that no man can take this great honor upon him but has to be called by God. If you were a Levite, the firstborn male, and a priest, that did not necessarily equate that you would ever become a high priest. God had to specifically call you or appoint you personally. You may have been happy just being a regular priest, but if God called you, then you took the office of high priest. I love history, so all of this is very interesting to me. I think it is important to understand how this process worked when you turn your eyes toward Jesus. It helps us to have a deeper understanding of the importance of the position He held.

What is most fascinating about how a high priest is chosen by God stands true even for Jesus. Just like a regular priest did not honor or exalt himself to be called by God to be a high priest, Jesus did not either. Hebrews 5:5 says that God called Jesus to, "become a high priest" (NIV). Jesus did not seek it out, but He was told by God that He would be one. This was the same process as for any regular priest. If I really think about this, it seems to indicate that prior to Jesus' death, burial, and resurrection, He was not a high priest. Afterward, He was perfected and became the source of eternal salvation to all who obey Him, and He was declared by God a high priest (Hebrews 5:9–10 NIV).

I have never thought about this before. God told Jesus in Hebrews 5:6, "You are a priest forever." Hebrews 5:7 gives us insight that God was able to "save" Jesus from death. That is an amazing concept. This is why Jesus asked God in the Garden of Gethsemane to allow the cup to pass from Him. Jesus knew His Father had the power to save Him, if it were His will. Jesus knew the will of the Father because they are one. Jesus accepted His Father's will as His own. If God would have saved Jesus, then He could have never taken the position of the eternal high priest. There would have been no one to take our gifts and sacrifices for sin through all of time.

Jesus came to earth for many reasons, but there is one that is often overlooked. We always think it was all about us. Jesus came to earth to become high priest because He was appointed in service to God for the people in order to offer both gifts and sacrifices for sins. Jesus has dealt with us gently as we have been ignorant toward His truth and have gone astray (Hebrews 5:1–2). God so loved the world that He appointed His Son to become high priest. Jesus' suffering was His service to His Father and His sacrifice for His brothers and sisters so they could be saved. We are Jesus' siblings (Matthew 12:50). His service was to God the Father, but His sacrifice was for us so that we could have eternal salvation if we obeyed His truth. Amazing. We needed an eternal high priest, and God provided one for us.

Listen to this closely. In Hebrews 7:12 it says, "For when there is a change of priesthood, there *must* be a change of law as well. When Jesus came, we all know that He became high priest. With His final gift and sacrifice for sin, we all entered a new covenant or "change of law." Jesus literally changed everything. He made the old and aging covenant disappear (Hebrews 8:13). Hebrews 7:14–28 to 8:1–6 acknowledged that Jesus did not come from the tribe of Levi in order to fulfill the legal commands but from the tribe of Judah. The reason for this is that Jesus was the only one of all the tribes past, present, and future that was chosen "based on the power of His indestructible life."

Only Jesus can hold His priesthood permanently because through His death, burial, and resurrection, "He remains forever." If the high priest's job was to offer the sacrifices of sin, only someone who can live permanently will be able to carry out these duties for all people through time. This is another reason that Jesus had to defeat death. This is why a mortal high priest could not have carried out this position and responsibility. We had to have an immortal High Priest. Jesus was chosen by God because He "became the guarantee of a better covenant that was perfect and long-standing." This covenant had "better promises" than the one men could have had the ability to provide.

While the information of Jesus being called to be a high priest is fascinating, it isn't all that hard to understand in my opinion. Hebrews calls this information, "basic principles of God's revelation, milk instead of meat, and an elementary message about the Messiah (Hebrews 5:12; 6:1). Hebrews 5:11 does indicate, however, some frustration with trying to explain the same material over and over again. The writer urges us to go into the deeper things of Christ. It says we can't do that because we are slow to understand. We don't try to understand; we are dull of hearing. Depending on what biblical translation you read, we are too lazy to understand (Hebrews 5:11). If you want Sarah Rowan's translation, this indicates that you are slumbering. If you have been a Christian for any amount of time, you should be progressively moving into the deeper things of God. If you are still very superficial in your life with Christ, you are slumbering. Praise God for His appointment of Christ Jesus to be our High Priest! He has certainly served His Father well.

Arise, My Love

Not a word was heard in Heaven as God watched His beloved take His last few breaths. The angels were still watching the events unfold. Thousands upon thousands upon ten thousand legions were standing by, waiting for God to say, "Fly faster than wind. Go get My Son." No word came. Michael, the mighty Archangel, stood ready as he hung his head and looked away. He knew Jesus would be left there to die by the Father.

God was on His throne as He had been from everlasting to everlasting. He was in complete control. Nothing unexpected had happened. Nothing would. Everything was going according to God's plan. With Jesus' last few breaths, He looked into Heaven and said, *Eli, Eli, lema sabachthani,* (My God, My God, why have You forsaken Me?). God's whisper was barely audible, "I will come for You, Love. My will be done on earth as it is in Heaven."

The angels watched as God moved to take His hand to cover the sun. Darkness fell over the earth. When God moved in Heaven, the earth quaked. The rocks were split under His movement. As God heard His Son say in a loud voice, "It is finished," the words echoed through Heaven and Hell. God appeared in the Holy of Holies in the Temple. This was His dwelling place on earth. He knew it well. God stood silent as He knew His Son was dead. He looked up to the top of the heavy tapestry that had been hanging for years. It separated access to Him from the common people. There would be no more separation. Never again. Jesus was High Priest now and for eternity future. All men had access to God the Father through Jesus Christ. God, Himself, tore the curtain from top to bottom. The priests in the temple fell prostrate as if they had fainted when they saw the curtain being slowly torn.

God's appointed time had passed: three days and three nights. It was after the third midnight that God moved from His throne again. All angels faced Him for their command. Right before dawn, God spoke, "It is time to wake My Son." God commanded an angel to descend to the garden tomb before Him. Immediately, when the angel's foot touched earth, there was a violent earthquake. The guards that witnessed the angel's descent fell like dead men at the appearance of the lightning-white being. The mighty angel rolled back the stone and sat upon it. God entered. He turned to see His Beloved lying wrapped in death clothes. Still.

The Ancient of Days' glory completely filled the tomb with the brightest light imaginable. God spoke over Jesus, "You have brought glory to Me, Son. I did not forsake you. I am here. I will not let You see decay. You have done My will. In a short while, You will be sitting at My right side. I will make Your enemies Your footstool. The stone that was despised by the house of Israel will become the cornerstone. There is salvation in no one else, for there is no name that I have given under Heaven by which people will be saved." God paused and then said

"ARISE MY LOVE! ARISE MY LOVE!"

When God finished speaking, the body of Jesus passed through the linen death clothes and floated to stand upright in God's presence. The clothes remained untouched. Jesus' body was healed of all markings except the wounds on His hands, feet, and side.

God looked into Jesus' eyes and said, "I will leave these scars as reminders of Your sacrifice and My will for salvation. Son, let them see your wounds and touch you. They are weak and have little faith. The women are coming. You can show yourself to them. Instruct them to tell the disciples to meet You in Galilee. I have appointed that You will remain there for forty days. After that time has ended, You will ascend and return to Your throne by My side. I will send the Holy Spirit to stay with My children, until I call Him at the appointed time. When I call the Holy Spirit home, My children will also come with Him, as He is in them. You will meet them all in the clouds to bring them back to Me at the appointed time." Jesus stood there in the whitest linen robe, with a big smile breaking across His face and a twinkle in His eye and said, "Yes, Father. It is all very well with My soul." God smiled back and said, "I love you, Son."

Alternate Realities

Sometimes, I believe we each have our own reality in which we live. We think things are one way when, really, they may not be that way at all. Take marriage, for example. A spouse thinks everything is going well in the marriage. This is his or her reality. This is what he or she wants to believe; everything is fine. Any issues contrary to this truth or perception are justified by whatever means it takes to maintain his or her own reality. The other spouse may feel lonely, disconnected, unloved, and neglected. How can one spouse justify everything is fine when the other person is an abyss away. One spouse is in one reality while the other spouse is in another. There can only be one reality.

Often, one spouse sacrifices his or her reality in order to maintain life in the other spouse's reality. At least it seems to keep the peace; forget about truth. It is more important to maintain the façade of reality than to address any real issues. One spouse accepts that living in the other spouse's reality is the only way that they can maintain any sort of normalcy. When one spouse doesn't want to sacrifice their reality any longer is when the trouble starts.

I used to maintain two realities in my marriage, but when they collided, there was only one truth on the other side. There is only one reality. My reality I held in my marriage was false. It did not line up with God's reality for my marriage. It was hard to accept that because of pride. With my husband's help along with the Lord's, I am now living in one reality with Kevin. It has been all the sweeter. If you have never had marital problems, you will not understand what I am trying to say. That's okay. In a way, I'm glad you don't have to learn this lesson the hard way.

Take the reality of a parent and child relationship. The parents are unaware of something the older child may be involved in. As a result, parents live in a reality that their child is pure and innocent, when in fact he or she is not. In reality, the child may be involved in something over his or her head, but the parents never know it. The older child will do what he or she can do within their power to make sure the true reality never collides with their parent's "false" reality. It is better for the child to keep his or her parents living in an alternate reality than for them to live in the true one. Eventually, the true reality will be discovered and will have to be dealt with. There are lots of pain and tears when a parent and child's realities finally collide, and the true one is known. I can also testify to this as well.

Take the reality of sin. When we sin, have we not entered an alternate reality that we have created for ourselves? Listen to me; just because you have entered the alternate reality that sin created for you, it never negates the true reality that still exists before you started the sin in the first place.

We know that it is wrong to be involved in the sin that we are in, but the new reality that sin creates is so much more exciting and stimulating than our old reality. Sin tells you a lie that your new reality can last forever, and it will bring you no harm. No, friend. Your new reality is just a façade. You will return to the real reality soon enough. May I add that it will be a very hard return, with lots of hurt and regrets, as well. Sin always comes to an end. It typically has devastating consequences that are far reaching. I can testify to the alternate realities of sin, as I am sure you can.

Take the reality of Jesus. He says there is a reality that He exists and is real. He exists even though we can't comprehend everything about Him. He exists even though people want to create an alternate reality that He doesn't exist. There is only one reality. There is a reality that Jesus is coming back to get those that are waiting and literally are looking for Him. He expects you to live in His reality as evidenced by your actions and behavior for the Kingdom. Jesus says that in reality, His return will be very soon.

Look around at our lives. Do we live in this reality that He is coming soon or have we created our own? We tell ourselves that we have all the time in the world to build a stronger relationship with Him. Your reality is that you are too busy and don't have more time to go deeper with God until later. When your reality collides with His reality, which one do you think is the right one? Who is living in an alternate one? Wake up, Christian.

I have slowly learned something, and it has been one of the hardest lessons of my life. There is only one reality. There is only one truth. There is only one truth in our marriage. There is only one truth in the transparency of a parent-child relationship. There is only one truth in the way sin really works. Jesus and all of these things, plus a multitude of others, all have one reality. Whether we know what it is or choose to live in it is the question. I can tell you right now, it is easier to live in your own reality. Why? Because you created it! You control it. As long as everyone else, including God, falls into your reality, all is well.

Christian, you live in your own reality because it's comfortable. Just because you are comfortable doesn't mean you are living in truth. I lived in all of my different realities because I didn't want to see the truth. This was the way I dealt with things to be okay inside. I don't want to live in a lie again. I don't want to live in an alternate reality. John 8:32 says, "Then you will know the truth, and the truth will set you free." You may not like the real reality for your life, but there is truth in it. You are free in it. The Lord only dwells in it.

Center Line

Recently I was told a story of a young person crossing the center line. Death and destruction of what a family once knew as their norm occurred. This morning in prayer time, I was thinking about this person and his family. The plans he had and the occasions he will miss is innumerable. The pain left behind is unfathomable for anyone to have to endure in their hearts. As I was pondering, the Spirit encouraged me to learn more from this, but what? He impressed upon me that death and ruin awaited anyone that crosses the center line of God's ways, not just the one on a literal highway. The thoughts started taking shape in my mind. I saw that every one of us is on a journey, Christians and nonbelievers alike. Christians, though, are supposed to be on a very narrow road because we chose to turn off the wide road sometime back.

Now the narrow road is unique in the fact that it does not have a center line to cross. When you are walking very closely to the Lord on the narrow road, you don't have to worry about crossing the line that could lead to your ruin. The Lord tells us, "Once you are on My narrow road, do not look to your right or your left. Keep your eyes straight at all times." What if, while we were on the narrow road, we did look to our left or the right? What does the Lord not want us to see?

Well, I know because I have looked both ways. I think we have all looked at one time or another. When I looked to my right or left, I saw another road. It was wider than the one that belonged to the Lord. The road though looked very nice, well taken care of, and it seemed like it was heavily traveled. That is always good to find a road like that because it gives you a sense of security that many others have also traveled that road before you. It gives one a false sense of security that it's okay for travel, even if for a short distance. I have noticed where the narrow road had no center line to cross, the wide road does.

The wide road seemed right for me to travel on different occasions when I have wanted to go my way. I would pick up speed and start traveling down that wide road a lot faster than I would have originally anticipated. Almost as if I was being pulled along and losing some control as I traveled. I would start swerving a bit and occasionally cross that center line. The farther I journeyed from the narrow road, the more I swerved. I have wanted to turn back from the wide road, but the pull was stronger the longer I traveled. Finally, as can happen without anyone's anticipation, I crossed the center line, which led to a spiritual head-on collision.

The Lord says, "There is a way that seems right to man, but in the end it leads to death and ruin." I think we are lied to or we lie to ourselves that we can travel the wide road occasionally and have control that we would never cross the center line. The Lord says that when you travel any road but His, you will eventually cross the center line. You will lead yourself into ruin when you hit what is on the other side head on.

When the line is crossed, there are multiple pains, heartaches, and fallout that await you. Sometimes it will take years before you recover from crossing that center line or when someone else close to you crosses the center line, which in turn greatly affects your life. You expect your spouse not to cross the center line. You expect your children not to cross the center line. You expect that you yourself will not cross that center line. The reality is they may, and you certainly may, as well.

I honestly wish I knew what initially turned our heads from right to left in the first place. How in the world do we turn off of the Lord's narrow road for our lives? Why is it so easy to do so? We fool ourselves that we can travel the wide road as far as we want because we have control not to cross that center line. How many times in my life have I crossed that line? The ruin that comes from it is something that you move through, but you don't forget the pain and disbelief it brings.

What makes us think we have that great of control that we won't cross it? Arrogance? Pride? Selfishness? Sometimes I think our minds just take over. We create an alternate reality to justify the travel of the wide road and to ignore swerving over the center line. We rarely wake up until we ultimately cross it and ruin awaits us.

As a Christian, I have learned that, even for me, it is easy to turn my head to the left or the right and turn off of the narrow road. It's too easy. The enemy makes sure of that. In my own life, I believe that my search for the deeper wisdom of why I sin and how I sin has opened my eyes to at least try to avoid the same wide roads again. There may be more turnoffs from the narrow road up ahead for me that I am unaware of right now. I am confident of that. There are things on those roads ahead that I would have never imagined catching my attention. I pray that when the roads present themselves that I am so firmly committed to the narrow one that they don't even turn my head.

I have traveled a few wide roads and crossed their center lines. The one lesson I have learned is that I never want to travel them again and hit the same ruin. I guess you could look inside your own Christian walk and see the times that you took a wide road here or there. You can also remember what happens when you crossed the center line. Maybe you were lucky and you almost crossed the line, but you woke up in time to just get brushed with some heartache or ruin. You quickly changed back to the narrow road.

There are still many lessons to learn from such a close call. Again, sometimes you may have stayed on the narrow road, but a loved one decided to divert his or her path and travel the wide road. When they have crossed the center line and met ruin and destruction, that involved some ruin and destruction for you as well. My only advice is for you to keep your eyes straight and stay on the narrow road so that the Lord can keep you, heal you, and love on you. The forgiveness the Lord provides for anyone that travels the wide road is immense. We can't even comprehend how badly He wants us back on His road. He is standing at the edge of it and calling us back constantly.

The question is how long will we hear His voice until we finally turn around? That is debatable. It depends on how badly you want what is on the wide road with the center line. Caution: there is a way that seems right to man, but in the end, it will lead to ruin.

Wedding Day

I received an invitation to attend a wedding. It was printed in red and gold. I heard that it will be heavenly. It will be like no other wedding I have ever attended. The invitations were sent out according to the names recorded in the Lamb's Book of Life. I gave my RSVP decades ago when I accepted Jesus' invitation. I have waited so long that, at times, I did not think it would come.

The world told me I was a fool to wait on the Lord. It told me that He didn't exist, and even if God did exist, that I could not be that important for Him to love me. It lied to me and told me that I was insignificant. The world told me that Jesus would never come for me. I know that I accepted an invitation sent by the Most High God, Himself. I remember the very day I did. I never lost faith that one day the wedding would come.

Today is the wedding day. The world has passed away, and it is no more. As I walk toward the glorious place where the wedding will be held, I notice the most beautiful things along the way. I see those very familiar tall swaying purple flowers that I have seen in all my prayers. It is in the middle of that very field that I met Jesus each morning. There are flowers as far as I can see. I see the transparent street beneath me. I look around me to see the most vivid colors that I have ever seen. They are almost too strong to look at, but yet I can't pull away.

I see the Tree of Life swaying with its leaves gently blowing in the wind. The fruit it produces changes with the season. I have never tasted fruit that satisfies me as much as the fruit that comes from this tree. There are mighty angels standing still like statues. They have their heads bowed and hands raised. They are holding large golden bowls of incense. White vapors are rising out of the bowls and traveling toward the direction that I am walking. The incense that is burning is the sweetest smell that I have ever smelled. There is nothing to compare it to. I want to take the deepest breaths to inhale as much as my lungs can hold. I breathe it out slowly, not wanting it to escape.

I reach the biggest golden doors that I have ever seen. I run both of my hands over the raised picture on it. It has the impression of a manger, a cross, and an open tomb. I know this picture well. It was the same one on the front of my invitation that I accepted while on earth. I am overcome with the recognition and what it holds for me. I gently slide down the door and lay my face against it. I have wet cheeks as I remember the Lord's story that He told me in a way I understood when I was a child. This is the story that saved my life. I whispered, "Thank you Jesus for Your story. I have loved every part of it since the day You told me."

Both of the great doors opened as if to welcome me. I looked around, but there was only me. It seems that everyone had already entered. I am the last one. The warmest glow is pulling me in. I stood at the threshold and looked down at my robe. I wore the best one that I owned that

I could find in my own righteousness. I hung my head, and the tears flowed again. I was so embarrassed. There is no way that I could attend the great wedding with my torn, tattered, and stained robe. It was not presentable, but it was the best I had. The warmth that I felt when the doors first opened pulled me in despite my appearance.

As I entered, I came into the widest and longest hall that I have ever seen. It was magnificent with tall, ornate columns holding up the great structure. First, I started hearing voices, but as I moved further down the hall, I could see one long line of people. I can't see the end of them. They seem to go on as long as the great hall did. It looks like it is some sort of receiving line. I fall in line after the last person. I looked at his robe; it too looked like mine. I was somewhat relieved at this. I looked at him and asked, "Excuse me, sir? Have I missed the wedding?" He looked at me and said, "No. Jesus is in the process of preparing the Bride now. You are just in time. Jesus will be coming very soon."

After a while had passed, I saw Jesus coming. I couldn't believe it. Jesus was coming toward me. A peace covered me as the anticipation of Him coming closer was too much to bear. Once I could see Him, I noticed that He was spending time talking with each person. Jesus smiled and nodded at them. He removed their robes and wrapped new ones around them. He had gold crowns in His hands. He placed one or more on their heads. I thought to myself that there is no way that I will get one of those crowns and white robes. I am so unworthy. If Jesus knew what I had done and who I was, He wouldn't want to give me those items. I am just happy that I am at the wedding.

When Jesus was about six people from me, I could hear some of the conversations. Jesus looked at the sixth man from me. Immediately, the old man dropped to his knees. The man was crying and weeping. Through his groans, he said, "I am a liar." Jesus smiled and nodded and said, "Rise, Abraham." Jesus took Abraham's tattered robe off and let it drop to the floor. It immediately disappeared. While Abraham bowed his head, Jesus wrapped the whitest linen robe around him. Many crowns were placed upon his head. I was in awe of what I had just witnessed! Abraham? He is the Father of all the Faithful.

Jesus moved to the next man. The man dropped. He said, "I am a murderer." Jesus said, "Rise, Moses." Jesus gave him a white robe and crowns. Jesus came to the fourth man from me. The man dropped and cried, "I am a thief." Jesus smiled and nodded and said, "Rise, Jacob." He received a robe and crowns. The next man dropped and said, "I am an adulterer." Jesus smiled and nodded and said, "Rise, David." Robes and crowns were given. When Jesus came to the second man from me, the man fell prostrate before the Lord. He heaved and heaved with a broken heart. I could hardly make out what he said with his face buried in the floor, "I denied you." Jesus reached down and patted the man's shoulder gently and whispered, "Rise, Peter." When Peter stood up, Jesus smiled. A white robe and many crowns were given.

Jesus walked up to the last man before me. The man that had talked to me earlier dropped to his knees and confessed, "I killed God's children who believed in You." Heartfelt cries rose up from this man. He was shaking in his grief. His sorrow was tangible. I could feel tears dripping off my cheeks watching him. Would this man have killed me at one time in his past? He would have done it or held other's coats while they did it. Yes. This man that I spoke to earlier would have killed me. I could not believe this man who seemed so gentle could have done such a thing. Jesus said, "Rise, Paul." Five golden crowns were placed upon Paul's head and a beautiful white robe with golden thread was exchanged for the torn, stained one. I could not believe Paul was standing next to me. Not only him, but Abraham, Moses, Jacob, David, and Peter. I was not worthy to even stand in the presence of these great men, yet they all wore the same torn and stained robes that I wore.

Jesus moved to stand in front of me. When I looked into His perfect and all-knowing eyes, I could not speak. It was like a force pushed me to my knees. Every knee shall bow. I was so weak; I could not hold my weight. It was the holiness of the Lord pushing upon me. My eyes started burning. The tears flowed like rivers as I tried to drown myself from His sight. Maybe somehow my tears could wash some stains away on my robe so that He couldn't see all of my sins. I was ashamed and wanted to hide myself from His gaze.

He stood there for what seemed to be eternity, just studying me. Jesus said quietly, "Who are you?" I spoke back in a shaky voice, "I am a sinner Lord! I am a sinner!" I was brokenhearted and sorrowful in His perfect love, confessing such a thing. He said sweetly, "Rise, My Bride." I couldn't believe what I just heard. I looked up and He held His opened hand out for mine. I reached up to grab His hand and stood. As soon as I rose, my old tattered and stained robe disappeared as the finest white linen one was wrapped around me. I asked, "Bride?" He was smiling and nodding. Gold crowns were placed on my bowed head. No words can describe their beauty.

Jesus said, "The last will be the first, and the first will be last. You were the last one here, so you will be the first one to enter into the wedding supper of the Lamb. Do you want to meet My Father?" I couldn't breathe. I just stood there speechless. I couldn't move. I thought, "Wedding? Bride? Do I want to meet Jesus' Father?" Jesus smiled and turned to my side. He held His arm out, smiling while looking me. I slipped my arm around His as we started the processional of the long line of people toward two large doors that I had not noticed earlier.

When Jesus and I reached the doors, two great angels opened them. The incense that I had smelled earlier flowed out all around us and filled the great hall. Jesus looked at me and said, "This is the throne room of the Most High God, My Father. By your acceptance of My sacrifice, you are worthy to enter His holiness. When My Father sees you, He will see Me with you. That is the only way He can accept you." I nodded and smiled back at Him, as I could not speak. I turned to look over my shoulder and saw Paul looking back at me. He gave me a warm smile, slow nod, and little wink.

Jesus walked me down the aisle to the very throne of God. His throne was high and lifted up. His appearance was like sapphire, jasper, and emeralds. The hairs of His head were white, like white wool or snow. His eyes were like a flame of fire. Around the throne were all the colors of the rainbow. There was brightness all around Him like the appearance of fire. Such was the appearance of the likeness of the glory of the Lord. And when I saw it, I fell on my face. I heard the powerful and majestic voice of One speaking like the roar of many rushing waters, "I AM. I am the Alpha and the Omega. The Beginning and the End. I accept you as My child, because when I look at you, I see My Beloved. Enter into My eternal kingdom where there is no more pain, suffering, or tears. There is no sun as I am light. I see you for who you are. You are in the image of Us. I will forever be with you. You will always have direct access to Me. Welcome home, My child."

I stood up and approached God's throne humbly. He leaned down and wiped my tears away. I would never shed another. I bent down at the corner of His robe, which filled the room. I whispered, "Could I give you something?" God leaned down again and put His hands out. I started taking one crown off of my head at a time and placing it with a grateful heart in His hands. After I was done, I walked off to my left. I found a place to stand as I watched Paul kneel and cast his crowns at God's feet, then Peter, then David, then Jacob, then Moses, then Abraham, and then you. You were at the wedding of the Lamb. You were part of the Bridal processional, too. All of the church was there.

When the processional was over, the Bride sang:

Holy, Holy, Holy is the Lord God Almighty. Who was, and is, and is to come. Salvation belongs to our God and to the Lamb, who is seated on the Throne. Blessing and glory and wisdom and thanksgiving and honor and power and strength be to our God forever and ever. We thank You, Lord God, the Almighty, because You have taken Your great power and have begun to reign. Hallelujah! Hallelujah because our Lord God has begun to reign. Let us be glad, rejoice, and give Him glory, because the marriage of the Lamb has come, and His wife has prepared herself. She is permitted to wear fine linen, bright and pure (Revelations 4:8; 7:10; 7:12; 11:17; 19:7-9).

Amen and Amen.

Image of God

The Spirit Himself testifies with our spirit that we are God's children. (Romans 8:16 NIV)

All of us have a mental picture of God when we pray. We just haven't thought about it before. For instance, one of my friends told me he pictures God sitting on His throne in like manner of Lincoln sitting on his memorial in Washington. If you have ever seen the Lincoln Memorial, you feel so small sitting at its feet. Lincoln is larger than life and towers over you with authority and strength. My nephew says he pictures standing in a warm bright light. These are only some of the images that people have when they go in front of the Lord. I am sure the images are unique for everyone who prays. I think it should be unique and personal to each Christian.

I have my own visual of how I appear to the Lord and how He appears to me. I would have to confess that it has changed somewhat though the years. The image I have now has remained constant for a long period of time. It is the only way I can imagine appearing before the Lord now in prayer. I take a few deep cleansing breaths as I enter the presence of the Lord. I am mentally preparing myself to be with Him for a good bit of time. What that will hold, I never know. Sometimes, as soon as I close my eyes, He pounces as if He has been waiting all night to tell me something. Then I stop and immediately write what He has said or shown me.

Sometimes, the Lord is standing there watching me walk up to Him. I know He has been waiting for me to come. That's for sure. I can't imagine missing the Lord in the mornings. Just think. The Lord is standing there waiting for me, and I never come. That one image is so strong in my mind that it keeps me accountable to meet Him every day. How often in the past have I left the Lord standing and waiting for me. As humans, we get so busy that we never think the Lord is waiting to meet us. How that must hurt His heart that such temporal things get in the way with our sweet time with Him. While He is longing and waiting for you, He may not have crossed your mind all day. Yet, the Lord is faithful when we are not.

I understand the Trinity is made up of God the Father, God the Son, and God the Holy Spirit. God the Father and God the Holy Spirit are spirits. The Bible is clear on that fact. Both are in fact invisible but very real nonetheless. That is a very hard concept for humans to comprehend. God knew that. We only understand what we can experience through our senses, so God the Son was sent. God took on flesh for our benefit, not His. I understand that the Father and the Son are in Heaven. I understand the Holy Spirit is on earth within me. He is in all Christians. The Father gave me to the Son. The Son gave me the Holy Spirit. Only by way of the Holy Spirit can I communicate to the Father and the Son. You can talk to God all day long, but without the intervening power of the Holy Spirit, you will not get far at all. You are ignorant to biblical truth if you think you can. Jesus was clear that He would only communicate through the Spirit.

Knowing all of this, when I enter the presence of the Lord, it is by the power of the Holy Spirit. I wouldn't have a desire to go to the Father and Son if the Spirit wasn't pulling me in the first place. If you never feel a pull to go to the Lord in prayer, that should concern you.

When I reach Jesus, I understand that there are four persons communing together, but only two are visible to me. I know God the Father is the light all around us and the Holy Spirit is within me. I cannot see either of these persons, but I can feel both of them as strong as if I could. I can visually see Jesus in front of me, and I am very much aware of my own flesh standing there. Four persons, two of which are invisible and two of which are visible. All are active participants in the time that we share together as we commune. I stand there sometimes with my eyes closed, trying to soak up the magnitude of who is surrounding me. I stand willingly transparent of everything that I am made up of in front of God the Father, God the Son, and God the Holy Spirit. Sometimes it feels like I stand there forever. They know exactly what I am doing. I am in awe of Them and my understanding of Them. It's almost like I feel They are examining me, hoping that I will go deeper with Them in my comprehension and desires of my heart.

The Lord understands the limitations of my comprehension of Him. It pleases and honors Him that I sit there and look at Him in deep wonder of His majesty. It honors Him that I praise Him. It glorifies Him that I thank Him. I have a deep peace that it brings joy to Him. I stand there and look at Jesus, and He looks at me. I am in the presence of the living God. Sometimes I kneel right in front of His robe. I get so close that I can feel it brushing against my cheek. Sometimes I picture the Lord sitting. I sit beside Him and lay my head on His lap. He puts His hand on my head. He has nowhere to go. I have nowhere to go. We just sit there quietly in complete peace.

While I am standing, kneeling, or sitting with Jesus, the Holy Spirit is moving inside of me, confirming that I am exactly where I need to be. The Spirit of God joins with my spirit to affirm that I am His child. There is complete assurance of whom I belong to. I have full understanding of why I am there. The love and the warmth of beholding the Lord in prayer time is difficult to put into words. It just is. Now you know why it is so hard for me to leave Him when quiet time is over. An hour passes like a blink of an eye. I love being with my Lord, and He loves being with His child.

The Books

I want to attempt to write about the books in Heaven. I say attempt because I feel unqualified to try to explain them as well as someone with a theology degree would. The crowns of Heaven have always fascinated me. The books in Heaven do, as well. If I should ask the Christian, "How many books are in Heaven?" What would he or she say? Two, three, four, or more? Everyone typically recalls at least one: the Lamb's Book of Life. That's the one you hear the most about in church. According to what I understand from my reading the Word, I have found the Bible talks about five books in Heaven. Five? Yes. That surprised me, too. There is the Lamb's Book of Life, Book of Remembrance, Book of Tears, Book of Wars, and Book of Works or accounts.

Let's start with the book that we know best, The Lamb's Book of Life or The Book of the Living. This book holds every single name that has ever been born on Earth through every generation. Not one name has been left off. According to Psalm 139:16, the Book of Life also holds the number of days the Lord appointed for you before you were born. The Word tells us that the Book was written at the foundation of the world (Revelation 13:8; 17:8 all verses are NIV). Talk about the Lord's display of omniscience!

A person's name appears in it before they have chosen Jesus as their personal Savior because everyone that has been born has the ability to be saved and go to Heaven. Their name stays in it until which time they make a decision against the acceptance of Jesus Christ as their personal Savior. Once that happens, it is if the Lord takes white-out and "blots" the name out of the book. Those are His words, not mine. It will be like hitting the delete button on the computer. It just vanishes right off the page (Psalm 69:28; Exodus 32:33).

If a person's name is blotted out of this book by their own rejection of Christ, then the Bible foretells of their worship of a Beast in the end times. This is the one the Bible calls Anti-Christ (Revelation 13:8; 17:8). People can believe that the Anti-Christ is a mythical creature, but this will lead to their own demise. Daniel 12:1 says clearly that everyone whose name is found written in the Lamb's Book of Life will be rescued from this time of great distress upon the earth.

I do know a couple of people that I have witnessed to that have told me that they have made their final decision against accepting Christ. That makes me shudder in fear for them. They are blinded, yet they feel that I am the one that has been "brainwashed" by a manmade religion of myths.

Each person has his or her own free will to keep his or her name in this book or remove it. The Lord may be the one who blots the name out, but it is only by the person's choice to do so. Once you authentically accept Christ as your Savior, you are sealed by the power of the Holy Spirit (Ephesian 1:13). Your name cannot be blotted out of the Lamb's Book of Life. You may sin in the biggest way possible and backslide to the lowest point in your life, but your name will not be blotted out. That is comforting to know. This is not a free pass to sin all you want to. You are very ignorant if you think that. You don't lose your salvation when you sin; you lose blessings, closeness, and intimacy with the Lord. Once you repent of your sin, that closeness will be restored. Your name will always remain in the Lamb's Book of Life once you authentically accept Christ with a true conversion from an old creature to a new one.

In the end, the only names that will remain in the Lamb's Book of Life, which will be after Jesus' Millennium reign on Earth, are the people who made a personal and deep heartfelt choice to accept Christ as their Savior (Luke 10:20; Philippians 4:3; Revelation 3:5).

Malachi 3:16 tells us of another book. If I am right, I think this is the only place in the entire Bible that it is mentioned. It is a very special book to the heart of the Lord. It is called the Book of Remembrance. Malachi says that the Lord listens to believers talk about Him. He hears what we say. When we talk about the Lord with one another, we honor Him. The names of the believers who honored, respected, and thought about Him so much so that they talked about Him were written down in the Lord's presence. Wow!

I wonder how many times you or I have had wonderful conversations about the Lord with friends at home, at work, or at church. The Lord is having those words recorded in the Book of Remembrance. Why do you think He is writing them down when His memory is perfect? He doesn't have to write things down. I believe He is writing them down for us so that when we have our one-on-one at the Judgment Seat of Christ, He will read the Book of Remembrance to us. He will open it up and say, "Sarah, I bet you don't remember the conversation between you and Natasha back in October 2013 on the way back from Atlanta! Oh, you guys talked about Me for four hours, all the way back home. You girls honored Me that night with your words. I wrote the whole conversation down along with your names so that you would know how precious you two were to Me that day!"

I'm not sure how or when the Book of Remembrance will be used. I do know that it exists. The Lord listens and hears those children who speak about Him in reverence and honor. I do know our names and events are recorded in the Lord's presence. This is one of my favorite books in Heaven.

There is another book called the Book of Tears or, as some may say, the Book of Sorrows. You have probably read right over it and missed it every time. I know I have. I only just discovered the Book of Tears in my preparation for this journal. I kept cross-referencing books and literally stumbled across Psalm 56:8. It seems that David believed that the Lord kept a book of all, wanderings, misery, sorrow, or tears of His children. David said, "You keep track or account of my sorrows. Are they not in Your book?"

It doesn't matter what translation you read this verse in, it is clear that David is referencing a book that belongs to God. This started my mind spinning a thousand miles an hour. God tells us that He will wipe away every tear and sorrow. If that is true, then according to David, God would have a Book of Tears or an account of each of them. It is amazing that the Lord keeps a record of all of our sorrows and tears, but it makes sense to me.

There is a book that is never spoken of. In fact, I have never heard it preached at church. It is the Book of Wars. Numbers 21:14 references this book by name. The verse says, "That is why the Book of the Wars of the Lord says, 'Zahab in Suphah and the ravines, the Arnon.'" I do not feel qualified to speak more about this particular book, but I know that it is specifically referenced in the Bible. Maybe we should all ask our preachers to teach us more about it.

What happens to the people who do not accept Christ by the time they die? We already know that their names do not remain in the Lamb's Book of Life. They do remain in another book of Heaven. Their names will appear in the Book of Works or Book or Deeds (Revelation 20:12–13). This book is named appropriately as it contains names of unbelievers and their personal works or deeds while on Earth, both good and bad. This book will be opened at the Great White Throne Judgment. Only nonbelievers will be at this judgment. This is a very different judgment than the Christians will have at the Judgment Seat of Christ. This will be time that Jesus judges the nonbelievers according to their works. The nonbelievers have already rejected Jesus. They will have an eternal separation from Him for their decision. That was made clear when their name didn't appear in the Book of Life.

The Book of Works will determine how they will spend eternity in Hell. I have not completed an in-depth study of Hell to speak much more about this at this point. At this point, all I know is the nonbelievers will be judged according to their works. There are some really good nonbelievers that did a lot of good for others; then there are the "Hitlers." All nonbelievers will be in Hell, but I do not believe they will receive the same level of judgment, but each will exist there according to their works. Why else would God spend time going through each of their works at the time of Judgment if all of them received the same judgment? It wouldn't make sense.

The book has a record of the deeds of the unbelievers as a basis for their judgment. The Lord will make clear how they fall short of His glory. They will not be judged with mercy and grace. They will be judged justly in the sight of the Lord. Whatever they deserve or don't deserve will be given to them according to their works as nonbelievers. Heaven will not be accessible to them as they have to have their name in the Lamb's Book of Life before the Great White Throne Judgment takes place (Revelation 21:27).

There are no second chances for Heaven once you die (Hebrews 9:27). I have actually argued this point, believe it or not, with a fellow Christian! Her whole premise is that God is love and once those nonbelievers see Jesus in front of them they will believe. Well ... What this Christian is forgetting is that while God is love, He is just. People seem to overlook that little fact. He has told you what to do while you are on this Earth, and He will not accept you into Heaven because you chose to do it your way. That is not how it works. Come on!

Let's not be foolish and dumb down what God clearly states in His Word. If you leave this world without Jesus Christ, then you can't get Him when you see Him in Heaven (Revelation 20:15). Don't try to work God out in your head and life to make Him convenient for you. Big, big, big mistake! It is one that could have eternal consequences for you. All of the other books in Heaven seem to be meant for the believer, but the Book of Words or Deeds will be reserved only for the nonbeliever.

The study of the books in Heaven is absolutely fascinating to me. I am writing this journal for my boys. I want them to understand more of the deeper truths of the Word as a child than I did, so their foundation will be solid as they grow in the Lord. I want them to understand the importance and significance of each Book in Heaven.

World-Centered Thoughts

What is the significance of our thoughts? Why are they so strong? I have never thought so much about thoughts before this last couple of years of studying the Bible. With my ADHD brain, I typically have about twenty thoughts running at all times, or so it seems. I have come to realize that thoughts actually can be fatiguing after a while. My brain seems to yell, "Enough with the thoughts already! Geez! I'm smoking here!"

I think that my journals have been the perfect way to get my thoughts out of my poor mind, and somehow, that allows it to rest. If I didn't write all my thoughts down, they would continue to run around in my head until I did. It's not like I want to have all these thoughts; it just happens. Sometimes I think of things that I should not, and other thoughts are about the most meaningless bunch of nothings that I'm mad that I even wasted my time thinking about them. Other thoughts are self-defeating and only meant to keep my eyes on the temporal.

I can see the enemy trying to run with some of my thoughts in an attempt to divert my attention from the truth the Lord tells me or to prevent me from knowing the truth. How many times have I fallen for the enemy's lies? It surprises me every time, too, which shows that I do not learn very well from my past mistakes. That in itself also makes me mad at myself. The enemy is so skillful in wrapping a lie, but in the end it is no different than all the other lies he tells.

What is the significance of our thoughts? I read once, "As our thinking goes, so goes our entire being." That is simple but full of absolute truth. When our thoughts are on the Lord and on the world, we have a divided mind. David talks about his desire to have a "united heart." He is referring to having one mind or heart for the Lord. This is not innate. It has to be taught by the Lord and accomplished only through His strength and grace. The more we walk in the truth of the ways of the Lord, the more we fear His name. The more we fear His name, the more united our heart and minds are to have the mind of Christ.

The enemy is fully aware of how this works. That is why he seeks to engage the believer's thought life. Once he loses a believer's divided mind, then he has lost the ability to suppress him or her. That believer wakes up and understands more of what Christ expects of a mind like His. Until a believer has Christ-centered thoughts, he or she will have world-centered thoughts and behaviors. It doesn't matter how strong of a Christian you are and how long you have been a Christian; if your thoughts are not kept captive by the guard of the Holy Spirit, you will think and act like the world.

I do not believe that Christians fully understand the power of their own thoughts. They can actually limit the work of the Most High God in their lives. You can only focus on one thing at a time. Multitasking is a lie; it is really how fast you switch between the tasks. I think thoughts are the same way. You can only think of one thing at a time.

I think that as Christians, we switch between Christ-centered thoughts and worldly thoughts. I think we convince ourselves that we do well with the balance. I think that is where my mistake has been in my own walk. I do not want to switch between these as I have in the past. I want to have a Christ-like mind with His thoughts. His thoughts never oscillate away from Him. Neither should mine. That is the sole reason I have found myself in sin.

If I would not have switched toward worldly thoughts and actions, the pain and grief I could have saved myself would be immeasurable. The second we switch our thoughts from the Most High God, they will focus on something the enemy wants us to think about. If he has my thoughts, then eventually he will have my actions, too. It may take a while, but it will happen.

It is a fact that your actions follow your thoughts. That is why the Holy Spirit starts convicting you at the thought level. He knows how dangerous it is if you don't get a hold of your thought life. All sin starts with your thoughts. All depression starts with your thoughts. All defeat starts with your thoughts. Do you know that not only does the enemy tell us lies, but we will tell ourselves lies as well? Shocking, I know. "I wasn't meant to be happy." "There must be something wrong with me." "If I only had her life or her opportunities, then it would be better." "I cannot do anything right no matter how hard I try." "Nothing good happens for me." "If only I could be more like him or her then I would be okay." "What did I do to make this bad stuff happen?" "Other people catch all the breaks."

These self-defeating thoughts or negative self-talk are toxic to the Christ-like mind of a believer. You might as well be drinking poison in a cup with a straw in it! Where do these thoughts lead? Joy, contentment, peace, and hope? No, those would be the thoughts of a Christ-like mind. Self-defeating thoughts lead to mental defeat, sadness, loneliness, and depression. This would be an enemy-like mind! Whether you buy the enemy's lies or your own, the same results will happen.

Why are thoughts so strong? I believe it is the gift of free will. I can choose to have the strongest thoughts for Christ, and my actions will be evidence for it. I can have that same strength of thoughts for the temporal world, what I want, and how I want things to be, and my actions will also be evidence of that. God built in us the ability to have strong thoughts because he knew we would need them to guide our actions.

Think about your thoughts being like your car steering wheel and your actions being like the car. That little steering wheel guides the entire vehicle. A couple of turns here or there and you have arrived. That car can go nowhere unless that steering wheel guides it. That is exactly like our thoughts. Our thoughts steer our actions. The question is who has more control of that steering wheel? Your thoughts? The enemy's thoughts? God's thoughts?

Lost And Found

Please read 2 Kings 22.

Josiah was a king of Israel. His grandfather, Manasseh, was a very evil, cruel, and depraved king who lived for self. He did not follow the Lord until his late years, but by that time, so much damage had been done to his kingdom that he was useless to amend things. Josiah's father was also an evil king. Josiah had been counseled by Manasseh and didn't want to go down the same path as his grandfather and father. He wanted to be godly. He wanted to be righteous in the eyes of the Lord. Manasseh also encouraged the young king to live for the Lord all the days of his life. Therein lies true blessings for not only himself, but also all of Israel. Josiah led the country in a godly way and ordered the temple to be cleansed.

While the Temple priests were cleaning and repairing the Temple, they found the Book of the Law! The priest even proclaimed, "I have found the Book of the Lord in the house of the Lord." Josiah ordered the book to be read to the people. There was a great repentance that came over everyone that heard the words of the Book. King Josiah cleaned all of Israel from every detestable idol. The king and the people were of like mind and sorrowful for their ways.

I have heard this Bible story so many times, but it never loses significance to me. First, you have Manasseh. He lived for himself. His priorities were always for his benefit and no other. They were not for his family, not his friends, not his country, and certainly not God. There was no room for God in Manasseh's life. Like so many who finally wake up from their own slumber, Manasseh woke up from his. He had so many regrets and consequences for how he lived.

Even though he had turned to God, the damage in his life was done. The damage in our lives that can happen by our delay of finding the Word of the Lord still stands true for us today. God forgives us and accepts us when we wake up from our slumber, but some of the things we did while we were slumbering may have long-lasting consequences in our life, lasting a lot longer than we thought. Some of us have to deal with things for years and years, even after we get our life back on track with the Lord, just like Manasseh. We may not be evil like him, but we have all slumbered. We have all had problems with prioritizing God in our lives. I have found God doesn't get put on the list sometimes. This should not be.

Josiah was an amazing person to read about. He knew at a young age that he needed to put God first. He never wavered once throughout his entire life. He was rewarded for this. God protected Israel from enemy attack all the days of Josiah's rule. God greatly rewards those who put Him first. I also think that God will protect us from our enemies the way He did Josiah.

What amazes me most about this story is where the Book of the Law was found. The priest said he found it in, "the House of the Lord." The Holy Scriptures were lost in the church? Yes. Think about the irony in that. In the one place that they should have been the safest, they had been lost. How does that happen? I have to ask myself if they were ever really lost. I don't think they were. No one had searched for them to read them. They had been sitting in the house of the Lord for all that time. No one desired to know what the Lord had said. The saddest part is they had not missed the Word of the Lord in their lives.

Do you know that Christians are called temples of God? Why? The Holy Spirit resides in us. That is incomprehensible. I am the temple of the Most High God. I am supposed to hide the Word of the Lord in my heart. For so many years of my life, I had not opened the Word to really study it like I should have. I never was wholly committed to daily Bible study. I thought what I got on Sunday morning was plenty. I have to confess the Word of the Lord had been lost in the temple of God that I call my life. Just like the Israelites, I didn't go search it out for myself. I didn't miss reading it once, from the time I closed it on Sunday morning, until I opened it again the next Sunday. This was when the preacher told me what to read.

Is it not true that as Christians we have lost the Word of the Lord in our own temple, just like in Josiah's day? The repentance in front of the Father for this should be great, just as it was for these ancient worshipers.

The Word of the Lord is alive. Our very spiritual life comes from the Word. God speaks to us through it. When we don't prioritize it in our life, we are spiritually stagnating, starving, and dying. We do not desire to hear the Lord's voice, yet we say with our mouth that we do. Our actions say something totally different. In the past, I will confess my priorities for the studying of the Word of God have not been right. Have I been a Christian the whole time this has happened? Yes, just like the Israelites were children of God when they lost their Scriptures. That doesn't mean that I grew the way the Lord would have intended. I certainly didn't hear the voice of the Lord.

Praise the Lord that the Word of the Lord has been found in my life. The journals that I have written are a testimony to that truth. The Lord continues to speak daily through His Word. Now, I can't imagine not reading it. It is truly alive. If the Word of the Lord has been lost in your own temple, go find it. Repent. Rejoice for the Word of the Lord has been found! Allow it to be alive in your own life, and never lose it again!

Pass Me Not

I recently found an old hymn called "Pass Me Not, O Gentle Savior." Until a few months ago, I had never heard of it. The famed songwriter Fanny Crosby talks about her understanding of the Lord looking over others, calling them to His side, and then smiling over those that accepted His call. There are those who are in disbelief, having wounded and broken spirits. They are in need of the Gentle Savior's mercy and the sweet relief it provides for the soul. A humble cry goes up to the Lord's throne, asking the Lord not to pass him by. He understands that the Lord is the source of all his comfort, and there is more life with Jesus than without Him.

I have listened to this song many times and meditated on its meaning. My mind keeps going back to the Book of Life that the Lord talks about. Do you know that every single person's name that has ever been born is in the Book of Life? That is how it got its title. The Lord places every name in this book for the sole purpose that not one will be passed by. His desire is that everyone recorded will spend eternity with Him. He died for every one of those names. Sadly, many names have been blotted out one-by-one through time. Those names that have made their own decisions to follow another way disappear from the Book of Life. This does not happen by the Lord's desires, but by those people who have made choices to follow another belief or no belief.

There are those people who are Christians in name only, but they do not share a personal relationship with Jesus Christ. This is a very dangerous place to be. They are the ones that will call, "Lord, Lord! Didn't we do all these things in Your name?" They are the ones that when the Lord searches for names in His book, their names will not be found. He will say, "You did it in My name. You had a mental knowledge of My name, but you never really knew it in your hearts."

I believe that many good people's names will not be found in the Book of Life when it is opened. If you could be good enough to keep your name in that book, then Jesus Christ didn't have to die. Only by your acceptance of His mercy and grace can your name remain in the Book of Life. It is only by this deep acceptance of Him that you will not pass the Lord by. He will never pass you by. This is an important truth to understand. You are the only one that does the passing.

In reality, the Lord is standing in front of everyone on Earth saying

> Please, do not pass Me by. Come to My throne of mercy. Find a sweet relief. I am Your Savior. If you kneel in your sin, I will hear your humble cry. I have called on many others to come, but now I am calling to you. Do not pass Me by.

Millions upon millions of people have looked right at Him and passed right by. As soon as they do, their names disappear from the Book of Life as they have chosen death. I pray that you will not pass the Lord by. Please, don't let it be you.

When we accept Jesus' invitation to be called a Child of God, we have come to the recognition of who He is. We are cleansed from our sin, and our names remain in the Lamb's Book of Life. The ink is permanent. Praise God! For some Christians, they always abide right by the Lamb, the Lion of Judah. They never pass by Him again.

Other Christians start to slumber a bit in their walk with the Lord. It is never purposeful, but nonetheless, they become inactive and neglect the will of God in their lives. They get busy. They stop listening for the voice of God. They get too comfortable where they are. Their priorities do not include an active prayer life and studying the Word of God daily. They get a little worldly, seeking self-will. They start compromising and justifying. They may or may not be sinning in this state of slumber, but they most certainly are not abiding closely with Jesus daily. They are not growing in the deeper truths of God. It can happen so easily. They justify that church is enough Jesus for them.

If you do any of these things, then you are slumbering. You are passing the Lord by in your life and missing His sweet fellowship. It happened to me for years. I have come to the realization that even though I did not pass by the Gentle Savior the first time He called me, which secured my eternal destiny, I passed by Him for years afterward from my daily destiny. He doesn't want you to pass Him by before or after you become His child. The Savior is standing there every day of your life as He watches you whirl around all day and whispers, "Slow down, Child. I am right here. Pass Me not."

Oftentimes, Christians act like the nonbelievers. We look right in the Lord's face and keep walking. Sometimes He never crosses our mind in a day. We justify that we will make time for Him later when we are finished with our other priorities. Remember, the Lord will never pass us by. Even as Christians, we are the ones who do the passing.

Duct Taped

He is before all things, and in Him all things hold together. (Colossians 1:17 NIV)

I was at the kitchen table the other night. The boys' books were all over the table. We were getting ready to eat supper. I picked up Andrew's history book off the corner of the table to move it. It looked horrible! There was thick, bright, yellow duct tape going down the binder. I opened it up and the tape was inside both front and back covers. I said, "Son! What in the world happened to your book?" He said, "It got stuck in my locker and the cover was torn off when I pulled it out. My teacher taped it. She said that without the cover to protect the inside, it would start falling apart."

Immediately the Spirit impressed upon me, "I have you covered." Just like so many other common things the Lord uses to teach me, I was in amazement that he would use my son's torn-up history book. So I said, "You have me covered, Lord! Thank you!" I started thinking of my life like that book. It is sort of like a history book. There are so many chapters of my life as I continue to walk through my mind. Each chapter is full of my history. It is composed of so many stories and memories.

Some chapters are full of big mistakes and regrets. Some tells of heartaches. There are those that I would like to read over and over. There are some chapters I never want to read again. I think of those times that I found myself in situations that were tearing my cover off, typically, by my own poor choices. I have felt like I was being torn apart before. Some of my pages were getting loose and were trying to fall out. I felt like I was losing a part of myself.

The Lord, in His grace, got His yellow duct tape and taped the binder of my life back together so many times. He held me together when I couldn't hold myself. He covered me, and every page of my life was protected. You would think He would allow the bad chapters to fall out, but He knows that I need them. He knows that I turned back to Him in repentance from the events that were recorded. I needed to remember those times. It's part of my history book and shaped me into the person I am today. The Lord saw to it that He was there for every page written, both good and bad. Even though some pages may not have made Him a priority, He was faithful to me. He has always covered me.

The book of my life may not look so good at times. It has been caught in the locker doors of the world more than once. I'm the first one to admit that I have duct tape down my spine! It may look worse than Andrew's history book. That is okay. I know without a shadow of a doubt that He holds my tattered and taped book in His hands. He knows what is written on all my pages. I want my life to be ready when He chooses to either read a chapter or write a new one. The Lord will always protect my book because it is open to Him. I know where to get duct tape if I need more! It's a comfort to know that I will always be covered and held together by the Lord.

Unseen Glory

So that the name of our Lord Jesus will be glorified by you, and you by Him, according to the grace of our God and The Lord Jesus Christ. (2 Thessalonians 1:12 HCSB)

I have had a strong image in my mind for a while now. I have not written about it previously, but this morning I had it again. I am standing in front of the throne of God. It is high and lifted up. It seems so much larger in proportion to me, but it feels intimate. It feels like there is an enormous expanse around me, yet I feel safe and warm in it. I feel tightly held. I am full of the sweetest peace and contentment that I can't begin to describe. It feels like I have been standing in silence for a long period of time. I know that I have not just arrived, but everything is fresh like I just got there.

When I look up to the throne, I can't make out a figure that I recognize, but there is Someone on the throne and something is flowing out all around the throne, almost like it is spilling over the throne. Nothing is big enough to contain what is on the throne. The Presence on the throne fills every part of the space around me. That is what is holding me. It is like it is literally holding me up as I would not be able to stand otherwise.

I picture my arms lifted with my hands open toward the throne. I see myself cupping my hands out in front of me almost like I am trying to fill them with water to drink. I then take my handful filled with the unseen and slowly pour it over my face. I put my hands out again and cup them in front of the throne. I hold them there for a second like I am filling them up again then I empty the handful of the unseen over my head. I keep standing completely still in the front of the throne and filling my hands up with the unseen and emptying it over my head. Over and over I refill and empty, refill and empty. There is stillness, peace, and love as I continue to refill and empty handfuls of the unseen over me.

I have an awareness that I am in front of the Father and that there is complete silence around me. There is no music sung and no words spoken. There is no need for them. I know that everything is very bright and open. I know that I am in a big space.

Up to this morning, I had no idea what I was filling my hands with. There was nothing in them that I can see. This morning in prayer time, I had the image again. I asked the Lord, "I see myself clearly. You know what image is in my head right now. I do not understand what I am doing. Why do I keep reaching out toward the throne and filling my hands with the unseen and then emptying them on my face and head?" He said quietly, "I am sharing My glory with you. You are holding your hands out because the glory of the Lord is round about you and all of My children. That is the way your soul has chosen to collect it and pour it over you. You are like a little child collecting raindrops in your hands as you look up at the sky. This time, though, you are looking up to the throne of the Most High God and collecting My glory that I have chosen to share with you."

Immediately tears started falling as the Spirit spoke these words to my spirit. How could He share His glory with me? As I write this, my tears that come from the realization of the Most High God in my life, His tenderness and closeness keep me in a state of awe. When I think of the enormity of God that He shares His glory with me, it is incomprehensible to me. I am learning that He wants to give me all the love, all the peace, all the contentment, and all the glory that I can hold in my hands. He wants me to empty as many handfuls over my face, my head, my heart, and my soul as I possibly can.

The source is eternal, so there will always be enough to take as much as I can hold. There is never a reason to be empty. Today, the glory that I am filling my hands with is unseen, yet I know it is there. One day I will see it for myself. We will all see it. The Lord promised in Isaiah 40:5, "The glory of the Lord will be revealed, and all people will see it together. For the mouth of the Lord has spoken" (NIV). I can't wait to fill my hands with the seen instead of the unseen glory of the Lord.

The most amazing part of the image is that I started doing this same motion of putting my hands out in prayer time. I allow my hands to be filled with the unseen then I pour it over my face. I put my hands out again and allow more of the unseen to fill them, then slowly empty it over my head to get every drop of His glory. The exact same peace, love, and contentment that I felt in my image is what I felt when I did the same motions in my quiet time. Amazing. As I held my hands out to collect the unseen glory, I sang, "Spirit of the Living God. Fall fresh on me. Cleanse me. Hold Me. Fill me. Use me. Spirit of the Living God. Fall fresh on me."

Lord, I'm Coming Home

They will not be punished for any of their sins. They now do what is right and fair, so they will surely live. (Ezekiel 33:16 NCV)

I visited my mom's church on Sunday. We go to different churches, but Sunday was a special day. I wanted to be with her. The preacher said that that the music director had chosen an old song to sing for the closing. "Lord, I'm Coming Home" was sung. I know I have heard this song before, but it has been so many years that I have forgotten the lyrics. The church started singing it so sweetly, and tears filled my eyes as the Spirit spoke to my spirit.

I never knew this song was about a Christian sinner coming home to the Lord. It talks about wandering far away from God as many paths of sin had been tried. There were many wasted precious years filled with bitter tears of repent. There was tiredness to sin and straying from the Lord.

At some point in the sin, there was recognition and renewed strength in the knowledge and hope of coming home to the Lord. There was a need to have His cleansing blood wash their heart and soul whiter than snow again.

When the Christians are coming home, they are tired and weary. Their souls are sick. Their hearts are sore. I have been in sin and far away from home many times. I never could put into words how I felt when I recognized my own sin and how far I had traveled from holiness. This song says it perfectly. My soul felt sick and my heart was sore. As I turned back toward the throne, I felt like somehow I was walking back on crutches and bandaged up. I was hobbling and falling down in my weakness of spending too much time in the world. In the past, I have allowed the world, by my own willingness, to take some of my integrity, focus on the Lord's will, and purity of thought and actions away. That makes my soul sick and my heart sore to think about now. I have learned that sin always takes the most sacred places of my soul and heart and only hands me back emptiness. I have made this trade over and over again. That makes a soul weary and a heart broken.

The song goes on to tell the Lord, "I'm coming home. No more to roam. Open wide Your arms of love. Lord, I'm coming home." Maybe this was the song the prodigal son was singing as he slowly made it up the walkway as his father had his arms opened wide running to him. I think as Christians, we get so beaten up by this world. If we just turned back toward home, the Lord will run to us and carry us the rest of the way home. He is just so glad that we are in His forgiving arms again. He immediately forgets where we have been and how far we have roamed. There is no condemnation there.

I know when I have come home to the Lord there has been great celebration and lessons learned from my roaming. He could have been so much harder on me than He has been in the past. I think if you ever want to see the most loving side of the Lord, go home to Him in repentance. The sweetness of His embrace makes it really hard to leave Him to roam again. The sins that caught my attention before do not have a pull on my thoughts and actions now. I'm not willing to trade home for emptiness again. Staying at home with my Lord is better than any shack this world tries to sell me. I just hate it took me all these years to learn that truth.

Go home, Christian. Go home with your crutches, your sick heart, and your sore soul. I promise He will meet you before you get all the way home. When you see a figure running full speed toward you, it will be your Lord. With His arms opened wide, embrace His forgiveness. Praise God! We can always go home no matter our sins. He loves us so much. Go home, rest, and get loved on. It does wonders for the heart and soul.

Searching, Knowing, and Trying

Search me, O God, and know my heart; try me, and know my thoughts. And see if there is any wicked way in me. Lead me in the way everlasting. (Psalm 139:23–24 KJV).

When I stand in front of a Holy God and I say, "Search me," what I am really saying is, "Lord, take Your time and very carefully examine me to find anything in my heart that does not bring You glory and can harm our close relationship. I may have something concealed from You that, as You explore my heart, You will discover. Uncover any wickedness by piercing, penetrating, and scrutinizing my heart. Leave no stone unturned until You find what is concealed. When I say, "Try me," what I am really saying is, "Lord, You are making a great effort to accomplish a great work in me. That always starts with my thoughts. Test them in order to determine their strength, effect, worth, and desirability. If that is by means of strain or stress, then do it. You have the right to open up my thoughts in order to find out whether I have locked any away from You for my own selfish reasons. I want You to determine the truth of my thoughts and pass judgment, if necessary, so that I may stand transparent in Your presence."

The Lord has taught me so much from different parts of this verse. It's truly amazing how He continues to show me freshness over and over with the same words. The verse never changes, but depending on what the Lord is teaching me, different words just leap off the page of the Bible as if to say, "Pay attention to me today!"

One morning in quiet time, I was saying Psalm 139 as a confessional verse. The Lord again magnified the words *search* and *try*. He whispered, "I am an active God in your life. I am always doing something. I never rest. I will do the searching, and I will do the trying. Your job is to let

Me!" Tears filled my eyes while I apologized for all the times I have not let Him. I had things I needed to hide because of my own desires to fill my heart and thoughts with what I wanted. It is difficult to stand transparent in front of a Holy God as He searches and tries me. The alternative will rob me from a close relationship from someone who loved me so much that He gave His own life for the right to do what He is asking.

Why aren't "know my heart" and "know my thoughts." the simplest things for God to ask for? "Let me know what's in your heart. What are you thinking?" These are clear and straightforward requests. Why do I feel sometimes that what I feel and think belong to me more than they belong to God? It's my heart. They are my thoughts. I guess that may be human nature of self that just jumps up and says, "They are mine. I can do as I wish. I can feel what I want and think what I want." God must be saying, "You most certainly can! That's called free choice. The question you need to ask yourself is, 'Is your mind and heart going to choose self or Me?'"

Every time I sin, I choose my will over the Holy God's. It sounds insane and illogical when I put it into words that way. Who am I to think I am right? It definitely defines my choices clearly. I should never deceive myself. My eyes should be wide open when I sin or move away from the Lord. I should never lie to myself about what is really happening when I sin. I should never minimize it, "Oh, I only did that; I didn't hurt anyone." God is looking down at me and saying, "You hurt Me, and you hurt yourself. You are just too far away from Me to feel it."

God wants to know my heart and my thoughts because He fully understands how He created them. My heart and mind are who I am. It's through them that I know God. What is in them is how I am and what I can become, either by my own will or by God's will. If these two things do not stay in check, they will affect my relationship with a Holy God. It's so important that my heart and mind are in one accord with His heart and mind.

I can't get past the part of the phrase, "wickedness in me." Wickedness is not far off. It is not even something that I have to go far to find. I don't have to search hard for it. Every time I put myself above God, the wicked way in me has been found in my heart and thoughts. Every time I say, "No, Lord, I want it my way" the wicked way has been found. When I have time for the futile things in this world that gives me temporal satisfaction in exchange for God's eternal will, the wicked way has been found in me.

Sadly, I understand that sometimes the wicked way is easier and more satisfying than God's way. When God says, "Stop doing that" or "Spend more time with Me instead of this world," and I don't, then I choose the wicked way. Make no mistake, the wicked way doesn't choose me, I choose it. The other thing is when I do choose the wicked way, I then justify it, which in my mind makes it all the more wicked. I continually strive to stand in front of a Holy God with transparency, asking Him to know my heart and try my thoughts. I hope that I can be strong enough in Him not to choose the wicked way, which in the end is choosing my will over His.

As I am increasing my understanding of the heart and whether it can be the source of my integrity or a source of my own weakness, Psalm 139 solidifies for me. Integrity comes from the inside. If God is on the throne of my heart, integrity is high and the spirit of truth flows easily. Decisions are better because of my obedience to the knowledge God has given me. This wisdom is promised because of my integrity. If integrity comes from the inside, then wickedness and evil come from the inside as well (Mark 7:20–23 NIV).

There is only one heart. It is the source of either one. If wickedness is in my heart, then self is on the throne. A spirit of deception settles and whispers, "What I want is what I should have no matter whether God says differently."

As my desires are met, it is harder and harder to move self off the throne. I believe Christians have been somewhat deceived on what degree Satan plays a part in this process. No doubt the spirit of deception is present, but let's never forget that every sin is volitional. I think we let ourselves off the hook a little too easily. We want to blame everybody and Satan, but we never want to take the blame. If the Lord whispers to you or me to spend more time with Him, and we don't, that's a pretty good indicator of who is on the throne of our hearts. If the Holy Spirit convicts us of something in our life that needs to change and we say "Not now" or "No," then that is another clear indicator of who is on the throne of our life. It's really simple, but Christians complicate everything. It's God or self. If you haven't tried to move self off of the throne in a while, it will be pretty hard. Today is as good as any day to recognize that self needs to move.

The Lord continued to reveal one last part of this verse to me. He showed me that He is an active God by searching my heart and knowing or trying my thoughts. I heard clearly that my job is to be transparent in His presence and allow the searching and trying. The Lord showed me that wickedness is not far from me, yet in me. Wickedness is always a choice away. Unfortunately, it is easily accessible as well. This knowledge should give me a healthy fear of this accessible wickedness that can have an immediate effect on my relationships with a Holy God, friends, and family.

Now, the last lesson the Lord wants me to know is He is doing all of this for a purpose. It is a time of preparation to meet Him where He dwells, which is in the everlasting. I cannot get there on my own, so after He searches my heart, tries my thoughts, and looks to see if there is any wickedness in me, only then will He finally lead me to where He is. *If I have allowed Him to lead me by being willing and transparent, then in the end, I have become more like Him along the way.* All of this is for my preparation for the everlasting. He expects me to be holy as He is holy. What excuse do you or I have not to be holy when He has instructed us so clearly?

You Are Beautiful

The Lord does not look at the things people look at. People look at the outward appearance, but the Lord looks at the heart. (1 Samuel 16:7 NIV)

Do you know that most people do not feel beautiful or handsome? They listen to feelings instead of Truth. In school or college, I never "felt" I was physically beautiful. I really did not feel beautiful even as a young adult. I looked at the world's standards of beauty, and I never seemed to measure up in appearance or talent. How I wish I knew 1 Samuel 16:7. If I would have been more diligent in the Word, I would have. I would have had the right perspectives.

I know now that I looked at the things that people looked at. I looked at outward appearance of others and myself. At the place I am now in my Christian walk with the Lord, I look back on all those wasted years of lost perspective. I will never get those years back. It makes my heart sick to know that I so easily adopted the world's meaningless standards of beauty. I see youth today doing the same things.

The Lord sees who I am. He only looks at my heart. He thinks I am beautiful and perfect. He sees His holiness in me. The Lord thinks as long as my heart beats for Him, I am beautiful. If I could relate how the Lord sees me, a few things come to my mind to put beauty in the right perspective. He sees me the way my mama and daddy saw me for the first time. This is the way they still see me. Since the first time they saw me until this day, I have been beautiful to them. My beauty never changes in their sight, no matter what I look like on the outside. The Lord sees me as my loving husband saw me when I walked down the aisle in the purest white gown to share a new life with him. I was the radiant bride walking to meet my bridegroom.

Jesus reminds me that I am His bride every day. When I come to the Lord in our quiet time, it is like I am walking down that aisle all over again, but this time it is to a throne of God. The Lord sees me as my little boys saw me when I rocked them to sleep at night and stroked their heads. They lay their heads on my chest and heard my heart beating for them. It was the perfect rhythm to calm them. I have an image of me and the Lord rocking. When I lay my head on His chest, I can hear His heart. I look up at Him and He smiles. I love His rhythm. He says, "You are so beautiful to Me, because I know your heart is only for Me. Lay your head back down, and listen to My heart beat for you, My child."

I can let this world lull me into a slumber, buy its lies about me, and steal my happiness only to leave me empty. I can be told that I am insignificant and not up to its standard. That is a choice, one that I have chosen too many times. I am awake now. I choose to lay my head on the Lord's chest. I listen as His heart beats in rhythm with my heart. With every thump, He is reaffirming to me, "You are mine! I can't tell you enough how much I love and long for you to stay with Me. I will never take My eyes off of you. You are breathtakingly beautiful to Me."

I don't know about you, but I would rather listen to the Lord's truth about my heart, instead of the world's or even my own lies about my appearance. First Peter 3:3–5 says it perfectly, "Beauty should come from your inner self, the unfading beauty of a gentle and quiet spirit, which is of great worth in God's sight" (NIV). Putting your hope in God is what makes you beautiful.

Simple Truth

Be diligent to present yourself approved to God as a workman who does not need to be ashamed, handling accurately the word of truth. (2 Timothy 2:15 NASB)

I am concluding that people are hungry for the simple truth of Christ. People do not want or need a fancy message. They love to be reminded of Jesus' love for them. They love to think about being with Him in His glory. They love relating to Him in a new way. They long to understand Him more deeply and more personally. They love to be reminded of the home He has created out of His love for them. They never get tired of hearing the old, old story of Jesus and His love.

I think a lot of Christians know this world dulls them, and they seek to become sharper, but sometimes they don't know exactly how to do that. The truths that Christians are seeking are so simple. Why do we move so far away from the simple things of Christ to the complex things of the world? Why do Christians get trapped in the snares that take them away from the simple truths of Christ? The Lord presented simple truth to us. We should share it with others.

The simple truth is that Christians turn their heads too quickly toward the world. They should keep their heads straight and walk down the narrow path with the Lord. They should be set aside from the things of the world. The truth is, they are so weak in their walk that all the world has to do is whistle to get their attention. They are easily led astray by their own fleshly desires and weakness of not being with the Father. The Spirit within them is willing, but the flesh is more driven to fulfill its own will than to seek holiness.

The simple truth is, some Christians have justified that they have just enough Jesus to be okay. They are foolish. You cannot have just enough Jesus like you have just enough to drink in your glass. Jesus says, "I will overflow you when you are in Me." Just enough Jesus and overflowing Jesus are not the same amounts. Just like a stagnating Christian life is not the same as life of vitality in Christ. The simple truth is that we are easily distracted from the Lord by our own lack of discipline.

The simple truth is that the Lord wants a Christian to lead a life of holiness. He wants the highest integrity that you possess. He does not accept your justifications that you sell yourself when you compromise with what He has told you is needed of your life. You buy these sorry excuses, but a Holy God does not. We have watered down a just and holy God to a withdrawn, sweet, elderly grandfather figure sitting in an overly cushioned throne in the clouds. Some Christians are sorely mistaken in their mental image of God. While He is the Ancient of Days, there is no comprehension by the human mind of His power. God doesn't fit in some jar on the shelf of your life for you to pull off when you need Him. You always need Him. God doesn't fit in your life! He is too great. You fit in His. Straighten up this simple truth in your mind and reprioritize your life.

The simple truth is that He has told His children to lead a quiet life. Your house may be full of children, work, and play, but it had better be quiet in the Lord. Do you know how to have a quiet life? Recognize sin and turn from it every time. Maintain a clear conscience. Obey the knowledge of what you know from spending consistent quiet time with the Lord through prayer and studying of His Word. Practice wisdom.

The more you pray and the more you personally study His Word, the quieter your life becomes. It's a mystery how this happens, but I can testify that it is true. The world around you quiets down more and more as you focus on the things of the Lord. Your perspective shifts, and things will be much clearer as you move through your day. Turn the noise of your life down in your heart. Do not miss quiet time with your Lord. You need it way more than He does. The simple truth is you are not doing Him a favor by spending time with Him; you are doing yourself one.

The simple truth is we have a river of life flowing out of us. It allows the lame to walk and the blind to see. It opens prison doors and lets the captive free. We've got a river of life flowing out of us. The well within our souls spring up from the Holy Spirit. It makes us whole. The waters that come from this well give us life abundantly. This holy well gives us the simple truth of who we really are in Christ. Christians limit their thinking of who they belong to and which river they are traveling down.

The simple truth is the day you accepted Christ, the Spirit of the living God started flowing in your soul and heart. We have built dams in our minds and hearts to guide the river where we want it to flow. No, Christian! That is not how it works. That will only create erosion in your life. The river that flows in us has a specific path that has been laid out by the same Designer that spoke this entire universe into existence. You can't control a mighty river like that; that is why you keep failing.

You are a part of the river. You are not the river. You don't control the river. The river controls you. You just lay on your back with your arms spread wide and float. The river will take you around every bend and through every rapid safely to calm waters ahead. The simple truth is the river leads to the throne of the Most High God. Stop going against it.

The simple truth is Christians limit the power of God in their life. We confess it with our lips, but we deny it with our actions. We don't understand how to harness it, so we ignore it or minimize it. How very foolish of us. Do you want the power of your God in your life? Bring everything in your heart and mind before His throne high and lifted up every day. Be transparent. Ask Him to search and try you. Ask Him for deeper understanding of how you fit in His will and not how He fits in yours. Ask Him to share His glory with you. Lift your hands up high in the presence of the Living God.

The simple truth is you need to be still and know the power of God in you. If you earnestly seek His power, He desires for you to see it in your life. He has made you so strong, yet when you use your strength; it only leads to great fatigue. We forget that we have to stay plugged into the Power Source of our strength in the first place. Our strength comes from His power in our lives. The simple truth is, most of the time, we are never plugged into the Lord to see His power, or we are too impatient to wait on Him to reveal it.

The simple truth is Jesus Christ loves every part of your heart, mind, and soul. He desires you to be close to Him. He sees His shed blood that covers you, and He sees His broken body that was sacrificed for you. The simple truth is Jesus Christ has done all of this so you could be with Him. He desires for you to be with Him so He can share His glory with you.

Jesus has prepared a mansion for each one of us. We will sit by His throne, walk with Him, talk with him, and He will love on us for eternity. As Christians, let us understand these simple truths. Let us be mindful that people and things can come into our lives to complicate the simple truths of the Lord. Finally, He wants each of His children to tell others about His simple truths as well.

Location and Volume

The Lord uses the most everyday objects to teach me His truth in such a down to earth way that it continues to keep me in a state of awe. I always have my phone with me in quiet time—not to text or play games, but to softly listen to my worship music. This morning, I was lying on my couch, which is where I have my quiet time. I was in praise time at the beginning of my prayer. I do not typically lay the phone up by my ear but rather to my side. Today, I laid it on my right shoulder. I was listening and praising the Lord like I do every day.

Even though the volume was on the last notch before mute, I could hear the music loud and clear because it was so close to my ear. After I while, I picked the phone up and moved it to my side. Immediately, the difference in volume from just my shoulder to my side was pretty dramatic. I picked the phone back up and put it on my shoulder again—loud and clear. Then I put it back by my side. I was fascinated at how much of a difference the volume went down at just an arm's length away from my ear.

Immediately, the Spirit started teaching me. I started thinking, if I put my phone at the same volume at the other end of the couch, how much would I hear? So I did. I had to be really still and concentrate to hear it, but I could. The words were much more difficult to make out. In fact, I really couldn't make out all of them. I was stunned. The ability to hear was greatly affected.

I thought to myself, what if I just moved my phone to the other side of the room? So I did. I could barely hear the music, and the words sounded like mumbling. I thought what if I moved it to just on the outside the room? I didn't really do that one, but I know what would have happened if I did, and so do you. I wouldn't be able to hear the music or the words. In my little experiment, the volume never changed, only the location of the device that was producing the volume was changed. It was amazing how it didn't take very much distance to dramatically affect the volume.

If we think of God speaking either in His Word or by His Spirit to us, we can conclude His speaking produces volume. The Bible uses "The voice of the Lord" over fifty times. "Hear the word of the Lord" is found twenty-four times. It would not be an external volume like my phone playing music, but it would be an internal volume. Sometimes, I have found that the internal voice of the Lord within me is so strong and clear at times that I would swear I heard it audibly. Knowing all this, I think the Spirit was teaching me a lesson this morning about location and volume.

If I have the Word of God and the Spirit lying close to my heart's ear, then I will hear the voice of God even when it is on the notch before mute. It will be loud and clear and be at the perfect volume for me to hear perfectly. If I move my location from the One producing the volume, even by one arm's length, I have decreased the amount of clarity of His words. If I moved away from the Lord by just eight feet or even across the room, I have significantly compromised the amount of detailed message I can hear. If I step just outside the door of Christ, so I can be in another room from Him, I can't hear Him at all.

Is He still talking? Sure. Just like my phone is still playing music, I just can't hear it. Interesting. I have justified that I can control the location, and He should speak up louder if He had something to say.

I have now come to believe that the Lord God has one volume. He sets it. He says, "If you want to hear what I have to say in your life, you better keep me right by the ear of your heart. I will never speak up, and I will never move. You are the one who moves your location, and you are the one that affects the volume of My voice, not Me. If you think you can be even an arm's length from Me and still hear Me clearly, you are very foolish.

If you wonder why you can't hear Me, you may need to check your location. Are you in another room of your life? Are you across the room? Are you eight feet away? Are you an arm's distance? Are you right next to My throne? What is your location? Child, listen to this simple message. Location affects volume."

Bond Servant

When I think of the word slave, it always had a negative connotation to me. When I think of how early Christians used it as they talked about themselves in relation to the Lord, it still didn't sit well with me. I want to think of my relationship with Christ as a child of God, not a slave. At least for me, a slave makes me think I am doing something against my will, and therein lays the mental struggle. Why couldn't they have used another word? I have struggled quite a bit with this word image.

Slave is defined as the property of and wholly subject to another. It is a person entirely under the domination of some influence or person. Peter understood the definition of slave. He said people are slaves of anything that controls them (1 Peter 2:18 NIV). If the fruit of the Spirit control me, then I am a slave to Christ. If a sin controls me, then I am a slave to self (John 8:24 NIV), and the Lord's face is against me. It doesn't get much clearer than that.

It is my way or Christ's way? Why do we as Christians minimize this simple truth? When I look at it like Peter, it helps me look at slavery in a fresh way. We are all slaves to something with the chains to go along with it, whether we like it or not and whether we acknowledge it or not. The truth does not change. We are all slaves to something.

Whatever controls us enslaves us. Those chains have been put there by you. No one has bound you. Jesus doesn't even bind you against your will. You have bound yourself to what enslaves you. This particular slavery that Peter is referring to involves free choice. So, in essence, we are free slaves. No one makes us serve what we are enslaved to, whether that be work, people, children, addiction, hobbies, certain sinful thoughts and or actions, busyness, sports, certain mental mindsets that keep us from living a victorious life in the Lord, and on and on. We have volitionally chained ourselves to these things.

This helps me to mentally look at this type of slavery as not doing something against my will but quite the opposite. I am fully involved in the enslaving. I have had it all backward in my mind. I have been volitionally enslaved to certain sins that had chains that I felt were heavy and unbreakable. I remember the feelings clearly. I felt trapped and wanted to escape. I have had several sins in my past that I have felt this way with, as I am sure everyone has. All along, I was the one putting my wrists out so the chains could be closed and locked around them.

The Lord commands us to strengthen ourselves so that we will live on earth doing what God wants, *not* the evil things that people want or we want (1 Peter 4:2 NIV). We should not be enslaved to ourselves, people, or the things of this world. We should not be enslaved to how we think things should be and trying with all of our might to make it so. All we are doing is making the chains tighter. I don't think we have a clue that we are even doing it! When we are enslaved to anything or anybody else other than Christ, it does not feel like we are free.

That's what I'm learning from all of this. I want to be a free slave to Christ and in bondage to Him like Paul talks about. I want to be wholly subject just to Him. I want to be entirely under the dominion of the Most High God. I want to feel His influence in every part of my life. I want to be a bond servant, a willing slave for Christ. You and I would be the most expensive slaves ever bought! We are worth far more than thirty pieces of silver. Our freedom of choice to be the Lord's slave was paid for with a King's ransom.

The Heart of the Matter

The Bible references the heart 743 times. We have heard and read about it so much that I think it has lost its significance. It seems like a lot of the verses I came across while studying had to do with the heart. With the Bible referencing it so many times, I saw why. I started wondering what, specifically, the heart is, what is in our heart, and how the heart affects who we are. Even one of those questions would be a journal in itself, maybe even a whole book.

Matthew 22:37 says, "Love the Lord your God with all of your heart, mind and soul" (All verses are NIV). Hebrews 4:12 speaks of dividing spirit and soul. It seems that He looks at each one of these parts individually. If we examined one part of us, what exactly is God referring to when He speaks about our hearts? After a lot of searching through references and sites, I have concluded that our hearts are simply our wills or desires. The Lord refers to men or nations having hearts which are their own desires and wills (2 Chronicles 7:14; Proverbs 14:33; Psalm 9:17). He is saying that we have a personal will and nations have their own wills. I like to keep things really simple. My heart represents my personal will and desire toward temporal or eternal things, righteous or unrighteous things, and holy or unholy things.

What is in our hearts? What are our desires and will? When I started cross-referencing what can be in our hearts, I was somewhat overwhelmed. I guess that is an understatement. I was dumbfounded by the amount of information I found from the scriptures. God wants us to know about the heart. He would not have been so exhaustive in His desire for us to understand the magnitude of what our hearts can hold.

There is no way I can write out the reference verses, so I have added the references for you to go back and study. I highly encourage you to do that. This journal will speak to you so much more if it guides you through the Word of God! This list is not complete, but look at what I found that dwells in our hearts: *wisdom* Ps 90:12; *eternity* Ecc 3:11; *seeking* Dt 4:29 6:6; *meditations* Ps 19:14; *cleanliness* Ps 51:10; *Word or Law* Ps 119:11, Rm 2:15; *trust,* Prv 3: 5–6; *purity* Mt 5:8; *treasure* Mt 6:21; Lk 21:34; Lk 2:19; *belief* Rm 10:9; *desires* Ps 37:4; *cheerfulness* Prv 15:13; *love* Mt 22:37, Rm 5:5; *The Spirit* Rm 5:5; *motives* Jer 17:10; *significance of your action driven by the heart* Lk 21:1–4; *thoughts and intentions* Heb 4:12, and *obedience and repentance* Dt 30:1–3.

God says six times "Return to Me with your whole heart." Did you catch the portion of our heart He says He wants? Christian, pay close attention! God doesn't waste His words. When He repeats anything, you better wake up and listen. He wants our whole heart.

Not all good things come from the heart. Think of the heart being a deep well. Whatever is in the well comes up in the bucket. You will drink from what the ladle dips from the bucket. You can try to hide what is in your well from all of us, but you will never hide one drop from an omniscient God. Don't fool yourself. Matthew 15:18 says, "The things that come out of a person's mouth come from the heart, and these defile them."

Defilement is an old biblical word that means to pollute, to dishonor, to make impure, to desecrate, or to make dirty. Defilement is a very strong word, and God says that it comes from our heart. If you broke down defilement, what would it look like if it dwelled in our hearts? How do our hearts get so dirty? Jeremiah 17:9 says deceitfulness can dwell in the heart. Synonyms for deceitfulness are untrustworthy, counterfeit, crafty, deceiving, deceptive, delusion, disingenuous, duplicitous, false, hypocritical, lying, and two-faced. Jeremiah said it like it was. This is one of the reasons he was rejected by his own people.

People typically can't handle being told their hearts are deceitful. God says they can be. Mark 7:20–23 says evil thoughts, wickedness, foolishness, greed, malice, deceit, envy, slander, arrogance, folly, and adultery can dwell in the heart. Luke 21:34 says mental distractions (dissipations), diversions, drunkenness, and the anxieties of life can dwell in our hearts, which dulls them and weighs them down

Hosea 10:2 says we bear guilt in our heart when we go our own way. Well, that makes my heart all warm and fuzzy feeling! I think I like the last paragraph better.

How does the heart affect who we are? If the heart is the source of our desires, look at how many ways those desires can manifest themselves, both good and bad. All desires come from one heart. Do you now understand why I was so dumbfounded? The heart is more complex than anything I have studied thus far. Jeremiah says in the last few words of chapter 17, verse 9: "Who can understand the heart?" I now understand that the heart was significantly affected by the first sins. It changed the makeup of the heart, what was in it, and what could come out of it.

Prior to the fall, we see all these godly and wonderful things I described, but after the fall, wickedness and deceitfulness seemed to reign supremely. This was the reason for the flood. This will be the reason for the destruction of the earth by fire in the future. It seems that sin made a once-tamed heart to be like an out-of-control animal. That is why Jeremiah said, "Who can understand it?"

I have been saying, "Wake up" in so many of my journals. What are we waking up from? Slumber? Yes. We are also waking up from our lack of knowledge of what is beating inside of us right now. Whatever our hearts are beating for can affect our entire existence this side of Heaven. If your heart beats for an intimate personal relationship with Jesus Christ and His Father, then holy desires that come out of your heart will spill out of your mouth and actions.

There's no way you can miss your quiet time with the Lord because you will go into arrhythmias when you are too far away from Him. You will have chest pain that will get your attention when you are out of the will of God. Will you be one of those people who ignore the symptoms of the tight chest and shooting arm pain? Will you be the one thinking your heart is fine while there is hardening of the arteries, restricting the life blood of Jesus Christ flowing through your words and behaviors?

After examining all the desires of my heart, I have experienced both sides. I have seen good things come out of my heart, and I have seen deceitfulness come out of my heart. Some of my desires have been for the temporal and some for the eternal, some for righteousness and some for unrighteousness, and some for holiness and some for unholiness. I know what I am capable of when I my heart does not beat in rhythm with God's.

If you have lived long enough, I think you have figured those same things out for yourself. It's scary what can come from our hearts, isn't it? Let's not stick our heads in the sand and ignore the power of the heart beating in us right now. Ignoring God's plain truth about our hearts is not going to wake us up. God wants us to take a long hard look at our current conditions. If there is any wickedness or anything outside of the will of God in our hearts today, He expects full repentance. He expects your heart to beat for the things of Him including eternity, purity, love, cheerfulness, cleanliness, wisdom, trust, motivation, meditation, and the Spirit, even in your thoughts and intentions. He wants to give us life and life more abundantly. He cannot do this when He only has half our hearts we hold one quarter and the world holds the other quarter. He says He wants our whole hearts.

What do we not understand about whole? He is a jealous God (Exodus 20:5). He doesn't share well. Our wills and desires, in our Christian walk, depend on who is controlling all of our hearts. Your current thought processes and your behavior make that clear to a God that is always your witness. Wake up, Christian. Let's get to the heart of the matter. Stop playing around with one of your most valuable resources that God has put in you.

Mystery of Christ

The Bible talks so much about the "Mystery of Christ." A mystery is something that is kept a secret, remains unexplained or unknown. Mystery also means any truth that is unknowable except by divine revelation. Personally, I feel that we have studied the life of Christ so intently that the awe of the mystery that was revealed, through Him, loses some of its shine. We are in no way minimizing Christ. I'm saying do we really contemplate how big it was that He showed up when and how He did? Has it been somewhat taken for granted after two thousand years?

If you told someone that had never heard the gospel message, they would be mesmerized by the mystery. With the older believers, the novelty wears off, and we just accept it as normal. I do not think we are mesmerized by it any longer as we once were. We have moved on to focus on other aspects of Christ or just other things in general. In the end, maybe I am the only one that has minimized it and filed this common truth away on a back shelf of my mind.

Paul stresses the importance of God's divine secret revealed in Christ. Paul preached it over and over again. He never stopped talking about being in awe of the mystery of Christ. It never got old to him. Despite as much truth as Paul knew, the mystery of Christ never lost its novelty. It was like he was opening a surprise gift every time he talked about it. It was central to the gospel that he preached wherever he went.

Do we know what Paul meant when he said, "mystery of Christ?" Paul speaks about it quite a bit in Colossians. Paul starts in 1:26 referring to "God's message" (NCV). God has had a hidden message from before time began. He held His message close to His heart as a mystery, until which time He said it was appropriate for man to know it. All the old prophets described parts of the message about a Messiah coming. They always longed to get the completed message from God, but it was so divine that they knew that it had to be revealed according to God's will. It was like God painted a picture of the coming Messiah, but they just needed a face and a name to go along with it.

People waited for literally thousands and thousands and thousands and thousands of years to hear God's completed message. Each generation closed their eyes in deep sleep as they slowly passed away through the ages. They were not the generation to see the mystery revealed. Colossians says in 1: 26 that God hid His message for "ages and generations."

Even though God lives outside of time, He had a divine appointment for His transcendence of time. It would not happen one day too soon or one minute too late. God had just the right time in history to "reveal the mystery to His saints." To know that we are His saints that He chose to reveal the mystery to should put you on your face in thanksgiving before a Holy God. We certainly could have lived prior to the revealing and been part of the people waiting for a face and name of the Messiah.

When Christ entered the world wrapped in flesh, the revealing of the mystery had started, but it was far from complete. The mystery took thirty-three years to be fully revealed to the world. Paul talks in Colossians 1:27 about the "glorious wealth of this mystery" (HCSB). There was no monetary value that you could put on this mystery. The wealth of what was revealed was not of an earthly standard to be measured but a glorious

Heavenly one. Paul was saying the wealth of what Christ brought to us was priceless. You could never afford it, so that is why the mystery had to be given as a gift. God doesn't accept monetary or behavioral payment to know the mystery of His Son.

Ecclesiastes 3:11 says, "Eternity is found in your heart" (NIV). How do you think eternity got there in the first place? God knew your heart was the only payment He could accept to know His mystery. Your heart was the only place big enough to hold what He would reveal. He made your heart to hold eternity because one day He knew it would hold His Son. That is why before you were saved, you felt a big emptiness, almost hollowness, inside of you. You searched to fill it up with people and things, but you couldn't. Only Jesus is big enough to fill all of eternity in your heart. This is another part of the mystery revealed.

Paul goes on in Colossians 1: 27 to reveal the complete mystery, "Christ in you, the hope of glory" (NIV). Every person that lived prior to the mystery being revealed would not have believed you if you told him or her that the Holy Messiah would dwell in your heart by the power of the Holy Spirit. The actual glory that would reside in your heart would have been too much for them to understand. There are countless people since the mystery has been revealed who still can't mentally process and accept the magnitude of what God did through Jesus Christ, His Son. They deny what they cannot understand and refuse to believe. That is certainly their free will to do so, just as long as they know that there will be no further mysteries revealed under which they will receive eternal life. It is always important to make informed decisions when you are dealing with your eternal soul.

Understanding the mystery of Christ takes wisdom and an unveiling by the Holy Spirit. People who do not have the Holy Spirit cannot understand the full mystery. Paul talks about in Colossians 2:2 that to have understanding is to have "all the riches" (ESV). It is not to be taken lightly and for granted. To have the gift of the mystery of Christ revealed is glorious wealth, and to have the full understanding of it has riches for us. These riches are hope, knowledge, and wisdom of the Most High God. Again, the mystery of Christ is absolutely priceless and worth more than the entire world. I know I have taken this for granted. Studying the mystery of Christ has really opened my eyes to what I possess in my heart and mind. To have the knowledge of God's mystery revealed opens up "all the treasures of wisdom and knowledge that were hidden" (Colossians 2:3 HCSB).

Blaise Pascal was a brilliant French philosopher who lived in the seventeenth century. He was also a mathematician, inventor, physicist, and writer. He had all the riches and treasures of the wisdom and knowledge of the hidden mystery of Christ. I want to end with one of His quotes that sum up the importance of the mystery of Christ in our lives. Pascal said, "Not only do we know God by Jesus Christ alone, but we know ourselves only by Jesus Christ. We know life and death only through Jesus Christ. Apart from Jesus Christ, we do not know what our life is, or our death, or God, or ourselves."

I ask you, without the mystery of Christ revealed to us by God, where would we be today? What kind of people would we be? Knowing all of this once-hidden mystery of God changes every part of who we are and how we relate to others and the world around us. To treat it like common knowledge is to rob ourselves of the glorious mystery of God. To ignore how it affects our thinking and action on a daily basis also robs us of all the treasures of wisdom and knowledge that are waiting to be revealed. Men who lived in the first and seventeenth centuries understood the magnitude of the mystery of Christ and never took it for granted; do we?

Tootsie Pop Heart

Does everyone remember Tootsie Rolls? How about the famous Tootsie Pops? Remember the owl licking and licking and licking the Tootsie Pop sucker? He said the famous words, "How many licks does it take to get to the center of a Tootsie Pop?" When I was little, I remember counting my licks, but then I would always lose count! The next one I would get, I would start recounting! I never did figure out the answer. It has been estimated that it takes about 600–800 licks to get through the hard candy lollipops to the chocolate-flavored Tootsie Roll center. They have actually had studies on the number of licks it takes!

I have a sweet friend who is very strong mentally, spiritually, and emotionally; however, she always seems guarded. She recently told me that she feels that she comes across somewhat "hard." She attributed some of this presentation to being raised with brothers. Her work ethic is bar none. She is driven and works without ceasing for her family and profession. She has put a harder front up for many years, but recently, she is letting it down a bit. Another friend said that she feels that our mutual friend is now showing a "squishier" side! We all laughed. I told her, "I always thought you had a soft side!" I think the Lord is really speaking to this friend right now, and she is seeking to become closer to the Lord's side. Maybe she is getting, "squishier" or I may say, "moldable" for the Potter's hand. Only good things can come from it, even though the molding may be painful sometimes.

Shortly after this conversation, I got in my car to leave for the day. The Spirit said clearly and simply, "She has a Tootsie Pop heart!" I said, "A what?" He said, "A Tootsie Pop Heart. You know the suckers that are hard on the outside but soft in the middle?" I just smiled and said, "I have never thought of someone having a Tootsie Pop heart before, Lord! That is going to be a fun journal to write when I get home! Thanks!"

We will never know what makes people present with a hard, thick outside. You may think you can break them down in your head. Until you have walked a mile in their shoes, you have no idea how they came to the hardness that you see and then sometimes judge them for it. People who present as hard may never have wanted to be that way in reality. Because of circumstances that were beyond their control, they started layering those hard outer shells. They may have not realized it, but those shells became thicker and thicker and thicker over the years. They have made it harder and thicker because this has protected their soft vulnerable centers. Their centers are all they have of who they really are, as the world has chipped away even at that.

You know the center of a Tootsie Pop isn't that much. I don't think there is really that much at the center of people, either. That is why they know they have to do whatever necessary to protect what they have, which is most valuable to them. If something happened to that center, their worlds would fall apart. They are quite sure mentally that they would not know how to pull the center together again. They are not going to take that risk, hence the thick, hard outer shells.

They may have not realized how the hard outer shells have affected their friends, family, co-workers, or even themselves. They have grown accustomed to its thickness and hardness. Where's the problem? The problem lies in relationships. I think the only thing that matters in this world is God and people. When someone has a thick or hard outer shell of any degree for any reason, I believe it can affect the relationship with God and people.

I believe it can affect the relationship with God because there is a controlling factor of keeping the outer shell in place. "It is my shell! It is there for my purpose! It has served me well and I am not laying it down. In fact, I have had it around me so long, I don't know how to lay it down." When you are in a God-child relationship, someone has to be in mental and emotional control. There can't be more than one person in control. We want to be the ones controlling how hard and thick our shells are. God may say, "Crack it open and let your soft center be vulnerable." You say, "I am in control here, and I am not going to be cracked open!" You see my point.

I know that having a hard and thick outer shell can affect your relationship with people. No matter how kind and nice you are, you are always seen as being an arm's length away from everybody. No matter how hard you try to connect with people, you can't. I have learned in life that to be in relationships with people, you have to be able to show your soft center. People really need to know who you are at your center. This builds closer bonds, trust, and respect. If you have always wondered if these things eluded you in relationships, it is because you have a thick and hard outer shell that you refuse to lay down or crack open. Until you do, you will never really connect to those around you in an intimate and real way. The relationships you desire will always elude you.

How many licks does it take to get down to the center of a Tootsie Pop heart? It may take many hundreds. What would a lick of that heart look like? A forgiveness of others or yourself lick? A deep self-reflective lick? A renewal of the mind lick? Letting go of bitterness lick? A deeper intimate relationship with the Lord lick? Letting go of past hurts and resentment lick? A binding up of a broken heart or wounded spirit lick? Letting go of regrets lick? A trusting lick? A leaning on the Lord despite your lack of understanding lick? Letting go of jealously or envy lick? An accepting of your emotional vulnerability lick? A peaceful lick? Casting your burdens on the Lord lick? Walking by faith and not by sight lick? A resting in the Lord lick? A giving of yourself to others lick? A listening to the Spirit's teaching lick? An obedience to the knowledge of God lick? A strong and courageous lick? A compassionate lick? A recognition of our eternal comfort and good hope through grace lick? A comforting lick?

How many licks does it take to get down to the center? I think it will be different types and number of licks for each Tootsie Pop heart. Each of these type of hearts became hard and thick for different reasons. It will take very special licks to get to the soft center. If you have a Tootsie Pop heart, do not be dismayed. God loves Tootsie Pops! He knows exactly how many licks it takes to get to your soft center because He made it! You have to give Him your Tootsie Pop heart first. You will have to want to break through the harder outer shell so that God and people can see your soft vulnerable center. I suspect it will take time for the layers to dissolve, and it may be painful. Just remember the soft center of your heart is the best part of the Tootsie Pop! You just have to get to it first, before it can be enjoyed by all!

My Heart Looks Like Your Heart

After removing Saul, He made David their king. God testified concerning him: 'I have found David, son of Jesse, a man after My own heart; he will do everything I want him to do'" (Acts 13:22 NIV)

Do you ever think of God having a heart? At the time of King David, Jesus had not been wrapped in flesh with a human heart that could be speared. God's heart is not flesh, like we understand a heart to be. God is spirit and is invisible (John 4:24; Colossians 1:15; all verses in this devotion are NIV). When the Bible talks about heart in this reference, it is referring to the will more than an actually beating heart. When Luke 10:27 says, "Love the Lord your God with all of your heart," it is saying, "Love the Lord your God with all of your will." If we look back at Acts 13:22, it is saying that David is a man after God's own will. That is clarified by the next part, "He *will* do everything I want him to do."

Everything that David wanted is the exact same thing God wanted. In a way, some may think that God comes across a little controlling when He says, "My way or your way." He is God, and He can make an absolute claim like that. Do not judge Him on His thinking unless you want to be judged by the same standard. Do we not say to God when we are in rebellion of sin, "My way, not Yours, God!" Sure we do. Are you not making an absolute claim, too, of who is in control? I have come to the realization that someone has to be in control of your will. It is either you or God. If it is you, then you are not following God's will or heart. If it is God, then you are following God's will or heart. How much simpler can this truth get?

Everyone brings up the fact that David committed murder and adultery. Sin is sin, but we humans tend to put murder and adultery higher on the things-to-avoid list. I am sure that David wishes he would have put those sins on his highest priority list of things not to do, also! That sin cost him his son's life. That sin cost him the privilege of building God's first glorious temple. After that, David was a broken man for God. He lived the rest of His days in the fear and adoration of the Lord. Go soak in the Book of Psalms and see for yourself. He followed God's will without compromise. Even when God said that David couldn't build the first temple, David obeyed. That had to be hard! That was God's will. David shared God's will, too. David could have easily built the temple, but he did not.

The thing I have learned about sin is that you never intentionally seek it out, but it seems you are over your head before you know it. It is not like you wake up one morning and say, "Today, I think I will have an affair" or "Today, I believe I will go murder someone." David did not set out to commit those sins; however, when he was tempted by them, he did not turn away. Even though he didn't set out to commit them, he still chose to engage the sins. We all know that David did not share God's heart when He did this.

What happened after David sinned in such a profound way? He confessed his sin in 2 Samuel 12:13: "David said to Nathan, 'I have sinned against the Lord.'" In Psalm 51:1–2, David cries out in repentance, "Have mercy on me, O God, according to Your steadfast love; according to Your abundant mercy blot out my transgressions. Wash me thoroughly from my iniquity, and cleanse me from my sin!" David was forgiven because he was aligning his heart with God's heart. David knew that their hearts had to be in one accord. He knew that someone had to be in charge of his will, and He chose God. He chose God's heart over his own. He never traded his will for God's again. He never compromised his heart again. God then said, "David was a man after His own heart."

What do we allow in our lives to make us exchange God's heart for our own? God says that wickedness is found in our hearts. Jeremiah 17:9 says, "The human heart is the most deceitful of all things, and desperately wicked." Isaiah 6:3 says, "Holy, holy, holy is the Lord Almighty." This is quite a contrast isn't it? Our will is wicked, and God's will is holy. No matter how good of person you think you are, if your heart is not after God's own heart, then you are wicked. This is very strong truth.

I have never thought of my heart being wicked. The Bible is clear. When I choose any other way than God's way, I am displaying wickedness. Why do we try to sugarcoat this truth by our own justification of going own way? You tell me! I have done it just like you. It makes me shake my head in disbelief of ever choosing my wicked heart over God's holy one.

Think about it this way. Everybody likes apples, right? What if I was holding a freshly picked apple from a tree in one hand and a stinking rotten, black one off the ground in the other one? I offered both my hands to you. You look at the shiny fresh one and then the rotten black one, and you choose the rotten one. Not only do you choose it, but you bite into the rottenness and enjoy it. That's a nice image isn't it? That is exactly what you do every time you choose your wicked will over God's holy one. You remember that image next time you go off on your own! Wickedness or holiness? Your heart or God's heart?

God remembers that we came from dust. If you choose wickedness, repent and be in remorse for your poor choice (1 John 1:9). Move so close to God's heart that your heart will become like His. You have to want to do everything that He wants you to do. Your heart, soul, mind, and spirit have to be in one accord with the Lord's will. That means you do not mentally or physically set one pinky toe outside of it.

The Lord said in Genesis 4:7, "If you do what is right, will you not be accepted? But if you do not do what is right, sin is crouching at your door; it desires to have you, but you must rule over it." You rule over the wickedness that is crouching at the door of your heart by being a gentleman or a lady after God's own heart. If you ignore this gospel truth of what I am telling you, then the roaring lion will devour you. You are very foolish to think otherwise. I don't know about you, but I want God to testify that, "Sarah, daughter of Jimmy and Johanna, is a woman after My own heart; she will do everything I want her to do."

Move That Body!

What completely amazes me, as I praise the Lord this morning, is the personalized touches He has put on my life. The people He brings into my life to make me a stronger and more godly person, have been strategically placed by the hand of God. We do not have a God of coincidences. We have a God of divine appointments and purpose. He does not waste one opportunity or person that we come in contact with. All have been ordained by His will to intersect our life's path.

He is a strategic God. Look around at our universe! Everything we see has purpose and cause behind it. Every person that crosses your life's path has been strategically placed for a purpose. It may be brief, but there is always a purpose. If you started looking at people like this, you can see why God allowed them in your life in the first place.

Take me for instance. If you are reading this journal, I am somehow in your life! I know that may make some of you jump and down and say, "Woohoo!" Others are probably still scratching their heads and asking God, "Why?" Each morning, by the Lord's grace, I send my journals to over 100 people in ten states. Some are in middle and high school, some are in college, some are professors, some are nurses, some are therapists, some are teachers, some are family, some are lifelong friends, some are random friends that I have met in the community, and on and on. I'm hearing now that some people that I send the journals to send them to their friends and families. The Lord is strategically placing them in people's lives who are supposed to have them for their growth and His glory!

It is not a coincidence that you are reading this today. The Lord, by His power, allows me to share what He teaches with you. I know some of you, and some of you I will never meet this side of Heaven, but God knows every one of you by name. He talks to you personally as He has things to say. He uses me to encourage you just as He has used so many of you to encourage me. He puts personal touches on your life just as He does mine. He is a God of detail. He wants all of us to wake up, to think deeper, and to set a more holy path toward Him. Sharing these simple journals is one Christian's life touching another Christian's life. That Christian's life will touch another then another then another, and on and on. God gets every bit of the glory when we intervene in our brothers' and sisters' lives.

That is called the fellowship of the believers. God says it is very good!

Let's open our eyes, move past the possibility of coincidences, and make personal touches in other people's lives for the glory of God. You are a part of the Body of Christ. Will you be His heart today? Will you be His warm hug and smile for someone today? Will you be His encourager? Will you be His ear and listen to others' troubles and heartaches? Will you be His messenger, and send a note from His Word to someone? Will you be his feet and carry the gospel to a co-worker or friend that needs Him? Will you be His mouth and speak a comforting word?

Who has He put in your life that you can touch for Him today? Can God use you to be a divine appointment into someone else's' life? All you have to be is available. He will do the rest. The blessings that you receive will be tenfold back to you, compared to the person that you will touch. Let's start moving around the Body of Christ and touching people for the glory of the Lord. If you have enjoyed my journals touching you, then go out and touch somebody else. It only takes one Christian moving around the Body of Christ to touch another one. What part of the body of Christ will you be today for the glory of God? Pick one then move!

Pleasing Man

When you look at people or even know people personally, you only see what they want you to see. You only know what they want you to know about them, their feelings, and their lives. They can paint any picture for you that they want. The question is, what are they like when no one is looking? Who are they truly when they are alone?

I know couples who paint one picture at church or in front of others as having a happy, lovey-dovey, close, and warm relationship, but they have anything but. I have worked with employees that present one way at work, but they are totally different behind closed doors. Their behaviors would shock everyone. There are some of our friends that act one way, but then depending on the circle they choose, change to mold to the expectations of the group dynamics. There are friends and family who lie because they want to maintain a façade of who you think they are. I'm learning some lie because they really want to be the person that they are presenting to you. They are not and don't know how to be. They know they have to lie because they think if you knew the truth, you may be disappointed and may even defriend them. They may think that you could talk about them behind their back or judge them. The problem that I find is that it takes more and more energy to keep up the façade that all is well, when in reality it is not.

In all of these scenarios, what drives us to please man so much? What makes pleasing man more powerful and more important than pleasing God? In the end, God is the one who really matters to please. Do you think all of the people that they tried to please will be standing around them at the judgment seat of Christ? Nope. It's a private one-on-one. God will say, "You could not please both man and Me. Why did you choose man, when I am the only One that knows everything about you? I loved you with all of your faults. You never had to present a façade to Me. I am the only One you could be real with. I accepted you like you were, but you still chose to please man."

Why do we desire to please man so badly? It is a sociocultural thing? Is it a respect thing? Do we want others to think we have it all together, no matter the cost? Is it so we won't be embarrassed? Is it to make ourselves feel better, if others think better of us? Is it so we will not disappoint others? I believe we please man for our own individualized reasons.

I am a people pleaser and perfectionist. I really want people to think I have it all together. I learned a long time ago I don't have the amount of mental energy to maintain that façade about me. I don't have it together. I am miserably disorganized, and it's not getting better the older I get. I am a procrastinator. It's hard for me to focus as much as I should. I can get overwhelmed pretty easily. God says

> Sarah, be yourself. You are hyper. You are disorganized. You are a procrastinator. Okay! So what? Child, be who I created you to be. I am the One that you should desire to please. When you are true to who you are and accept your faults, you please Me. When you work within your weakness, you are strong in Me. I don't ask a thing from you except to be real.

Some people expect a façade. They seem happier knowing a façade of us than really knowing us. We know this is true with some. This is why we have to maintain what we are not, at all costs. This is why we hide our deepest emotions and fears. How tiring that is. Guess what? You don't have to act like you have it all together if you don't. Just be real and ask for someone to come alongside of you and assist you if you need help. That will contribute to a deeper relationship that is real, rather than keeping your façade up.

As far as marriages are concerned, it's not for man's benefit to be pleased by your marriage. It is for God's benefit! Those people don't go home with you. God does! Who cares if people at church think your marriage is great when you and God know it is not. You don't want to be embarrassed understandably, but you are not fooling God. Get help for your marriage so that it can be truly solid and satisfying in all ways. Why fake a great marriage when you truly can have a great marriage! I was there once so I know what I am talking about! Sometimes we try to put a façade up for our own spouses; however, that is still trying to please man. In the end, whether we have a façade of a marriage, façade of a stronger Christian life than you really have, façade of having things together when we know we don't, façade of hiding an addiction with lies, and on it goes. I have to conclude that façades are to please man.

Maybe it is even easier to please ourselves with a façade than to be real. Maybe we start believing our own façades. That doesn't change reality. God said that is it a choice as to who we will please. Self will rise up and try to be the dominant one, it seems, but you have to make a choice. Façade or real? Man like façades, and God likes reality. The one you view as more important or intimidating will be the one you will please. You may be the one in a relationship who is being real, and the other one is living the façade. In whichever case, God will never demand that you please Him. He desires for you to choose Him over man or yourself. He knows His blessings can flow when you are being transparent and authentic. Sometimes it's harder to choose God because you have to be real.

Sometimes it has been so long since we were real with our spouses, friends, family, and ourselves, that it is scary and even emotionally unsettling. You may have to admit that you need help in some areas or that you don't have it all together. It's okay. It is all a process. If we do nothing and choose to please man or ourselves, I believe we will miss potential blessings God has intended for our lives.

Judge Not

Do you know what we have enough of in this world? Judges. We have so many people who judge. I guess somebody told them along the way that they had some authority over others. I'm not sure who that somebody would have been, certainly not God. I wonder who led them to believe that lie. God says He is the Judge and is no respecter of persons.

It seems to me that to judge someone would automatically make you superior to them. If you judge someone in your head, you have immediately elevated yourself above them somehow. I don't care if your judgment may be accurate; you are still placing yourself higher than them on some elevated mental or physical level. We can deny that we do that, but when we judge others we have made ourselves superior to them.

God says, "I am no respecter of persons." What does that mean? It means that all people are equal in the Most High God's sight. He is impartial. If that is true, then when we judge, we are putting ourselves higher than Him. When we judge, we become partial to our opinion of another. God says He is impartial, but we become partial in our judgment. If He is no respecter of persons, shouldn't we be the same? God teaches us not to judge, but to love one another. The problem with typical Christians is there is very little love but an abundance of judgment. Why do you think the church is dying? People do not want to fellowship with a group of judges but with a group of loving sisters and brothers. Which group am I in? Which group are you in? Which group is the church in?

The question is, "How much have we contributed to the church's death by our own judgment of others?" How innocent are we if we were honest and transparent?

"Oh. Look at her. You know she is crazy."

"Oh look at him. He is homeless and will never amount to anything."

"Look at him. Can you believe he left her?" "Look at her. You know her husband was a druggie and alcoholic."

"Don't waste your time witnessing to that person. He is hopeless."

"Have you heard about what her son has done now?" "She needs to get a hold of that child. What kind of parent is she?" "I haven't seen that couple at church in a while. I knew they wouldn't be faithful in coming."

"She is different than I am. I can't see being her friend."

"I wonder if her husband knows how his wife acts."

"If I had that position, I could do it ten times as effective."

"Look at the mess his or her life is in."

"Did you hear they are declaring bankruptcy again?" "I can't believe they are running that area that way!" "They never volunteer for work at the church."

"You heard there was a fallout between some choir members, right? You know it has to be the same lady that is always making trouble. You know how she is."

"Look at her. She has never been married and there are probably good reasons for that."

"Did you hear that so and so's daughter is a druggie? Can you believe that?" "Look at him. He has been divorced forever. He is still not remarried. What's up with that?" "Look at her. She is on her third marriage! There has got to be something really wrong with her."

And on and on the judging and gossiping goes. Love? No, that has never crossed some Christians' minds. Wrapping their lives around the one they judge to help them through a situation or trial instead of judging them for it? No, that has never crossed their minds, either. As a collective church body, don't sit there and say we are no respecter of persons when we elevate ourselves above others and judge them. Don't sit there and say we love like God told us to love. We want to be our own gods in our lives and pass judgment on others. Why? Maybe it is to make ourselves feel better or maybe we truly think we are superior to them.

One way of acting as our own god is by judging others, but we have never looked at it as such. It's really simple. Do you want men to judge any part of your life or how you are? No? They don't either. God is the only one that has the authority to judge man, not you and me. We have to stop doing His job. I can promise you, He doesn't need our help. At least when He judges, He does it in love, mercy, and grace. We never do.

Have I been guilty of the sin of judging others along my life's journey? Absolutely. Have I been convicted by the Holy Spirit? Absolutely. How about you? The world is full of enough judges. Let's be different. In fact, God calls us to be different. Matthew 22: 37–39 says:

> Jesus answered, "Love the Lord your God with all your heart, all your soul, and all of your mind. This is the first and most important command. And the second command is like the first, Love your neighbor as you love yourself." (NCV)

Christian, there is no love in judgment. When you judge, you are breaking God's second greatest commandment. Hold your judgment for your own actions and thoughts, not others. Work on keeping yourself accountable to God. Don't worry or judge other's choices, problems, or lives. They don't need it or want it.

I am reminded of that song, "They Will Know We Are Christians by Our Love." The title is not "They Will Know We are Christians by Our Judgment." Which song, though, do we quietly sing more often in our churches? If people are judged by you, then are they to assume you are a Christian by the love that you have demonstrated toward them or by your judgment? We say, "Oh, we never judge anyone to their face!" Does it really matter how we do it, or that we just do? Christians are so good at justifying their own behavior. Everything we do is in the presence of the Most High God, including our judgment of others.

We wonder why we are stagnating and dying as a collective church body. The answer is the world does not know we are Christians by our love. The world sees that we are just like it. I write such harsh words. I know. If I am not speaking truth, then you tell me why the church is dying and the Christian is stagnating, if we are not behaving exactly like the world. Colossians 2:20 says, "If you died with Christ to the elementary forces of this world, why do you live as if you still belong to the world?" This verse was written 2,000 years ago. Is it still relevant for Christians today? Sure it is.

Lord, I See You Standing There

Lord, I see You standing there. I know you are waiting just for me. I'm not sure how You make me feel like I am Your only child, but You do. You spend so much quality time with me and show me such deep love. When I am with you, I feel like I am the most special child that You have ever created. You have a way of making things fade from around me. The meaningless and temporal seem to be pulled off of me when I am walking toward You.

It is almost like someone is pulling off a heavier, outer garment. Sometimes that outer garment feels too small as it is difficult to remove when I am walking toward Your presence. It is like I have to fight to remove it at times. Once I do, the lightest white linen robe flows around me. It is so soft when I rub my hands across the material. I feel absolutely beautiful swirling around in Your presence. I love how it drapes around me when I kneel in front of You. Thank You for dressing me in finest linen of Heaven.

Lord, I see You standing there. You always wear a welcoming and warm smile. There is not a line on Your face of discontent in me. There is no condemnation. You are so smooth in appearance. You have such a graceful ease when You move. You are the most beautiful person I have ever seen. I want to keep looking at You. I stand in amazement that You exist. The glory that surrounds You makes You appear the purest white. It is as if You are glowing. You are beautiful to me, Lord. I know I tell You that all the time, but it is the only thing that keeps coming to my mind when I see You standing there. I want to tell You all the things that are on my mind, but when I see You, I can only think of how beautiful You are to me. I'm speechless. What I had to say fades away as I look at You in awe.

Lord, I see You standing there. I often wonder if you got the wrong person. What could I have done to deserve You? I know; I know. You have told me so many times that I did nothing. You chose me before I chose You. You waited from before time began until this very day, so that I could see you standing there in all of Your glory. My whole existence is based on Your existence. You tell me every day, "You live because I live." I hear Your words echoing throughout my day. You never let me forget that truth. After Your resurrection from the dead, I was the one who was dead; You were the One that was living. You sealed me with the Holy Spirit and breathed Your life into my dead body and spirit. You baptized me and raised me with You. I was without hope, and You flooded me with eternity. When I live within Your will, Your grace and mercy overflow within me.

Lord, I see You standing there. I want You to know that I am ready for You to come back and get me, my brothers, and my sisters in Christ. We are all so weary and very tired of living in this place. Please, Lord, we want you to come get us. The older I get the more I know I do not belong here. I look around me and see death, hurt, rejection, pain, loss, heartache, suffering, loneliness, depression, and hopelessness. I want to comfort everyone and ease what is in their life, but I cannot. I try to be Your hands and feet, but there seems to be so many people who need so much more than I have the ability to give.

You have taught me to stay in Your will and to work through the power of the Holy Spirit. You have taught me the best that I can do for people is to encourage them, inspire them to think of You more, and to be available for them. You have taught me that people just want to be loved on and listened to. You have taught me that there are enough judges in this world. I should never have judgment in my heart, as that does not show love toward my brothers and sisters. I am to accept all people through Your own demonstration of love and acceptance.

You have been the perfect model for me to follow all the days of my life. I understand that You will come get us when your Father tells You the time is right. I just want You to know that we are ready when He is. You go tell the Father that we are waiting for You. Tell Him that we are ready to see Your holiness and glory in the clouds. You go tell Him that we are ready for You to wrap Your arms around us. We are waiting.

Lord, I see You standing there. Thank You for Your faithfulness when I fail to be faithful. I'm sorry that I have hurt You so many times. My heart breaks when I return from sin and have to lay it in front You. I am embarrassed when I am selfish and think my way is best. I am so very sorry. Please see how sorry my heart is for hurting You even once. I know I have hurt You more times than I can count. You love me so much. To think that I have caused You any hurt in return makes me recoil in my own ignorance of how to live as Child of God. To think of all the times I have left You standing there waiting for me to commune with You and I never came.

My heart breaks with sorrow for my treatment of You, Lord, and the priority that I have shown You in my life. Thank you for Your faithful forgiveness over me. Thank You for welcoming me back home with the most accepting embrace. I am so underserving of You and what You offer my life. Thank you for giving me a standard in which to live my life. Help me to not only speak about the power of God but to live within it. I picture myself climbing in Your power as if I am climbing in a small boat. As the boat crosses calm or rough waters, I am sleeping in the back with my head on a soft pillow. I have peace no matter what kind of water I am passing through because I am resting in Your power.

Lord, I see you standing there. Do you see me looking back at You?

I Thank God for You

I was reading the first chapter of Colossians. I couldn't get past the third verse before the Holy Spirit brought my attention to something. It was a simple theme that I kept seeing over and over again in all of Paul's letters. Why haven't I put it together before now? I always get so excited when I find new truth! I am sure the Spirit has been trying to teach me this for a while now. Today, I finally got it! Some of the verses written in this theme are (all verses are HCSB):

We always thank God, the Father of our Lord Jesus Christ, when we pray for you. (Colossians 1:3)

We always thank God for all of you, remembering you constantly in our prayers. (1 Thessalonians 1:2)

We must always thank God for you. (2 Thessalonians 1:3)

I thank God when I constantly remember you in my prayers night and day. (2 Timothy 1:3)

I always thank my God when I mention you in my prayers. (Philemon 1:4)

I give thanks for my God for every remembrance of you, always praying with joy for all of you in my every prayer. (Philippians 1:3)

I always thank my God for you. (1 Corinthians 1:4)

First, I thank my God for all of you. (Romans 1:29)

Do you notice a pattern? Paul was the greatest apostle the world has ever known. He was highly educated and trained in the Law and then had a dramatic conversion to Christ. He saw Christ on that dusty road to Damascus, and it changed him from the inside out instantly. He lived the rest of His days serving Jesus until his death. He never wavered once. He was, no doubt, God's man.

Do you think for one second that if Paul said something that was inspired by the Lord that we should not take heed and also follow it? Paul clearly said over and over and over again, "I thank God for you when I pray." How simple is that? Do we faithfully do it? Did we even know that we should consistently thank God for people when we pray? I didn't.

This new truth will have a dramatic impact on the way I pray for my friends and family from this point on. That is exciting to me that I can start praying as Paul prayed. I am faithful in intercession on behalf of any friend or family in need. I have never consistently thanked God first for people then prayed for them. I just didn't know that was something that I should do.

In the past, I would have prayed, "Lord, put Your hand on my two boys. Bless them and keep them. I pray that they will follow You all of their days." Now I pray, "Lord, I thank you with everything in me for my two boys. Thank you for allowing me to have them for a short time. Thank you for their health and happiness. I pray that you put Your hand on them. Bless and keep them. I pray that they will follow You all of their days."

In the past, I would have prayed, "I pray that my sweet friend is able to conceive and carry a child; she is a blessing to me and would be sweet Godly mother. She would honor You and raise her child in Your ways." Now I pray, "Thank you so much for my sweet friend. Thank you for allowing our life paths to cross. Thank you for her sweet spirit. I pray that she is able to conceive and carry a child. She is a blessing to me and would be a sweet, godly mother. She would honor You and raise her child in Your ways."

The Word of the Lord tells us that having thanksgiving in our hearts brings peace. I know there is nothing more important in our lives to be thankful for other than people. They are each unique and made individually by God. People are like snowflakes; no two are alike.

The Bible teaches a multitude of things. It is endless. The one thing the Bible does well is teach us how to pray. If Paul, being one of the greatest men of God that has ever lived, thought he should thank God in his prayer for the people that he came in contact with, shouldn't we? I would love to list all of my friends and family's names out in this journal that I am thankful for, but it would go on forever. Just have confidence to know that when I pray for you by name for now on, I will thank my God for you first. Not only will I be following in Paul's footsteps of how to pray, but the Lord promises great peace upon me as well. I always thank my God for you!

Scriptural Flavors

I woke up this morning, thinking about the flavors of the Bible. I started thinking what an interesting topic it was to ponder and write about. The Bible talks about flavors in some detail. The Lord guided me to new knowledge by studying the flavors of the Bible. I am again reminded of Ecclesiastes 3:14, "God works so people can be in awe of Him" (HCSB). I am in awe.

Let's start with exploring the flavor of salt. God speaks about the flavor of salt quite a bit. Job 6:6 refers to things being unsavory if not eaten with salt. Matthew 5:13 says, "You are the salt of the earth. But if the salt loses its saltiness, how can it be made salty again? It is no longer good for anything, except to be thrown out and trampled underfoot as worthless" (all verses are NIV). A Christian loses his or her saltiness by being complacent. A complacent Christian is slumbering. A complacent and slumbering Christian is saltless and useless.

Do you know what happens to a human body when it is low in sodium? It causes weakness and can even make you unresponsive if low enough. Isn't that interesting? That is exactly what happens to Christians when their spiritual salt in their lives is low. Coincidence? I don't believe in coincidences. Mark 9:50 says, "Salt is good. Have salt in yourselves, and peace one with another." Colossians 4:6 says, "Let your speech be always with grace, seasoned with salt, that ye may know ye ought to answer every man." Leviticus 2:13 instructed, "All offerings should be made with salt."

Did you know there was a very powerful covenant of salt (Second Chronicles 13:5; Numbers 18:19)? When we accept Jehovah God, we agree to become His salt flavoring to the world. By accepting this covenant of salt, we are agreeing to be holy. As long as I have been a Christian, I have never known about the covenant of salt. Fascinating! We are to be mindful to be just enough salt so that we can be the right flavor to others. We know that not enough salt or too much salt does not taste good. We want to turn people toward God because we are salted perfectly.

Another flavor of the Bible is sweetness. When God fed the Israelites manna in the wilderness, it tasted like wafers made with honey (Exodus 16:31). Proverbs 24:13 encourages people to, "Eat honey, for it is good, and the drippings of the honeycomb are sweet to your taste." Psalm 119:103 says, "How sweet are your words to my taste, sweeter than honey to my mouth!" God says He and His Word are sweeter than honey. Did you know that honey is sweeter than table sugar? God is saying, "I am sweeter than sugar."

The Lord encourages us in Psalm 34:8 to, "Taste and know that the Lord is good." First Peter 2:3 says, "If so be ye have tasted that the Lord is gracious." Hebrews 6:5 says, "And have tasted the good word of God, and the powers of the world to come." Nehemiah 8:10 told the people to, "Go and enjoy sweet drinks." Solomon's wife refers to her beloved as sweet to taste (Song of Solomon 2:3). We clearly see from these scriptures that God prefers the good taste of sweetness. He is sweet to us, and He expects us to be sweet to Him and others at all times.

The last flavor of the Bible is bitterness. Job indicates that complaining can be bitter. Ephesians 4:31 pairs bitterness with wrath, anger, evil speaking, and malice. The verse says, "It should be put away from you." Hebrews 12:15 says bitterness has a root, and it can spring up and give you much trouble and even defile you. James 3:14 pairs bitterness with selfishness and jealousy. He also said the source of bitterness is in your hearts. That means it is within your will to be bitter or not. You choose bitterness. No one does it to you. You do it to yourself. Wake up, Christian. Stop blaming your bitterness on what people did to you. Start looking at what you are doing to yourself. James goes on to say, "Where jealousy and selfishness are, there will be confusion and every kind of evil."

I believe all of these emotions or states of being that I have mentioned can become idols in your life. Anything that takes your eyes off of the Lord being the center of your life is an idol. I know people who have the idols of complaining, bitterness, resentment, anger, evil speaking, selfishness, and jealousy. I see it devouring them. I bet you know of people in your own life that have some of these idols. Maybe you have some idols that you need to take to the Lord and crush like King Josiah did in 2 Chronicles 34:7. The Bible says, "He crushed the idols to powder!" I love that! Any emotional, personal, or physical idol that we have in our life, we should crush them to powder! These idols will only continue to hold power over you as long as you allow it. *Crush them!*

The Bible distinguishes the difference between the last two flavors of sweet and bitter. Isaiah 5:20 says, "Woe to those who call evil good and good evil, who put darkness for light and light for darkness, who put bitter for sweet and sweet for bitter." When you justify your sins or harbor wrong emotions and knowing the good to do but not choosing it, you are allowing darkness, sin, or bitterness to take root. When it springs up in your life, it will overpower you and control you. You will eat of these fruits in your life. No one likes to eat something bitter, so why do we eat it so much?

If you were holding a spoonful of honey, would you exchange it to swallow a spoonful of vinegar mingled with gall? No? The Lord says we do make this exchange. When we sin, that is exactly what we are doing. It is interesting to look at it this way, isn't it? Do you know why we sin? I have figured it out by studying the flavors of Heaven. Sin goes down like honey. It tastes sweet to us. When it hits ours stomach, it becomes bitter. It changes flavors, just like when John ate the little scroll in Heaven (Revelation 10:10). There is a direct correlation. What cool new understanding!

The study of these scriptural flavors has absolutely astounded me. The Lord knew it would when He told me the theme this morning. I have learned new truth. Some of the truths I did know are now deeper. I spent several hours in the Word to understand and write about these flavors. It is imperative to understand what flavors we have in our Christian life.

Are you salty? How much? Are you sweet all the time and to everybody? Are you bitter? What is the root? Are you exchanging your sweetness for bitterness? Self-reflect and answer these questions transparently before God. He will help you answer them honestly! I thank my mighty teacher, the Holy Spirit, for spending the afternoon with me, guiding me through the flavors of God's Word.

Bunker Hill

I was at church this morning. We always have a quiet time as a church body prior to the beginning of the service with soft piano music playing. The lights are turned off. I love how the natural light comes through the stained glass windows. Everyone is bowed in silent prayer. We are one Body with one mind. This is my favorite time of the service. I pray for many things, but I always end with a global request to cover my church family during the next hour from any spiritual attack of unseen forces.

I imagine my prayer being a covering or a shield around my church so that my sisters and brothers can worship the Lord in body, spirit, and mind. I always feel my church family is covered by the power of my one prayer. I know that I pray this each Sunday morning in the power of the Holy Spirit; therefore, I believe my prayer is answered as I have petitioned. Jesus says ask anything in His name and it shall happen. As a side note, I encourage you to be the one in your church who prays for its protection each Sunday morning as you join in worship. You be the one who thinks about the whole Body and covers it in prayer.

This morning as I was praying in church, a very clear picture of a bunker appeared in my mind. I saw it slowly spinning around just as I was finishing my prayer of protection over my church. I said, "I see it Lord. I will write about this when I return home today." The picture disappeared from my mind, yet the impression it left did not. This is a way that information is given to me to write about sometimes. I see an image that I was not originally thinking about, and it is typically irrelevant to what is happening around me. Then I write about it. This does not happen all the time, but many times it has. I know that makes me sound a little off, but I am just being transparent. I have no reason not to be.

I have no reference to write about a bunker. The first thing that comes to my mind is that a bunker is some sort of a military object. It is used in times of war for protection against enemy attack. It is meant to secure whatever is inside from whatever is on the outside. Something on the outside hates what is on the inside and has intent to harm it. In times of war, men run full speed for the closest bunker for their protection. It is their only hope for survival if they were on the battlefield. Bunkers are buried in the ground for further protection.

What if you were in a war in your life? What if the enemy is closing in and has won the last few battles, and you are on the defense. What if even though you are a Christian, you feel weak and vulnerable from being beaten down by the burdens of this world? The powers that have come against you may be one of disease, loss of a loved one, divorce, depression, self-doubt, anxiety, addiction, loss of direction, heartache, loneliness, deepest hurt, uncertainty, fatigue, marital struggles, loss of an opportunity, loss of a job, past abuse, loss of income, or consequences from a recent bad decision or sin. You look around you and see that you are in the middle of a battlefield that you never anticipated. It may be a battlefield that you had some responsibility in creating. It could be a foreign battlefield that that you never saw coming and could have never prepared for. You were just dropped in it. Either way, it is very, very real to you.

You have been wounded, and you are looking around for shelter. You know that you are not going to make it emotionally much longer. You know that you are not in a physical battle, but an emotional or spiritual one. Those are the worst kind because you feel like you can't get a firm hold on where the enemy is going to attack you next. You may even attack yourself next with all the anxieties of living in the past or future. You feel very raw and vulnerable.

You need a bunker: one that is fortified, tested, and true, one that you have used before but have mentally strayed from its protection. There are many bunkers out in this world promising you shelter, but they are not all equal in the protection of your heart and mind. They present themselves as strong, but they are façades that will force you to seek another shelter later. Why do that when you can rest in the one shelter that you never have to leave again? It makes sense when I say this, but how often do we sit in the wrong bunker because it promised us protection.

Sometimes we have created our mental bunkers where we hide from realities, hurts, and emotions that we do not want to face. Those realities are not going away once we come out of our mental bunkers. You know this is true, despite telling yourself and wishing something different. I think our own mental bunkers that we hide in are way worse than any worldly ones. This is due to the fact that we have the key to our own mental bunker going in and coming out. We control when the door opens or closes. We control how long we stay. We control who comes in and out.

My Christian sisters and brothers, creating mental bunkers to help ourselves be safe from others, hurts, and emotions most likely do more harm to us than good. They are not in our best interest. When you are in there, you are not only closing out help from people who love you, but you also closing out the Lord's healing power for your battle wounds. How often have I hid in my own mental bunker, thinking that, in time, my battle wounds from some of my life choices or heartaches would pass? As soon as I would venture too far out of my self-erected bunker, the wounds were just as painful and fresh as ever. So the cycle went on for me. I went in and out of my own mental bunker with no healing and no changes. How could I glorify the Lord and work as His vessel in such a condition? I ask, "How can you?"

Hiding out in the mental reclusion of a bunker is not the answer. Hiding out in the physical bunkers of addiction, depression, anxiety, affairs, alcohol, human logic, work, and whatever else you can find is not the answer. God reached down out of Heaven and gave us a bunker that is stronger than the mental or physical ones that you could ever hide in. This bunker was made out of pure rock. He puts you in the cleft of the bunker, and He personally covers You with His hand. Nothing in His bunker can harm you. It is only the stuff on the outside that can. This is a place of safety and healing.

In His bunker, He has a little hospital set up. He knows that you have just come off the battlefield, and you are weary. Psalm 147:3 says, "God heals the brokenhearted and binds up their wounds" (all verses are NIV). Where did our wounds come from? I have already told you earlier, "From the powers that have come against us." I don't know about your mental or physical bunker, but I bet you my lunch that it doesn't have a triage center in it. God says in Psalm 147:6 that He "Sustains the humble." He supports, holds, and helps bear the weight of our wounds that we sustain in life.

The most hopeful news is that our wounds will be healed by the piercing, bruising, chastisement, and stripes Jesus endured for us while He was on the battlefield (Isaiah 53:5). There was not a bunker for Him when He went to battle. Because of what Jesus did, one was created for us, though. We no longer have to suffer from worldly or our own self-inflicted piercing, bruising, or chastisement. We no longer have to be in the battlefield of our minds and emotions and have nowhere to seek shelter. Just do as Moses did. Obey the Lord and step in the cleft of the rock. Wait there until He binds yours wounds and heals your heart, then come out again in His power and the renewal of your mind.

You can enter the bunker. It is located in the cleft of the Rock. It is impenetrable to enemy attack when you are inside. He will strengthen you and fill you with His peace as you spend more time there. In my opinion, Calvary could be called "Bunker Hill." It is there that your bunker rests. You never have to wonder where it is. You never have to search to find it. It is high and it is lifted up. Look; do you see it? Christian, get off the battlefield of your mind and emotions. *Run* to the hill! Go get in Christ's bunker and rest in it. It is your only hope for your mental, spiritual, and physical survival. The best part is you never have to leave His bunker again. You are safe and secure there. May God receive all honor and glory forever and ever for the gift of His bunker. Hallelujah and amen!

The Difference

The fellowship of the believers desires discussions and deeper truths. I think sometimes that occurs when we listen to each other's ideas of how the Bible presents different points to us. This also happens when you listen to what other people are mentally and emotionally struggling with. We are hungry and thirsty for more of the Lord. I believe we are hungry and thirsty for deeper fellowship.

I am not a theologian. I am a speech therapist—slash—full-time mother—slash—full-time wife—slash—Sunday school teacher—slash—new writer! I am one of you. My life is as full as yours. I am on a journey the same as you are. I am trying to figure life and our God out just like you are. I am a regular Christian who is tired of slumbering. I desire to move away from the milk of the gospel and sink my teeth into the meat of it. I think you are the same as I am. We all want to grow, but how?

I think we have become dependent on the preachers, topic-driven Bible studies, and the church too much to teach us what God wants to teach in a one-on-one relationship. Please, do not misinterpret me! All those things are good. I partake in all of them. Preaching, teaching, and the church are all ordained by God. I think, sometimes, He just wants you and me to Himself. I think we can get lulled to sleep with too much organized religion, and we don't even realize it. It gives us an arbitrary spiritual ration that we check off in our head as complete. Sometimes, we finish the week with not another blink about our Lord until somebody else is teaching us on the next Wednesday or Sunday morning. John 14:26 says the Holy Spirit will teach us of everything that Jesus spoke about. I have felt the Holy Spirit tell me that my job is to read the Bible in quiet time, and His job is to interpret it and teach me. If I do not do my job, how can He do His? He can't, and I stagnate.

So often we want that spoon-fed truth, but we will not go seek it out ourselves. Why? What is stopping us? Are there people out there that enjoy my journals or other devotionals but never open their Bible that day to study truth on their own? Sure there are. Why? They have had their spiritual ration for the day and they are good to go. They had "enough of God" for the day. Our spirits have to be fed more than they have been fed thus far.

I think that is exactly how we get ourselves in the mental and emotional situations along with the spiritual stagnation that we may be in. We need to dive in the Word ourselves, without having someone telling us to turn to a certain spot in our Bible or ponder an interesting thought. We need to have a personal Bible study without someone telling us the theme for the next six weeks. Again, those things are not bad, but you have to have a personal time just with the Lord so you can be Spirit led and Spirit fed. I am faithful in church and Sunday school, but I can tell you there is no comparison between when I am Spirit led in my personal quiet time and when I am people led at church. Both are beneficial, but there is a great difference.

I always thought I was getting enough God from going to Sunday school and church. I really did. Even teaching Sunday school, I thought I was getting enough of Him. What a fool to think such a thing. You and I can never get enough of God. How could I sell myself that lie and then be okay with it for so many years? How could I be starving my spirit and not even know it? That scares me to think about it. I take such good care of my flesh, but my poor spirit has been much neglected in the past. I have given it "enough God" to sustain it but not enough to make it flourish and grow and not enough to stay alert and awake. Again, there is a chasm of a difference. Until you experience this difference for yourself, you will not understand what I am describing or explaining. If your thinking is anything close to how mine was, why don't you check out the difference for yourself?

Holding Firm

Hold firmly to the Word of Life. (Philippians 2:16 NLT)

We know who the Word of life is. John 1:1 tells us that Jesus is the eternal Word. He tells us that Jesus was God. I really do not think this truth can get much clearer. Jesus told the disciples that when they saw Him, they saw God the Father. God is spirit. He is invisible. How do you "hold firmly" to something you can't see? Jesus came wrapped in flesh, so through Him we could hold firmly to God. We can actually lay our hands on Jesus and His Word of truth and hold on tight.

Why does Paul say to hold securely to Jesus? It is not like something is going to snatch Him away from us, right? Are we going to be snatched away from Him? No. We are sealed by the Holy Spirit, and God never breaks a promise. God says there is a crooked and perverted generation around us, though. This generation can be very influential in our lives. Just like we have seen teenagers led astray, we as adults can be tempted off the straight road and onto the wide and crooked one just as easy. You arc a fool to think otherwise.

I think of it like this. Let's say there is a storm coming. You have been warned to prepare and to seek shelter. You think you have things under control. The wind starts picking up, and the rain comes. The wind of temptation is so strong, and it starts to lift you off the ground and move you into its direction. You recognize how much danger you are in of falling so you firmly grab on to a strong tree. You hang on to that tree for your dear life. When the stormy trials come, if it were not for you holding firmly to that tree, you would have destroyed parts of your life. You would have destroyed relationships in your life. You would have destroyed your witness to others. You held firmly to the tree, and you were not carried away with the wind.

We have all had regrettable times in the past that we have not held firmly to the tree, haven't we? What happened in those times? You were blown around and hurt badly in the storm that you entered, most likely of our own choosing. You thought that you had enough control over the situation that you could handle the storm without holding on firmly to the Lord's truth and way. You learned quickly that your way was wrong. The next time the storm came, you held on a little tighter and were protected from further consequences of poor choices.

We have all done this. We have all tested the wind to see if we can handle it on our own. How arrogant of us to think we were strong enough to go it alone. How ignorant we were to think we wouldn't get hurt. We think we can turn our heads and walk on the wide and crooked road a mile or two and not become misguided ourselves. Christian, sin is nothing to play around with. God warns us and warns us to hold on to Him firmly. He is saying to hold on to His truth and His way. He is saying to hold on to Him no matter how good the winds feel to us. They always pick up hurricane force as you go deeper in them. You just can't see it when you enter it. He has good reasons to tell us to hold on firmly.

We tell our children to not touch a hot iron. We know what harm can come to them in advance. The Lord is the same way. He knows what harm can come to us in advance. What happens when the child disobeys and touches the hot iron? It is the same thing that happens to us when we don't hold firmly to the Word of life. God never wastes His words or His warnings to us. We just ignore them, and we get burned. Let's stay awake! Hold firmly to the Word of Life.

I Believe

I believe in the Father, the Son, and the Holy Spirit. I believe that I was created in Their image. I believe that God knew me in my mother's womb when I was without form. I believe by His power alone that my heart beats and my lungs breathe. I believe I am unique, special, and beautiful because God says that I am. I believe that I have an eternal spirit. I believe in one salvation by way of the broken body and spilled blood of My Lord and Savior, Jesus Christ. I believe I was predestined by the Lord's omniscient power to become a child of God before time began.

I believe the same Holy Spirit who hovered over the deep at the dawn of time is the very same Holy Spirit that has been placed within my heart by Jesus. I believe the Spirit testifies with my spirit that I am a child of God. I believe that the Father and the Son has come to make a home in my heart and life. I believe through the interpretive ability and power of the Holy Spirit that I commune with the Most High God of Heaven and Earth. I believe that He allows me in His throne room to sit before Him and gather handfuls of His glory to pour over me. I believe that I bring Him honor by my fear and love of Him. I believe that as long as I stand transparent in His presence, asking for the searching and the trying of my life that He will heap abundant blessings on me.

I believe that I have the ability to be holy and righteous through the knowledge of God the Father, God the Son, and God the Holy Spirit existing and living through this flesh. I believe through wisdom and spiritual maturity that I can turn away from evil and wickedness that is found in me and the crooked and perverse generation that I find myself in. I believe, as Paul, that I may be blameless, pure, and faultless. I believe that I shine like the stars. I believe in the perfection of Jesus as my high priest. I believe in His forgiving love. I believe that I must hold firmly to the Word of life.

I believe that there is no other name under Heaven in which to be saved than the name of Jesus Christ. I believe He was high and lifted up for the entire world to see His sacrifice of sin and His obedience to the Father. I believe God raised Him from the dead on the third day just as Jesus had said. I believe Jesus is preparing a mansion for me. I believe He is interceding in front of the Father's throne for me. I believe He is standing by the gates of Heaven waiting for His Father to say, "Son! Go get My children." I believe His return is imminent, and time is very short. I believe that I will leave this earthly flesh and receive a new body in a twinkling of an eye when I meet My Lord in the clouds.

I believe I will be dressed in the finest white linen of Heaven. I believe when the Lord said He is coming soon and I would spend eternity with Him. I believe I am ready to meet the Most High God. I believe in You, Father! I believe in You, Jesus! I believe in You, Spirit! I lift my hands up high to You, Lord, and fall to my knees in awe. My soul, my mind, my heart, and my spirit all cry out to You, *"I believe!"*

Hopelessness

I will put my hope in Your name, for it is good. (Psalm 52:9 NIV)

One would think that a Christian could never become hopeless. It's almost like you cannot use the words "Christian" and "hopeless" in the same sentence. Sure, we all know the world is without hope but not us. We are God's children. Everything will always work out somehow, right? Second Corinthians 4:16–18 says:

> So we do not lose heart. Though our outer self is wasting away, our inner self is being renewed day by day. For this light momentary affliction is preparing for us an eternal weight of glory beyond all comparison, as we look not to the things that are seen but to the things that are unseen. For the things that are seen are transient, but the things that are unseen are eternal. (ESV)

This passage is full of comforting words for the Christian. What if that "light momentary affliction" isn't light at all? What if that light momentary affliction doesn't feel momentary to us? What if that light momentary affliction blinds us so that we feel and believe we are without hope? We don't want to believe it can happen, but it can. When the verse says, "We look not to the things that are seen but to the things that are unseen. For the things that are seen are transient but the things that are unseen are eternal," we may sometimes look at only the "seen," despite the Lord advising us not to. We look at only the things that we can reason out in our own mind, and if we can't make sense of things, then the door is cracked open for hopelessness to come in.

Some of our trials do not "feel" transient to us. We have allowed our emotions to convince us that they may be permanent. Hopelessness builds. We can't see past our temporal situation to glimpse the eternal that is right in front of us. Hopelessness will blind a Christian. It is like quicksand to them. They are in over their heads before they know it.

Their perception changes, and they exchange reason for the illogical and unthinkable. No Christian sets out to take this path. It is like a shadow that slowly covers them a little at a time. They look around them, and see they are in the dark. They "feel" there is no hope for light again. It is like they are on a small boat in rough seas, and their boat is taking on water too fast for them. Instead of a bucket to scoop the problems out, they only have a small thimble. Even though land is just over the next big wave of life, they cannot see over it. It's all too much. All they can see is the water in their boat raising.

We think because we are Christians that we are immune to hopelessness. We are not. We live in this temporal world, and we have real emotions. There are so many people, trials, and situations in this place where we live that keep dumping water or problems on us and after a while we cannot come up for air. No matter how hard we try to keep our eyes on Jesus, the water is just too much. The weight is just too heavy. God knows that we try, and He doesn't count it against us for our emotions. There is no condemnation in Christ even in times of our hopelessness.

He remembers that we come from dust. He knows how hard life can be as He also lived it Himself. He loves us no matter where we are mentally in our thinking. His peace is there for us even though we see it elude us. Whatever our choices are when we find ourselves in a sea of hopelessness, God will be there to hold us together. In your darkest hours of hopelessness, God will pick your whole boat up out of the water and carry you to shore. Sometimes you cannot help your emotions. They just are. Lean on the Lord as hard as you can in your times of hopelessness. Remember, He does not condemn you. He loves you completely, no matter where you are and what you do in these times.

Sometimes, emotions can take you deeper than you need to go. When your emotions are drowning you, and you are taking on too much water, put you hope in the good name of Jesus. He will gently guide you to safety when you are in the deep end of the ocean.

The Exchange

They exchanged the truth about God for a lie. (Romans 1:25 NIV)

I was praying this morning, and thanking the Lord for my life. I know of other lives that have so many trials and heartache in them. Some of these lives were inadvertently affected by others exchanging what they wanted for what the Lord would have wanted for them. Some of these lives willingly made their own exchanges. Some of their decisions of the exchange were permanent. When there is an affair in a relationship, one of the spouses exchanged what the Lord would have wanted for what they wanted. When there are lies or distrust in any relationship, one party exchanged what the Lord would have wanted for what they wanted. When there is hopelessness and a temporary blindness in someone's life to the light of a solution, they exchange what the Lord would have wanted for what they wanted.

When we live outside of God's will, for whatever good reason we want to justify, we are exchanging what the Lord would have wanted for what we wanted. I have never considered it a true exchange. This means that we have given up a part of something for something else that we perceive as equivalent. When we make an exchange, we replace whatever we currently have with an equivalent of something else. There is a replacement of one thing for something else. There is a mental, emotional, and/or physical switching or swapping. There is an exchange.

The one theme that I am picking up on about this exchange is there is a perceived equivalency of that which is being exchanged. We see it as equal or oftentimes better than what we currently have. Somehow when we go exchange what the Lord would have wanted for what we wanted, we illogically reason that it is equivalent. What makes our exchanges with the Lord look good to us is a complete mystery to me. To think our will is that strong to affect the logical and reasoning parts of our minds is almost too much to comprehend. Honestly though, what else is there?

When we see something our way so strongly that we are willing to compromise everything for it, there has to be some disconnect somewhere. I am right here with you in these illogical God-self exchanges. Every time I make the exchange and only later come to my senses, I am amazed that I made the exchange in the first place. I sit back and chastise myself, *"What were you thinking? Where was the equality in your exchange?"* When I realize there was absolutely no gain in my exchange, I feel cheated and hurt. Who is cheating and hurting me? *Me!* I look around to be mad at somebody for giving me such a bad exchange. I would have to look in the mirror if I really want to see that "somebody."

If you look for the equality of what you received in return for the exchange of God for your self, you will not find it. You can try to search and justify as much as you want; you will not find the equality in it. You will not find the logic in it. Why? It simply doesn't exist. When you exchange God's will for your own in any situation or relationship, you lose every single time. You will not gain one single thing. You can tell yourself you will all day long, but that doesn't make it reality. When you exchange God's will for yours, what you are exchanging is holiness, closeness with God, purity of thinking, blessings in your life, and deeper wisdom for nothingness.

Let me give you an example of nothingness. Take you right hand and make a fist. Turn your fist so the palm is facing you. Now open your hand. You can do your both hands if you want. What do you see? That's right. You are seeing exactly what you get when you make an exchange of God's will for your own. Equality? I think I will let you answer that for yourself. The amazing thing is this is what you get every single time that you make the exchange. Guess what? We make this exchange over and over and over again. We call ourselves spiritual, logical, and educated. How can we be when we exchange the glory of God in our lives for handful of nothingness?

For You

I had communion with the Lord this morning. I saw Him holding the bread. He was holding His hands out in front of Him. He slowly broke the soft bread down the center. He held it out to me and said, "This is My body broken for you." He then held the most beautiful silver goblet out in front of Him and said, "This is My shed blood for you." He said, "Remember Child, I did all this for you." As I was listening and watching Him this morning, the Spirit stirred inside of me and echoed, "For you

… for you … for you."

I stood there with my hands folded as the Lord came and enclosed His hands around mine. I said, "You did everything for me. You created the universe for me so that I could live on Earth. You created the first man out of the dust of the earth so that I could be born one day. You created the Jewish nation so that You could come through it to save me from my sins. You defeated death so that I could live. You wrote Your Word for me so that I could know about You and my future. You wrote the Word so that I could live a victorious, holy, and pure life through the wisdom you have given in it.

You waited thousands of years after Your ascension so that I could be born, grow in maturity, and see that I needed You in my life. You care that I become who You created me to be. You waited for me. You stand in a field of the most beautiful, tall, purple, swaying flowers that I have ever seen, waiting to commune with me every day. You show me fresh truth in Your Word by the power of the Holy Spirit that you placed within me. You have dipped out the coolest water from Your well for me to drink. You have shown me your narrow path because You want the best for me.

You hold nothing back from me according to Your will. The blessings You have to give were created for me. You told me that you were going to build a mansion for me. You told me that you intercede in front of the Father for me. You told me that you will come get me so that where You are, I can also be. You told me that you would give me a new body. I know that I have the most beautiful white linen robe waiting for me. You reached down from Heaven to cover me with Your hand. You did all of this and even more than I can contemplate for me.

The Lord stood there with His hands outlining mine as He covered my prayer-folded hands with His own. He said, "I did not have to do one of these things. I was perfectly contented and peaceful before the first star was created. I am in need of nothing to complete Me. I never have been in need and never will be. I AM. I have received glory from the work of My hand. I have worked that you can be in awe of Me. You are right in your thinking that I did this for you. I wanted you with Me for eternity. I made provisions for that to happen. You are unique to Me. You are like no other I have ever created. I came to Earth, showed you the Father, provided a love offering and sacrifice, took your place of pain and suffering, forgave your sins, died, rose, and am coming back again. For you … for you … all for you."

A Comfort to Know

It is a comfort to know that we are not alone. We were once alone in our lostness. We were stumbling around in the darkness. We exchanged what was right for what was wrong, and we had no awareness that the path that we were walking would have ended in death. The Holy Spirit spoke a word to our spirit to "come." Some of us had to be called several times before we could understand the light and head toward it. We came out of the muck and mire of the lost state that we were sinking in. We exchanged the temporal for the eternal. We exchanged our life for God's life for us. We are all the richer for the exchange.

It is a comfort to know that Jesus understands our human emotions. Despite being enlightened by the Holy Spirit, we experience true feelings of sadness, loneliness, confusion, and hopelessness. The trials that come into our lives leave us feeling alone at times with no light shining for us to follow. Even though we know the Lord is there, because of our situations blinding us, it is hard to see Him. This world fights for our attention. The enemy wants nothing more than for us to take our eyes off of our Savior, our light in the darkness. Once this happens, our emotions take on a life of their own as we sometimes spiral downward, looking for something to grab on to slow our descent.

There is a listening ear that hears you call out. There is a strong hand that catches and holds you. Isaiah 59:1 says, "Surely the arm of the Lord is not too short to save, nor is His ear too deaf to hear you call" (NIV). No matter the human emotion you are experiencing, the Lord understands and is there.

It is a comfort to know that when I exchange the sweet things of the Lord for the bitter things of the world, even after coming to the saving knowledge of Jesus Christ, that by His shed blood and broken body, I am forgiven. I can choose to get off the narrow path and take the wide path, despite hearing my Savior calling me back. Once I come under the conviction of the Holy Spirit and repent, I can return once more to the narrow path. My poor decisions do not have to define my life or negate me from living a victorious one. I do not have to listen to the enemy tell me that I am not worthy of the Lord when God calls me His child. I am grateful for the Holy Spirit teaching me, giving me knowledge, and understanding so that by obedience I can become wise. I can walk away from wickedness when it comes to tempt me. I can live a life with the highest integrity, purity, and holiness through the indwelling of the Spirit. I do not have to live a life where sin controls me. I can lay up treasures in Heaven by what I do for the Lord on Earth. I do not have to be defeated by only what I can see and feel when the unseen is so much more glorious.

It is a comfort to know that this world and body is not my home. I have the most unimaginably beautiful mansion, waiting for me. I have a Lord who will call me to the clouds to dress me in a perfect resurrected body and white linen robes. Even though the enemy lies to me and tries to tie ropes to my mind and understanding of what is really waiting for me, I can easily slip out of them and be at the Lord's side anytime I want, even now. The enemy does not have dominion over me any longer. I am not of this world. I am a child of the Most High God who calls me to His side, talks to me, forgives me, and loves on me so sweetly. I have a Lord who gave His life for me, so that I could be with Him for eternity.

It is a comfort to know all of these things. The realization of not only these comforting things but so many more keeps me on my knees before my Lord. The more I understand and learn of Him, the more I crave His comfort. He gives it in abundance if we stay right by His side. Do not travel even an arm's length from Him. The further you travel, the less comfort you will experience. It is a comfort to know the Truth. It is a comfort to know that I have been set free. It is a comfort to know the Lord as my personal Savior.

God's Resting Hand

I was praying this morning, and several things were running through my mind, including the road to publishing my journals, my relationships, guidance on how to proceed on some things, pondering situations to figure out the why of, and looking at my family dynamics of how best to contribute to a peaceful path, among many other things. God clearly spoke in the midst of all of this. Each thought that came to mind He said,

"My hand is on that. I have it covered. You can rest."

I know His voice so well now. I love it when He talks. He does typically talk, but sometimes He allows me to hear Him through His Word or through a certain situation. Believe me; that is fine. Many times, though, He will tell me things in prayer time through the interpretation of the Holy Spirit.

This morning with full authority and confidence it was, "My hand is on that. I have it covered. You can rest." I said, "You have all of this covered. Besides being God and You can do that, why do you have Your hand on all of this?" He said, "If you stay close to Me and abide in My will for your life, then every decision you make, every desire that you have, every hurt you feel, every thought you think, every aspiration you can dream of, and every relationship you make—My hand is resting upon it. Since I can do all of that, it allows you to rest in Me, knowing that I have you covered with My mighty hand. I promised you peace, and I always honor My promises to you. You may not have all the answers of the whys and what-ifs, but you do know that while you rest in My will, you will be well taken care of." I just started smiling and said, "Lord! I love when you talk to me. People think you don't exist, yet here You are talking to me. I don't understand exactly how you do it, but You certainly make Yourself clear when You do speak."

Since I am a visual person, I picture the Lord's hand gently resting on my head. I picture His hand resting over my journals. I picture His hand resting over the relationships He has given me. I picture His hand resting on every situation I have in my life. With that resting hand, there is peace. I pray that I do not step outside His will by my own choice so that the covering of His hand is removed. I don't only desire it, I literally need it to stay resting on me. I have learned that He is not the one that removes His hand, but it is me that slides out from underneath it. When I do this, His peace is taken from me. I may not like everything that happens in my life, but it sure does run more smoothly when His hand is resting on me.

Questions of Sin

Recently, I have been on an unintended journey toward understanding sin. Honestly, I haven't thought too much about sin through the years in my Christian walk. I have never studied sin from God's perspective to have a deeper understanding of why I sin, the length of sin, and the consequences of sin. I really never had a reason to. I think that was my mistake. I think if I would have, I could have avoided some of the sin I have chosen in my life—maybe not all of it, but some of it at least. I think that God can use our sin to drive us to our spiritual and literal knees in humility and broken-heartedness. I know this can only happen if you are in place of the deepest repentance and remorse of your hurt that you have caused yourself, others, and the Lord. It is not that you got caught in sin and you have to come clean, it is that you are hurting because you hurt the Lord's heart with your sin.

I think those secret sins that Psalms talks about can bring us to a new place of understanding. In those times that this new understanding occurs, the lessons the Lord can teach are immense and seem innumerable. Who knew? I think you have to have a willing spirit to analyze your sin and have your heart pliable so that the Lord can work in and though your life. You have to have the ability to seriously self-reflect in an objective way. I think one of the reasons this does not happen earlier in our Christian lives is spiritual immaturity.

I believe it takes a certain amount of sin through the years to finally realize the power of it. I think it takes the "bigger" sins that affect the deepest part of your heart that wakes you up the most. Those "bigger" sins would be individualistic for sure. Just for the record, there really is no "bigger" sin. Sin is equal because it is all disobedience to a Holy God. It's hard not to rank sin in bigness, though, as that is so natural for us to do. We may be gossiping over in our corner while we point our finger at the one who may be cheating in the other corner. They in turn are pointing their finger at another, drinking in the far corner. And so it goes.

I have learned that, as humans, we do a poor job at accepting our sins for what they are—disobedience. Someone is always doing worse than what we are doing, so that somehow makes what we are doing wrong not that bad. That is all foolishness, but we justify it in our heads. "We may be doing this, but at least we have never done that!" It is all disobedience, no matter what you tell yourself. Sin is really sin, in the end.

I want to take this journal and answer the three questions I posed at the beginning according to what I have learned in my own search for the understanding of sin. Why do we sin? How long does sin last? What are the consequences of sin? We sin because we want our flesh to be satisfied. We mistakenly believe that when our flesh is satisfied, then all of us are satisfied and content. What a lie!

Sin feels amazingly good, and the fun is immeasurable. What truth! The why of sin is actually not that difficult to comprehend. We want what we want when we want it, with disregard for anyone and anything including the Lord. God says in Romans 1: 32 that there is pleasure in sin. There has never been a truer statement written! We sin because it is brings us pleasure. Let's never deny that truth to justify our sin any deeper. The why of sin is quite basic.

How long does sin last? This isn't as simple, yet I have an analogy that I believe sums it up. Think about a fire. There are some components that have to be present for a fire to continue to burn, including oxygen and material. Without these two minimal components, a fire would go out instantly. Well, sin is just like fire in so many ways. First of all, it will burn the heck out of you! That's obvious.

More importantly, sin requires some basic components to continue to be sin: ungodly thoughts and actions. That's it. Two components. How can these two little things get us in so much hot water? You take ungodly thoughts and actions away, and just like a fire, the sin stops. It's pretty amazing how that works. Before a person changes his or her thoughts and actions, the actual time frame of sin that could occur may be a day up to many years. The sin will stop instantly just like the fire only when the two components are removed.

The sin will continue to burn as long as the two components are present. Just for the record, sin can occur with just one component, as well: your thoughts. Sinful thoughts rarely continue very long without subsequent sinful actions. Be very careful, Christian, as all sin starts with just a thought.

The last question is the problem. What are the consequences of sin? No journal can hold the answer to this question because it is too immense. Just because the sin has stopped, there is an unmeasurable amount of time for the longing for that sin to continue or reoccur. The dealing with this longing is a consequence of sin. Since sin is fun, you miss it when it is gone. I know that is hard to understand, but it is truth. I don't think you miss all the sins you have done, but there are some that, if left unguarded, you wouldn't mind returning to.

There are a hundred examples of this. I heard of a story of a man who ended up in the ministry. He had an addiction to pornography. When he got married, he confessed his addiction to his wife and told her that he needed her to help him not to return to it. She has passwords for every electronic device he owns; at any time, she can key into whatever she wants. She can check the sites he has visited. Now this man is serious in his desire to turn from this sin, yet he still longs for it at times.

He longs so much for it, in fact, that he needs strict accountability to keep him from returning to the sin once again. This is what I am talking about. Other examples would be drinking, drugs, adultery, or any compromise of integrity. Why do you have a man who commits adultery once, repents, gets his life straight, yet returns to adultery again years later? The longing for the satisfaction of that particular sin is so strong that it calls him back. It is the same of any of our own sins.

I think as Christians, we need to wake up and really understand how sin works in our lives. As soon as the enemy knows our deepest weaknesses, don't be foolish to think that he will not use this longing as bait to return you to the sin you once enjoyed. This would be the only explanation of why the alcoholic goes back to drinking, the adulterer goes back to unfaithfulness, the drug addict goes back to drugs, and the pornographer goes back to pictures and videos, and we go back to any former sin. That longing is stronger than the sin sometimes. Once the flesh has tasted what satisfies its weakness, it will battle against this for an undetermined amount of time. This is a horrible consequence of sin.

The consequence of sin that we completely ignore is the harm it will cause our personal relationship with the Lord. The Lord says, "Do not grieve the Holy Spirit." We never think about that when we sin. Other consequences of sin would be the more obvious such as loss of family, of work, of relationships, of health, and so forth. These could hold long-term consequences for you, as well. There are extremely harsh consequences for choosing our own way for temporary pleasures. The cost far outweighs the pleasures every single time.

We do not see the cost because not one of us thinks about the consequences of sin when we enter it. We fool ourselves just like all the humans before us thinking, "I am fine. I'm just going to see how close I can get." How close to a fire can you get before you get burned? You have to touch it. You can't get close to a sin before you are already in it. Once burned, there are consequences. If you do not think there are, then you are a very foolish and naïve person. That exact thinking is what gets you in the sin in the first place.

Why do we sin? How long does sin last? What are the consequences for sin? Maybe you need to answer these same questions for your own Christian walk. Answering these questions for my own life has given me a new perspective on the power of sin. I also feel that it has laid down a layer of accountability between me and the Lord. Wisdom is being obedient to the knowledge the Lord has given. I want to be a wise person; therefore, I cannot ignore the lessons the Lord has taught me and that I have painstakingly learned.

State of Being

As we are walking along in life, I have come to the conclusion that you are in one of three states of being. You can only be in one state at a time; however, one state could precede another one. You are either in a state of sinlessness, temptation, or sin. I used to believe, before an intensive year of study, that you couldn't help but sin each day somehow. I understand that while our righteousness is as filthy rags and we are sinful beings, that does not necessarily mean that we will automatically sin each day. In fact, I may go many days or months without sinning.

Will I eventually sin? Most likely. Why? I know that I have sinned and that I will sin again eventually because my flesh is so strong, and it doesn't stop badgering me until it gets what it wants. The chances are always there that I may give in. First John 1:8 says that if we say we have no sin, we are deceiving ourselves (all verses NIV). Sin keeps looking for the path of least resistance to seep in. It may be in just a thought that is dishonoring to God. It may be a "little white lie" that we justify as acceptable.

Sin will usually find its way in eventually, based on the weakness of the flesh and the poor attention we give to the Spirit. While I understand that, it doesn't give me a free ride to just accept sin as okay when it does happen. "Oh, I haven't sinned in two months, but whoops, I had a thought today that wasn't honoring to the Lord. Oh well, that's not so bad! Look at how good I have been." Don't pat yourself on the back when you haven't sinned in a while and then justify that you are okay when you sin a little. Sin is disgusting to a Holy God no matter how little you convince yourself it is wrong or how long it has been since you sinned last.

Now with that clear, I want to talk about this interesting "sinless" state. I believe that as you grow closer to and stronger in the Lord, you will sin less and less. I believe that is a natural occurrence. The opposite is also true. I believe when you really see sin as the stinking trash heap that it is, and you finally see your sin how God sees it, you wake up to some new reality. You start evaluating your weak areas that you sin in. By the convicting power of the Holy Spirit and your full willingness to be holy like God says to be, your mindset and desires start changing.

Slowly that stronghold in your life starts losing its grip. I think this takes time and deep commitment to the Lord to overcome. I believe the Lord works with you as He sees you are making great efforts to be victorious over the flesh. You have to be fully committed. Your focus gets clearer and clearer and then you have laser-beam focus on the Lamb of God. You only desire is to seek holiness. Your eyes shift less and less from left to right to see what else is out there because you are so afraid that if you do see something, it will break the intimate relationship that you have taken so long to build with the Lord.

You may say, "Sarah, you have to sin. That is just what we do as humans because we are not perfect." I understand. I am saying I believe that you take one sin that binds you at a time to the throne every day. You and the Lord dissect your sin and get to the root of why you are doing it in the first place. How did you "fall" or "choose" that sin in the first place, and what is the stronghold behind it? I do not believe Christians ever do this or do it consistently. How do I know they don't? They go right back to it later.

It may even be years later, but they return to the same sin none the less. Obviously they didn't understand the root cause, so the same sin sprouted back up. If you use the excuse, "I *have* to sin because I am not perfect," I believe that is a lazy cop-out excuse that you don't care enough to work through what is in your life with the Lord. You have to sin because you want bondage to the sin more than you want freedom from it. Let's be real with each other. You want your way more than the Lord's way. You have to sin? Live in bondage if you want to. You will be in the majority of people for sure.

I love the Book of Job. God said that Job caught His attention because he was blameless and righteous. Had Job ever sinned? Of course. Job obviously became serious about his sin, understood the root causes, and got rid of the strongholds. He walked so close to God that he didn't want to do something that could hurt God's heart. Job disciplined his mind and actions to walk blameless.

Remember in John 8:11 when Mary Magdalene was going to be stoned for adultery? What did Jesus say, "Go! Try not to sin again?" No. He said, "Go. Sin no more." Why would Jesus say this if He didn't believe that Mary could be victorious over that particular sin in her life? Alternately, is it possible that Jesus was referring to absolutely no more sin in her life? Interesting thought. God said Noah was, "Blameless and righteous." Had Noah ever sinned? Of course, but like Job he had completed a root-cause analysis. He didn't live in sin, or he would have been no different than those on the outside of the boat, beating on the door to get in.

All these people started me thinking about righteousness and blamelessness. Righteousness is being absolutely genuine and morally right. Is it possible that the longer you spend time in the absolutely genuine presence of the Most High God that He can start influencing you stronger and stronger to live in disciplined uprightness in all areas of your life? I believe more and more it is possible. Is that easy? Uh—No! Noah, Job, and Mary would all tell you that it's not easy, but they obviously did it. If they can do it, why can't we? I believe we can. It is just that the majority of us are not willing to be disciplined enough. This world is way too fun, and the Lord is way too boring. I guess it goes back to free will. Whose way do you want more in your life, yours or God's?

Let's talk about the "temptation state of being." You try so hard to live a genuine upright, moral life that is pleasing and honoring to the Lord. You keep your head straight ahead on the narrow path. Out of the clear blue, something unexpectedly catches your attention off to your right. You turn your head. That is the best way I can explain temptation. Are you still on the narrow road living the same righteous life? Yes. You *briefly*, and that is the key word, turn your head. Immediately, the Holy Spirit snaps His fingers in front of your face and says, "Child of God. You are holy, and that is not. Keep your head straight and walk on." You look in the Most High God's face, and you immediately pray for a covering for strength that your head is kept straight and that you will not fall into temptation. You physically, mentally, and emotionally put as much distance from that temptation that you possibly can.

Once the enemy sees that he turned your head, he will throw that same temptation back into your path over and over again to see if he can get you to do more than turn your head the next time. He might just be successful, too. Don't be arrogant and foolish to think he won't. You are weak in the flesh, and if you are just as weak in the spirit, then you are nothing more than a sitting duck for the enemy. Being tempted is not a sin. Jesus was tempted and He did not sin. No matter how strong the temptation is, by the power of the Holy Spirit and your willingness to listen to His counsel, you do not have to enter into sin following a temptation. It is so easy to enter sin after a temptation.

Beware of temptation as it always precedes sin. Remember the state of temptation is brief. You will either quickly fall back to a sinless state or fall forward to a sinful one. Temptation can at least last forty days as we know from Jesus'. It may last shorter or longer than this, but still it will be an overall brief period time. Why? Your spirit or your flesh will win out eventually. It all depends on which one is stronger. It all depends on who you have been hanging out with more: God or the world. That is why God says we are in a battle.

The last state that we find ourselves in is of course the sinful one. Again, I think this is one that we fully accept as inevitable. I do not believe that we can be sinless in our lives. If we could, then Jesus Christ did not have had to die. That's a fact. I have boiled sin down so many times in my journals. We sin because it is fun having our own way, and we like being in control, period. Sin satisfies the temporal needs of the flesh, whatever they are. Since most people are ruled by their flesh and not their spirits, sin happens pretty naturally.

Sin will take everything from you and hand you back nothingness every single time. Christian, think about it. You get nothing in return for all the time and energy you put into sin. Think about spinning your wheels in a pile of mud. You can push the gas pedal as hard as you want, but when you get out to see how far you have gone, you have traveled no distance. Sin takes everything from you but takes you nowhere. You are just sitting there, burning gas with nothing to show for it. What a waste. I wonder how tired our Lord gets of seeing His children spin their wheels in the mud?

If there are three states of being, which one does God say we should dwell in? There are so many verses in New Testament about the expectations of living in a sinless state after an encounter with the Lord that I cannot ignore them. I think we Christians dismiss them so easily. I think we have been conditioned to assume that we will sin and so, therefore, we do. I believe it may be one of the biggest lies bought from our enemy, and we didn't even know it. I think a Christian lives a defeated and stagnated life to think that he or she cannot live a holy life. It has nothing to do with being good enough, worthy enough, or work-based. That is not biblical. It has everything to do with staying in the will of God and caring enough for holiness to avoid anything that He calls sin. It has to do with understanding the good you are supposed to do and then following through consistently.

I do not think we spend enough time with the Lord to equip us for defending and preventing ourselves against sinning. He has given us the means to be like Noah and Job through the Word of God and power of the Holy Spirit. These men served the same God that we do. They both caught God's attention because of their determination to be blameless in the Lord's sight. They are obviously very special as we are talking about them some 4,000 to 5,000 years later. They had to make choices just like us about what to think and how to behave. They consistently made righteous and godly decisions. They stayed so close to God that when temptation made them turn their heads, they listened to the Holy Spirit snap His fingers in their faces.

What about you? What state are you in right now? We will all find ourselves in each of them, depending on where we are in our closeness with the Lord. I just have to praise the Lord that He has already reconciled our sin and forgiven it under the cover of His blood. He became our sin so that we would be able to live in another state if we so choose. That is the key, though. Which state you live in is a choice—whether you are going into one or coming out of one.

It is your choice. God has made it very clear which state you should choose no matter how hard it is. God said He has not called us to impurity (1 Thessalonians 4:7). He wants us to live a life of godliness and holiness (1 Timothy 2:2). God said we know how we ought to act in His household (1 Timothy 3:15). God commands to stay pure and pursue righteousness (1 Timothy 5:22; 6:11). God says He has written all of these things to us in His Word so that we may not sin (1 John 2:1). God says that no one that abides in Him sins (1 John 3:6). God says no one is born of Him and practices sin (1 John 3:9; 1 John 5:18).

I could go on and on, proving my case of what state God fully expects us to live in. I think 1 Timothy 6:14 sums it up best, "Keep the commandment without spot or blame until the appearing of our Lord Jesus Christ." What commandment? "Pursue righteousness and godliness." He is clear on which state He prefers for you. Does He love you any less when you are in a sinful state? No. I want to make clear His love is not conditional on what you do, but His love is based on what He already did. His love is unconditional, and that is where grace and mercy comes in. Plead the blood of Jesus on your current sin state, and move quickly to a sinless one! He says in 2 Timothy 2:19, "Everyone who names the name of the Lord *must turn away* from unrighteousness."

Listen closely. If you are an authentic Christian, you should not be able to live in a sin state for very long without being harassed by the Holy Spirit. You can't live in a perpetual sin state like you did prior to accepting Christ. You can't live like the old creature but claim to be new at the same time. That's not how it works. Your façade will become transparent rather quickly. God is no fool. If you call Him Lord, you *must* come out of the sin state.

If you are not being bothered by Him while in a sin state even for a short time, something is seriously and dangerously wrong. Red flags should be waving like crazy in your head. You should be extremely worried and in need of some deep soul searching about whether or not you have ever been sealed by the Holy Spirit in the first place. I am in no way trying to make you doubt your salvation. I am just giving you a sure-fire way to check it. With time so short now, this is nothing to play around with.

I have been long-winded in this journal, and that was not my original intention. There seem to be many things that needed to be said. These states need to be thought about and discussed. I believe that we should be constantly monitoring our lives to determine what state we are in and what state the Lord wants us to be in. We should be making every effort by the power of the Holy Spirit in us to pursue righteousness and godliness. We can't do this in our power. If you are so arrogant to try, you will fail.

I want to close with this. You achieve a sinless state not because you are good or by works, but by your obedience to the Holy Spirit and God's set ways. You can choose to obey Him and be in a sinless state or disobey Him and be in a sinful state. That is as simple as I can make it. Prior to having the power of the Most High God in you, you would not be able to achieve a sinless state. It would be utterly impossible. After He dwells in you and you are in Him, that is a game changer. Then He says, "Be Holy as I am Holy." He wouldn't tell you this if He didn't expect it was possible.

You are holy and sinless when you abide so close to the Lord that you can hear every word The Spirit says to guide your life. Your spirit is quickened immediately as He guides you away from a sinful state into a sinless one. It all depends on how carefully you are listening. It all depends whose will you want more: His or yours. The majority of people may disagree with me. That is fine. I know what I feel the Lord has impressed upon me for my life. I think I have included enough scriptural references that support what I have written.

Am I a sinner? Yes. Is it possible that I will sin again? Yes. Does He forgive sin? Yes? Will I sin less and less the closer I abide in the Lord? Yes. Can I live in a sinless state to which point I choose the Most High God's over my own will? Yes. Does God expect me to go and sin no more? Yes. Will He love me in whatever state I am in? Yes. Does He expect holiness? Yes. What state are you in? What are your excuses for living in a sinful one? God doesn't much care about your excuses. Trust me, He has heard them all. He loves you and tells you, "Be Holy."

Hold Together

He is before all things, and in Him all things hold together. (Colossians 1:17 NIV)

Have you ever been in a situation that you have no answers to, no guidance in, no understanding of, and no clue how it's going to work out?

All you are doing is going along for the ride because you have no other choice. All you are doing is trying to hold it together. At times you can feel yourself breaking apart. A piece of your heart breaks off over here, or a piece of your life breaks off over there. At any moment, you feel that you will break up completely.

The next morning comes. You open your eyes and wish somehow you could have disintegrated before the next day started. You do not want to struggle one more day. You keep putting one foot in front of the other to get through it. You are surprised how you made it. You actually held it together. To this very moment, you are still holding on.

The question is, who is really doing the holding? Is it really you? Could it be Someone much stronger and mightier in you? The Lord tells us in Colossians 1:17, "I hold all things together." If you did not have Jesus Christ in you with the consideration of what you have been through or currently going through, you would have disintegrated by now. Poof! Burned upon re-entry—disintegrated. Yet, you are still here. How is that possible?

The centrality of Christ in your innermost being despite your circumstances, despite your lack of understanding, and despite not "feeling" the Lord working holds you together. You are certainly not doing well by yourself as the world would have you believe. God holds this universe together. He holds this Earth together. He holds everything visible and invisible together. He holds the Church together. He holds all of creation together. You are His creation. He holds you together. Isn't it comforting to know that Christ in you is holding you? He holds you from the inside out.

You are not going to fall apart today. You will not cease to be. You may not like your situation and may be floundering around a little bit right now, but as an authentic Christian with the power of the Most High God in you, disintegration is not going to happen on His watch. One of His primary jobs is to hold things together. Of all of creation, you are His top priority. He will hold you. How am I so sure? Simple. He tells us in His Word that He has the inability to lie. He tells us in His Word that He holds all things together. If I believe the Word of God, then I have to completely trust that He will hold you and me together no matter what this life throws at us.

In the end, holding together is not all for our benefit. It is for God's glory! When you have every right to disintegrate based on your situation, but you still hold it together, the world sees Christ in you! Wrap your mind around that one!

Spoiled

See what great love the Father has lavished on us, that we should be called children of God! And that is what we are. (1 John 3:1 NIV)

The longer I spend time with the Lord in prayer and in His Word, the more spoiled I feel. Men do not usually think about being spoiled. Typically, women are the ones who desire to be spoiled. I think inwardly that men wouldn't mind if their wives or family spoiled them a bit. They would never express that desire but would take the rewards of being spoiled without putting up too much of a fuss. Humans generally like to be taken care of.

This being "taken care of" may be in the form of a strong, peaceful, inviting, loving family, and home environment. It may have nothing to do with receiving material possessions. One could become spoiled if this is what you lived in all the time, especially when you never had it consistently before. To be fully accepted for who you are and what you have to contribute to life by others could give you a feeling of being spoiled. Sometimes the feeling of being spoiled comes from behavior by another toward you that you feel is undeserved or greater than you deserve. I think we could put together a short list of what it would take to make us each feel spoiled.

Have you ever stopped in your Christian life and thought, "Wow! The Lord has spoiled me." Have you ever made a list of how the Lord has spoiled you? Have we taken all of His gifts for granted? Have they lost their newness? Have we had them so long that they have lost their "bigness" in our lives? You know that saying "spoiled rotten"? That is what the Lord has done for His children. We fail to recognize and really put together what He has done for us.

I love 1 John 3:1 (all verses in this devotional are from the NIV). It says the Father has "lavished" us with His love. I looked up the definition of the word lavish. It means to expend or give in great amounts or without limit. Synonyms are heap, pour, scatter, and thrust upon, devote, favor, and to honor with. The Most High God, who owes us absolutely nothing, lavishes things upon us. Who are we that He is mindful of us? Can you explain why He would care enough to heap and pour blessings without limits upon us? 1 John 3:1 simply says it is because of the Father's great love for us. It is not just Jesus' love, but the Father's great love, too.

What makes Him show such great love for us? He says it is because we are His children. Think of your own children; do you lavish great love for them? It just comes naturally, and it is without limits. Our children have done nothing to make us shower them with our great love. We have done nothing for God to shower us, either. It is the exact same, except God's lavishing should make you feel spoiled rotten. "Your Father in Heaven gives good gifts to those who ask Him" (Matthew 7:11). He gives gifts to His children that only He can give.

How does God spoil us? When He lavishes us with His great love, what does it look like or feel like? I cannot include everything, but I will try to tell you as many things as I can fit in a journal! John 1:12 says when we receive and believe in His name, we are lavished with an adoption as children of God. When we become adopted, we have full rights as a daughter and son of a King. Nothing is held back from us. If God has it to give, He will give it according to His will. One thing that He gives us as adopted children is freedom (Galatians 4:5). Our freedom nor our adoption was free to Him, but it was free to us. We are free from condemnation. We take that for granted. You were given a great gift when God placed His Spirit in your heart when you were adopted. Through His Spirit communing with your spirit, there is affirmation that you are His child (Romans 8:14–16).

You should have complete peace of mind of who you belong to and who calls you His child by the power of the Holy Spirit. There should be no doubts. Do you know of people who have no peace and are full of doubt? I do. Their lives are tossed to and fro with each wave of life. We take God's gift of peace for granted. God spoils us with joy and strength (Psalm 68:6; Nehemiah 8:10). Through God's great love for us, He makes us competent. We are equipped for every good work. We become competent in the work the Lord has for us. (2 Timothy 3:17). Have you ever been around incompetent people? Have you ever thanked God for lavishing you with competence to achieve all good things? No? We have taken our own competence for granted.

God spoils us with wisdom and understanding if we will only be obedient to the knowledge He has given us through His word (Job 28:28; Proverbs 4:5–7; Ecclesiastes 7:12). Wisdom is ours for the taking, but so often we disregard or squander it. God lavishes the correct directions you should take in your life. Proverbs 3:6 says, "He will show you which path to take." How comforting to know you never have to feel lost again on which way you should go. Have you seen people wandering around without direction in their life? Some wander aimlessly for years. They never seem to be able to find a path that leads anywhere good. God has given His children a path or a way to follow. It is not His fault that we do not follow His directions. It is ours. The lavish gift of the right directions is huge in a Christian's life.

One of the most wonderful gifts He gives His adopted children is healing. Do you know what one of the most painful parts of the body is to heal? The heart. If you have ever had a broken one, then you will agree with me. Before God heals anything physical, His gift of healing goes straight for the heart every time (Psalm 147:3). It seems that is the first part of the body to always get hurt by the world and people. God binds our wounds. What a gift!

As daughters and sons of the Most High God, we can't just live in any old shack. Jesus says in John 14:2 that He will personally prepare for you a mansion to live in for eternity. Feeling spoiled rotten yet? Or are you so spoiled now that you take all of these gifts for granted?

How many other people that you have ever known in your entire life have given you even half of what God has lavished, heaped, poured, honored you with, favored, or scattered upon you? Let me help you out—zero. No one in heaven or earth will spoil you like your Father. Proverbs 10:22 says, "The blessings of the Lord makes a person rich and He adds no sorrow with it." You were poor and without a path, but He adopted you into His family. You are now His daughter or His son. You are now rich without sorrows.

One last gift has to be mentioned, or my list would be incomplete. Romans 6:23 says, "The *gift* of God is eternal life in Christ Jesus our Lord." The what? The *gift*. If the Father would have held this first gift from us then we could have never been adopted. He could never have lavished us with all the other gifts without Jesus being given to us. From the first breath that Jesus breathed to His last—that was a gift to us. His entire life was the ultimate gift, one that opened the doors for us to become spoiled-rotten, eternal children of God! I don't know about you, but I like being spoiled!

Innocent

So now there is no condemnation for those who belong to Christ Jesus. (Romans 8:1 NLV)

Remember the story of the lady who was caught in the act of adultery in John 8? How embarrassing. It is one thing to sin, but it is quite another when people catch and confront you. Would you want to be caught in your sin and pulled in the middle of a crowd? The Bible actually said she was "caught in the act." If that is true, then they would have been able to catch the man as easily as they were able to catch the woman. Have you ever wondered what happened to the man? Why wasn't he pulled in to be condemned and stoned by the more righteous Jews? The Bible does not answer this question. I always thought that was interesting.

I can picture the scene of people laying hold to this sinful, sinful, sinful woman and dragging her to where Jesus was teaching in the temple courts early one morning. They made her stand in front of the group of people. The people named her sin. They yelled, "She has the sin of adultery! We should condemn her!" Jesus looked at the woman and the people, bent down, and wrote in the sand with His finger. What He wrote has always been a great mystery as the Bible does not record it. We will never know until we can ask Jesus in Heaven, which I plan to do, by the way. Is it possible that He bent down and wrote, "You are not condemned by Me"?

After they kept questioning Him about what to do with the punishment of this woman, who was obviously a sinner to everyone, Jesus stood up and said, "All right! Let the one who has never sinned throw the first stone!" After He said this, He stooped down to write in the sand again. What could He have written this second time? Maybe, "I will take the condemnation upon Myself. You are innocent." We know the story; all the people drop their stones and left.

Can you imagine the woman standing there, looking at Jesus who had just saved her physical life? She had never met Jesus and most likely did not know who He was besides being a teacher of the Scriptures. Jesus stood up and asked her, "Where are your accusers? Didn't even one of them condemn you?" She answered, "No, Sir." Jesus, the sinless and perfect Lamb of God, said something profound, "Neither do I condemn you." Of all the people who had a right to throw a stone, it was Jesus. What Jesus was saying was, "I do not accuse you. I place no blame on you. I will not pass judgment or sentence you. There is no damnation for you."

Did the woman deserve the condemnation because she broke the law? Yes. Someone had to take the condemnation for the sin committed. There always has to be a payment or sacrifice for sin. Someone has to wipe the slate clean. Someone has to pay. If it was not the woman, then who would it be?

Jesus didn't excuse the woman's sin. He instructed her to take a new sinless path. Jesus didn't condone her sin, but He did not condemn her personally. She would go without punishment. She would, in essence, go free. The Lord gave His innocence and freedom in exchange for her sin and the condemnation that went along with it. It was not His to take, but He was the only one that could take it. All the people who were holding the stones had been infected with sin, too. That is why they threw their stones down. The accusers could not exchange their innocence for her condemnation as they were just as guilty as the convicted. Even if they had the ability to, they would not choose to.

Understanding this truth, Jesus does the exact same thing for us today. He exchanged His innocence for the condemnation that we deserved. Would you ever exchange a convicted criminal's life sentence in prison so he could have your life of freedom that you enjoy now? No? Why not? You pass judgment that the convicted criminal was not deserving of the freedom. He had broken the law and now had his justified condemnation. You reason that you deserve your freedom, and you should not have to give it away.

We are so quick to reason this out until we are that prisoner. God says in Psalm 68:6 that He sets the prisoners free (NLT). Who are these prisoners that He set free from condemnation for breaking His law? That would be you and me. While we would never exchange our lives for a random prisoner that we didn't know in some prison somewhere, that is exactly what Jesus did for us. Not only did He not throw stones at us and condemn us, He gave us His innocence so that we could stand in front of His Holy Father.

What did He get in exchange for taking our condemnation? Calvary. That doesn't seem like a very fair trade does it? That is because there was nothing fair about it. It was only because of the Father and Son's great love of us that this uneven exchange of innocence and condemnation occurred. Listen. It had nothing to do with our great love for them. We had no love for them as we were still their enemies when the uneven exchange occurred. Slow down and think about that. Stop taking your undeserved innocence in this exchange for granted.

The only reason you are innocent today, despite your sin, is that Jesus took your deserved condemnation (John 3:18 NIV). If you are not an authentic Christian, then you will face full condemnation and the wrath of God at the Great White Throne Judgment (John 3:18 NIV). You will be found guilty. Your own disbelief in this happening to you in the future will in no way negate the biblical truth of this statement. Many people wrongly reason that if they do not believe this judgment is coming, it will not happen. That would be like me saying, "If I jump off a skyscraper, I do not 'believe' I will die when I hit the ground, despite people telling me the truth of the matter." I will hit the ground, despite what I reason and believe in my head.

Likewise, you will be found guilty, despite what you reason and believe in your head about denying God. If I were you, I would let Christ take your condemnation and guilt in exchange for His innocence. It's your choice whether you truly accept this uneven exchange with Jesus, but it is the wisest one you will ever make.

Second-guessing

During my quiet time, I was praising the Lord by marveling at His works, including the Creation, flood, Jewish nation, His time on Earth, sacrifice, and more. It's a bit much to take in. I was sitting with Him and pondering these things. He said, "With all of that, I never second-guessed Myself." I said, "Second-guessed?" What an odd thing to say. The Lord has never second-guessed Himself. I was thinking, "Of course not. You are perfect." I was trying to understand what the Lord wanted me to get out of this statement. The Spirit said, "If you know this truth, then why do you second-guess Me?" Oh my gracious.

The Lord is always within His perfect will, and as long as that occurs, there is no reason to second-guess Him. If I, as a dedicated Christian, am in His perfect will, then when He asks something of me or shows me a new direction, I should not second-guess Him. It is even harder when something I see as bad happens in my life, and I second-guess if the Lord knows exactly what He is doing. But I do. If I am living the way He has appointed, according to what I know to be right in my thoughts and actions, then when the Lord moves, there should be no second-guessing on my part, no matter what happens. I should move forward immediately and completely without hesitation. I should not wonder if His hand is on me and the situation. I know it is.

Why is it so hard to not second-guess the Lord? I think it goes back to making sure we are comfortable. If we are okay with what the Lord has impressed in our spirits to do and it goes along with the plans we already have, then we will agree and won't second-guess Him. If we are not okay, then we delay in our willingness to immediately follow and listen to the Lord. We wonder if the things we didn't want to happen could still be part of His will. We have all done that. If the Lord tells us to talk to this person or that about something or even Him, we second-guess it. If the Lord tells you to do something specific at church, maybe make a move here or there, you delay and second-guess it—sometimes for years! We delay and second-guess it because we are not comfortable with what the Lord is saying. We, in essence, hesitate. Whether you want to call it delaying or hesitation, it is the same thing as second-guessing.

I am coming to realize that the Lord may not want us comfortable. He wants us to be so strong in Him. God wants us so close that we never second-guess His perfect will. Yes, it will make us uncomfortable. You work best in His strength and not your own. Think about it. If you only move when you are comfortable, you will not move very far. Any movement you do make will be in your own strength. Don't expect to experience the Lord in your life. If you can do it in your own strength, then why in the world would you ever need any of His? Isn't this how some Christians think: "I can do this in my strength. I will let You know when I need Yours!"

Do you have any idea who you are really talking to? We second-guess the Lord and do things in our own strength while staying very comfortable. This epitomizes why the church in America is dying and some Christians walk around wondering, "Is there more to this Christian life?" Nope. You get the Christian life that is mundane because you choose it.

God created everything. He is powerful enough to destroy it all because of sin and His holiness. He separated the world into two groups of people, so the Savior would come through the Jewish nation. He sacrificed Himself for all people, and on and on. *He* did all of this! The same Lord that did this in His perfect will is the same Lord that says to each one of us, "I never second-guessed Myself and neither should you. Move with Me inside My perfect will for your life. I know exactly what I am doing."

Cookie-Cutter Love

Remember when we were little and we would call someone a "copycat" if they imitated something we said or did? As old as that saying is, we still use it today. Our kids still call each other copycats! It simply means someone who mimics another's actions. If someone is being a copycat of you, that means they want to do exactly what you do and how you do it. Have you ever been around someone whom you admired and would like to have some of their same qualities? You talk to them a lot. You watch their mannerisms. You do not want to be them, but you would like to copy some of their better qualities. Have you ever met a person like this? I have.

I am an avid people watcher. I can hear myself say things that I have heard other people say and now is part of my vocabulary. I have even picked up some other people's mannerisms. My co-workers copy me with a few of my statements that I copied from other people like, "What I hear you saying is …," "Be mindful," or "That depends." Now when other staff hears someone say one of those statements they say, "You sound like Sarah!"

I am a manager in a rehab center, and I supervise numerous employees. When one of them needs help in a certain skill area like improvement in active listening, I will encourage them to copy other people on staff who are naturally good active listeners. It has worked so well. We all watch and copy certain sayings and mannerisms from others around us. As long as those models are good, moral, and strong, we should be fine. However, be mindful who you are copying!

Have you ever noticed that Jesus is a self-proclaimed copycat of His Father? Think cookie cutter or carbon copy. Anything the Father does, Jesus says He does. John 5:17 says, "My Father never stops working, and so I keep working too" (NCV). The Father works tirelessly so Jesus works tirelessly. Did you know Jesus never took a vacation once in three years of His ministry? Some may consider Him a workaholic! That is because His Father never stops working, either. Jesus says in John 5:19–21:

> The Son does only what He sees the Father doing, because the Son does whatever the Father does. The Father loves the Son and shows the Son all the things He Himself does. Just as the Father raises the dead and gives life, so also the Son gives life to those He wants to. (NCV)

John 5: 26 says, "Life comes from the Father Himself, and He has allowed the Son to have life in Himself as well" (NCV). Jesus says in John 5:30, "I can do nothing alone. I judge only the way I am told, so my judgment is fair" (NCV). God judges; therefore, Jesus judges the same way. John 14:10 reveals the words God speaks are the words that Jesus speaks (NCV). Jesus says in John 17:8 that He copied the teachings that the Father had given Him (NCV). He adds in John 17:10 that what they possess is the exact same Jesus says, "All I have is Yours, and all You have is Mine" (NCV).

Jesus indicates in John 14:9 that He looks like the Father. Phillip asked Jesus to show them the Father. Jesus responds, almost hurt, "Don't you know me, Phillip, even after I have been among you such a long time? Anyone who has seen Me has seen the Father. How can you say, 'Show us the Father?'?" (NIV). Jesus was saying, "I am a carbon copy of My Father in every way."

Jesus doesn't copy God because He wanted to adopt some of God's mannerisms or sayings. He copied God because He is God. John 10:30 says, "The Father and I are one" (all verses in this paragraph are NIV). John 10:38 says, "The Father is in Me, and I am in the Father." The people became upset as they knew that Jesus was saying He was equal to God. Jesus, in the flesh, copied what the people already knew of God, in the spirit. This should prove to them that the Father had sent Him. He says in John 5:36, "The things I do, which are the things my Father gave Me to do, prove that the Father sent Me." He goes on to clarify this point in John 17:26, "I showed them what You are like, and I will show them again." He showed the people what God was like by copying Him. Why did Jesus work tirelessly to show everyone His Father? He continues in verse 26, "Then they will have the same love that You have for Me, and I will live in them." Jesus went to great extremes to ensure this happened.

Jesus turns the "Copy Cat" game around on us in John 5:23. "All people will honor the Son as much as they honor the Father. Anyone who does not honor the Son does not honor the Father who sent Him" (HCSB). He is saying if you want to honor the Father, then you had better honor Jesus. Without copying that honor for the Son, people do not honor the Father. We should be copy cats of Jesus' forgiving nature. Colossians 3:13 says, "Just as the Lord has forgiven you, so also you must forgive" (HCSB).

I hear Jesus explaining that He copies the Father, then we copy Jesus, and by doing do that we copy the Father. If Jesus is a cookie cutter of God, and we are cookie cutters of Jesus, then we can be cookie cutters of God. It has to go in that order. If we all are copy cats and carbon copies, then we are all the same. Do not misinterpret that we can be God as Jesus is God, but we will be in God and He will be in us. I think John 17:21–23 sums up my point nicely. Jesus prays:

> Father, I pray that they can be one. As you are in Me, and I am in You, I pray that they can also be one in Us. I have given these people the glory that you gave Me so that they can be one, just as You and I are one. I will be in them, and you will be in Me so that they will be completely one" (NCV). Listen to the end of verse 23 very closely as it blew my mind, "You loved them just as much as You loved Me.

God's love for us is a perfect copy of the love He has for His only begotten Son. That gives me chills. Dwell on that for a second. As filthy sinners and unfaithful children that ignore our Lord so much in our life by not spending consistent time with Him, God still loves us just like He loved Jesus. Cookie-cutter love. It's the exact same love! God loved His only Son so much that He promised Him that He would never decay in the clutches of death. God was true to His Word. He tells us the same thing. We will never perish but have eternal life (John 3:16 NIV).

God's love is the same, and His promises are, as well. What complete peace fills me to really understand the copying that occurs from God to Jesus to me and back to God! Jesus says we are all, "one." If I had to be a carbon copy of anyone, it would be Jesus. He said if we loved Him, then we would copy Him. He said we would want to copy the things He did. We would copy His love for others. We would copy His teaching, preaching, and sharing the truth. I will close with the perfect cookie-cutter, copycat, and carbon-copy verse! Ephesians 5:1 says simply, "Be imitators of God." Why? "Because, you are His dearly loved children" (NIV). If you truly love God the way you claim to, then imitate Him at all times in front of all people.

Sexual Immorality

The Lord has laid a more uncomfortable theme on my heart to speak about. I knew what He wanted, but I have been avoiding the topic. This morning I opened the Word to do my daily reading. Colossians chapter 3 was the study for the day. Verse 5 says, "Therefore, put to death whatever in you that is worldly: sexual immorality ..." (HCSB). The Spirit was like, "I am going to keep showing you this until you write about it!" I let out a sigh.

Sexual immorality can be defined by a corrupted character or conduct according to what God intended the sexual realm to be. It is a twisting of the original intent. It is a compromise or justification at some level of what God has deemed as right. It is an iniquity, misconduct, offense, transgression, violation, degradation, and impurity of what God had in mind when the sexual desire was created in us. It is a breach or violation of God's way. No matter how we justify the smallest sexual immorality in our thinking or behavior, it is truly all the things that I just described. It truly carries that much weight, despite forcing ourselves to believe it any other way. No matter how good it feels when we are engaged in thinking or behavior that compromises our sexual morality, God calls it sin. Sin is rebellion against holiness. God says clearly that sexual immorality in a Christian's life must be put to death.

God is so strong on many topics of the Bible, but sexual immorality has to be one of the strongest. God's expectations of us are amazingly high. He calls us His children. He has great love for us and desires for us to be pure, holy, and sanctified. He says we have been set aside out of this world for His glory, pleasure, and work. When we corrupt ourselves with things of this temporal world, we might as well take a bow and arrow and shoot it right through Christ's heart. We might as well go wallow in the trash heaps of this world, as that is exactly what we are doing when we play around with sexual immorality.

Jesus clearly says in John 15:19 that we are not of this world. If we are not of this world, then we are not to take part of worldly things, thoughts, and behaviors. Why is it that we have death grips on different parts of this temporal world and the meaningless pleasures they offer us? Even the strongest among the Christians can fall. I read a statistic about pastors. Close to 40 percent confess they have had an extramarital affair since beginning their ministry. Forty percent? If they are supposed to be the ones closest to God, is there any hope for the Christians who are spiritually asleep and in stagnation? Are we all sitting ducks, just waiting for the perfect storm of sexual immorality to present itself? Perhaps.

Every one of us has a weakness, and sexual immorality may be one without your even realizing it yet. Do people wake up in the morning, stretch, and jump out of the bed to say, "Today seems like great day to be sexually immoral! Yeah!" No. It never happens like that. Before sexually immoral behavior can occur, there has to be the first sexually immoral thought. There has to be the first mental compromise. All sin starts with just a thought. The more you play with the thought, the more emotions are hooked to it.

God made these sexual feel-good emotions for our pleasure as long as they are inside His boundaries. The brain is a chemically-based organ. It doesn't know why the stimulus is there. Its job is to create the sexual emotions to react to the stimulus. We mistakenly think, "Oh our brains are happy with this picture, video, girlfriend, boyfriend, friend by the water cooler at work, friend on the Internet, and so forth, so it must be okay to explore this a bit deeper." The same emotions are going to be there whether you are engaged in sexual morality or immorality. The sexual emotions can't distinguish if they are being used in God's will or your will. The emotions are strong, and they are very real just like God created them to be. What happens when the sexual emotions lead you to a fork in the road between immorality and morality?

What would make you, as a Christian, take that turn toward sexual immorality? The lack of a fulfilling and consistent sexual relationship in a marriage has led many a wife and husband down that road. That is why Paul said to husbands and wives in 1 Corinthians 7:5

> Do not deprive each other of sexual relations, unless you both agree to refrain from sexual intimacy for a limited time so that can give yourselves more completely to prayer. Afterward, you should come together again so that Satan won't be able to tempt you because of your lack of self-control" (NIV).

When a man and wife are in a sexually satisfied marriage, this verse indicates that they each have a level of self-control. When they are not, then there is a lack thereof.

When there is a lack of self-control, then there will be temptations. When there are temptations, sin usually is close behind. That seems logical. A man and wife actually help protect each other from the world as they increase self-control in the other, by their own obedience to loving their spouse faithfully in a sexual way. I think if married couples would deeply understand this truth, it would be the first defense they could put around their marriage to protect it from the roaring lion right outside their doorsteps or in their home by a click of a computer.

Spouses who deprive their spouses of regular sexual relations set them up for temptation and possible fall. Those spouses reason that their spouse should be strong and faithful no matter how things are going in their sexual relationship. They are very foolish, and may I say blatantly ignorant of the truth of God's word. They are in disobedience to God's way and thinking as they live in their self-created alternate realities. Both spouses have God-given responsibility to protect each other from the sexually immoral temptations that *will* come knocking.

Don't be naïve to think opportunities will not present themselves. Satan can smell this weakness in a marriage a mile away and creeps in, ready to set up the perfect scenario to lull the spouse way. We are truly in a spiritual battle for our marriages, and Satan has won many of them in this exact way I am describing. Husband! Wife! Wake up! Do not be ignorant! You are going to have an empty marriage and miss the abundant blessings that God promised if you are not sexually faithful to each other. Stop making excuses then justifying them in your head then compromising your marriage! Wake up! Wake up! Wake up! Sound the alarm!

Many, many marriages end in divorce from the above-described course of events. Sadly, many more will. Your marriage does not have to be one of them!

The other thing that would make you take the wrong turn in the fork of the road is the novelty of the sexual immorality that presents itself to you. You may be sexually satisfied in your marriage, but you just want something new and different. You want it all! Why not have your cake and eat it too when you are in control of your life and not a Holy God? Many couples truly have a sweet marriage, but you hear of a divorce due to a choice of exploration in places and people they should have never been engaged with. Someone like a person or countless photographs and videos catch their eye. They just want to spend a few minutes or few hours exploring possibilities of what it would be like on the other side of the fence.

Oh, they do not want to leave the security of their good marriage, but what will it hurt if they just explored a bit? They reason that it would not be hurtful at all. Satan is watching the whole time and tightening the snare around them without them even knowing. Thinking, looking, meeting, and talking, slowly turns into something that they did not set out to happen and is a natural occurrence of what happens when someone compromises their standard of integrity with sexual immorality. The flesh always demands more of the stimulus to keep the pleasurable emotion alive. The brain is an extremely powerful organ and will supply the chemicals as long as the flesh supplies the stimulus. After that person falls, only one thing waits for them at the bottom: utter destruction of their lives and emotions in addition to their family's lives and emotions. There is a significant blow to your Christian witness and your relationship with God!

Whatever stimulus that is invoking these strong sexual emotions outside of your marriage, is—in the end—stealing from your spouse. You may have never thought about it that way. Those emotions that you are expending on pictures or other people inappropriately are being taken from the one they truly belong to.

A spouse will justify an affair because the sexual emotions they would like to or try to direct toward their spouse have not been received. This spouse's self-control is severely compromised. It may be a hard conversation to have with your spouse, but show this journal to your spouse. Use this as a means to open up your heart to your spouse to let him or her know that you are struggling, and you don't want to be. You do not want to misplace your sexual emotions. You would never want to take something that belongs to them and place it elsewhere. It may be your spouse is the one struggling, and you are the one who has not received their sexual desires. If it is you, then you need to understand what the Word of God says and go apologize to your spouse and love on them. Abundant blessings will occur in your relationship.

For those singles out there, do not let the temporal pleasures fool you that they are just too good to wait for. If the pleasures are partaken of outside of God's design, then you have entered sexual immorality. Forget having sexual immorality in the marriage, when you are already experiencing now. There are so many things the Bible says to stand and fight against, but it clearly tells everyone, which includes singles, to run from sexual immorality (I Corinthians 6:18 NLT). If you ever have the most seemingly innocent sexual emotion outside of the boundaries of what God ordained, then you flee as fast as you can away from the stimulus. The devil is dangling a carrot in front of you to see if you are going to bite it. Christian, it is a trap. *Run!*

First Corinthians 6:18 says that all other sins are outside the body, but whoever sins sexually, sins against their own body. Think about that for a moment. Sin means rebellion. Does anyone really desire to be in rebellion against themselves? Does anyone really desire to hurt themselves in the deepest part of who they are? People don't set out for rebellion and hurt to happen to them. Most people are not thinking of the consequences of sexual immorality when they enter it. Everyone may want to wake up a bit because there are very harsh consequences when you hurt your own body by engaging in sexual immorality. Be wise. Protect your heart and body. Put a hedge of protection around your marriage. Honor God in purity of every thought and every action.

Never think sexual immorality can't happen to you. Why do you think the Bible teaches the Christian about it? Stay alert. Be ready to run!

Powerful Word

I have heard a preacher say once that the strongest thing on earth was not governments or military or people. The strongest thing on earth was the truth. We, as authentic Christians, know that the Truth has been revealed in the Word. I will confess that as a long-time Christian, I took the Word of God for granted. Only within the last few years has the Word of God become the Living Word to me every day. The Word was always living; I just wasn't living it. I thought I was, though. How many Christians can relate to this, I wonder? How many of us think we have just enough of the Word to be okay?

We are each on our own journey to stop living for ourselves and start living for the Truth. This journey takes longer for some than others despite us all carrying the name Christian. I understand this now. The Truth in the Word of God is not innate. You have to go get it. Once you keep going and getting more Truth, the Holy Spirit will interpret it for you. This is based on how committed and serious you are. Many Christians are content with what they know now when there is so much more to learn. The desire to get deeper Truth has to come from the inside of each of us.

Once we have the desire, the Lord starts revealing how really alive His Word is. I think He does this differently for each person. For me, the power of His Word has been revealed through assimilating the truth that I understand into my written journals. I have said once to friends that I feel my journals are gifts each morning from the Lord. That is why I can't miss quiet time. He is standing there with a gift, and I have to show up to receive it. He has gifts for each one of us in quiet time. People who love us give us gifts. The Lord heaps gifts on us every day for one reason. He loves us. We are just too busy to be loved on sometimes.

The Lord has allowed me to see the power of His Word through others receiving some of my journals. I have seen some people read my journals and be convicted. I have seen some read them, who are comforted. There are some that have read them and received instructions. Some say they receive inspiration and encouragement. All the journals are based on Truth, or at least Truth the way I perceive it. I have learned so much about the power of the Word by observing others read some words I feel the Lord allowed me to write. That in itself has been a witness back to me about the power of the Word of God.

In the past, I had never "experienced" the Word of God. I had only read it. Christian, they are not the same. It is one thing to read flat words on a page, and it's quite another for the Word to be wrapped around you and in you. The Word of God tells us that it is convicting. I have experienced this and have seen this to be true for others. Hebrews 4:12 states "For the Word of God is alive and active. Sharper than any double-edged sword, it penetrates even to dividing soul and spirit, joints and marrow; it judges the thoughts and attitudes of the heart" (NIV).

The Word of God tells us that it is comforting. Paul would speak the Word of God to people and end with, "Brothers, comfort one another with these Words." The Word of God brings instructions into our life. Second Timothy 3:16 says, "All Scripture is God-breathed and is useful for teaching and training in righteousness" (NIV). I have experienced this and have seen this to be true for others.

While I was praying to the Most High God this morning, I heard Him say, "My Word is alive and powerful." I responded, "Yes, Lord." I knew that I was supposed to write about this. My gift today was the journal that His Word is alive and powerful. He wants us to know and dwell on that truth. He wants us to experience His Word so that it is more than words on a page. He wants you to know that He is the Word and what that really means for your life.

John 1:1 says, "In the beginning there was the Word. The Word was with God, and the Word was God" (NIV). When we pick up the Word, we are literally picking up Jesus. When we experience the Word, we are literally experiencing Jesus. When we hear from the Word, we are literally hearing from Jesus. Jesus is God. We are with God when we are in His Word. Again, this staggers my mind.

The power of the Word of God is in my hands and life. This is made possible by the Holy Spirit revealing it to me. I am the only one that can control how much conviction, comfort, and instruction that I receive in my life. I receive them based on the priority I give the Word in my life. This is the same priority I give God in my life. The Word and God are one. He never limits these things; I do. I do not think most Christians contemplate these truths. I think it's time that we refocus and reevaluate what exactly we are holding in our hands and life. I think it is time that the Word becomes 3-D for us and stops being flat and taken for granted.

First Place

He is first in everything. (Colossians 1:18 NLT)

Why does it always seem that things in our lives fight to be first place? At least in my life, it seems to be a struggle. Spouses? Work? Clean house? Extracurricular activities? Children? Homework? Church? Friends? Other life duties? Do any of these sound familiar? It seems like there is never enough time. Everything needs its chance to be first sometimes. That is fair, right? The harder you try to divide your time and your mental priority list of what will be first today or even this hour, other things quickly flood you.

I always seem overwhelmed with things. I want to give 110 percent to everybody and everything. Since that is my thinking, I want to make everybody and everything first. Seeing how that is impossible, that is most likely why I get overwhelmed. That makes logical sense. Despite that I understand that makes logical sense, I still wake up the next day and go full force with the same thinking. I feel driven to do so.

This morning, I am reading over Colossians chapter one. Verse 18 jumped off the pages and screamed, *"Look at me!"* The end of verse 18 says, "He is the beginning, the firstborn from the dead, *so that He might come to have first place in everything.*" You know people say the Bible is hard to understand. Really? Jesus is saying, "There is nothing before Me. I am the beginning of all things. I died. God raised Me from the dead. There is no struggle about what should be first place in your life. I told you clearly that I am to be first in everything." How much clearer can the Word be?

God tells you what to put first as clearly as the sky is blue and grass is green. There is no guesswork in it. There is no contemplation about it. There is no internal struggle. When I understand the centrality of Christ in my life, I also understand He is my first of everything. Period. There is no debate on what comes first. Everything after Christ is second, third, fourth, and so on. There may still be a struggle ranking those, but there is no struggle on ranking what is first. Do you know the most amazing thing I have discovered? When I put Christ first, like He said He should be, everything else in my life seems to naturally fall in order with little to no effort.

There are no more struggles with what comes second, third, fourth, and so on. I do not have full understanding how that is possible. All I know is it is true. The minute you put Christ second is the very minute your struggles of ranking things in your life will start. The minute you obey Him and put Him first is the very minute everything else you have in your life will fall in natural order. Don't believe me. Believe Christ. He is the One who said it. We are the ones that complicate what He says because we want to be first in everything.

Listen Once

This morning I had to take my husband to work. I took a road that I do not typically take so that I could drop him off. Strong memories flooded my mind as I came to this one particular four-way stop.

It was just down from here that an event happened that I have never forgotten. It was probably fourteen or fifteen years ago. I was on my way to work, and it was pouring rain. I came over the bridge, and I saw lots of police and ambulances at a red light intersection. This would be an intersection that I would have to pass through on my normal route to work. I quickly took a side road for a detour around so that I wouldn't get stuck in traffic. This detour took me to this current four-way stop.

On the road ahead, I saw a car broken down right on the road. It was stuck in the lane and couldn't pull over. Just to show my age a bit, this was before people had cell phones! Anyhow, it was pouring down rain so hard, and this person had no phone to call for help. There were a few cars ahead of me pulling around this broken down car. No one was going to stop and help. It was my turn to come up to the car. Because I was in a van, I could look down into her car. It was a young woman with a young child in the back. She had her head resting on the steering wheel. Later on, I found out that she was praying.

Right when I looked down in her car, the Lord spoke clearly, "Help her." I quenched the Spirit and said, "Lord, surely not. I have to get to work, and it's raining." I drove slowly by and crossed one more road. I slowed down and said, "Lord surely someone else will come along and help her." He said, "I have appointed you to help her." I stopped the car. I sat there for a second in disbelief of what the Lord had said. I slowly did a U-turn on a side road and drove back to the car. Sure enough other cars were just going around her like she wasn't even there.

I parked my car in a side parking lot. I ran over to her passenger side window and knocked on the glass. She rolled the window down with rain coming down and stared at me in disbelief that I was standing there. I yelled over the sound of rain hitting her car, "God has sent me to help you!" She looked at me and said, "I was just praying that you would come! Thank you, Lord." I said, "Let's get you and your baby in my car and I can take you wherever you need me to take you. I can't help you with your car. I can only help you and your baby."

As soon as I was moving her and the baby to my van, several men, who appeared out of nowhere, stopped their car. They got out and pushed her car out of the road. They got back in their cars and left. Within minutes of my obeying the Lord, she and her baby were safely in my van, and her car was pushed to safety so it wasn't blocking traffic anymore. I took her baby to daycare; then I took her to her work. We talked the whole way. I told her that I was a Christian and needed to ask for her forgiveness.

I started getting choked up a bit because I felt so guilty. She put her hand on my arm and said, "Why on earth would you need me to forgive you when you have helped me so much?" I told her, "I had originally not obeyed the Lord and passed you by like all the other people because I didn't want to be inconvenienced. The Lord had to tell me twice to help you. I am so sorry that I didn't stop immediately." She said, "It's okay! I understand. The most important thing is that you did listen, and you turned around to come back. Thank you, and may God bless you." I dropped her off at work and I have never seen her since.

When I was at the stop sign this morning, it was like I was right back in the rainy morning when I passed that sweet mother and her baby. Immediately, I knew that I wanted to write a journal on obedience. What keeps us from obeying the Lord when He speaks? We can say it's a simple matter of inconvenience, not good timing, not comfortable with the situation, not prepared enough, or not something that we want to be involved in. It would take too much of energy, somebody else will do it, and the excuses continue. I can sum any excuse you and I can think of for not obeying the Lord when He has asked us to do something in a four-letter word: S-E-L-F. Every excuse will fall back to self. Every single one. How easy do our excuses start flying right when the Lord asks us to do something? After the excuses, don't forget the justification of those excuses.

We are very foolish if we think the Lord buys our excuses and justification for disobedience. *He never will!* Let's get into a little bit of reality. We are the only ones buying them. After just seconds, we have bought the lie of those excuses and accepted the justification, then we go on about our day. The next time we pray at church, we say, "Oh Lord, use me for your purposes." *Really?* We are hypocrites!

I can imagine the Lord looking down on some Christians saying, "I only use the willing, and the last three times I have asked something—whether that be for a witness of Me or help one of My children out in their time of need—I found no availability and obedience in you. While you are My vessel, you are not a usable one for My Kingdom. You are too wrapped up in your own self to obey when I need you for My work!"

The Lord has never let me forget that lesson I learned that day. I was embarrassed to go into His presence afterward. I was so ashamed that I have asked to be used by Him so many times in the past, then I saw how easily it was to brush Him off when He really needed me. So though I helped the lady and her baby, I couldn't get over the Most High God had to ask me twice when I heard Him crystal clear the first time. I thought I would be more obedient when He asked something of me, but I wasn't. I let myself get in the way.

The Lord has long forgiven me for my delayed obedience, but He has made sure that it has always stayed fresh in my mind so the next time He will only have to speak once. I never want to say "No, Lord. That doesn't work for me." I only want to say, "Yes, Lord. Whatever You need. I am here." I pray that I am always available and obedient the first time the Most High God speaks so that He will continue to use me for His purposes. There is nothing more important in my life I have the honor and privilege of doing than the Lord's will. We all have to be ready to listen and respond to His request at a moment's notice. That is His expectation of His children. Lord, help us to listen the first time you speak.

The Rescue

This morning started out just like any other morning. It was time for me to head to work. I pulled out of my road onto a four-lane road and traveled down until it ended into a three-way intersection that has twelve lanes converging at a red light. I have been traveling this same path to work for over seventeen years. Nothing much happens on the way to work; I am sure not much happens when you travel your same route to work each day. This day would be different than all the others. As I think back on the timing of my morning before I reached this intersection, it had to be timed perfectly. The Lord wanted me to see something very special.

I came down the road, which ended at a red light. As I was sitting there waiting for the light to change, I saw a woman who may have been in her fifties or sixties. She was walking from a convenience store that was located on one corner of the intersection toward the middle of the intersection. She was heading toward where the traffic light hung over the road. I thought she may be disoriented and was wondering exactly what I should do, if anything. I know I was not the only one watching her walk right into the intersection. I couldn't take my eyes off of her.

I was thinking, "What in the world is she doing! The light is going to turn any minute." This is one of the busiest intersections in my town. She walked very calmly into the middle of the intersection as if she was in complete control. As she almost reached the middle, she bent down for a minute. This was the first time that I saw the object of her attention. It was a small- to medium-sized turtle sitting in the intersection.

She bent down to check on the turtle. I said, "No way! I can't believe I am seeing this. How in the world is a turtle in the middle of this intersection?" The lady reached her hands around the turtle's shell and picked it up. She stood up, held it out in front her, and looked around to see where she could put it so it would be safe. She saw a grassy field with a small fence on one corner of the intersection. Holding the little helpless turtle away from her, she walked out of the intersection and placed the turtle on the other side of the fence so it would not be able to crawl back into the road.

She stood there and watched the turtle to make sure it would crawl away. The little turtle stuck his head out and slowly started crawling. She smiled then looked back at the intersection. She walked back to her car. Not one car moved through that busy intersection until she had rescued the little turtle and crossed back over to safety. Writing this out makes the story seem longer than it really was. It happened within a few minutes.

When the traffic light turned green, the Spirit instantly said, "I rescued you just like that. I wanted you to understand." I got really teary-eyed for my short drive to work in awe of the Lord's timing and caring enough to teach me lessons in such a way. I thought about that lady rescuing that turtle in the middle of the intersection for the rest of the day. I could not get the scene out of my mind.

There was only one reason that the lady did what she did. She had compassion and love for that little helpless creature. She knew that without a doubt that the turtle would not make it across the intersection without experiencing death. There would be a crushing of body and soul. The turtle would not have lived the life it was meant to live in the green field just past the fence. Somehow, the turtle had lost its way and traveled deep into very deadly territory. The turtle did not have full understanding that he was on a very wide road—twelve lanes wide to be exact.

That's a wide road for such a little creature. The reason the turtle took the road is that the road seemed right to him, but in the end it would lead to death. When he set out that morning, he did not anticipate taking the wrong road; nevertheless, he was right in the middle of it. The little creature had lost its way, and I doubt with its limited perspective that it had any idea of the large and fast dangers that surrounded it on every side. It did not understand the depth of danger it was in. Even if it had kept crawling, it would have never found the grassy field behind the fence. He couldn't see safety.

He could only see what was right in front of him. The turtle became so scared that it pulled its little feet, tail, and head in. He was just sitting inside a shell that he mistakenly thought would protect it from the outside world. The only way out of this very dangerous situation was for someone to have enough compassion and love for him to sacrifice his or her own safety to step into the twelve lanes of traffic to rescue him. The turtle could have certainly been left there to fend for itself and most likely not make it across the road. That was a fate it could have had, but because of the lady's intervention into the turtle's life and dire situation that it found itself in, the turtle was saved. The turtle could not have saved itself, no matter how hard it tried. He needed to be rescued, and he was.

I think you understand why the Spirit wanted me to see this very special rescue. We were just as lost as this little turtle. Our lives were on a road with twelve lanes of intersecting traffic. We were missing the grassy field just over the fence and traveling down a road that seemed right to us. We did not have full understanding that death was on the other end. No matter which way we turned, we were not going to make it off that wide road by ourselves, due to our limited perspective and wanting to be within our own control. Jesus left the safety of His throne and walked right into that deadly intersection to rescue us. He didn't have to rescue us. He had great love and compassion for us, despite all of our faults. He chose to rescue us. He protected us from the impending and permanent consequences of our lack of direction. He picked us up and put us in the safest place imaginable: by His side.

You are always the same. (Hebrews 1:12 NLT)

In the course of a one's life, nothing ever stays the same. Your parents, your spouse, your children, your job, your appearance, and your health never stay the same. Why? We are temporal beings living in a temporal universe. We live in time; therefore things can never stay the same. No matter how much you want them to remain the same, it is impossible.

What keeps our lives grounded when we live in the temporal that guarantees constant change? It would have to be something that exists outside of time that doesn't change. It would have to be something, or better yet, Somebody, who is eternal. The Bible says Jesus is the same yesterday, today, and forever (Hebrews 13:8). By very definition, this makes Jesus eternal. This one constant gives security to our temporal lives. In fact, this is our only constant security. This one eternal constant anchors the temporal human life so that it can have an unchanging centrality in the person of Jesus Christ.

The eternal is the center of the temporal. If I had to create a visual, I think of the sun. It is the center, and everything else in our solar system spins around it. The sun would represent the eternal, and the planets would represent the temporal. Jesus is the light of the world. He is our eternal center sun. Isn't it interesting that a sun is the center of each solar system as God the Son is the eternal center of our life system? Is that a coincidence?

The solar system couldn't exist without the sun anchoring it and warming it. We can't exist without the eternal Son anchoring and warming our lives. We depend on the Son to be the unchanging center of our existence. His gravity will eternally pull us toward Him as He keeps all things together. It is reassuring to me that as I see parts of my life change with time, the eternal centrality of Christ keeps my soul and heart from the changing effects of this temporal world.

The Promise

For you need endurance, so that after you have done God's will you may receive what was promised. (Hebrews 10:36–39 ESV)

The Christian walk is not for the weak. The weak will draw back from faith, and they will be destroyed. Those who endure and have faith will obtain life. You will only receive what has been promised, after you have done God's will—*after*, not before. There is no promised reward for those that follow their own will. I wonder why Hebrews 10:38 speaks about those who "draw back" or fall away (KJV). I wonder how that can happen. I think I have some greater understanding now than in the past.

Following God's will, rather than your own, is hard and takes immense endurance and strength. Following your own will is like taking the path of least resistance. The Lord says in Luke 13:24 "Try hard to enter through the narrow door or gate" (NCV). This does not imply you can work hard to enter Heaven. The narrow gate is laying down your will and picking up God's way or God's will for your life. Since it takes more effort and self-sacrifice, many will enter the wide gate, which is the path of least resistance. Many will have too much pride and love for sin and their own will to enter the narrow gate. If you don't strive hard like Jesus instructed, you will enter the wide gate.

The path of least resistance is always the easiest to take. It's one thing to recognize who God is, but it's entirely different to follow His will. Jesus directly correlates loving Him with being obedient to His will. Where is our love when we are obedient to our own will? Our love is focused on ourselves. Lucifer and the fallen angels recognized who God was, but that didn't save them. They even knew His name. They did not recognize His sovereign will for them, and they were separated from God for eternity. I think this is a foreshadowing of the picture of Heaven when everyone gets there and judgment begins.

All the people who recognized God's name and even did things in it but never followed His sovereign will do not receive the promise. Just as the fallen angels had to depart from God's glory, He will say to those people who knew His name only but refused to lay their own will down to follow His, "Depart from Me, I never knew you and where you come from"(Luke 13:25–27 NASB). When God says this He is ultimately saying, "I claim no ownership to you, and I know you never found your origin of who you are in Me." Again, the very sobering thing is it seems that He is talking to people who claimed to know Him. They are begging Him to remember all the things they did in their own will. It comes as shock to them that God will not accept that as payment for entrance in Heaven.

The time is at hand for the Christian to wake up and self-evaluate whose will they are truly following. If they know God's name, yet followed their own will, then they will be shocked when their Christianity was not as authentic as they believed. They fooled or lied to themselves that they truly had a personal relationship with God. It's one thing to know His general name; it is quite different if He knows yours. All they knew in the end was God's name but never cared to know His will or heart. They will not receive what has been promised. Remember that saying, "If you snooze, you lose"? That may be applicable here. Lose what? The promise.

Sacred

God considers everything that He has been selected, appointed, or commanded by God secure against violation, pure, sanctified, cherished, and regarded with reverence. What are some things that God has selected that He cherishes and regards in the above manner? Our worship, fellowship, discipleship, witnessing, deepening personal relationship, integrity, and obedience to His will are just a few examples. We should guard these things with every bit of mental and physical energy that we have. What God considers sacred, so should we.

Sadly, these are the very things that we put last in our lives. We say with our lips that we love the Lord, but our actions minimize those things that God says are sacred. No wonder God's heart aches when He says we have forgotten our first love. I am convinced that the Lord cares very little about our good intentions or flattering words; rather, He cares about what we actually do in Him and for Him.

I find it very interesting that the devil typically goes after what God has ordained as sacred. He lies to us that these things are not that important in our lives. That cannot be a coincidence. We may compromise our integrity and hurt our family and God. We may not engage in Christian fellowship as we deem it is not necessary. On a larger scale, 3,500 churches close their doors every year. On a smaller scale, look at the dwindling church attendance in the local churches. How is attendance on Sunday nights? Where are the committed Christians? We rarely if ever tell one other person about Jesus Christ, outside of talking about Him at church.

We lay our Bibles down after church on Sunday only to pick them up the next Sunday. We never miss the Word of God during the time in between. The Word is Jesus. In essence, we are not missing your Savior once during the week. We are satisfied with the amount of the Word we get on Sunday mornings and do not desire to go deeper. If we do say we want more of the Word, our actions do not match our words. We typically only open the Scriptures when the preacher tells us to turn to a passage on Sunday morning but rarely during the week. We follow our time schedule. We give God time, if by chance we have some left over after we finish our priorities for the day. Often, there is no time left for the Lord. Most of the time, He never crosses our mind, and we are certainly not bothered by missing Him. All is well.

If we are say that we treat the things God has ordained as sacred, then the whole truth is not in us. For us to honestly think we are fooling a Holy God is unimaginable, yet this is how we operate. We mistakenly think, "God is a good guy, full of love and patience! He understands how real life operates these days. There's no accountability for my actions." The key word here would be "mistakenly." We want to forget that He is a God who is sickened by the lukewarm Christian and wants to spit them out of His mouth. All the while, they are feeling great (Revelation 3:16). We don't like to talk about this verse, do we, even though it is describing the majority of the Christians.

What God has ordained as sacred, we can't change because it is inconvenient, uncomfortable, and not desirable to follow on our part. Many of us blatantly disregard what God considers sacred as we are living in our own little world. The scary thing is that some of us have been lukewarm for so long that we don't realize we are missing the sacred things of God. We are so out of touch with Him that we never consider we are possibly making God sick.

Joy

Keeping our eyes on Jesus, the source and perfector of our faith, who for the joy that lay before Him endured a cross and despised the shame. (Hebrews 12:2 HCSB)

I love this verse. Some interpretations say it was for the joy of Heaven that He endured suffering so that He could sit down at the right hand of God's throne. I believe Jesus is God and already had the joy of Heaven. The only thing He didn't have before He came to Earth was me and you. I interpret this verse that I am the joy that lay before Him. Anyone that has a personal relationship is the joy that lay before Jesus.

If I could paraphrase this verse it would say, "Keep my eyes on Jesus, the source and perfector of my faith, who for the joy of Sarah that lay before Him, endured a cross and despised the shame." Read it again and put your name in it. He endured the cross and despised the shame for the joy of me and you! Think about that.

We bring Jesus so much joy that He endured a cross and despised the shame. We sometimes think our lives are so insignificant and unworthy, but He obviously doesn't feel the same way. When they scourged Him, He got back up because He saw that we lay before Him. When they spit in His face, He wiped it out of His eyes because He saw us lay before Him. When He stumbled and fell carrying the cross, He got back up because He saw that we lay before Him. When they laid Him in the grave, He got back up because He saw that we lay before Him. Hallelujah! He got back up for me and you!

We were His joy then, and we still are today. He kept going for us. He was focused on showing me though His actions, not His words, that He is the source and perfector of what I should believe in. He had His eyes on me through all of His suffering and shame so, in the end, I would keep my eyes on Him. Knowing all He has gone through for me to know Him and all the things He has promised me, how is it possible that I ever take my eyes off of Him to look at anything this world could offer me in exchange. He has never taken His eyes off of me. How can I take my eyes off of Him? How can you? Nothing should turn our eyes away from Him. We are His joy. He is our suffering Savior.

Try to live in peace with all people, and try to live free from sin. Anyone whose life is not holy will never see the Lord. (Hebrews 12:14NCV)

We are called to live in peace with all men and holiness with God. Hebrews says that God has set this as His personal standard, and no one who rejects this will see the Lord. This is an extremely strong verse. Sin, bitterness, falling short, troublesome times, defilement of many things, irreverence, and immorality have their roots in not consistently pursuing holiness with God as He has instructed. The correlation is clear and inarguably true.

Why do Christians seem so shocked to find themselves in the above situations? Do they actually believe that they have been pursuing holiness with God? They believe somehow they have been blindsided by sin or trouble finds them, but they are totally innocent? They ignore the fact that they haven't pursued holiness with God recently or even in the remote past. They may not recall the last time they pursued holiness. Then they cry out, "Oh, God! Why are all these things happening to me, and how did I wind up here?" Christians do not take responsibility for following God's set standards of pursuing holiness with Him. They don't take it seriously. They are foolish and do not recognize the correlations.

How can this be when God has made Himself abundantly clear? I think it all goes back to your own level of spiritual maturity in recognizing that you have to lay down your own will and consistently pick up God's will. We have to keep our attention on Him. If you look at one important word that is repeated twice in the verse, it may shed light on the problem. The word is *try*. Do you see it? Try to live in peace with all people, and try to live free from sin.

I think people disregard God, and they do not think they have to try. I think Christians have been dulled by the monotony of their Christian life and think that holiness is a natural outcome of just carrying the name Christian. Well, if it says you have to try, then holiness is not just going to happen on its own. Stop thinking it is. It takes attention to the finer details of your thinking and actions. It takes endurance and patience. It takes time in the Word of God. You have to try and stop minimizing what it will take to meet His standard.

We have all tried and fallen short of living at peace with all people and holiness with God at times; most likely, we will again. Repentance is part of a humble heart and part of holiness in the Lord. God expects a lot out of His children. Just remember, He knows you can't achieve His standard on your own. You can only meet His standard by the power of the Holy Spirit that dwells in you. He will guide you in peace with men and holiness with Him.

The Shaking

Please read Hebrews 12:25–29.

When Jesus, God in flesh, walked upon the Earth, people rejected Him as Savior. That is based on their God-given right of free will. Jesus came to speak to us about His saving grace and to warn us. He highly encouraged that we not reject the Kingdom that He freely offered us. If we did, there would be no further way of escape that would be given under Heaven. He told of consequences for the rejection of Him

There will come a time, according to Hebrews, that God will shake not only the earth, but also the heavens. He will shake them, as if He put His hands around an apple tree and started pulling and pushing it as hard as He could. As the limbs begin to move back and forth, some apples hold on tight to the branches because they have been bound tight, but some apples start to let go as they have been loosened or fall from the tree. Those apples (or people) that are bound will remain attached to the Branch or the Vine. The removal of what can be shaken takes place so that what is not shaken might remain. Think of it as a separation.

As true believers that have a close, intimate, and personal relationship with Jesus Christ, we cannot be shaken loose. We have received a kingdom that has been bound in our hearts. We should be thankful that this eternal Kingdom, which holds our citizenship, cannot be shaken. When situations start to shake our lives, let us hold on God's unshakable hold on us and the acceptance of His grace and mercy. The knowledge of what He has already done for us binds us so that we can never be shaken free.

This shaking that Hebrews is talking about has yet to take place. It will happen very soon with the coming of the Lord. You have to be prepared. Do not be foolish and play games with your relationship with the Lord. You will not be able to hold on if you are not truly a child of the Most High God. There will be one shaking and after that judgment. If you are a child of God, you are not appointed to wrath, but if you are not, then His full wrath will come upon you.

Hungry and Thirsty

When is the last time you have really been hungry—not when you just wanted a bite to eat, but felt famished? The slow burn of your stomach is the first indication that you may need to eat. You get busy and forget. Then, a little later, it feels like someone lit a small campfire in the middle part of your body that if you touched it, you may get burned. Well, you still have a few more things to finish, so you keep going. You try to ignore the burn. No one really can see or hear the burn. You are the only one that feels it. Sometime later, you are sitting in a meeting, and *growl, growl, growl*! You grab your stomach and look around to see everyone looking at you saying, "Hungry?"

How about being thirsty? You get up in the morning, and you are running late. You are rushing around like crazy, trying to get out the door. You don't have time to even drink a cup of coffee. The only liquid that touched your tongue had toothpaste mixed with it. You get to work; things hit you right when you get it in, and you start working diligently.

You talk to this person and that one, and then you feel like your mouth is a little dry. You know you need to grab a glass of water, but you will get it eventually. After a while, with more talking and time, you are pretty sure that you have cotton in your mouth. If you keep going without water, you will eventually show some external signs of headache. You may have to take an Advil to help it go away.

Our flesh has physical needs. It will slowly give you quiet signs that it is hungry or thirsty. Eventually, it will make some noises, so others know what you need, too. Why do we ignore the flesh's needs sometimes? I think it is the same reason we ignore our spirit's needs. We are just too busy. We have every intention to getting to it eventually. There's really not too much more to it. We have too much we have to do, so we will eat and drink when we can.

It may not be what is in the best interest of the flesh or our spirit, but that is not our concern at the present moment. We have things to do. We will get around to it when we have a chance. At some point, the flesh will not wait much longer and will stop you if you do not care for it. It will make its needs known if you ignore it. Soon you will be looking for water and food as fast as you can. Then you are ravaging.

If our flesh can become malnourished, how much more malnourished can our spirits become? The spirit has needs to eat and drink, just like the flesh does. The Lord knew the Samaritan lady at the well was very thirsty. She had no water. Her life choices reflected her dryness of spirit. Did the Lord offer water to her flesh? No, only to her spirit. He offered her the Water of Life. He offered Himself. As long as her spirit drank this Water, its hydration needs would be met.

The Lord knows the spirit He created not only has hydration needs, but nutritional ones. He told Peter, "My sheep need to be fed with milk first, then meat for their growing spirits' needs. Remind their spirits that I am the Bread of Life." When our flesh gets hungry and thirsty, it shows external signs. After a while of being ignored, it becomes ravenous. Others know it. I often wonder if some of us feel that slow burn in our hearts because we haven't fed and watered our spirits in a while. Our spirits may have been fed a little, but they are still malnourished. They are not as full they need to be.

Think of it this way. If you haven't eaten all day, would you be satisfied for just a bite of food and sip of water? No. That is not satisfying. You still walk away hungry and thirsty. It's the same with our spirits. How often are our spirits ravenous? We only spend a few minutes in prayer and God's Word. Our spirits walk away almost as hungry and thirsty as before they received a few sips and bites of the Word.

I wonder if others have seen some external signs of our spiritual malnutrition and dehydration by our behavior and choice of words. I wonder if the Lord has noticed our thoughts and priorities getting further away from His, the hungrier and thirstier our spirits get. No one is going to make you feed your flesh. You have to do that on your own. Likewise, no one is going to make you feed your spirit. You have to make time to do that on your own as well!

When a spirit is malnourished and dehydrated, bad things can happen. Sin can happen. Depression can happen. Hopelessness can happen. Emptiness can happen. Loneliness can happen. Discouragement can happen. Stagnation can happen. Could it be so long since our spiritual needs were met that it is ravaging? Our spirits have to be fed and watered just like our flesh. That is probably the only thing our two natures share in common.

Compromise

Compromise can be good, but the minute we justify an uneven one in our favor, then it can bad. Let's say Kevin and I are having a disagreement. I see it one way, and he sees it another, not that this scenario has ever happened before! We will just pretend for the sake of my point. In order to have a positive and meaningful resolution to the problem, we will have to compromise. Kevin may be right just a little, and I may be right a lot—oops. I mean a little! We come to a middle ground and work it out. Compromise can be an excellent way to work toward conflict resolution.

Compromise does not work so well with God, though. When you are going God's way and living a holy life that is pleasing to Him in every area, you don't have to compromise. The only time you think you need to compromise with Him is when you step outside the way He wants to do things. You may call it a nice word like *compromise*, but God is not your spouse! He calls compromise sin. Big difference. You typically use compromise to agree. That is why it is useful in conflict resolution.

There is no conflict to resolve with God if you are doing every single thing in your life His way. The only conflict is the conflict you have created on your side by failure to do it His way. God is not interested in compromising with you. In fact, He doesn't have to because He's perfect. You don't compromise perfection. You either do it His perfect way or your fallible one. You are the one that is imperfect, so you are the one who tries to compromise with Him. It doesn't work! Knowing this, it doesn't stop us from trying.

We sugarcoat our compromise, thinking He doesn't notice or would agree with it if He did. How very foolish we are. It seems we are somewhat ignorant with the things of God. The enemy is eating it up. He is whispering, "That half-truth you told to your customer—you remember the one—you were compromising. You reasoned what you thought was best and you are fine." He may say, "Remember that half-truth you told your husband or wife? It will be best in the long run. He or she doesn't need to know every single thing. You are doing what is best for everyone," or "That half-truth you told your friend—if she knew everything, she wouldn't understand anyway. It's better this way. She couldn't handle knowing it all. Compromise is a good thing. All is well."

We can compromise ourselves into seeing things exactly how we want to see it and make it right. A synonym for compromise in the way I am using the meaning now could be *justification*. "I am justifying what I told that customer was right. I am justifying what I told my spouse was enough. I am justifying how I treated my friend was acceptable."

Why do we justify so hard? Why do we try to reason and compromise with God? Three simple words. Are you ready? We know best. We know best with our customers, spouses, and friends. We know best with God. We are just that good. When we feel the need to justify, thereby compromising by telling half-truths or however else you compromised God's way, we have sinned.

Your desire to control and need to be right will disregard the Spirit's conviction, so He will not affect you as much. The way you see it is the right way. If you had to use a half-truth or justify your behavior to make things work out in your favor, so be it. In the end, you did what you thought was best because your way and methods were the best. I don't know about you, but the word *arrogant* is coming to mind. When we compromise God's perfect way, we are being sinful and arrogant. Being prideful, foolish, and arrogant typically go along with being sinful. Whoever you compromised with, due to your need to be right, should receive an apology. It goes against every single fiber of your human nature to apologize for the compromise you thought was best.

The one thing that will prevent you from following through is the first sin of all creation. It is the strongest in my opinion. That is the sin of *pride*. Every time you compromise your way is better than the Lord, you have said to His face, "I know better than You, Most High God." Is that not the same thing Lucifer did? Pride goes with compromise. Sin goes with compromise. Foolishness goes with compromise. Arrogance goes with compromise. Self goes with compromise. God does not go with compromise. I always talk about God's way and my way. There is no other way to look at it, if I am honest. The second I choose my way, I have compromised God's way for my life, no matter how small.

God says, "I will not compromise with your fallible way no matter how you try to spin it. If you think for a second that I will, based on your own justification of your way, you need to remember that I am no fool. That would be you. I do not compromise." He doesn't compromise with us because He loves us and is perfect. I confess that I have tried to compromise God's way for mine many times in the past. We all have. We need to wake up and call compromise what it really is—sin. The sooner we do this, the less foolish, prideful, and arrogant we will become.

Visitor

I have never thought about God just being a visitor. I heard this phrase at church, and it really caught my attention. Another word for visitor is a guest. I know when I prepare for a guest to come to my house, I clean it, fix food, and become the hostess. I know that when my guest is coming, I look forward to it. I know we will have a nice time, but I have understanding that they will eventually leave. Sometimes, I've had enough visiting and am ready for them to leave! Once they leave, I can really get laid back and kick my shoes off to relax. I'm done entertaining. I get settled back to how it is when no one was there. I get comfortable.

I have to ask myself, "Can I compare this same mindset to God. Do I treat God like a visitor or like a family member in my life?" We treat those so differently. If I were honest, I would say that I used to treat God like a visitor in my life. He could visit on Sundays. He could have a short visit here and there during the week with a quick prayer in the shower or before drifting off to sleep. God typically wasn't called over to the house during the week for one-on-one time, and certainly wasn't treated like a family member.

Family members like to be talked to at least daily. They like time spent with them, or they can get kind of edgy. If you went through a whole day not acknowledging their existence, I don't think you would be received very warmly. How about if you did not talk to them once or spend time with them for six days in a row, but you would visit once a week for an hour or so? Outside of that, they never crossed your mind. Why don't you try this with your spouse or child this week? Let me know how that goes for you.

Oh, we would never do that to a family member would we? No, we love them, and we show them by our actions of talking and spending time with them. We want to engage them and hear their thoughts on a consistent basis. We want their attention, and we want to give them ours. We want our relationship to be strong. No. We would never treat our closest family members, such as our spouse and children, like guests. Yet, we call God "Abba, Father."

At the same time we say that with our words, we treat Him like a visitor in our lives by our actions. Maybe it was just me who did that, but I do not think so. You know why? I am no different than you. I know how the majority of Christians think and behave. I was one. Do you really think the church would be dying right now if we would wake up and treat God like a close family member instead of a visitor in our lives? Do you really think we would be living the same Christian life as we did one year or five years ago if we treated God like a close family member? If we talked to Him and acknowledged Him daily like a family member, it would completely change us.

Whether we really want to be changed may be the question. Do we really have the time and the desire? Our lives are so comfy and full just as they are and as they have been. The bottom line is, you spend time with, talk with, and want to hear from those you see as valuable and close to you. You make time for those people. The rest are just visitors. Why is it so difficult to treat our Father as more than a visitor in our lives? If we spent enough time with God to move Him from His current visitor status to close family member status, that would require restructuring of our lives. It's easier if He just visited. If the truth be known, it's much easier to fit Him into our schedule that way.

I am transparent and will confess to you that even as a long time Christian, God had only been a visitor to me. I never understood that I treated Him like that. I treat Him like a family member now because I call Him Father and mean it this time. We speak daily now, just like my husband and children. I don't ignore them, and I don't ignore God. They are equal now in my mind. I urge you to not treat God like a visitor in your life, when in fact He is the most important family member you will ever have. How ironic that He treats us like His child every day, yet we treat Him like a visitor.

Experiencing God

If we truly believe that JEHOVAH YAHWEH exists, then why do we not behave in such a way to reveal that in our actions? I believe my husband exists; therefore, I talk and interact with him. I expect him to talk and interact with me. I believe my friends exist; therefore, I talk and interact with them. I expect them to talk and interact with me. I have always believed God existed, yet I did not talk and interact with Him consistently. In essence, I treated humans better than I treated God.

What a thought! His invisibility and undemanding nature made that really convenient in my life. If I didn't talk to my husband, there would be consequences. If I didn't talk to God, there would be none. At least there would be none that I would deem immediate and threatening to me. He is our Divine Salvation. He expects to be interacted with consistently.

If you truly believe that EL-SHADDAI exists, then why do you not fully expect to experience Him? Why do you feel that experiencing God would be those rare mountain-top experiences and not a daily occurrence as though somehow He is too big and we are so unworthy. If you have two or three really strong experiences with God before you die, then you will be satisfied. You don't wake up each morning, excited to run to Him. There's no anticipation of an experience. Often there is no running at all, because you are still asleep, if not physically, then at least spiritually.

How can we experience God if we put Him at such a low priority in our life? We think it is all nice to experience God, but let's be real. It is not and should not be a normal occurrence. If God exists, why do we think we can't experience Him in a profound way daily? How have we justified in our heads that experiencing God is not to be expected in such a routine way? Maybe we believe He is just too holy, and somehow, we are not eligible to experience Him in a consistent way. The problem is we have justified all of our reasons; therefore, we do not experience God. He hasn't prevented us from experiencing Him; we have. He is the Almighty God.

If we truly believe that JEHOVAH-RAPHA exists, then we should expect a healing of our bodies and hearts. When we hear of someone laying on hands for the sick or possessing the gift of healing, a majority of us have that skeptical attitude and the rolling of our eyes like, "Oh, they are one of those edgy weird Christians who believe that far-out stuff of laying on hands and healing." There are so many Christians who judge others for laying on of hands for the sick and afflicted along with the belief of true healing. I have been convicted that I have been one of them.

I say that I believe an omniscient God exists, yet without the true power to heal, based on my own lack of understanding. I don't understand how all that works so, therefore, it doesn't work at all. If a healing occurred, the person wasn't "really" that sick in the first place. How very human of me to think such. God said, "I cannot lie. If I say I can heal, I can. I have all authority and power, why do you have such little faith?' He is the Lord our healer.

If we truly believe that JEHOVAH-MACCADDESHEM exists, then how do we miss that our lives are sanctified vessel in His kingdom to be used for His Holy purposes that we can't begin to fathom in our limited human minds? Why are we shocked that He chooses us to make a difference in other lives on His behalf? Why do I continue to be shocked that the Lord could be using me as His vessel and that people get anything out of my journals? We tell ourselves that we are nobody in particular. That's our primary problem, isn't it? That thinking is what limits our use, even though we tell God to use us. Besides us really thinking He will not use us, we have little to no deep understanding of how God sees us.

We only see ourselves with our limited human perspective. We lean on our own understanding, despite Him telling us not to. We fail to see how God really sees us and our possibilities for Him. One day, we will reign with the Lord. He will set us above dominions to rule over. We are joint heirs with Jesus Christ. We are worthy of a King's life. God loves us as He does His own Son.

If all of these things are true as told to us by Someone who has the inability to lie, then why do we not expect to be used as holy vessels to further the Kingdom of God at this point of our existence? We have been predestined before the foundations of the earth to be part of God's plan, not for our benefit but for His. When will we start believing that and be available for service for Him and not us? He is the Lord thy sanctifier.

We all serve a God who exists in more power than we can comprehend, but to limit Him for our own understanding is to limit our full capability of what we are supposed to be in Him. He never limits us; we limit ourselves in Him. He wants to give all power and glory to us, but we say, "Just a thimbleful, please. I truly don't believe in too much more than that for my simple life." He is standing there holding overflowing handfuls of blessings and possibilities for us to have. I have fully bought the lie from the enemy to believe that we are less than what God says we are.

Why do you think Satan fought so hard for Jesus to fail? If Jesus failed, He would have lost us. There was a major spiritual battle fought over our souls because God and Satan know how valuable we are, despite our lack of understanding. We operate our lives with this lie as our norm; therefore, we have suppressed ourselves more than we can understand. We all act like we do not serve the Mighty God that He says He is. It's like we redefine God to make Him fit in what we can understand of Him.

If we truly believed that God existed in the ways He says He does, then the church would not be dying, and we would not be experiencing stagnation. We would be experiencing God Almighty! We have cheated ourselves out of experiencing God thus far because of our own human thinking, not the Lord's. He is:

EL-OLAM "The Everlasting God."
EL-ROI "The strong one who sees."
EL-ELYON "The Most High God."
JEHOVAH-SHALOM "The God of peace."
JEHOVAH-JIREH "The Lord will provide."
JEHOVAH-TSIDKENU "The Lord of our righteousness."
JEHOVAH-SHAMMAH "The Lord who is present."

JEHOVAH-ROHI "The Lord my Shepard."
ELOHIM "God has all power and might."

When will we, as children of God, truly act like God exists in the ways His names says He does and stop limiting Him in our lives. When will we start experiencing God daily in ways that He says we are worthy and eligible for? When we start experiencing God continually, and when will we stop being surprised that we do?

If you want to feel the Holy Spirit's touch today, repeat the powerful names of our God out loud over and over again. Say them out loud like you are calling His name personally. You will feel His peace settle over you. It is intimate, amazing, and powerful. We serve a God who is real and desires to be experienced.

Obedience

I was talking to my brother-in-law yesterday by phone. He was telling me some specific things that the Lord had told him to do. They were bold things that most people would never do. He said in a quiet and humble voice, "I know what the Lord is telling me to do. Will you pray for strength and that I will be obedient?"

As I was praying this morning, I told the Lord, "Help me to obey what You tell me." My mind drifted to just pondering the word *obedience*. Simply stated, it is doing something that someone else has asked you to do. I will assume those requests are always in the positive, as we are not to listen to unwise counsel. If obedience is that simple, then why is it one of the hardest things in our lives to do? Why can't we just follow through? What is it that rises up in us when someone asks us to do something? This voice comes up and screams, "No!" Why is no so much easier than yes? Yes carries commitment. Yes carries energy that you have to expend. Yes carries time that you have to find. Yes carries relinquishing what you want to do to follow the will of another.

I do think obedience was easier before the fall. Once humans understood they didn't have to do it anybody else's way, that opened up a whole new world to them. Whether that is God or someone else, so be it. They had their own voice; in finding it, they wrongly concluded that they knew best. And so it has been from the first generation of humans to us. We are all the same. Obedience goes against our grain. Why? We know best. We doubt God and others have our best interest at heart.

I don't need some fancy psychology degree to figure out human behavior. It's simple, when you tear all the fluff off. We are convinced our way is right, and we don't want anyone, including God, to tell us differently. We are willful beings who are self-centered. We have no desire to self-reflect that we could be wrong in our thinking and direction. It's innate. That is why the Lord has given us so many stern verses about rearing a child. He knows what is in us, and He knows that same "will" can lead to our ruin.

Let's say you are driving a car in the mountains. I know the road to the left dead-ends into falling off a cliff, and the road to the right leads safely to a wonderful mountain village. You are driving along, and you see me standing on the side of the road. You ask, "Which way should I take at the fork in the road?" I say, because I know what is ahead and where each road leads, "Take the one to your right! The one to your left will lead to your own ruin and destruction." You say okay and drive off down the road.

When you get to the fork in the road, you see that the road to the right is very narrow. You see the road to your left, and it is nice and wide. You remember what I said, but will you obey? Will you think your way is best? How willful you are will determine which road you take. It's all about choices. You have the information that was told to you. You have no reason to disobey it, except that you think a different way is better. You justify your logic and disobedience, so you turn to the left. As you are driving along, all of the sudden the road gives way, and you join numerous other cars at the bottom of the canyon as they chose to disobey, too. Is this not what we do? Sure it is.

God has only good for us and tells us which road to take. We take the opposite one. Stubborn and defiant don't even come close to describing humans. As God sees car after car or life after life fall to the canyon floor, due to their own willful disobedience, what must He be thinking? I can just see Him shaking His head, saying, "I tell them clearly that there is way that seems right to them and in the end it will lead to their own destruction, and nine times out of ten they take it anyway. The strength of their will is unlike anything on earth. The amazing thing is they do it to themselves over and over and over. It beats all I have ever seen!"

When we get tired of our ruin, God in His grace gives us another chance to travel the road again. He gives us another chance to be obedient. He never gives up on us. He just hates that it takes so long for us to learn our lessons. Lost time can never be found again. What amazing things could He accomplish in our lives, if each time He speaks, we are obedient to His will and not out own? What will it take to finally lay ours down permanently? How old do we have to be to figure all this simple stuff out, when God told us this from the beginning of time? Willful? Stubborn? Defiant? Us? That's an understatement.

White-Washed Lives

The Lord does not look at the things humans beings look at. People look at the outward appearance, but the Lord looks at the heart. (1 Samuel 16:7 NIV)

In biblical days, and even up to this day in some countries, people buried their dead in tombs. In biblical times, they would make sure the tombs appeared nice and beautiful. They called them "whitewashed" tombs. They scrubbed the stone on the outside to get it as white as possible to give the illusion of cleanliness, but they held death and uncleanliness on the inside. The appearance on the outside was a façade of what was truly on the inside.

As I talk to more and more people, they tell me some of the things they struggle with inside themselves, with loved ones, or in their home. This same analogy of whitewashed tombs comes to my mind. Just recently, a friend disclosed that she and her husband were having serious marital conflict. I would have never known it. It is a whitewashed marriage. The appearance on the outside is a façade of what is truly on the inside. You hear of Christians who present one way in the church but do not live that way at home in front their family or at work in front of their co-workers. They are whitewashed Christians.

The appearance on the outside is a façade of what is truly on the inside. You hear of churches that look and feel unified on Sunday morning, but as soon as the rest of the week starts, there is bickering and discourse. People want their way to be done. There is continual hurt behind the stain glass windows. The Holy Spirit is being grieved. Some churches are whitewashed churches. The appearance on the outside is a façade of what is truly on the inside.

Some families are revered as strong, and others wish their families could be like the others. Inside the family, there are major problems from finances, the parents, and the children. It is a whitewashed family. The appearance on the outside is a façade of what is truly on the inside. There are so many people who present themselves as having everything together. They are falling apart on the inside and are hopeless that things will get much better. Some people are whitewashed. Some whole lives are whitewashed.

I could go on, but I think you get the point. We work so hard to make sure that we scrub everything so diligently so the outside of our lives looks tidy, white, and clean to those around us. We want the outside world to have full confidence that we have it together because we all feel that the whitewashed world has it together. We don't want anyone to know that we are dying inside over a problem or even an ongoing sin in our life. We strive with all our strength to hide the truth from others. We want them to think we have it all together. Why? Why does our culture put so much emphasis on having a façade up at all times, when in reality we are all struggling with something? There is a façade that real-life problems don't exist, and if they did, what is wrong with you for having them?

I think it is a ploy by the enemy to keep us bound mentally from experiencing the freedom in the Lord. Think of the strain, pressure, and fatigue it takes to keep up whitewashing your life for other people. Guess what—we do have serious problems. We do get depressed, and it is hard to shake. We can't be happy all the time. We do get hopeless here and there. We aren't the best spouses at times. Our children are not perfect little angels. Our families aren't as they appear. We are not the strong Christians that we present ourselves to be. We don't like everybody, and that doesn't make us bad people!

It's like the world doesn't expect us to be real-life people. It has come to expect whitewashed lives for so long that we think we have to be cleaning them up to present ourselves to whoever is watching. We may think if people only knew our real struggles inside, they may think poorly of us. If they only knew how I really am. If they only felt the deep pain that I feel. If they really knew me then they may find the secret that the appearance on the outside is a façade of what is truly on the inside of me.

Sometimes, I am trying to figure out what is truly on the inside of me just like everyone else. You may be dying inside from the burdens you are carrying, but you are going to be whitewashed on the outside. The world has sold this lie to us, and we have bought it. I have bought it. I had a whitewashed marriage for many years. I presented that my marriage was strong when no one knew that we were in counseling, not once but for many years. I was a whitewashed Christian. In my case, I presented that I was a stronger Christian and closer to the Lord than I actually was. There's some reality for you. Did I talk about these things? No! Why? The pull of keeping everything whitewashed and all the imperfections hidden that I wasn't living up to some standard was too strong.

The whole time I was wearing myself out, whitewashing my life for the world, the Lord was whispering:

My sweet child, I see it all. I know what you are doing. I know where you are. I know how you are feeling. I know how hard it is. I know everything in the deepest recess of your tender heart. You can put down the bucket and sponge and stop cleaning now. I know the whole truth of you. I made you. You are so weary. I died so that I could make your inside whiter than snow. You can clean your life all you want to, and you will never be as white and clean as I can make you. You truly are limited on how much cleaning you can do. I transform you from the inside out. Once I clean you, it will cross over to what the world sees as well. No more whitewashing. You will only be authentic.

Stop worrying so much about cleaning up for the world. Worry more how you present yourself, your marriage, your Christian walk, and everything else you keep whitewashed to Me. I give all I have to you, but the world only takes and demands more. I should always be your primary concern. Once I am, you will not care so much about what the world thinks of you. Let me wash everything in your life for now on while you rest in Me. I will make you and every part of your life whiter than snow, even the parts that you feel are dying or too far gone to clean.

First Samuel 16:7 says the Lord only looks at our heart, but people look at the outward appearance. If we spent more time getting our heart right for God to look at, we may stop caring so much about whitewashing our lives.

The King Is Coming

I woke up out of a sound sleep this morning with four clear words repeating over and over in mind: "The King is coming. The King is coming. The King is coming." I asked, "Lord, how close are you?" Without hesitation, He said, "I'm standing at the door."

Isaiah 66:8 prophesied in 740 BC, "Who has ever seen anything as strange as this? Who ever heard of such a thing? Has a nation ever been born in a single day? Has a country ever come forth in a mere moment?" (All verses are NIV). People thought Isaiah was crazy, as a nation had never been born in one day nor could it. With the dispersion of the Jews from their homeland in AD 70 to every part of the world, the reality of Isaiah's prophecy seemed like a false one. Two thousand years would pass without fulfillment.

In Jeremiah 33:7, God promised to bring Israel back from captivity and rebuild them as they were before. In Amos 9:15, God promised to plant Israel in their own land, never again to be uprooted from the land He had given them. All of these fantastic promises. God says, "All of this will come to pass as I have the inability to lie. Reality is based on what I say it is, despite what you believe will or will not happen or what you can or cannot understand" (Hebrews 6:8; Numbers 23:19; I Samuel 15:29). Israel had to be reborn, against all possibility, in order for the King to come. How could it be? With man this would have been impossible, but with God all things are possible (Matthew 19:26).

Has a nation ever been born in a single day? God's promise came true on May 14, 1948. Has a country ever come forth in a mere moment? At 4:00 in the afternoon, the gavel came down to declare Israel's statehood. After David Ben-Gurion finished signing the Declaration of Independence, he declared, "The State of Israel is established!" It was prophesy fulfilled in front of our very eyes. God's promises about Israel were made reality for the whole world to see.

The disciples asked Jesus, "What will be the sign of Your coming and the end of the age?" (Matthew 24:3). Jesus told the disciples, "Now learn this lesson from the fig tree: As soon as its twigs get tender and its leaves come you know that summer is near, even when you see all these things, you will know that the Son of Man is near, right at the door (Matthew 24:32–33). The fig tree is Israel and it has physically bloomed. The Lord said that the generation that sees this shall not pass away until they see the coming of the Lord (Luke 21:32; Matthew 24:34). Although the Lord has had a dwelling place in all generations (Psalm 90:1), it is the last generation that has been set aside to see the coming of the Lord. A generation lasts approximately seventy to eighty years according to Psalm 90:10. If we can apply the psalmist's time frame for generations and the last generation started on May 14, 1948 at 4:00 in the afternoon, then I believe that we are in the time frame to see the Lord's return. No one could know the last generation until Israel was reborn. The King is coming.

Ezekiel 38 prophesied that a great king, full of power and strength, would rise up in the North in the last days. This king is called Gog, meaning ruler. The land to the north of Israel was referred to as Magog in ancient times. Magog was in Rosh, which is the ancient term for Russia. Ezekiel said that Gog would gather the countries around him, making allies of them and exerting authority in the region. Is any national leader's name coming to your mind?

Does any of this sound familiar to what is happening today? No one will be able to stop him at the appointed time of his rising. Do you see any country of the world stopping him now? Gog and his allies will rise against Israel in a coming great war called the War of Gog and Magog or Ezekiel's war. This is why numerous countries are changing regimes as they are preparing for war. In order for the armies to come against Israel, there had to be a nation of Israel first.

Ezekiel stated in 37:14 that the Lord had to place His children in their own land first. He has done this. The stage is being set now as we see key players or countries fall into the place during the last few years at blinding speed. We are seeing Gog gather the specific countries named in Ezekiel together through diplomacy and brute force. Who are some of these countries that the Bible says will rise up in the last day unifying in power and like mind? Russia, Iran, Iraq, Afghanistan, Ethiopia, Sudan, Libya, Egypt, Eastern Europe, Southeastern Europe, Turkey, Bulgaria, Romania, and other current Arabic countries.

What have we been witnessing inside these countries over the last few years? Regime changes, one after the other. You would have to wonder why they are all changing at the exact same time Russia is rising back to a superpower. This is happening all in the same time period. Coincidence? Gog is strengthening and making plans. The countries are unifying as prophesied in Ezekiel.

Surely when Israel is attacked, she will have her allies, right. It is prophesied that no one will come to protect Israel. She will be all alone going into this coming war. Israel's biggest ally is the United States. We are quickly abandoning Israel on all fronts, just as the prophecy revealed. God says, "I will defend her. Israel will know that I am the Lord their God." The King is coming.

We are moving toward a world government. This too has been prophesied. You can't stop it. I can't stop it. Listen to some of these quotes which should make the back of your hair stand up on your neck. James Paul Warburg, a banker, on February 17, 1950 spoke in front of our US Senate, "We will have a world government whether you like it or not. The only question is whether that government will be achieved by conquest or consent." Former Deputy Secretary of State under Clinton Strobe Talbott stated, "The 21st century will be the time that national sovereignty would cease to exist; that we would all answer to a single global authority." He went on to say, "In the next century (now), nations as we know it will be obsolete; all states will recognize a single global authority and realize national sovereignty wasn't such a great deal after all."

Nelson Mandela said, "The new world order that is in the making must focus on the creation of a world democracy, peace, and prosperity for all." Richard Gardner, Former Deputy Assistant Secretary of State, stated in April 1974, "We are likely to do better by building our house of world order from bottom up rather than from top down ... an end run around national sovereignty, eroding it piece by piece, is likely to get us to the world order faster than the old fashioned assault." David Rockefeller said, "We are on the verge of a global transformation. All we need is the right major crisis and the nations will accept the new world order." The King is coming.

Why am I telling you all of this? It's not the typical journal. You may want to ignore everything I am saying, wishing to stay cozy in your slumber and your own little world. The Lord wants you to wake up and take the blinders off. Wake up from your daily routines, and look past what you see in front of you. Wipe the sleep out of your eyes, look with spiritual eyes, and see what time it is! Matthew 24:44 says, "Therefore, stay awake, for you do not know on what day your Lord is coming."

Why does the Lord have to keep telling His own children to stay awake? Because they won't! We are all in our own little slumber land! Our spiritual knowledge of the things of the Lord and His agenda for this world is so weak. We are so worried about making it through our current problems or the day that we miss the forest for all of our trees! If we are identifying key players in the coming Ezekiel's war, and we have identified a 2,000 year old prophecy being fulfilled by the establishment of Israel, then it is past time to wake up. There are many more prophecies, but these are some of the biggest and clearest to see right in front of your eyes! We need to know what time it is! The King is coming.

Jesus says in Revelation 3:20, "Here I am! I stand at the door and knock; if anyone hears My voice and opens the door, I will come in. They will be with Me." Listen! If we are truly living in the last generation, and I believe we are, based on the above prophecies, you will want to be with the King when He comes. Do not think that the Lord will stand at your door and knock forever. He won't. You are very foolish and have a great lack of wisdom to think differently. If you have never made a decision for Christ, you need to do it before it's too late. Open the door, so you can be with Him. As fast as everything is moving, it will be too late sooner than you think. In a twinkling of an eye, it could be too late for you.

If you have already opened that door to Him, then continue to wake up from your slumber and be watchful. Get out of your comfort zone and stop keeping Christ to yourself! You don't want to stand in front of the Most High God's throne, when He asks you, "I saved your soul from eternal damnation. How many others did you tell of My saving grace of their soul also? Who did you bring with you, because of your personal witness of Me?" When you have no name to answer with, what will be your justification?

Brothers and Sisters in Christ, what time is it? Wake up from your slumber! The King is coming. The King is coming. The King is coming.

Life's Measurements

He also raised us up with Him and seated us with Him in the heavens, in Christ Jesus, so that in the coming ages He might display the immeasurable riches of His grace in His kindness to us in Christ Jesus. (Ephesians 2:6–7 HCSB)

Think of your life as a measuring cup. You can be filled to 1/4 cup, 1/3 cup, 1/2 cup, 2/3 cup, 3/4 cup, or 1 cup. These are your possibilities. Your life cannot be filled with more than 1 cup of anything, as that is all it can hold. Whatever combination you want to use to add up to one cup is acceptable. It is your measuring cup, so you get to control how much of each ingredient you use and what particular ingredient you put in it. No one else should put ingredients in your measuring cup. Only what you allow goes in it, as it belongs to you. Now 1 cup is the most you can have, but that doesn't mean you have to or will fill it up. You may be hovering around 1/4 cup and feeling pretty empty inside. Again, you control how much or little goes in.

Knowing how your life's measuring cup works, let's talk about what ingredients you can put in it. You can add any combination of love, joy, peace, patience, kindness, goodness, faithfulness, gentleness, forgiveness, and self-control. There are more positive emotions you can add besides those. You can also add any combination of sadness, despair, loneliness, hopelessness, low self-esteem, rejection, doubt, jealousy, resentment, anger, regret, vengeance, hostility, unforgiveness, hurt, and any other negative emotions you can put in, as well. You can also add some that you can't find the words for but are very real. See, you control what you put in your own measuring cup and how much of each ingredient goes in it.

I understand that things happened in your in life that you never deserved. A certain amount of negative ingredients were put in your cup. It seems like those negative things kept you afloat at times, as you just tried to get through another day. Other people have almost forced you to take some of their own negative emotions in your cup. The world loves to fill your cup with negative ingredients of its own. You have to protect your measuring cup from this world by covering the cup opening with your hands.

Sometimes, you may not know what is in your cup. You are just trying to keep life somewhat balanced the best you can. You have tried to level the negative out with more positive, but mixing positive ingredients and negative ingredients in your measuring cup is like mixing oil and water. They will never mix, no matter how much you will it to be. You desire to be filled with positive ingredients. The benefits that would come into your life are immense, but you don't know how to level the ingredients out or mix what you have in the cup with different ingredients to make things better.

Child of the Most High God, the reason you can't level it off or remix it correctly is because it is impossible within your strength. No matter how strong you think you are or want to be, you can't do it. Sometimes, when you have so many negative ingredients from events in your life that God has to pick up your measuring cup and pour everything out. He has to empty you completely. Can you picture Him literally emptying out everything the world has poured in? The world didn't have the right to pour ingredients in and affect your cup, but that is how the world works. It takes and never gives back. It pours into you what it wants you to take.

God has to actually wash the worldly ingredients out of the cup from the inside out. He does this by offering forgiveness to you. He does this by offering renewal to you. He does this by offering a personal relationship with you. He does this by creating a new cup for you. He understands how you were filled with some negative emotions and memories in the first place. You collected them along life's journey, just like the rest of us. He doesn't blame you. He doesn't hold it against you. You did the best you could with the ingredients you had in your cup at the time.

The Lord loves you so much that He offers a clean measuring cup back in exchange for the old one. No matter what ingredients the cup once held, He will give you a new one. He offers to fill your life with positive ingredients, including the Fruit of the Spirit. These ingredients can only come from Him. The most amazing thing happens when God fills your measuring cup. Before, you could never overfill your own cup as it had self-limitations. God is not bound by such limitations. When He fills you, your measuring cup will completely overflow with the things of Him. You will have to partake of God's ingredients from the saucer that the cup sits in! Imagine that! The filling by the Most High God can never compare to what this world has filled you with or will fill you with again, if you allow it.

It grieves Him more than you can imagine that you ever had to be filled with anything negative in the first place, but He makes all things new. That is His promise to you. He pours out ingredients that are not from Him. He pours out what He sees as not part of His will. God refills you only with things that will prosper you and brings you closer to a relationship with Him. Whether you are a new Christian or an older one who still needs more godly ingredients, He is the one that fills you to overflowing.

I said at the beginning that the cup was yours to control. That is absolutely true. If you want to relinquish control, you can hand it over to Him. Be mindful that He is the only One you would ever want to give your measuring cup to. He is the only One that you can trust with filling it with goodness, forgiveness, mercy, grace, truthfulness, love, and full acceptance of who you are. May God bless the filling of your life.

Amazing Grace

Amazing Grace. How sweet the sound that saved a wretch like me. I once was lost, but now I am found. Was blind but now I see. Twas grace that taught my heart to fear and grace my fears released. How precious is that grace appears the hour I first believed. When we have been there ten thousand years, bright shining as the sun, we have no less days to sing God's grace, then when we first begun.

Why is grace so amazing? Grace is receiving something that you don't deserve. The Eternal King of the entire universe, Creator of Heaven and Earth, including everything above and below the earth, left His Holy Father to shed all of His pure blood for your filthy, undeserving, sinful soul. Jesus was just fine in Heaven. He didn't need you; you needed Him. Big difference. He didn't have to choose you, but God so loved you that He put you first and His Blessed Child second. Your sin killed God's Son.

Jesus was slowly tortured to death for you, despite Him seeing your unworthiness and unrighteousness in front of Him. You deserved that cross, not Him. He covered you while He received the wrath of His Father that was not due Him. Jesus literally protected you with His own body. He had never been separated from God. Your sin separated God the Son from God the Father for the first time in eternity past. Your sin did that to Them. Jesus died while you were still His enemy.

Amazing Grace. Those words are sweet to me like honey. They sound sweet to me like music. Before grace, I walked around blind, as I continued to get more lost in my darkness. Jesus' grace taught many lessons to my heart, so I could elevate Him and respect Him for who He truly is. All of my fears that this world can cast upon me were released the very moment Jesus appeared to me. The very hour that I believed that He was who He said He was and could do what He promised He would do in my life, I received all forgiveness of sin. I became a new creature in Christ. I am now worthy to spend eternity with Him.

There is no time in Heaven. Ten thousand years will pass like a day. There will be day after day, then more days after that for me to sing about God's grace. I will never stop singing. I will never run out of time to sing to My Savior the songs of grace that are so amazing to me from the very first hour I believed. How precious eternal grace is to me. It flooded my soul, heart, and mind, so that I am in Christ and He is in me. All mystery has been revealed. I am a child of the Most High God. Praise the Son for His blood that saved my soul and filled it with the most amazing grace I could ever imagine. Thank you God for your amazing grace! Praise God. Praise Jesus. Praise the Holy Spirit. Thank God, I'm saved! His grace is truly amazing!

Brick Walls

You know, I have never thought that I was trying to force the hand of God when I sinned. He has said, "No." I badger, sneak, and justify, trying to make Him see that this sin feels good to me. I am trying to get Him to approve of something that He has said no to. I deserve to have what I want. I go about my own way knowing that He disapproves. The Holy Spirit is doing cartwheels inside of me trying to get my attention to warn me of danger, danger, and more danger.

I, in my rebellion, disregard and ignore the godly counsel of the Holy Spirit. I am in defiance of Him when I choose my own way and then justify it. I'm not sure which one is worse. Telling God that He is wrong or showing Him all the many ways He is wrong. When I am out of sin, I gasp at my thinking. When I'm in sin, I badger, sneak, ignore, and justify. I really am no different than an obstinate, defiant child in my thinking. No wonder why we are always called children of God; we act like children!

In the past, I have told my own children that their father and I were to be looked at like a brick wall. They could come against us all they want, but we "ain't" moving, so give it their best shot. I will not say it's not exasperating when they come to test that brick wall, but I don't move it because I love them. The brick wall is only there for their protection.

God puts up brick walls for me just like I do for my boys. I remember the times I was pushing with all my strength against His wall. Maybe it was a wrong direction that I wanted to go, a bad decision I was trying to make, or a sin I wanted to engage in. I pushed and pushed and pushed then pushed some more. It left me way more exasperated than God. I can imagine Him, as He sat on top of the wall looking down saying, "Are you tired yet, Child? If you would like to keep pushing against Me, you can, 'cause I "ain't" moving! Give it your best shot! There is no good waiting for you on the other side of this wall. I love you. When you are done trying to push through Me, I will show you where I want you to go. I can't do that until you are done trying to go your own way. I have all of eternity, but you don't. Let Me know when you are done!" I don't know about you, but this is what happens to me.

When I am out of sin, I see so clearly. I see the wall. Not only do I have no desire to go push against it, I don't have a desire to even go near it. It amazes me that I can fall right back into sin so quickly and my clear thinking goes out the window. There I am, pushing against the stupid wall again. I have to wonder what God must think. He may say, "Would you look at that! Sarah is down there pushing against that wall again. I thought she learned her lesson the last time she pushed on it, and I didn't move. Oh well. She will figure it out again. Bless her." It's almost comical isn't it? I love thinking what God must be thinking and saying in Heaven. It helps lighten a serious sin problem.

I honestly believe the best way to beat sin is to really understand it. It is important to really understand ourselves, and what pulls us in sin in the first place. When the enemy dangles that carrot in front of us, what makes us take a bite? It really is fascinating—not so much when I am biting the carrot, but more so when I am studying why others bite the carrot. The amount of mental reasoning we expend when we try to justify sin so we can meet some deep want or desire, no matter what it costs us, is really mind boggling. We seem to lose the ability to focus on what is right because all we see in front of us is something that will satisfy us. It really is amazing how the mind reasons what you want is what you should have. Thank goodness for walls.

I picture the Holy Spirit being many things to me. He is a counselor, teacher, comforter, and a brick wall when He needs to be. I pray that you and I will listen to Him counsel and teach us, so He will not have to become a wall to protect us from our poor choices. There are much easier ways of doing things that require much less expenditure of energy. It's called listening and obeying. Shockingly simple, right?

The Beauty of Simplicity

Who of you reading this journal can say they have a simple life? Who desires one, but this world prevents it from being a reality? You try to be the gatekeeper of what comes and goes out of your life, so you can have a simple life. How's that working out for you? Sometimes, it seems like the gate opens and closes at its own will, not yours. It seems like others want control of your gate or already have control. They may determine what enters, when it enters, and how it enters. You have things come in even though you hold the gate shut as hard as you can. It comes in anyway. It seems like you are powerless to stop it.

We are simple people at heart. We do not desire to have complicated lives, but the world we live in is pretty complicated. When the Lord created us, He made us to live simple lives in a perfect garden. Simple. He never intended for us to be to be gatekeepers. That was His job. I think our lives are complicated because we have come to a place in our lives that we don't know how to relinquish His job back to Him. We have controlled the gate for so long. We wouldn't know how to give it back to Him if we wanted to. We have been gatekeepers so long that we wrongly believe the control of it belongs to us now. We can't trust someone else to do as good as job as we do it. We alone hold the key.

It's possible that you have given the job of gatekeeper of your life to another person in the past. Your gate was wide open to that person, and they hurt you so badly that you shut and locked it. If it is shut so tight, how can you let the hurt, anger, loneliness, despair, and hopelessness out? The truth of the matter is—you can't. Your mind and heart have to process all of those emotions as they swirl around locked deep inside of you. If it is shut so tightly, how can you share the deepest parts of who you are with others or the Lord? How about that close loved one or friend that you have to keep at arm's length at least emotionally? You guard your gate so closely now. You have learned how not to get hurt. You have learned how to balance the complexity of your situation. The amount of mental energy and heart strain demanded for this balance is unimaginable and immensely fatiguing, but what choices do you have?

One of the reasons our lives are so complicated is because the Lord did not design us to be gatekeepers. He did not design us to carry the heavy lives that we do today. He designed us for simplicity. You know that I speak the truth. You can feel it. When Jesus walked upon this earth, He saw our struggles.

He said, "Child. Listen to Me. Let me control the gate of your life. I only want you to focus on two simple things. First, I want you to love Me with all of your heart, mind, and soul. Second, I want you to love others as yourself. That is all." I picture Him saying, "Whatever tries to come and go through your gate is all temporal and seeks to take your joy and focus off of Me. I understand that hurt has entered your gait at some point. I created you to love deeply, and with that, there is a possibility to be hurt deeply. I understand. I could not create you to love deeply without the possibility of the other happening, too. Open your gate again. Open it wide to Me. Let Me restore healing and freshness in your life. Remember the only two things that I told you to focus on? There's beauty in simplicity."

The Plank of Faith

Have you ever felt like you were walking out on a plank? With each step, you are closer to the unknown. Maybe there are situations in your life that are pushing you closer to the edge, even against your will. You look over the sides to see, but there is just air. Only when you get to the very edge, with your toes tightly curled around the end, do you look out and see Jesus.

He is there smiling, while holding His arms up saying, "You are okay, My Child. Jump. I'll catch you. You have been doing so well step-by-step coming out this far, even though you don't understand how you arrived here in the first place. You have reached the end of yourself now. This is why you are getting nervous and scared. That is why you doubt. It's okay. You are exactly where I need you.

I am right here. I have been here for every step you have walked so far. I allowed you to walk many steps in your own strength because it takes a while to get to the end of your capabilities. I created you very strong. I allowed you to control things a bit along the way, as I gently controlled the outer boundaries. You needed to see the gifts and talents that I placed in you. I wanted you to feel them and have faith in them. I needed you to refine them by really using them. I didn't give them to you just to enjoy, as they are not really for you in the first place. They are My gifts and talents that I placed in you, but they really never ceased to belong to Me.

I have always planned to challenge you with those same gifts and talents when you were ready. I challenge you only because I love you and want you to grow. I challenge you because I need you ready for My work, not yours. Yes, I know it's scary as you are reaching the end of yourself now. You are starting to realize that you are really going to need Me more than you ever have before. I cannot allow you to do all things in your strength. If I did, you wouldn't need Me.

You see, I have allowed you to go this far to expend your own strength. To be perfectly honest, I have been waiting for it to run out. When you do all things, you will do them in My strength, never your own. I would have never started a work in you that I had no plans in finishing. That's not My nature. You only understand what you can see and control. That is exactly what limits you. Anything after that point, you have to have faith."

The Lord continued, "You have been so self-sufficient all of your life, that you never had to fully trust Me with the unknown. Yes, you have always acknowledged Me and loved Me. I know that. You have claimed to have trusted Me, too, but you always held back complete faith in My ability in catching you. Why? You had to hold onto your last bit of control. You can never fully trust Me and have faith in Me, if you even have one finger holding on to your control. That means you are still working in your own strength. That is not where I work. You are just now realizing this truth and it scares you. It frightens you to let go of that last finger."

The Lord added, "You have the fear of the unknown, even though I am telling you that I'm in it. There is no fear in you that comes from Me. There is no fear in perfect love and trust. If you allow fear and doubt to rise up in you, then you will never work outside of your own strength. The enemy would love nothing more for you to buy the lie of fear. In that lie, he knows he can paralyze you, and keep you from jumping off the end of the plank to where I am. You cannot even imagine the spiritual battle around you right now. The enemy does a good job instilling fear to keep you bound to only what you can see, touch, and understand. Fear does not contribute to your growth, but only to your stagnation."

The Lord said, "The enemy and I desire two very separate things for you. He wants bondage and self-reliance. He wants you to believe that you can do nothing outside of your own strength. He wants you to cling only to what you know and can understand. He wants you to believe that I will not be there when you jump off into the unknown. They are all lies. I want your freedom, strength, and reliance only in Me. You can't have it both ways. It is either My way or his way."

The Lord finished by saying, "You have to decide who has your best interest at heart. Who do you trust and have more faith in? It's easy to say that you have faith in Me, as long as you are working in your own strength and comfort zone. It's hard when I tell you to jump. Child of Mine, I am telling you to jump. I am right here. Trust Me."

Just Like Children

Children, obey your parents because you belong to the Lord, for this is the right thing to do. (Ephesians 6:1 NLT)

For those with children, have you ever understood why they disobey you? All you want to do is to love them and show them what is best. They go their own way. They think differently than you. Their ways are not your ways. They see a way that looks right to them and jump in with both feet. They will stop at nothing, until they obtain what they desire.

They only live for the moment. They seek self-gratification. They make decisions based on what they see and think is best for them. They disregard your instructions. Their desire for what they want is greater than the poor outcomes that come from those same desires. Your heart and goodness that you want to provide is not their top priority. In fact, when they disobey, you are the last person on their mind. They are certainly not thinking of how this would affect you. They are thinking, "How long can I get away with this with nothing bad happening?" The only thing that concerns them is getting caught.

I will repeat my question, "Have you ever understood why children disobey?" God, in His wisdom, has allowed me to understand the answer by giving me two boys! Children disobey their parents for the exact same reasons that I disobey my Heavenly Parent. It is for the same reasons you disobey Him—the exact same reasons. We elevate ourselves above our children because we are older. Why do we think by being older that we somehow outgrow disobedience? We somehow think we outgrow wanting things our way. You and I both know that isn't true.

We think since we are older, then we are wiser. Why don't we act wiser sometimes? How do we get ourselves so far off the road that the Lord would want us on? It's simple; we do not outgrow disobedience. We are not as wise as we first thought. We still want things our way just as much as when we were little. If you want to understand your sin a little better, see how the disobedience of your own children correlates with your own disobedience as a child of God. How really different are we from our own children? We may not disobey our mom and dad anymore, but we do a pretty good job of disobeying the Lord.

It was amazing to me when I put this together. It was very enlightening to help me understand my own sin. I now understand one of the reasons the Lord calls us "children." Allow me to personalize Ephesians 6:1, "Child, you were bought at the cost of My Son's life. When you accepted the gift of grace, you belonged to Me. I, the Most High God, am your Father. I have a great desire that you would obey Me. This is not for My benefit, but it is the right thing for your life. Through your obedience of Me, I will bless you with wisdom." When will we stop acting like children?

Symbol of Life

Jesus amazes me with the power He has to change things. He changed nothingness into a universe. He changed dirt into a man. He changed a people into a nation. He changed fishermen into world evangelists. He changed water into wine. He changed nonbelievers into believers. He changed a symbol of death into a symbol of life. The power that it took to even change one of these into another is beyond comprehension. Each change could be a journal all its own.

The Lord caught my attention with the last change I listed. I have lots of necklaces, as any good girl does! I wear one every day. One day, I put my cross on. It is so dainty with little diamonds in a shape of a cross. Very simple. When I put it on this particular morning, I caught a glimpse of it in the mirror. It stopped me, as I was looking at it hanging around my neck. I just stared at it in the mirror. The Lord spoke so quietly, "I died on a cross. It was a symbol of fear, intimidation, control, torture, agony, dishonor, shame, humiliation, hopelessness, and death. You are hanging all this around your neck.

Nobody would have made jewelry out of an execution device in the first centuries. No one wears a noose as jewelry. No one wears a gun as jewelry. No one wears a stake as jewelry. No one wears a guillotine as jewelry. No one wears stoning rocks as jewelry. No one wears any of these means of death as jewelry, yet you wear a cross. Do you know that the Roman used to crucify thousands of people a day across the hills on crosses? People were left there to suffocate to death. They were left there for the fowls of the air and animals to eat their remains right off the cross. Today, you wear a cross proudly around your neck."

The Lord continued, "How did it go from a symbol of death into a symbol of life? I, alone, have the power to change death into life. I, alone, have the power to change people's perspectives that a cross could mean life instead of death. So much so, that you want to proclaim it unashamedly to the world. There is power in the cross, not only because I died on it, but because I changed it from a symbol of death to a symbol of hope, love, and sacrifice. I changed it to a symbol of life. What other man walking on the earth before or after Me has had that same power? I, alone. The cross is like a door. You have to come through the blood that I shed on it, in order to have the life on the other side of it. I change people from who they are in themselves, to who I want them to be in Me at the cross. There is immense power in the symbol of the cross."

Need Gas?

I hope that my husband will skip reading this particular journal, because he will fuss at the content! The analogy is just too good, so I have to write about it. One of Kevin's pet peeves is I allow my car's gas tank to get too low. I wonder if any ladies reading this can relate to my struggle. I see the gas gauge getting lower, but I am just so busy. I have places to go, things to do, and people to see. I am busy, busy, busy. Sometimes, a few days will go by and I will happen to glance at gas gauge. I am shocked that it has dropped so fast to right above E!

I tell myself that I will have to get gas very soon or bad things will happen! What do I do? I keep going. The reality is that I forgot that the car is hovering just at E, and I continue to go about my busy schedule. I have the best intentions to get gas. I have nothing against getting gas, except I just don't have the time to get it! It periodically crosses my mind to get some, but it is sort of like one of those high-speed train sort of thoughts. As soon as you think about it, it is gone. I even pass many gas stations as I am busy being busy. I'll do it later.

This week, I was picking up one of my sons after school, and then I had to take the other one all the way across town to piano lessons. My car is dead on E. Time was short, and I could not be late for either one of these appointments. I kept going, hoping that the bad things that could happen would not as my poor car kept going. I was not sure on what. I picked my son up from school and had the other one in the car heading toward piano. The all familiar, "Ding, Ding" sound came on. I knew immediately my car was calling out to me, "Help me! I need gas!"

I was halfway to the piano lesson, and another sound came on that I had never heard before! That immediately caught my attention. My car dashboard read, "Low Range!" Yikes, I had never got that low! I had no idea how far I had when it said, "Low Range." I wasn't interested in finding out. I dropped my son at piano lessons and drove to the gas station at the corner. I breathed a sigh of relief when I reached the gas pump. The only thing I was thinking was, "What would have happened if I had to call Kevin to bring me gas one block from a gas station!" I don't want to imagine that conversation.

To cap this true story off, I was sitting at a red light a couple days later and looked across the intersection to see three men pushing a white Tahoe out of the road. There was a lady trying to steer a dead car. Guess where the men were pushing the Tahoe toward? You guessed it! A gas station! The guys pushed the car to the tank, shook hands, and got back in their cars and left. The lady got out, looked around hoping no one including her husband saw, and then started pumping gas. The whole time I am watching this, one thought came to my mind, "That could have been me!" The lady ignored the "Ding, Ding," just a little longer than I did. She even ignored the "Low Range" warning. Maybe she was just busier! Either way, bad things happened. Her car stopped in the middle of the road within two lane widths of a gas station. She almost made it. Bless her heart.

I kept rolling this over in my mind. I believe God laid out a clear analogy of what we do as Christians. We are the driver. Our life is the car, and He is the gas. My vehicle cannot voluntarily take itself to get gas. Even though the sounds are going off and the gauge is spelling out clearly what it needs, it has to be driven to the gas station. If I give it what it needs and fill it up, then my vehicle can run very well for me. My life cannot voluntarily take itself to the Lord for gas. Even if it is groaning out, falling apart, and making all sorts of noises saying, "If you don't fill me up soon, I will not be fully functioning for you. I can't go on much longer like this."

What do we do as Christians as we get weaker? We keep on going. We do not voluntarily drive our lives into the Word of God. Who needs gas? We have things to do, places to go, and people to see. We have our own priorities, and refueling up with the Lord is not one of them. We reason that it would take too long to refuel. There's no time. We tell ourselves we are okay, just keep going. We foolishly think that we can pass all the gas stations or opportunities for the Lord to fill us because we still have a little fume left to run on.

As long as our lives are still going, what is the problem? We ignore how far we have driven from the Lord's gas station, until one day your life stops. No more gas for you. Your lack of time to refuel with the Lord finally caught up with you. You look around, and you wonder why your life is in the shape that it is. You wonder why you feel so empty. The Lord is saying, "You have got to stop and refuel with Me daily. I keep you running! You need Me in your life. Stop running on fumes."

Is your life full of the Lord? Is it dinging to alert you that you are low? Is it saying "Low range?" Has it finally stopped functioning in the way it needs to be? What is your life's gauge saying? You may want to keep a close eye on it, as it can drop really fast.

Straddling the Line

Do you ever feel pulled as a Christian? You have one foot in the world because there are many things that you really love and enjoy there. You have one foot in the Eternal because you know that the things God has for you are incredible. It's almost like there is a line drawn between the temporal and the eternal. Instead of picking a side, we straddle the line. When you have a divided mind like this, sin and desires of the world already have one of your feet and legs on its side. Half your body—and, more importantly, half your mind—is on one side with the world. It's so much easier to cross your whole body back over and sink into the familiar, enjoyable, and comfortable things of this world. Everything fits you like a glove. That is why it is so hard to leave it completely.

You reason and justify that the music you listen to has a good rhythm, but the words are not important. The artist is a professing member of the occult, but you don't judge people's personal lives. It's okay. You reason and justify how you saw that movie because there were only a few times that it profaned the name of your Savior, had profanity that you are numb to so you don't hear anymore, had explicit fornication and adultery scenes, along with other things God calls an abomination. You say, "Well, I can ignore all that because it had a really great story line."

Do you realize that the Holy Spirit was occupying a seat next to you the whole time? He is thinking, "You crossed back over to the world so easily, and you didn't even realize it. You pulled Me right in here with you to watch this. You never considered Me." You reason and justify that you have all the time to live for Jesus later while you live for yourself now. The Lord says, "You fool, tonight your soul could be required of you."

You reason and justify how you can spend two hours catching up on posts on Facebook because you want to stay in touch with your friends. You have never spent a solid two hours with the Lord or even two hours at church. Is it too much to ask spending just two hours with Jesus one-on-one uninterrupted, just like you spent on the computer reading the things about people's lives that you won't remember in a week. Why don't you read about Jesus' life, instead of the lives of your friends all the time? What a greater impact that would have on your own spiritual life! There's nothing wrong with Facebook or the other social sites if you give the Lord the same amount of quality time. If you don't, which side of the line are you on? Who is more important in your life? God or the world? Eternal things or temporal things?

I'm learning that we can say with our words that we want to serve the Lord and be blessed by Him. How can we do that if we are straddling the line between the world and Him? You were once of the world, but as a confessing Christian, you have been called out of world (John 15:19; all verses HCSB). You are not expected to compromise. You are not expected to reason and justify your crossing the line back into the things of this world. When you do, you really can start seeing the strength of the world on you. When I teach my two boys between right and wrong, I tell them if you can play that video game, watch that movie, look at that Internet site, watch that home video, look at that magazine, listen to that music, send that email, spend valuable time in whatever way you want and ask, "Holy Spirit, will you do it with me?" If He says "Yes," then you should jump in with both feet and glorify the Lord that you are honoring him. You are on the right side of the line.

If He says, "No," then you should thank Him for His conviction and obey. We don't like the word no; therefore, we do not ask the Holy Spirit a thing. In fact, He rarely crosses our minds when we make worldly choices. We don't like being made to come back completely across the line toward God's side. We can even get resentful and mad that we can't do those things that we used to like to do. When you feel those feelings of missing the things of the world that you once enjoyed, you are feeling the true power of the world in real time. As long as you go the way of the world, you will not feel its pull. The second that you try to go against it, the pull is incomprehensible.

One of the reasons Christians' lives are in the shape they are in is because they have justified that they can still have one foot in this world and one in the Kingdom of Heaven. Have you ever heard that phrase, "I am completely sold out?" If you are straddling the line and justifying your behaviors that are associated with the world, who are you really sold out to? Which side of the line are you really on? I think as we continue to wake from our long sleep, we need to be mindful that we need to be sold out at 100 percent for the things of God. We need to stop justifying our worldly behavior.

If we, as Christians, look just like the world, what would make the world want to ever look like us? They wouldn't, and they don't. If we are supposed to be the salt of the earth, how can we make a difference if we taste just like the world? (Matthew 5:13). We can't! It is our job to stand out and taste differently than them. They should desire what we have so badly they ask, "Why are you different? Why do you make different choices even against things that you once loved?" What a testimony it would be for you to say, "I finally stopped loving the world. Let me tell you about it."

John 15:19 warns us that once you mentally and spiritually put both of your feet on the solid ground of Jesus Christ, the world will hate you. Jesus said that the world will hate you because they hated Him first (John 15:18). They hated Him because He showed us how to separate from the world. Satan rules this world, and he doesn't like to lose that which once belonged to him. Even if you were a Christian, but still had one foot in the world, he was stealing your victory and strength in the Lord. You were too busy justifying and reasoning your actions to even notice. Wake up, Christian. This world is very powerful because of who rules it. The enemy and the world's pleasures will place an unnatural pull on you. Remember, as soon as you justify or reason why you are doing things on the world side of the line, you have just felt the enemy's pull. It's real.

"Oh Sarah, you are such a conservative fanatical Jesus Freak. Not all Christians are going to live and think like you. That is okay. We can't all be cookie cutters of each other! Just because you don't love some of this music, movies, and other things in this world doesn't mean I can't. You can take it overboard, you know! Not all of it is so bad. Besides I am having fun." I do not have to respond to this statement. I'd rather use the Lord's words. He says it so much more convincingly than I ever could. First John 2:15–17 says:

Do not love the world or things that belong to the world. If anyone loves the world, love for the Father is not in him. For everything that belongs to the world—the lust of the flesh, the lust of the eyes, and the pride in one's lifestyle—is not from the Father, but is from the world. And the world with its lust is passing away, but the one who does God's will remains forever.

When you have so much pride in your lifestyle that you justify that you can have one foot in the world and one foot in the kingdom, just remember this verse. The question you need to seriously ask yourself is, "Is the love of the Father in you or the love of the world?" You can't have it both ways. Choose this day whom you will serve.

Life's Chips

And in Christ you have been made complete. (Colossians 2:10 NASB)

I have been married twenty years. We were still using our original everyday dishes that we were received when we married. They came from a grocery store. I'm not kidding. Kevin and I were married right after college, and we had nothing. My mom saved grocery store coupons for a year to buy my set of dishes. She was so proud of them. I was, too. I didn't care that I had grocery store dishes. They had apples on them! Who couldn't like dishes from a grocery store that had apples?

We used those grocery store apple dishes for nineteen years! They have gone through many moves, two boys, church functions, reunions, and many family meals. They held up great, but I wanted new dishes. I justified after nineteen years that I deserved to have nicer everyday dishes. I could afford a new and more modern set. I was really tired at looking at apples on my plates!

I went to a nice department store and bought a beautiful pattern for dishes. They matched my kitchen. They had all my favorite colors in them. They were the prettiest dishes I had ever seen. I knew instantly that they would be going home with me. I bought an eight-piece setting with all the cups and serving pieces. I thought I was something. I was so proud of them. I gladly gave away all my apple grocery store dishes and put all my new dishes up.

A few weeks later, I was washing dishes after supper. I was putting one of my pretty new coffee cups in the dishwasher and didn't clear the corner of the counter. I instantly looked at it and sure enough a little chip around the edge. I just stood there and thought, "I never chipped one of my cheap grocery store coffee cups. I can't have my new cup chipped." Even though the coffee cup was still very usable and the chip was tiny, I was not going to have it. I went back to the store and bought another coffee cup! I wanted my dishes to be perfect.

All was well again, until a few weeks later I was putting dishes up after dinner and noticed a chip in one of my bowls! Ahhhhh! Who did that? When did that happen? Kevin said, "Honey, you can't get a new piece every time one chips!" I took one of my serving pieces to a church function. I wanted my food to be on my pretty new dishes. I hit the door coming out of the church—another chip. Aaahhhhhhhh! I have had the dishes now for one year. I have several chipped coffee cups, plates, and bowls, as well as a serving piece. How is that possible? All the dishes are fully functional, unless you count that one pretty coffee cup that I dropped on the floor and busted in seven pieces. Unbelievable.

I started thinking how I can't stop more chips from coming. I have now given up trying. These pretty new dishes are like my life. I strive for a pretty presentation. I desire to look fresh and up-to-date. I want to be complete, not only for how it makes me feel, but how I want others to perceive me. I do not think it's wrong to strive for this as I do not harbor vanity in my heart. I just want things to look nice. I don't want chips in my life, but I get knocked around by this world and some of my own poor choices pretty regularly.

When the chips do come, it seems to affect my mental completeness. I just hate having it as a part of me. There are some chips I have to live with, as they are the consequences for going my own way instead of God's. He has forgiven what caused the chip, but He doesn't remove the effect of the chip. That's just part of living. Just like seeing only my chips in my pretty dishes, that is all I can see in me as well. I may be doing pretty well, but all I focus on is my chips. God sees how beautiful and functional I am for His use. My perception is so limited by focusing on how I am, not how He sees me. My usability in the Body of Christ is greatly affected by my own perception of myself.

I was reading Colossians 2:10 (AKJV). The verse just about leaped off the page. "You are complete in Him." God knows that I am going to get lots of chips as I walk through this world. The broken hearts and hurts create chips. Loneliness creates chips. Hardships of marriage create chips. Raising children create several chips! Frustrations of not having things like they should be create chips. Losing loved ones create chips. Worries of what the future holds create chips. The pressure of living in this world in general creates chips. Illnesses create chips. Work creates chips. Family difficulties create chips.

We are all like my new dishes. No matter how hard we try to be gentle with our lives, the chips will come. The question is where we find our completeness again after chips appear. In Christ. We can't find our completion in anybody else or anything else. We try, though. We try so hard to find completeness within our own strength. The Lord says, "No. You are only complete in Me." Such simple truth. The Lord doesn't see our chips in our lives. He only sees our completeness in Him. Think about that. If we can ever fully believe these words, it would be life altering. We can stop trying to cover up the chips we have and stop caring so much about the chips we will collect along the way.

We are self-focused. We need to be more God-focused. I would rather trust Him with my completeness than any other truth I know. The enemy and our self-talk lie to us that we can never be complete and sufficient the way we are right now. The Lord says, "You are already complete. It happened the day you accepted Me into your heart." There is so much rest and peace in this truth. I can just stop. I don't have to keep going and gluing all those chips back in place in my life when He says I am already complete. I can just exhale. Praise God, I am complete and so are you.

Holy Spirit, Rain Down

It rained so hard last night and even until late today. I was sitting at my little desk, writing a few journals, while I looked out my window at the rain. I watched it for a long while. I love watching it fall. I love hearing how the rain sounds on the roof and as it drops off the eaves. We have had so much pollen recently, so I was glad the rain washed it all away. The rain is cleansing to the earth. When I went out to the garage a while ago, I could smell that fresh rain smell. There's nothing like it.

I was thinking how many things are in bloom right now. The flowers will drink this rain up to come out brighter and stronger. The rivers and lakes will be replenished. I love that verse in Psalm 65:9 that reads, "You visit the earth and water it, making it rich and fertile" (NLT/HCSB) When it rains, I tell my boys that God is visiting. One time when my youngest son saw it raining day after day, he asked, "How long is God going to visit?"

As I was sitting here watching the rain, I started thinking about the song, "Holy Spirit, Rain Down." It is one of my favorite songs. The Holy Spirit is called Comforter and Friend. The song talks about asking the Holy Spirit to rain down on us. The words speak of how we need the Rain. It's not that we just want Him; we need Him deep in our souls and minds. We need to be outside with our arms stretched out in the Rain. With this invitation, power falls within us from on High. When the power of the Holy Spirit falls upon us, His voice is heard by our hearts. There is communion. There is conversation. There is life inside of us. There is freshness and renewal. There is sharing of truth and deeper understanding of the Most High God.

The Rain falls on us in abundance. He changes our hearts through the foundation of the Word of God. The song continues, as it asks Heaven to open wide and to rain down the Spirit over God's church and our lives. No one knows what God has in store for us. We need the touch of the Holy Spirit to make it possible to know God's will for our lives.

So often in my life, I have dismissed the Spirit's power. I knew who He was, but I always thought that He was the weakest of the Trinity. He is the one that kind of got left behind as God and Jesus lived in Heaven. I kind of felt sorry for Him. God gets Jesus back in Heaven, and the Holy Spirit is stuck with us. Poor Holy Spirit. I always focused on Jesus and God. I paid little attention to the Spirit. When you are a child, you think like a child. It seems like I drank spiritual milk for a very long time before I truly understood just who the Holy Spirit really was. When I did, I asked for His forgiveness of my disregard and lack of understanding of Him.

I started studying about the Holy Spirit. Since that day and for the rest of my life, I will be in awe of who He is and the power He possesses. The Hebrew word for Holy Spirit is *Ruach* pronounced Roo-akh. It means wind. The Greek word for breathe or breeze is *Pneuma* pronounced Pnyoo-mah. The Holy Spirit is God's literal breath in us. God is in us by the power of the presence of the Holy Spirit. While we are on this earth,

He is what we breathe in order to commune with the Most High God. We know that God fashioned Adam from clay. He breathed in his nostrils. If the Holy Spirit means breath, who actually breathed into Adam? God the Father or God the Holy Spirit? Who hovered and vibrated over the deep during the days of creation? The Holy Spirit.

Often we think of God the Father and God the Son as persons, but we think of the Holy Spirit as a force of some sort. He is just as much a person of the Trinity as the Father and Son are. He is equal at all levels. When you leave your children with someone, do you leave them in the best care possible? Sure you do. That is exactly what Jesus did at His ascension. He said He would send someone that would teach us, comfort us, and never leave us. Someone is not a force; it is a person. The Holy Spirit is the person that Jesus entrusted our care to.

Jesus told us in John 16:12–14 (HCSB) that He had so many things to tell us, but we wouldn't be able to handle it all while He was with us. He would send the Spirit of Truth or the Holy Spirit to continue the teachings. Jesus made it clear that He would communicate with us directly through the Holy Spirit. There is no other way. If you don't have the Holy Spirit, you will not hear Jesus. It is impossible. Jesus says the Holy Spirit will take what He had to say and tell us. When you don't care to listen to the Holy Spirit, you are telling Jesus that you don't care to listen to Him either.

The Holy Spirit is a very important person in our lives. He is not One to be dismissed. He is not One to be belittled in our thinking as being less important in the Trinity. He is not a force. He is certainly not One that you want to grieve by your own sins. He is not One that you want to ignore spending time with. If you don't spend time with Him, how do you figure on hearing Jesus?

The Holy Spirit is breathing in my soul right now. When He is removed from the earth to meet Jesus in the clouds, I will go with Him as I am in Him and He is in me. This is the mystery that Jesus has made known. The Holy Spirit and I can never be separated. He has sealed Himself around me. I am His, and He is mine. Where I go, He goes. What I see, He sees. What I say, He hears. What I write, He reads. What I do, He watches. What I listen to, He hears. What I think, He knows. What I feel, He feels. We are one.

I am standing with arms stretched out toward heaven in the Rain singing, "Fall as much and hard as You need to down on me. I want to hear Jesus talking. Spirit! Tell me what He is saying. Speak to me! Breathe in me, so Your breath is mine. I pray I will never grieve You. Spirit, when You leave this world, take me with You."

Crouching Close

If you do what is right, will you not be accepted? But if you do not do what is right, sin is crouching at your door; it desires to have you, but you must rule over it. (Genesis 4:7 NIV)

There are so many lessons to learn from the story of Cain and Abel. Genesis 4:7 is a verse that I keep coming back to because of the strong life lesson I believe the Lord wants us to learn. I have read Genesis many times, like most people, but the Lord keeps bringing me back to this particular verse.

I have studied sin in depth because I wanted to understand how it had a hold on me. I wanted to understand how I had a hold on it. I wanted to have a Christ-like mind, but how could I, when I struggled with sin? How could I make headway in becoming a stronger Christian in thought and deed if I was going in circles with meaningless things? That includes the lust of this temporal world in whatever it had to offer me. I finally came to the conclusion that I couldn't made headway. I was no more than a fast spinning tire bogged down in mud. I was spinning as fast I could go, but I wasn't moving in the deeper knowledge of God. Why? For the same reason Cain was spinning his tires—the pride of life. He wanted to do things his way, and he expected that his way was just as good as God's way. Shockingly arrogant, but that is exactly what we do today.

We all know what Cain did to Abel. I do not need to retell this story. The part I want to focus on is before Cain called his younger brother to the field. God saw what was on Cain's heart and mind. God saw his intentions.

God came close to Cain and said some of the most powerful words in the Bible, as it relates to understanding sin in our lives. He said, "If you do what is right, will you not be accepted? But if you refuse to do what is right, then watch out! Sin is crouching at your door, eager to control you.

But you must rule over or subdue it and be its master." Do you know that the Most High God came to Cain to try to get him to think about his actions and understand how sin works? If you look at the interchange, Cain didn't even respond back to God. After God tried to teach him and help him, Cain still called Abel to the field to carry out what was controlling him. Cain was not in control.

Sin is crouching at the door. Don't you find it odd that God uses the word *crouch*? He could have used standing, sitting, or lying at the door. When you think of crouch, what do you immediately think of? An animal. Not a domesticated animal, but a wild and uncontrolled animal looking for something to devour. That something would be you! Crouch means to bend close to the ground, as an animal preparing to spring for attack. Animals lie in wait as they stay close to the ground. They only move when they are sure that the target is vulnerable. They look for the animals that are on the outside of the herd so they increase their success rates of taking it down.

The target animal is never aware that the predator is even there. Why? They are very quiet and crouching low. They don't make noise like, "Hey! I'm watching you. I am coming after you to take you down!" They will crouch there quietly for long periods of time just waiting for the right opportunity. Isn't that how sin works? Sin works just like a wild animal. It will not announce itself because pretty much it is always there crouching and waiting to take you down. God says, "Christian, sin is stalking you! Be watchful!"

Not only is sin crouching, but where is it located? On the other side of a door. How thick is a standard door? Less than two inches. Look at your finger. That is about the length two joints of your finger. Christian that is how close sin can be to you this very moment! Does that alarm you a bit?

Sin is crouching ready to devour you, and it is two inches from you. We go about our lives in la-la land, falling into sin over and over. God tells us how it works and how close it is, but we are oblivious to this truth. We wonder why our lives are not stronger. We keep opening the door and letting the crouching, uncontrolled sin right back in. We might as well put revolving doors in our lives. Sin comes in, we fall, we repent, sin comes in, we fall, we repent, and round and round the door goes. God said sin is eager to control you. If there is a revolving door of sin in your life, then sin is in control.

Is there any hope for us with this close, controlling, and crouching sin? God came to Cain, just like He comes to us today and says, "You must rule over sin. You must be the master of it." God knows how close sin is to us. God knows how sin is like a predator. That is why He warned us to be watchful. He has given us dominion over the animals of the earth. He has also given us dominion over sin by the power of the Holy Spirit. We act like we are not capable to have the dominion that He says we have. We act like we have to sin as that is what people do. Why would He say we could master it, if we couldn't? Is God a liar?

The problem is not that we can't master sin, but that we like opening the door back to it. It's sad, but that is what we do. Instead of mastering it, we expect it. After all, we are fallen people who sin. That is just what we do. When God comes to me and says, "Sin is crouching at your door. Its desire is to devour you. You must control and master sin or it will control and master you. Listen to Me," will I refuse to answer God and walk off into the field, like Cain, to do my pleasing?

Will I give power to the enemy, because of my refusal to obey God (Ephesians 2:2 NIV)? Or will I answer back, "Lord God Almighty, cover, strengthen, and protect me against the temptation and sin that is two inches away from my life. By the power of the Holy Spirit, I am in control. I will not open that door." Cain could have had a different outcome. So can we. Ephesians 6:10 says, "Finally, be strong in the Lord and in His mighty power" (NIV).

Freedom of Thought

Do you ever have thoughts from your past come to your mind out of nowhere? They are usually faster than a speeding train as they travel through your mind. Some are from twenty years ago, and some are more recent. Thoughts of what you did in that past bring back intense emotions and are immediately distracting from the life you have now. You remember the wrong you did, those poor choices you made, those regrets that you can't let go of, and those "What-ifs." It's like if you replay the thoughts long enough in your head that somehow you can change what happened and make it right. If you can figure out the why of your behavior, then maybe it will give you some peace to release what is holding onto you, so that you can be free from it. Yet, year after year, the same thoughts periodically come. The amount of mental energy you are expending is exhausting. These past memories keep you from living with freedom in the present. They bind you to your past. It's like they are shackled to you somehow.

What does the enemy keep throwing in your face from the past? Fornication? Promiscuity? Drugs? Alcohol? Being in the wrong place at the wrong time? Anger and hurt over an abusive childhood? Failed marriage? Affair? Stupid decisions? Hurting people's hearts? Failed relationships? Poor behavior toward loved ones? Being estranged from family because of poor communication, misunderstandings, or abuse? Disobedience toward God? Pornographic addiction? Lust of the flesh? Lust for materialism? Poor self-worth and self-esteem? Being hard on yourself for taking behavior toward you in the past that you didn't deserve and trying to figure out why you endured it for as long as you did? Maybe it's the opposite. Being hard on yourself for having behavior toward others in the past they didn't deserve? Your prior weaknesses in a situation that you know you should have been stronger in? Your past dishonesty with people or in situations?

Christian, what did you do or what happened to you that the enemy won't let you forget? You know exactly what I am talking about. It's probably coming to your mind right now. It comes back so easily, doesn't it? It's right under the surface. It's always right there, just an uncontrolled thought away. You could be walking along in your life looking straight ahead and within seconds, the enemy allows a fleeting old thought packed with every emotion imaginable to race across your mind.

Your head instantly turns to the right or to the left. Your focus is immediately taken from the present as you start turning that old familiar thought over and over in your mind. You have come to hate when the thoughts come because they take so much of your mental energy to think about all over again. You don't want to think about them; if you could stop them, you would. You feel powerless. It's like the thought has to run its mental course, and then it starts fading away only to return later when your head is straight again. And so goes the bonding cycle to your past.

How do I know how to explain this so well? It's like I know how it feels. Oh, I know exactly how it feels. I have my own past. I did a great job of making my own mistakes. It seems like the enemy knows every one of them. I have my own thoughts that invade my private and inner place, just like you. Those thoughts know exactly where to land, so that knife of regret is twisted a little deeper in my soft, vulnerable heart. The older I get, the more I understand that there are very few people without regrets. There are very few people that don't have thoughts that come back to them, looking to turn their head.

What is their purpose? The old thoughts come back to steal your joy. John 16:22 says, "And ye now therefore have sorrow; but I will see you again, and your heart shall rejoice, and your joy that no man taketh from you" (KJV). Joy and happiness can be taken from you if you allow it. I don't know about you, but when my old thoughts come back, joy is not the emotion I feel. The enemy takes it and it makes me so mad! My joy is replaced with anger and resentment that I am back in the same place again.

The thoughts come back to steal your focus. God says since you belong to Him, that you should set your mind on what is above, not what is on the earth (Colossians 3:2 HCSB). What is in our minds? Thoughts. He is saying, "Set every thought only on Me and the truth that I have given to you from above." If your thoughts and mind are focused on the things you did in your earthly past, then the enemy has succeeded in stealing your focus from the Lord. The old thoughts come back because the enemy hates you and wants you to suffer deeply. John 15:19 says since you are not from the world, there is only hate for you now (HCSB). You have no idea how much the enemy hates you.

Why do the thoughts keep happening after all these years? The enemy seeks to make you miserable. If he can keep you miserable in your own regret, despair, and remorse, then he can take your victory in the Lord away that day. He doesn't care about the next day. He wants to see if he can make you miserable today. As long as he can steal your joy and focus when he dangles that old thought over and over in front of you face, he will. As long as you allow those old thoughts to rule over you, the enemy will use them. That's all the ammunition he has on you. Stop responding and reacting to them; stand in the knowledge of God.

Will we ever be free from them? The enemy knows our lives are short. He knows the Bible better than we do. Psalm 103:15–16 says, "As for man, his days are as grass; as a flower of the field, so he flourishes. For the wind passeth over it, and it is gone; and the place thereof shall know it no more" (AKJV). Our life is like a vapor that appears for a little while and then passes away. The more time the enemy takes our joy and our focus, the less life we have left to devote to God and the things He needs us to do for and with Him. We are all given a certain number of days. If Satan takes a lot of them by tricking us to dwell on the past, then what is left for us and God? Do we really want to spend our limited time left focusing on things from our hurtful past?

We can never change our past. The Lord has thrown all the iniquities of our past into the deepest sea (Micah 7:19 AKJV). The enemy goes fishing in that sea all the time. He catches our thoughts and throws them back in our face. God doesn't do that to us. God has a no-fishing sign posted, but yet the enemy fishes there anyway. When these thoughts come from our past, they are not from our Loving Father. We need to consider the source and know how to deal with them. We need to stand on the Truth.

Romans 8:37 says, "No, in all these things we are more than conquerors through Him who loves us" (NIV). First John 5:4 says, "For everyone born of God overcomes the world. This is the victory that has overcome the world, even our faith" (NIV). God tells us in Luke 6:45 that we have good treasure stored in our heart and his heart produces what is good (KJV). The enemy knows we have good stored in us; he just doesn't want us to tap into it. He wants us to tap into the bad because he knows how powerful it is. Good thoughts are more powerful than bad ones; we just believe the lie that they are not. We dwell on what we did bad and forget about all of our good.

We have to understand how the enemy thinks and works. We have to know him as well as he knows us, or we are defenseless. God has given us the full armor and knowledge to be victorious against the enemy. We just have to pick it up and use it. The enemy makes us think that we have no control over our thoughts. They just come and go out of our minds as they please. That is another lie that we buy.

Second Corinthians 10:5 says, "We demolish arguments and every pretension that sets itself up against the knowledge of God, and we take captive every thought to make it obedient to Christ" (NIV, emphasis added). Who takes our thoughts captive? The enemy? This verse says the truth of the matter is that we take our thoughts captive. We are the hunter! Not the prey. Hallelujah! Praise the Lord! Knowing the knowledge of God puts power pack in our hands and takes it out of the enemy's hands.

This truth is life changing! We don't have to be the prey ever again. The freedom in this truth is unfathomable. We can have freedom from this repeating torture of having our past thrown in our faces by the enemy.

I'll end a declaration, extracted from some very familiar verses that you can use the next time the enemy attacks and tries to capture your thoughts, joy, and focus. You speak with full authority back to him, audibly if you want to, "I am a child of the Most High God. I resist you, by the power within me. The One who loves me, which has no condemnation for me, is greater than you and this world will ever be. I know the truth and I have been set free. I am victorious in Christ Jesus. Flee from me" (1 John 4:4; John 8:32; Romans 8:1; James 4:7; Galatians 3:26–29; 1 Corinthians 15:57 NIV). Give God all the glory. Stand in truth. You are completely free in Christ Jesus. Amen! Amen! Amen!

Ordained Steps

Man's steps are ordained by the Lord. How then can man understand his way? (Proverbs 20:24 NASB)

Have you ever wondered how Lazarus walked out of the tomb when he was wrapped from head to toe in preparation for burial? Have you wondered how Moses led over a million people from Egypt to the Promised Land? Have you wondered why Ananias healed Paul of his blindness? Have you ever wondered how Abraham left his own country to arrive in the land of Canaan? Have you ever wondered how Peter walked on water? Have you ever wondered how the story of Christ spread from a little town in the middle of nowhere to every part of this world? Have you ever wondered how every disciple, except John, walked to his death confessing Christ? Have you ever wondered what drives a person from the comforts of their homes to take the gospel in inhospitable locations? Have you ever wondered how you found the church body that you are a part of? Have you ever wondered how you came to Christ at the exact time you did?

The other day, the Lord asked me, "How did Lazarus walk out of the tomb?" I thought this was a strange question. I know that Lazarus was raised by the power of the spoken word of Jesus, "Lazarus, come forth."

The Lord responded, "Yes, but how did he walk out, when he couldn't see where he was going?" I started thinking that Jesus told the people to loose Lazarus after he came forth. No one went into the tomb to loosen him before he was raised. He would have had the traditional wrapping from head-to-toe of strips of fabric. His body would have been wrapped separately from his head. Since Lazarus was loosed after he was raised, he would have had to walk out with his head wrapped in fabric. He would have walked out blindly. I have never thought about this before. The Lord knew that. As He allowed me to ponder what I knew of the story, He said, "I ordained his steps when he couldn't see." I love it when the Lord speaks new truth to me.

Other stories of people's steps being ordained flooded my mind. When Paul was brought to Damascus, blinded from His encounter with Jesus, he was taken to the house of Judas. We don't know a lot about of Judas, except he was Jew who lived on Straight Street. This was one of two major intersecting roads in Damascus. Paul was left there blind for three days. He did not eat or drink. He was a broken and blind man. All of the worldly authority and passion that drove Paul was emptied out. God had poured it all out. A new authority and passion had flooded Paul. He was a new creature in Christ.

The Lord called upon his faithful disciple, Ananias, who had the gift of healing, to go see Paul. The Lord told Ananias exactly where Paul was staying, right down to the street name. The location was not the problem for Ananias. Unlike Lazarus, Ananias could see where he was going clearly. Ananias questioned God about going to see a person he felt unsafe and whom he was uncertain and fearful of. Paul, known at the time as Saul before being healed, had full authority to arrest all Christians and put them to death. In fact, the only reason he was in Damascus in the first place was to do just that.

Ananias knew this. The Lord had to tell Ananias twice to go heal Paul. When Ananias set out toward Straight Street, his steps were ordained by God, as he was fearful of the uncertainty of the situation. The faith it took for Ananias to obey God in this directive is some of the strongest faith that I have witnessed in the entire Bible. That would be like your being asked to go to Iran to a house that Ahmadinejad was in and tell him Jesus Christ sent you. Would you go?

Honestly, the Lord would have to tell me more than twice to go! I really don't know how many times the Lord would have to tell me. There is a distinct possibility that I would disobey this request by the Lord. Ananias obeyed, and we know that He healed Paul, filled him with the Holy Spirit, and baptized Him. The Bible said, "Immediately, Paul began proclaiming Jesus as the Son of God in the synagogues." God ordained Ananias' steps when he was fearful and uncertain.

Abraham, friend of the Most High God, was a righteous man. He had a very affluent life in Haran. His father, Terah, had moved his family from Ur about five years before God called Abraham out to be the Father of the Jewish nation. God told Abraham, "Leave your country, your relatives, and your father's home, and go to a land that I am going to show you." Unlike Ananias, God told Abraham once. During that time, he traveled through many unknown lands until he reached Canaan. Abraham had no other reason to leave his comfortable life in Haran, except the Lord was ordaining his steps. Abraham never questioned God or asked for clarification for directions. He had full faith that he and his family would be taken care of based off of God's promises.

Do I have full faith in God based on His promises? When bad things happen in my life, do I trust His heart when I can't see His hand? When my heart is broken, do I trust His promise that He will bind it? When I sin and fall so far from holiness, do I trust Him that He will scoop me back up once again and bring me close to His bosom, just as if I had never sinned? Abraham is called the Father of Faith. I am a child of that same faith. God ordained Abraham's steps when he left his comfort zone to go into the unknown.

There are so many specific stories that I could tell of how and in what ways God ordained people's steps. No matter how many stories of ordained steps that I give, they all have one thread in common. These people were always in God's holy will. They lived with clear consciences, obedience, a deep love for God that He knew best, a faith to step out of what they knew, and a trust in God that they would be protected. They walked when they could not see one foot in front of them. They walked when they were filled with all sort of uncertainties. They walked away from their comfort zone and what they could understand to enter God's zone. They walked to the exact place and in the exact timing that God needed them to be in for His glory and purpose, never their own.

I think we as Christians miss that truth so many times. We have to remember that God knows where we are heading, but when we are supposed to arrive, we don't. We have to trust the path when we can't see. We have to have faith when we feel that we are unsafe and uncertain. We have to be obedient when God tells us to walk outside of our comfort zone. I pray that each step I take is ordained by the Most High God. I trust Him one step at a time. I pray that I stay in His holy will, so where I step, people will see Jesus' footprints, not mine.

Praise the Lord Now

Psalm 113:2 tell us to bless the name of the Lord now and forever (NLT). What if now is a bad time in your life? What if now your heart is broken? What if now you are confused on which direction to turn next? What if now your faith has run out? What if now you are in a trial that you don't deserve? What if now you are in the middle of falling apart? What if now your health is failing? What if now, you are in the midnight hour of your life, and you cannot see past the next minute? The Lord tells us if we are to be in His will, we are to give thanks in all circumstances (I Thessalonians 5:18 NIV). There is no indication that He is leaving you a choice in this. God is not asking you; He is telling you. But, what if you are in pain and suffering right now?

All pain and suffering have causative factors. If God can't be one of them, what factors cause our pain and suffering? Just by living in a fallen world you will have pain, sickness, and death. These three things will either affect you personally or someone that you love. That is a guarantee. If you live long enough in this world, you cannot escape them. Are you responsible for them? Is there something that you did or didn't do that caused them? No. They are the consequence of living in a world affected by sin.

Pain and suffering can enter your life as the result of other's poor choices of their free will. Is it right that we have to suffer because of others? No. Does it happen every day, and will it happen again? Yes. This is a reality of living and breathing. Pain and suffering can enter your life as the result of your own poor choices of your free will. Could they have been avoided? Yes, by your obedience to the Holy Will of the Most High God. Let me tell you some truth. If you live for yourself, according to your own will, then you are guaranteed pain and suffering. Again, I would like to reemphasize the word *guaranteed*.

If you think you know better than the Lord, then you are a complete fool. You deserve to be called one. I deserve to be called one as well. I have been a fool for more times than I have fingers and toes to count. Don't get offended for me using the word *fool*. A fool is defined as someone who lacks judgment and is weak minded. If you put aside a Christ-like mind and judge your way is better than Gods, then, by definition, you are a fool. You are guaranteed to cause your own pain and suffering by your own foolishness. Be very mindful of the power of free will in your life. It is a gift to be used very wisely. Remember, you don't want to be responsible for causing pain and suffering in others' lives or your own.

The Lord tells us to bless His name in all circumstances. Those circumstances could involve pain and suffering. Most likely they will. There is freedom in thanking, praying, and singing praises in our pain and suffering. How can this be? It takes our eyes off of us and refocuses them on where they should have been the entire time. This keeps from giving the enemy a stronghold, thus throwing you into despair. We can honor and glorify the Lord despite our circumstances. We should have our eyes firmly focused on Him. He makes an impossible circumstance possible to bear. You make it another day when you didn't see how you could take another breath yesterday.

When you bless the Lord's name, those chains of that circumstance loosen to where it is bearable. Sometimes, the chains completely fall off. Even if they don't, we don't stop blessing the name of the Lord. Your circumstance not going away doesn't make God less loving. What Christians still have such a difficult time understanding, as we live in such a self-centered world and culture, is it is not about us. We can praise God in our pain and suffering because the praise is not for us or about us. No matter what we are going through, God is the Holy Creator Savior of our souls. Our lives are all about—and only about—Him, despite our circumstances.

He doesn't cease being the King of Kings and Lord of Lords, losing one ounce of His authority, when you are in pain and suffering. He doesn't cease because He didn't cause it. It doesn't come from Him. If we thought it came from Him, what logic would there be to praise Him for it. That would be ludicrous. Since He didn't cause it, and our lives are not about us, we therefore praise Him in all circumstances despite our lack of understanding.

Another reason that is imperative to praise God in our pain and suffering is because other people are listening and watching. Their lives can be positively or negatively affected, depending on what we say and do in our own pain and suffering. Acts 16:16–34 tells one of my favorite stories. Paul and Silas entered the town of Philippi. While there, they cast out a demon from a girl that enabled her to tell fortunes. When the owners of the girl found out that they could not make money off of the girl any longer, they assembled a mob to attack them.

Even the leaders of the town ordered Paul and Silas to be beaten with rods. The Bible is clear that many blows were inflicted on them. They were thrown in prison and shackled to the floor. At midnight, in all of their pain and suffering, Paul and Silas remembered what King David said in Psalm 34:1 (KJV). They remembered to be thankful and bless and praise God continually in all circumstances. They were bleeding and bruised, so I can imagine that they were not in high spirits. The Bible says they started singing and praying.

I can see Silas starting a sweet hymn to the Lord, then Paul smiling and joining in on the chorus. While one kept singing, the other one would pray out loud. They were not blaming or cursing God. They were thanking God for their chains. They were thanking God for their suffering on behalf of Him. They were singing hymns of adorations to God. He loved them so much despite their current circumstances. I have read this story so many times, but this time seven words jumped out at me, *"And the prisoners were listening to them."*

Other people were there in their own pain and suffering. They were watching and listening to see how these professing Christians responded differently than the world. When the earthquake happened, their chains fell off and the doors opened. The prisoners were in such awe of Paul and Silas and how they handled their own pain and suffering, their lives were affected. They didn't run out. They stayed right where they were. Why? They had to know what made Paul and Silas respond this way.

They were listening and they wanted to know more about the Lord. Many lives were changed that very night for one simple reason. Paul and Silas praised the Lord in their pain and suffering. What a powerful testimony! You need to be very mindful who is listening and watching you in your pain and suffering. You are being a witness while you are enduring your trial. The question is, what are people hearing and seeing in your pain and suffering? Are they hearing hymns and prayers or blaming and despair? Remember Paul and Silas. We are to be mindful of our responses. We can have a powerful impact on many people around us that we may never realize.

Do not compromise God's way for any person or circumstance. People in your life that are not living in obedience to God's way can cause you great pain and suffering. Reevaluate who and how people are affecting your life. If there needs to be space placed between their lives and your life to lessen the pain and suffering in your own life, then that needs to be evaluated. That doesn't mean you care for those people any less, but you know that you have done everything you could at this point. It depends on how close the relationship is to you with how far you can back away. It may only be for a time, until their behavior is in obedience to God's way.

You may need to readjust the role and the depth of the role you have in their lives. It may mean that you distance yourself physically, but always be an active prayer warrior for them. Some people never line their lives up with God's way. They are guaranteed continue pain and suffering, but that doesn't necessarily mean you have to share in that. You can talk to them and be a model for them, but you can't change people. Only God can do that. I have learned that the hard way. Pray for discernment in those situations where other people cause pain and suffering in your life. May the Lord order your steps as you make the best decisions.

Where is our hope? When will our pain and suffering end? We have a living hope is Christ Jesus. Read 1 Peter 1:3–7 to see all of your promised hope (NIV). It is too long to write here, but the words are perfect in describing the promised hope we have. Pain and suffering sometimes last for a season and sometimes they last for many seasons. All you can do for your life is to ensure you are living in obedience to God's will. While we are here on Earth, Christ is our hope through the pain and suffering we have, despite who or what causes it.

The encouraging news is that we will not always be on this earth. One of the greatest promises of the entire Bible is in Revelation 21:4. The verse says, "And God shall wipe away all tears from their eyes; and there shall be no more death, neither sorrow, nor crying, neither shall there be any more pain; for the former things are passed away" (KJV). Have hope,

Christian! Pain and suffering will end completely one day. We have to trust the Lord for this promise when we think we will not make it one more day. Keep thanking and praising the Lord until this promise is fulfilled with His return.

Fluctuating Faith

Do you think it is possible for your faith to fluctuate? Can it be really strong one moment and really weak at another? If it can fluctuate, what are the causative factors? Or do you believe once you reach a certain level of faith that you maintain that level, and then build on top of that level to make faith stronger for the future? If the second scenario is true, then you would not be able to return to a lower level of faith, no matter what situation came up.

Have you ever thought about faith in this way? No? Me, either. I was driving to church one Sunday morning, and out of the blue, I started pondering whether faith can fluctuate. If it could, what were some examples? I wanted to understand more about this. The Lord, in His wisdom, was watching my mind's wheels start turning faster and faster. He said, "Look at Peter and John."

Faith can be defined in several different ways. I'm going to piece together a few words that make the most sense to me. Faith is sureness, an allegiance, loyalty, hope, dependence, conviction, certainty, belief, and acceptance. When I say I have faith in God, all of these words can be interchanged with faith. I have acceptance in God. I have dependence on God. I have hope in God. If you think of some of these words, can you start wondering how they can be interchanged in the lives of Peter and John?

Let's look at Peter first. Everyone loves Peter. I picture him as the tallest disciple and broad-shouldered. He is a big guy, far from wimpy. I would never want to confront Peter when he is mad! We remember what he did to that guy's ear in the Garden! Remember, he was going for the man's neck and missed! I see people moving out of his way when he walked through crowds. He was the strong-willed child that his mother barely got raised without killing him. When he was involved in something, he was committed entirely. He was the take-action disciple.

When Jesus came into the area of Galilee, He saw Andrew and Peter fishing. Jesus said, "Follow Me." Immediately, Peter jumped in with both feet. He was committed, believed, loyal, and depended on Jesus. Peter had a large amount of faith in Jesus. In fact, of all of the disciples, he had the most faith in Jesus at some point in the ministry. What proof do I have for this statement? Who had the faith to get out of the boat in the storm? I don't remember the disciples fighting over who was going to walk to Jesus first, do you? Walking on water had to take more faith than all the other disciples had put together. Simon Peter was the only natural man in the history of the world to walk on water.

If we go back to some of my original questions (faith fluctuation or reaching a certain level and building on top of that), what will we see in Peter's future? If Peter had the level of faith to walk on water, and if faith didn't fluctuate, then we should never have seen Peter at a lower level of faith. Right? But we do. Not only do we see him at a lower level of faith, we see him with none. How can Peter go from having enough faith to walk on water and even willing to fight for Jesus in the Garden to not having faith to stay with Jesus in His darkest hour? Honestly, this has always confounded me.

I bet no one was more confounded than Peter, himself. He had to be in disbelief every single time he uttered the words, "I do not know Jesus." What happened to him? Peter had trusted Jesus so much that he left his livelihood to follow Him. He had seen the miracle and healings. He trusted Jesus to keep him from drowning on the Sea of Galilee. This last experience should have allowed him to build a good amount of faith to be able to handle more fearful situations in the future.

What happened to Peter's allegiance, loyalty, dependence, hope, and certainty in Jesus? What happened to Peter's faith? The only thing I can figure out is Peter lost his faith due to unanticipated, paralyzing fear. He was ready to fight to the death earlier in the garden. Just a few hours later, he disowned Jesus. Peter did not set out to lose his faith that night. He would have never thought it was possible. I think he was faced with a situation that that was just too much for him to handle. I do not believe that he loved Jesus any less than when he was with Him in the Garden.

How can we apply what happen to Peter's faith to our lives? I really do not know the exact circumstance it would take to instill paralyzing fear into Christians today to affect their faith in Christ. In a real sense, Peter could have been facing martyrdom if He confessed Christ the night of the arrest. He knew that he could have been called to stand right by Jesus. The High Priest certainly had that power. I think if today's Christian was faced with martyrdom, that would naturally instill paralyzing fear. We each hope that we would not deny Christ even unto death, but we know that it is possible. If our life was threatened, would our faith fluctuate? Don't be arrogant to think it can't. Peter's did, and he saw Christ first hand.

I know of people personally who have lost their faith in Christ because of the pain and suffering they have endured. They blame God. They reason if He was a loving and caring God that He could have stopped it all. Since He didn't, they disbelieve in Him. They have no hope in Him. They no longer accept Him. They lose their faith and, unlike Peter, they may never find it again. If we receive that terminal medical diagnosis, if our spouse says they want to leave, if we lose a child, or they travel to the far country, among other trials, would our faith fluctuate? Would it cease and would we recover it if it did?

John was just a teenager when Jesus called him. He was the youngest of the disciples. I am sure he was the least respected among the older men because of his age. Jesus certainly didn't treat him any differently. When the storm came upon the water, John did not have the faith of Peter to get out of the boat. Even so, John's faith didn't fluctuate like Peter's. John's slowly built, based on the events that he witnessed. Even though he didn't walk on water, he witnessed Peter and Jesus do it. Can you imagine the amount of faith that must have built?

After seeing this, he witnessed feeding of 4,000. He witnessed miraculous healings. He witnessed the Transfiguration. He witnessed Judas' kiss. He witnessed Peter's denial. He was the only disciple who witnessed the crucifixion up close. He witnessed the empty tomb first. Every single one of these events and the countless others that he saw that are not recorded built his faith slowly and firmly.

There is not one instance in the Bible, that I am aware of, where John's faith fluctuated. I believe there are many reasons why Christ allowed John to be the only disciple who wasn't martyred. Jesus had set John aside to write Revelation. Why was he the one who was chosen to write it? I believe it was because no matter the circumstances that faced John in his life, his faith never fluctuated. When faced with unanticipated paralyzing fear, which John was faced with, his faith did not fluctuate. When faced with pain and suffering that was undeserving, John's faith did not fluctuate. When faced with the uncertainties of life, John's faith did not fluctuate. John's faith built slowly and firmly at each level. It never dropped down to a previous level. It only increased with each trial.

How can we apply John's faith to our lives? I have had the honor to watch strong women and men of God as they have gone through intense trials of life. These friends have been the strongest testimony to me and others around them as their faith stood firm. They didn't know how they were going to get through the day, much less the week, but their faith never fluctuated. They may have not known what to do, but they had faith that God did. The only way they could have faith like this is if they had already witnessed Jesus in their lives over and over. They internalized every event. The foundation was laid which became thicker and more solid with time. I have stood back in amazement wondering if I were ever in their shoes, whether I would carry myself as well. Is my faith as solid as John's and my friends? I hope so.

As authentic Christians, we need to remember that situations will come into our lives that will shake our faith and paralyze us with fear. Some of us may have gone through trials like this already and know exactly what I am talking about. Some of those trials may be in our future. The scary part about faith is that you won't know how you will fare until that trial comes. I pray I can be like John, but realistically, I could react like Peter. No matter which disciple we are like when our trials comes, we need to remember that the love that Jesus has for us and God's faithfulness are not dependent on our fluctuating faith.

His love and faithfulness are based on what He has promised us and who He is, not who we are. This is a very important truth that Christians miss. There are times that we may be faithless. We do not slip out of God's hands during those times. He just cups His hands around us tighter and holds us closer. Jesus never let Peter go. He never stopped loving Peter, despite his fluctuating faith. Jesus will treat us the same way. Let us all rest in God's faithfulness; it never fluctuates.

The Color of Sin

Have you ever thought about the color of sin? All things have color. Try to think of one thing that doesn't. Even things that are white are still called a color. God sees in color. How do I know that? Look around. He is the one the picked out all the colors you see in nature. We didn't do that. I have often read of people who come back from near-death experiences say the same thing. They agree that the colors in Heaven are all intensified compared to Earth. The colors are brighter, beyond their comprehension. When they look at colors now, the colors are never as vivid as they are in Heaven. I have no doubt that there is color everywhere in Heaven. Everything has color, and so does sin. What color is sin?

The Lord continues to guide my mind to think about all sorts of things I have never contemplated before. The color of sin is certainly one of them. I was singing "Jesus Paid It All" along with our church one Sunday morning. The chorus goes like this, "Jesus paid it all, all to Him I owe. Sin has left a crimson stain. He washed it white as snow." While I was singing, I kept going back to sin having color. If it leaves a crimson stain, then sin must be red. I was immediately reminded of the verse, "Though your sins are like scarlet, they shall be as white as snow; though they are red as crimson, they shall be like wool" (Isaiah 1:18 NIV). Scarlet is defined as a bright red color. Crimson is defined as a deep red color. I thought of the spectrum of red. Sin has the entire spectrum covered from the deepest to the brightest color red. God wanted to make sure that you saw your sin as any color red.

Have you ever washed one little red thing in the washing machine by accident with your other white clothes? What happens? The power of that one red item changes everything else in that washer to a shade of red. Isn't that exactly what sin does in our lives? If we have one "little" red sin in our lives, it affects the colors of all the others things in our life. Nothing is untouched by the little red sin. The intensity of the color of sin has a life-changing effect doesn't it? Sure it does. Everything has a reddish hue. The sad thing is that we justify our new color, "Oh, that pinky red hue on everything isn't that bad."

What is the only thing that gets the reddish color back out of our clothes? Clorox. You have to literally put the clothes back in the washing machine and put Clorox in the water to get your clothes white again. That is exactly how God gets the red back out of our lives. God is the washing machine that we are put into. Jesus is the Clorox. The Holy Spirit is the agitator. He holds us and moves us around as we are being convicted. Jesus goes deep into the fabric of our lives to cleanse every spot of red from one spectrum of color to the other.

When God pulls us out, He says, "Now, your robes are as white as snow and wool. They are made of fine linen" (Revelation 19:8 NLT). "My Son's blood has washed you and you are not the same color that you used to be." He goes on to say, "Not only were your other garments crimson, they were like filthy rags to Me (Isaiah 64:6 NLT). Your righteous acts, the pride of your lifestyle, and thinking that your way was better than Mine, made you the deepest red. You have been washed and made clean. Remember, every sin you commit is like taking one drop of red food coloring and dropping it into in a washing machine that holds the white linen robe that I have given you. You are in charge of dropping the red color in your life. Only you. It will turn the whole robe red again."

Not only can our sin be crimson and scarlet, I believe it is black as well. How can it be both? It's a mystery. Listen to these verses:

Proverbs 2:13—Who leave the paths of uprightness, to walk in the ways of darkness. (KJV)

Proverbs 4:19—The way of the wicked is as darkness; they know not at what they stumble. (KJV)

Ecclesiastes 2:14—The wise man's eyes are in his head; but the fool walketh in darkness. (KJV)

Isaiah 29:15—Woe unto them that seek deep to hide their counsel from the Lord, and their works are in the dark, and they say, Who seeth us and knoweth us? (KJV)

1 John 2:11—But he that hateth his brother is in darkness, and walketh in darkness, and knoweth not whither he goeth, because that darkness hath blinded his eyes. (KJV)

Let's say you walk into a black closet. There is absolutely no light. What color do you see, even if the closet was filled with the brightest colored clothes? Black. The color black is actually the absence of color. When you have sin in your life, you are crimson and scarlet on the inside, while everything on the outside is complete black. The Word of God said it is so pitch black that you actually stumble around. Picture yourself holding your arms out in front of you, slowly swinging them from side to side as you try to walk around in the darkness.

You are blinded by sin's blackness. You call right wrong and wrong right. You exchange the light for the dark when you sin (1 John 1:6 ESV). You are so blinded when there is sin in your life that you don't realize what you are truly doing to your life. The longer you stay in the darkness of a sin, the more you justify that it is light. Your eyes adjust to the darkness, and you continue to stumble around.

A nonbeliever is in constant darkness. Christians choose darkness even though they have been in the light. Even though they have worn the white linen robes, they exchange them for filthy crimson rags over and over again. Don't say you don't exchange your garments. Every time you sin, you exchange them. You have just never thought about the color of sin before. Why would you give God His white linen robe back to walk back into darkness to turn red inside again?

You may say, "I can't help myself." I would say, "Yes, you can. That is an excuse. You have the power of the Holy Spirit in you." You may say, "We all sin." I would remind you of Romans 6:1–2, "Shall we go on sinning so that grace may increase? By no means! We are those who have died to sin; how can we live in it any longer" (NIV)? The Bible is saying that the darkness of sin is no longer a lifestyle that is acceptable after you have walked in lightness.

What I have finally accepted, which has changed my way of thinking, is that sin is my personal choice. Nobody can make you sin. As a Christian, you have been taught God's way. You have been made whiter than snow and wool. You would have to choose to change your color back to red or black. When you do make this color change, you then justify it. When you are not in sin and look at this color process, the trouble we can get our lives in due to the pride of our lifestyles is pretty alarming. When you are in sin, none of this will make sense. You are blinded by what you think is best. It's like you are color blind. You see nothing wrong with the color you are.

What color is sin? Maybe the more important question is, what color are you right now? Are you crimson? Are your scarlet? Are you black? Are you whiter than snow and wool? What are you wearing right now? Filthy rags? A white linen robe? I want to make it very clear that once you know Christ, and you exchange these colors and garments, you do not lose your salvation. You are losing your daily victory, closeness to the Lord, and usability in the Body of Christ. What is worth enough, in this temporal world, to have that much stronghold on you to change your color? Repent of the colors red and black. Put white back on, and walk in the finest linen.

Glass of God

I picture my life with God as a simple glass. People can picture the most complex things to figure out how God "fits" into their lives. First, God shouldn't fit in your life. God should *be* your life. Christians typically don't understand this as they have so much of the temporal world in their thinking. "It's me and God." Wrong. It is just God. There is none of you, if you have truly died to self. Again, until Christians understand this truth, they will struggle to put God in the place that He is supposed to be in their lives.

It seems like we always have a little self in there left. While we say we have died to self, we are secretly doing CPR to keep it breathing. We always sing that old hymn: "I surrender all." We don't surrender all. We don't pour all of ourselves out of the glass. We never have and, frankly, most of us don't know how to turn every single thing over to God, yet we expect great blessings from God. He sees all. He sees what we are holding on to. You are not fooling God. You are only fooling yourself.

Picture a glass. It can only be filled up with two things. Self and God. How much of you is in the glass of your life? How much of God is in the glass of your life? They are simple questions but so hard to be truthful about. You say, "I'm a born again believer in Christ Jesus!" I ask you, "How much of God is in your glass?" You add, "I go to church and tithe. I even go on Wednesday night." I will repeat, "How much of God is in your glass?" You think, "I have been saved since I was a child or a teenager and I love God." Again, "How much of God is in your glass?"

What I have learned, since I have said all of these same statements to convince myself that I am living a victorious life in Christ, is I had a whole lot of self in my glass and just a little God. Was I saved? Yes. Was I living one foot in the temporal world and one foot in the eternal world? Yes. How much of God was truly in my own glass of life? I justified that it was a perfect balance.

God said, "Perfect balance? Justified? Who, may I ask, is holding the balancing scales? You don't balance yourself with Me. In that thinking, you are more off-balance than you can imagine. You have justified that all is well in your life. You have just enough of Me in your life to think you are fine? You are only balanced when there is none of you and only Me. All through time, people have tried to balance themselves in the same glass with Me. Look at Saul. Look at David. Look at Solomon. Look at Lot. Look at Judas. Look at the Sadducees and Pharisees. When your whole life is in Me, I do not share the glass of life with you. I completely fill it."

Luke 9:23 teaches about denying yourself for Christ (NIV). How can we deny ourselves, if we still recognize that some of ourselves are still sharing the glass with God? We can't. Hebrews 12:29 says that "Our God is an all consuming fire" (ISV). I try to pour myself out of the glass, but the world and self are so strong. I have to retain some control. I think the only way for God to remove what I share with Him in my glass of life is to consume it by fire. He needs to heat Self up so high that it evaporates. He can do what I cannot in my own strength. When we can't empty self out, because of our own weakness and pride of lifestyle, God can. We have to allow Him to.

When I think what my glass of life looks like when He has completely filled it, I cannot imagine the possibilities. What He fills up in my glass, my life will drink. What He will give me to drink comes from a well of water springing up that has an eternal source. My glass of life will never be less than overflowing when I allow Him to fill it.

Reasonable Service

When I started writing my personal journals, I had no idea what the Lord may do with them. Honestly, I didn't think He would do anything with them. I never conceived that others would ever read them. I only thought they were something that I did as an outlet for what the Lord was showing me. As the journals have deepened and spread to others, I am trying to figure out what is exactly going on. The Lord has said the same phrase over and over to me, "This is your reasonable service." When I am confused on the direction this is all leading, He says, "This is your reasonable service." When I doubt that I can finish what I have started, He says, "This is your reasonable service." When I feel like I am getting into something that is too deep for me, He says, "This is your reasonable service."

I now understand that He doesn't much care about my reservations or apprehensions when I have prayed for Him to reveal His will for my life. Once I know His will and the ministry He has given me to do, it is my reasonable service that I carry it out. He doesn't want to hear my excuses or hesitations when He has given me a task to complete. He doesn't care about my human frailties. God only cares what He can do through me, which is my reasonable service to Him. I'm beginning to understand that the journals are not for me or you, but they are my reasonable service to the Lord.

Romans 12:1 says, "I beseech you therefore, brethren, by the mercies of God, that ye present your bodies a living sacrifice, holy, acceptable unto God, which is your reasonable service" (KJV). I think for us to understand God's will for our lives, we need to understand this verse much more deeply. We do not need to briskly read over it. Beseech means "to urge, to beg, to encourage, and to plead." Paul is urging, begging, and pleading for the Christian to listen to him. He is not addressing the nonbeliever as the things of God are foolishness to them (1 Corinthians 1:18; 1 Corinthians 2:14–15 KJV). Paul is begging or encouraging only the Christian, as he has something very important to say. Beseech is a very strong word. When someone begs or urges you to do something, what power does he or she have to support that which is being asked for? What should make us listen?

Paul says, "You better listen, brothers and sisters, by the very mercies of God." What does that mean? Psalms 136:1 says, "O give thanks unto the Lord; for He is good, for His mercy endureth forever" (KJV). Psalms 103:17 says, "Mercy is from everlasting to everlasting" (KJV). We should listen to Paul, based on the mercies of God, which are eternal. All things that are eternal are powerful and incomprehensible to the human mind. Mercy is eternal, yet we take it so lightly and for granted. We have no idea the power of God's mercy. No idea. Paul was making his whole case that you should listen to him, because of God's mercy.

Let me ask you a few questions. Did God show mercy on the fallen angels? Could He have chosen to? Sure. God did not choose to show mercy on the fallen angels. Did God show mercy on fallen man? Could He have chosen not to? Sure He could. That truth right there should put you on your face in front of Most High God's throne and keep it there. If you never learn another truth of God, the power of His mercy should make you listen to every word that comes out of His mouth until you take your last breath.

Christians and this unbelieving world have yet to comprehend the power that the Most High God possesses. The prophets and the disciples have tried to explain it to us, yet we still limit it in our lives. We don't understand God's power. We certainly do not think twice about the power of His mercy. While you are down on your face, make sure you thank Him that mercy is eternal. You really, really don't want His mercy to ever run out on you. Just go ask one fallen angel. So when Paul says, "Listen to me. I tell you these things by the mercies of God," you might want to sit up a little taller and pay closer attention. For Paul to use that phrase, "mercies of God" is to say he is speaking on one of the eternal characteristics of God's power.

Paul says, "Listen to me very closely. I speak on behalf of the eternal power of God's mercy to tell you this. Present your body a living sacrifice, holy, acceptable to God." Your body is the temple of God, the Holy Spirit. Did you hear me? God, the Holy Spirit, physically resides inside of your heart, mind, and soul.

First Corinthians 3:16 says, "Do you not know that you are God's temple and that God's Spirit dwells in you (ESV)? Do you know where the Holy Spirit resided in the Jewish Temple? The Holy of Holies. If God is saying that the Holy Spirit is residing in us, that means we are a walking Holy of Holies. We have the most sacred part of the entire Temple within us. If understanding the power of the mercies of God didn't put you on your face before God, then understanding that you are the literal Holy of Holies on this earth should put you down. No? Pride will hold you back every single time, and the enemy loves it! Christian, what will put you on your face before an Almighty God? If these two truths don't, what will?

How do you become a living sacrifice that is holy? Ezekiel 36:27 tells us clearly, "I will put my Spirit within you and cause you to walk in My statutes and be careful to obey My rules" (ESV). As soon as you walk in the Lord's ways, you have instantly become holy. You don't have to figure out how to be holy and make it all complicated, which we do so well. Walk in the Lord's way and you are holy. Simple. When you put your ways away and elevate God, that is your sacrifice. When you do this, He says, "You are holy like I am holy." I think it is interesting that He uses the phrase, "Causes you to walk in My ways." He assumes that since He has placed the Holy Spirit within you that by His power and knowledge, it will cause you to walk in the Lord's ways.

The only time you are living for Him is when you are doing what He has caused you to do, by the Spirit He put within you. When you are at the spiritual maturity level to understand this and not grieve the Holy Spirit by your disobedience of His will, God says your sacrifice is acceptable to Him. When you try to please God, yet you know that you are still doing things in your own strength and way, that is not considered a sacrifice. It is far from acceptable. When you are not offering an acceptable sacrifice, does that negate your salvation? Absolutely not. You are just stealing your own blessings. No big deal. You keep telling yourself you are fine.

All of these things that I have described combine to make our reasonable service possible before a Holy God. He knows you can't do this on your own; this is why He put the Holy Spirit within you. I can say to God right now, "I am not going to write another journal. If I do, I am not going to share them." I could say that, and I could even do that. The only way my reasonable service stops is if I say, "No." I certainly have that power, because God gave me free will. Will I use that free will to serve myself? Could this be reasonable? If I justified it and put my way above God, I could. It would be pretty easily, actually, as this is what we typically do anyway.

God says that He put His Holy Spirit within me and will cause me to walk in His way. When I walk His way, my living sacrifice is holy and acceptable to Him. Because of who Jesus is, what He has done, and how He has demonstrated His love and faithfulness to me, my minimal reasonable service, at this time, is to be obedient to writing and sending journals about Him, if that is what He wants. I am confident that when this particular service is over, He will show me another service that He deems reasonable. Remember, it is not if you feel that the service is reasonable, but if He does. There can be a big difference in that. I did not think it was reasonable to write a book, but He did! Don't hinder the Holy Spirit's work in your life by your own human excuses and justifications. You will miss God's abundant blessings.

Life's Temperature

Behold I am coming soon. (Revelation 22:7 ESV)

Jesus is coming soon. We have heard that said over and over again. Our parents have heard that all of their lives. Our grandparents have heard that all of their lives. You don't know exactly when Jesus is coming, so let's just trust Him at His Word. If He says He is coming soon, what are you doing to prepare for His imminent arrival? What's on your mind? What are your actions? Are you doing the same thing in your life as you have always done? Are you still wrestling with sin that has a strong hold on you? Are you just about in the same place in your Christian walk as you have always been? Is your personal relationship any deeper with the Lord than a year ago? Do you trust Him with your life to do great things?

Some people may take Christ at His Word, but the majority doesn't. Why? They do not believe Jesus Christ is coming soon. They believe He is coming, but they have loads of time before He arrives. They are procrastinators. They think that this world and the life they know will continue on as they have always been. They don't need to get serious with the Lord. They have believed the enemy's lie that they have all the time in the world.

They say they believe the Bible, but they act like what it says isn't really going to happen. If they did, their actions would show it. They would be driven to prayer daily. God would be foremost in their minds, not an afterthought. God would come first in their day, not what was left over, if anything. They would be driven to the Word of God and soak their spirits in it. They would have great passion and desire for the Lord. They would have a power in their lives that fills them with peace and joy that no circumstance can shake. They would know more about Him. They would have fruit that was ripe for the picking, so others would know that they had been with the Lord.

Look around. What do you see more of? Stagnant and defeated Christians. Churches are dying. Christians stuck in the ruts of life, just like the rest of the world. There are Christians who are just trying to make it through, though they have no fruit, no witness, and no outreach into other's lives so that they can grow as Christians. How can you help others grow in Christ when you are not growing yourself? It is impossible. How can you be prepared to be used for the spreading of the Kingdom of God when you are comfortable where you are? God doesn't want you comfortable.

I previously thought if I was comfortable, then I was doing right in the Lord. No, that's backwards. If you are comfortable, then you are doing nothing in the Lord. If you are not growing in the Lord, then you are stagnating. There's no in-between. God doesn't work in your comfort zone; He works in His. It amazes me how ignorant Christians are of the Lord's Word, or maybe they just ignore parts they don't like.

He says, "I am coming soon. When I get there if I find you lukewarm, then you will make Me physically sick. I will want to spit you out of My mouth" (Revelation 3:16 NIV). Wake up, Christian! This isn't a game. You don't get to make up brownie points at the end of life. That is what He said! Our stagnation, desire for our comfort zone, and our life's temperature of being lukewarm for the things of Christ makes the Most High God sick.

If you say that you believe Jesus is coming soon, but your actions say He is coming much later, then you are a lukewarm Christian. If you believe Jesus is coming soon, but you have no desire to witness to one other soul about Jesus Christ, then you are a lukewarm Christian. If you say Jesus is coming soon, but you are satisfied to stay in your comfort zone of life, then you are a lukewarm Christian. If you think quiet time with prayer and study of the Word is optional, something you do *if* you have the time and can remember to fit it in your life, then you are a lukewarm Christian. If you think as long as you are personally doing well while forgetting about loving others, then you are a lukewarm Christian. If you think the only time you need to spend time with God is an hour a week on Sundays, then you are a lukewarm Christian. Will you make God sick upon His return?

Wipe the sleep out of your eyes and rise up. Time is short. If you know you are lukewarm, light a fire and boil the waters in your life. You have to get your life's temperature up. He is coming soon. The Word of God will instruct you on how to build an intense fire to heat things up to be ready for His return. Jesus Christ has told you clearly that He is coming soon.

Stupidity, lack of preparedness, busyness, and laziness will not fly as excuses to a Holy God who knows the truth. Don't get caught standing in front of His throne with your hands up in the air saying, "Lord! Lord! I just didn't know You were coming so soon or else I really would have started living for You!" He will say to you, "Remember My Word that you never read? Remember your contentment in your own comfort zone? My Word told of My imminent arrival. You just didn't take it seriously. You are fully accountable. You were told I was coming. I am a just God."

Christian, I don't know how else to tell you that you need to check the temperature of your life. Do it now! When He dips His finger into your life to check the temperature, which He will, will it feel lukewarm to Him, or will it burn Him? You have got to wake up and heed His words. Trust what He says is really going to happen. Heat your life up. "Behold, I am coming soon."

Seeking Wisdom

When I was a child, I talked like a child, I thought like a child, I reasoned like a child. But when I became an adult, I set aside childish ways. (First Corinthians 13:11 NETB)

I accepted Christ in my heart at the tender age of nine. All I knew of God was that He loved me so much that He died to have me live with Him forever. That's all I needed to know. I'm reminded of the time the disciples were arguing over who would be the greatest in the Heaven, and then Jesus scooped a child up in his lap. I can imagine Him looking at this child that He loved so much, smiling, and saying, "This child will be the greatest. Be like this child." When I was little, I always knew that God loved me because I pictured that I was the child that He scooped up in His lap. That is a powerful image for a little girl to carry in her heart.

That little girl grew up though. I grew into a young lady and then to a woman. I love I Corinthians 13:11 (NETB). The Lord gave us the gift of our childhoods. We had to pass through them before we could be fully mature in whom we would become as an adult. I grew up in the Lord with faithful parents who loved the Lord. I am thankful for them.

They provided a strong example of how to become an adult and put aside my childish ways. Even though I had wonderful, godly models, putting childish ways aside was not as simple as I thought. Even as a teenager and adult, I found myself thinking and behaving in childish ways. I define childish ways as seeking self and my ways above God's way for my life.

When I started to develop some deeper knowledge of the Lord as a young adult, I prayed earnestly for two things. I prayed for wisdom and discernment. I have prayed for these two things since I can remember. Honestly, I really didn't know what wisdom and discernment were when I started praying for them. Looking back on it, I can't pin down a reason that I picked them. I just know that I did. The hardest thing about wisdom and discernment is that they are not part of childish thoughts and behaviors. Far from it. They are in direct contradiction to anything childish. When wisdom and discernment collided with my life, it was very difficult to put away my childish thoughts of wanting things to be about me instead of God.

It would take the majority of my Christian life to finally put away childish ways. While I was a woman on the outside, I thought like a child in a spiritual sense. Self didn't want me to grow up and gain wisdom and discernment. The enemy certainly didn't. Even though I was a Christian, that didn't necessarily mean that I put away childish thoughts of wanting things my way. I look around at some Christians today and try to figure out why they act and talk at church or in front of me one way, then act and talk totally differently other times. It took me years to figure that out. Then I looked at my own life. They do it for the same reason that I did it.

Many Christians are adults on the outside but have never laid their childish ways aside. Why? Once you lay your thoughts and behaviors aside, you have to relinquish your control over to God. You have to do things His way. We say we want to do that, but the spirit child in us is screaming, "NNNOooooo!" When you do things God's way and you do not hear a voice screaming "NNNOoooo" at you, you have put away childish ways and thoughts. It is also possible that you could be engaged in ungodly thoughts and behaviors. When you are involved in a sin, and the Holy Spirit says, "Stop that right now," but you keep doing it because, like a child, you are having fun, then you have not put away childish ways. I am so guilty of doing this. I justify to the Holy Spirit that when I am done having fun in my disobedience, I will then comply with His request. If this doesn't sound just like what our own children do, then I don't know what does.

Wisdom is the obedience to the knowledge of what God has taught us in His Word. I had loads of knowledge of God growing up and even up to where I am today. You can have all the knowledge of God in the world and be an utter fool. Why? If you do not obey the knowledge that God has given you, then you are not wise. Wisdom requires obedience. It is not until you shun sinful thoughts and behaviors that you will understand (Job 28:28 KJV) and think like a mature, wise, spiritual adult.

The Bible says, "Fools despise wisdom" (Proverbs 1:7 KJV). Fools despise wisdom because they refuse to grow up spiritually and obey the knowledge of God. Fools want things their way, despite knowing God's way. They hate wisdom because they know God will make them follow His way. The truth of the matter is that God never makes people follow His way. They have to desire it themselves.

Wisdom is never forced; it is sought after. God will allow you to remain a fool until the day you die, as this is part of your free will. Many of us, even as Christians, will. You can be a Christian and not be wise. You can be a Christian and not have put aside childish thoughts and behaviors. My question is, "Why would you want to?"

Many Christians will struggle all of their lives to put God first. They love Him, but they can't seem to make Him a consistent priority. They find it so difficult to do things His way over their justified ones. I know people who live together but are not married. Wise or foolish? I know people who become drunk with wine. Wise or foolish? I know people who can't seem to find the time for God in a consistent and devoted quiet time. Wise or foolish? I know people who can't say no to a sin that meets some fleshly need. Wise or foolish?

All of these people are confessing Christians. Just because they make foolish decisions doesn't negate their salvation. It doesn't make them obedient to the knowledge of God, though. It doesn't indicate that they are mature Christians. There is no wisdom in their choices. It doesn't demonstrate that they have put away childish ways of justifying what they want and how they want it. Again, wisdom is evidence of someone following God's way above their own desired ways. Wisdom is evidence of spiritual maturity.

How do we gain wisdom? James 1:5 says, "But if any of you lacks wisdom, let him ask of God who gives to all men generously and without reproach, and it will be given to him" (ESV). Where should we seek wisdom? God. Where do we typically seek wisdom? The world and other people. We wonder what is wrong with our lives. The world tells you fornication is not a big deal. The world tells you that being drunk is your choice, and as long as you stay off the road, no one cares. The world tells you that you are too busy for God to spend quiet time with Him. The world tells you that fulfilling the needs of the flesh in whatever way is your right. The world does not have wisdom, Christians. It only has foolishness.

God says His wisdom is pure, peaceable, gentle, reasonable, full of mercy, and good fruits, unwavering, and without hypocrisy (James 3:17 NASB). What a contrast it is to foolishness. We have to have the discernment of the Holy Spirit to know the difference between dancing too close to the line of foolishness and planting both of our feet in wisdom. I have learned that foolishness comes so easily, but wisdom takes time and commitment to the Lord. Anything worth having should be sought after.

If you self-reflected, would you say you are knowledgeable or wise? They are not the same. Don't justify that they are. Are you a Christian adult with a child's spiritual mind who wants to cling to their own way? If you are, do you think you fooling God while you are hiding it from the rest of us? I thought I was hiding my foolishness for a long time—until I woke up from my deep slumber.

I will tell you; the truth hurts. Moving from childish thoughts and ways to a spiritual mature man or woman of God is a process. Moving from foolishness and justification of our actions and thoughts to wisdom takes time. I do not think it happens overnight, because the self-part of us doesn't want to relinquish control. Childish ways are harder to set aside than you may think, but it is achievable. Proverbs 14:8 says, "The wisdom of the prudent is to understand God's way" (KJV).

You have two choices. You can stay in your childish thinking and own ways which leads to foolishness, or you can understand and obey God's way which leads to spiritual maturity and wisdom. If you are not consistently and actively seeking wisdom, then you have made your choice. I have learned that words do not matter when it comes to distinguishing between these two states of being. It's all about your thoughts and actions.

"Go In Peace"

Peace I leave with you; My peace I give you. (John 14:27 NIV)

I finished my hour of prayer this morning, and the Lord said something as I was leaving that He has never said before. He said, "Go in peace." I looked back at Him, and He knew that I picked up on that new phrase. All of these hundreds and hundreds of hours of prayer and just today He said, "Go in peace?" The first thing I started wondering is, "Oh no. What is going to happen today that He wants me to go in peace? He must know I will need it for some reason today more than any other before."

His phrase definitely intrigued me. I started searching the Scriptures for the understanding of peace. You always hear of peace, but what does it really mean? I found that it is an actual state of being. It is how you are. It is harmony, union, friendship, and love found in your heart and in relationships. If you have peace, you feel contented and calm despite your circumstances. You have no worries or unsettled feelings as you rest in the Lord.

Where does peace come from? Isaiah 32:17 says that peace is the fruit of righteousness (NIV). Righteousness comes from holy living through the power of the Holy Spirit. Peace from this righteousness produces quietness and confidence. How long? "Forever!" John 16:33 teaches us that knowledge of the Lord will bring us peace (NIV). The more knowledge of the Lord I have, the more peace I will have. I can testify that this is an absolutely true statement.

Please be mindful that the opposite is just as true. Psalm 29:11 tells us that the Lord blesses His people with peace (NIV). He always tells us that He will give us abundant blessings. One of those is peace. Trusting in the Lord brings you peace (Romans 15:13 NIV). Pleasing the Lord, which means following His will over yours, brings peace. This peace will extend to even your enemies (Proverbs 16:7 NASB). Having a steadfast mind for the Lord brings perfect peace (Isaiah 26:3 NIV). David said that there is safety and good sleep in peace (Psalm 4:8 NIV). Loving the Word of God brings great peace (Psalm 119:165 HCSB).

When your heart looks like God's heart, then He will actually turn His face toward you. When He looks at you, peace is given (Numbers 6:25–26

NIV). Did you know that Christ's actual punishment for our sins brought us peace (Isaiah 53:5 NIV)? Philippians 4:7 says that God's peace actually guards your hearts and minds (NIV)! Peace comes from the all three parts of the God head (Philippians 4:7; Colossians 3:15; Galatians 5:22 NIV). I never knew that! We can pray for peace for people and nations (Psalms 122:6 NIV). We should be thankful that we have been called to peace (Colossians 3:15 NIV).

I have always heard about peace, but I never knew that it came in our lives by so many sources. Not only does it depend on all of these sources, Romans 12:18 says it depends on us, too! It reads, "If it is possible, as far as it depends on you, live at peace with everyone" (NIV). I can look at all of my relationships and ask the question, "Is this relationship with this person peaceful?" If it is, then we are both sharing in making it so. If it is not, then the next question is, "Am I doing everything on my side to make the relationship peaceful?" If the answer is yes, then I will rest in that knowledge. If the answer is no, then the Lord says that I have a responsibility to uphold peace as much as I can on my side of the relationship.

If the other person does not hold up his or her side of peace, I cannot control that. In the end, the relationship may not be what is best to have in my life. Especially if it is a Christian relationship, both sides should be obedient to the Lord to maintain peace. We are actually called to peace as Christians. If you are the one that takes peace away from a relationship, you are far outside the will of the Lord. I would recommend you mend your ways immediately. However you mentally and emotionally justify your unpeaceful behavior in your relationship with friends and family, you are in the wrong according to the Scriptures. Be spiritually mature and grow up. These are harsh words but very true. You are to live at peace with everyone.

My sweet Lord told me to, "Go in peace" this morning when I left Him in prayer time. Those three powerful words prompted me to write this journal and, in turn, have deepened my understanding of exactly all that He said. The Lord doesn't waste His words with us. I have found He only has to speak a few words; the meanings behind them are abundant. We serve such a mighty God who desires for us to go deeper in His Word. He has so much to teach us before His return. One of the most important lessons is to understand and have peace.

SARAH ROWAN

*May God Bless You
and Your Family*

About the Author

Sarah Rowan is a medical speech language pathologist with a Master's degree in Education. She is a Cum Laude graduate of Valdosta State University. She assists in managing an inpatient rehab facility with Phoebe Putney Memorial Hospital in Albany, Georgia for approximately twenty years. She is married to Kevin Rowan. They have two boys, Jonah and Andrew. They are members of First Baptist Church of Leesburg in Leesburg, Georgia. Sarah loves teaching Sunday school to middle school girls.

Through writing and publishing, many doors have been opened for Sarah to speak at churches, youth groups, women's ministries, rehabs, and jails. She has witnessed the Holy Spirit encourage many lives and seen many new additions to the Family of God. She will go anywhere and speak to anyone who will listen of the power of the Most High God in people's lives. If you are interested in her speaking to your group, please email her at srowanslp@yahoo.com. There is never a speaking fee. God always provides.

Sarah is the Director of Heart Vision Ministries, Inc. This is a non-profit encouraging women's ministry who share the same God-given passion for youth girls, women in recovering addiction rehabs, jails, and prisons. Heart Vision Ministry encourages women, who are the most crushed in spirit and broken hearted in their personal time of trial. If you are interested in more information on Heart Vision Ministry, please email Sarah. She would love to talk with you personally.